Knowledge in Contemporary Philosophy

The Philosophy of Knowledge: A History

General Editor, Stephen Hetherington

'*The Philosophy of Knowledge* is a truly remarkable work. In addition to its vast breadth, the set is commendable for the expertise of the contributors and the clarity and rigor of their essays. The set has three chief virtues: it provides a clear understanding of Western epistemology; each individual volume makes for an ideal resource for courses focusing on that period; and the individual essays themselves are perfect complements to primary works of the philosopher(s) addressed. Summing Up: Highly recommended. Lower-division undergraduates through faculty; general readers.' *CHOICE*

'*The Philosophy of Knowledge: A History* is a tremendous achievement. Its four volumes cover the entire scope of Western epistemology, from the ancient world through the medieval and modern periods to the contemporary scene, with essays on the most influential figures in each of these periods. The result is a splendid overview on how fundamental questions about knowledge have been thought about over the millennia. These volumes will be the standard resource for all those interested in the history epistemology for decades to come.'

Richard Foley, Professor of Philosophy, New York University, USA

'This ambitious fourfold work aims to provide an overview of Western epistemology, from the Greeks through contributions on the contemporary scene . . . An invaluable resource on epistemological topics and on the development of Western thought about them.'

Ernest Sosa, Board of Governors Professor of Philosophy,
Rutgers University, USA

The Philosophy of Knowledge: A History presents the history of one of Western philosophy's greatest challenges: understanding the nature of knowledge. Divided chronologically, these four volumes follow conceptions of knowledge that have been proposed, defended, replaced, and proposed anew by ancient, medieval, modern, and contemporary philosophers.

Each volume is centred around two key questions. What conceptions of knowledge have been offered? Which ones have shaped epistemology in particular and philosophy in general? Together, these volumes trace the historical development of knowledge for the first time.

Volume I *Knowledge in Ancient Philosophy*, edited by Nicholas D. Smith

Volume II *Knowledge in Medieval Philosophy*, edited by Henrik Lagerlund

Volume III *Knowledge in Modern Philosophy*, edited by Stephen Gaukroger

Volume IV *Knowledge in Contemporary Philosophy*, edited by
Stephen Hetherington and Markos Valaris

The Philosophy of Knowledge: A History

Volume IV

Knowledge in Contemporary Philosophy

Edited by Stephen Hetherington and Markos Valaris

BLOOMSBURY ACADEMIC

LONDON • NEW YORK • OXFORD • NEW DELHI • SYDNEY

BLOOMSBURY ACADEMIC
Bloomsbury Publishing Plc
50 Bedford Square, London, WC1B 3DP, UK
1385 Broadway, New York, NY 10018, USA
29 Earlsfort Terrace, Dublin 2, Ireland

BLOOMSBURY, BLOOMSBURY ACADEMIC and the Diana logo
are trademarks of Bloomsbury Publishing Plc

First published in Great Britain 2019
Paperback edition published 2024

Cover image © The Yellow Books, 1887 (oil on canvas), Gogh, Vincent van
(1853–90)/Private Collection/Bridgeman Images

A catalogue record for this book is available from the British Library.

A catalog record for this book is available from the Library of Congress.

ISBN: PB: 978-1-3504-4663-2

Typeset by Jones Ltd, London
Printed and bound in Great Britain

To find out more about our authors and books visit www.bloomsbury.com
and sign up for our newsletters.

Contents

Contributors

Scott Aikin (Vanderbilt University, USA)

Claudio de Almeida (PUCRS, Brazil)

Heather Battaly (University of Connecticut, USA)

Michael Blome-Tillmann (McGill University, Canada)

Berit Brogaard (University of Miami, USA)

Peter J. Graham (University of California, Riverside, USA)

Stephen Hetherington (University of New South Wales, Australia)

Clayton Littlejohn (King's College London, UK)

Kourken Michaelian (University of Otago, New Zealand)

Duncan Pritchard (University of Edinburgh, UK)

Stathis Psillos (University of Athens, Greece)

Weng Hong Tang (National University of Singapore, Singapore)

Julia Tanney (independent scholar; formerly at University of Kent, UK)

Markos Valaris (University of New South Wales, Australia)

General Editor's Preface

Stephen Hetherington

The Philosophy of Knowledge: Introduction to a History

Welcome to philosophy – to part of it, at any rate. A powerful and pivotal part of it, though: *epistemology*. Welcome to this survey – a tour, across four volumes – of a significant segment of epistemology's history. Western philosophy began in ancient Greece, before travelling far afield, still prospering. And whatever it is now is at least partly a consequence of whatever it has been. Within these four volumes, we meet much of whatever epistemology has been and is.

Why is this form of historical engagement philosophically important? Why is it important *now* to have some understanding of what epistemology has *been*? One reason is the possibility of current epistemology's being more similar to some or all of its former selves than it might at first seem to be, in productive and destructive ways. We should not merely be reinventing the epistemological wheel; nor should we repeat past epistemological mistakes – design flaws in earlier epistemological conveyances. To know epistemology's history is to know better what contemporary epistemology could be and perhaps should be – and what it need not be and perhaps ought not to be.

Epistemology is usually said to be the philosophy of knowledge and of kindred phenomena. But what makes it *the* philosophy of such matters? Well, epistemology has long been a collective endeavour – a gathering of individual efforts, by a plethora of epistemologists over oh-so-many years – to understand the nature of knowledge and those kindred phenomena. (Some of those efforts even ask whether there *is* a phenomenon of knowledge in the first place.)

How does that collective endeavour take shape? A first – a partial – answer is that epistemology is ineliminably *theoretical*. It is one theory, another theory, yet more theories, and so on. And so it is theories linking with, and departing from, other theories. It is theories living, developing, dying, reproducing, influencing, succeeding, failing. It is new themes replacing old ones. It is old themes replacing new ones.

And these four volumes will introduce you to such theories – competing conceptions of knowledge and those kindred phenomena, conceptions from across the ages. Volume I introduces us to theories from parts of the ancient world, the fount of all Western epistemology. Volumes II and III trace theories of knowledge as these arose over the following two millennia, late into the nineteenth century. Volume IV then tells a tale of the past century or so – while gesturing also at how epistemology might continue into at least the near future, taking us there from here. Not all of epistemology's past or present theorists and theories appear in these pages; but many do. The result is a grand story of sweeping intellectual vistas with striking conceptual foundations and ramifications. It is living philosophy. It is here, with you right now.

Introduction: Theorizing about Theorizing about Knowledge

Stephen Hetherington and Markos Valaris

The term 'contemporary epistemology' – when used now, as part of this volume's title – is typically interpreted as encompassing the past 100 or so years of philosophical reflection on knowledge and kindred phenomena. This volume introduces you to many of the more developed ideas, issues, and theories from this past century of epistemological reflection.

The ensuing chapters will speak for themselves. In this introduction, we have two aims. We highlight some influences and emphases that, because they have characterized this period in epistemology's history, permeate the volume's chapters. Before doing that, we introduce you to some *meta*-epistemology. This will help you to reflect in a more nuanced way upon the point of those discussions in the volume's chapters.

The term 'meta-epistemology' can be used in at least these two ways:

- to denote epistemological discussion of the contours and applicability conditions of what seem to be the most explanatorily fundamental *concepts* that would be featured in a finished epistemology;[1]
- to denote epistemological evaluation of epistemological discussions, asking about their epistemic *credentials*.[2] For example, what is needed if a theory of knowledge (or evidence, or rationality, etc.) is to be genuine understanding, actually insightful, or even knowledge itself?

Most contemporary epistemology is meta-epistemological in the first of those two senses. We may call this *meta-conceptual* epistemology, since it seeks philosophical understanding, by using and discussing epistemic concepts, of epistemic phenomena. Those epistemic concepts are purportedly about epistemic phenomena or attainments. Most of this volume's chapters are explicitly trying to understand some element of the epistemic universe.

But these chapters also implicitly seek to attain or achieve some pertinent epistemic status (such as by being knowledge, or understanding, or the like). So, we can set the scene for those chapters by remarking on that second sense of 'meta-epistemology'. We might call this *meta-achievement* epistemology. It aims to describe whatever actual or potential epistemic statuses are *achieved* by various epistemological theories of epistemic phenomena or attainments (knowledge, understanding, evidence, etc.). In formulating a theory about knowledge, for example, does a given epistemologist *achieve* knowledge – about knowledge?

Imagine an ethicist and a metaphysician proffering their favourite theories – about, respectively, personal moral goodness and free will. Presumably, they wish to know whether their theories are true. (If so, they are wishing for the theory to be knowledge.) How is this to be achieved? These philosophers would be asking whether their theories amount to real understanding or insight, instead of being *only* theories – mere words, more words, even if seemingly intelligently used ones. These philosophers might therefore consult philosophical peers within their respective sub-disciplines – other ethicists, other metaphysicians. Nonetheless, how do those further philosophers know when their own philosophical efforts, let alone others', amount to genuine understanding, insight, or knowledge? The immediate moral is that the ethicist and the metaphysician would need to consult more widely – specifically, by including *epistemologists* among those to whom they turn for advice.

Will that then be enough? Not quite. Suppose that an epistemologist tries to be helpful, by replying in this way: 'Your theory is knowledge if it has the following features: X, Y, and Z. For knowing *is* always the combination, X + Y + Z.' (We are keeping this epistemologist's tale generic.) The epistemologist could well be professionally successful – a distinguished professor, an 'expert', an acclaimed member of the 'guild' of contemporary epistemologists. Her reply will probably be taken seriously by our ethicist and our metaphysician. After all, in practice, what else *could* we reasonably ask of the ethicist and the metaphysician, as they wonder whether their theories give them real philosophical understanding, insight, or knowledge? It is epistemologists who tell us what understanding, insight, or knowledge even are.

But a lingering philosophical presence shadows those efforts. For the same sort of question arises about any epistemologist, too, who is consulted. How is she to know that her own story about those features X, Y, and Z is *itself* real understanding, insight, or knowledge? She tells the ethicist and the metaphysician that a philosophical view is knowledge *if* it is X, Y, and Z – 'because that is what knowledge in general is'. This might be professionally prudent on her part: she might be alluding to some widely respected epistemological publications – papers, books – by herself or other eminent professors on the nature of knowledge. Even so, her assurance to the ethicist and the metaphysician is true only if her claim about knowledge's nature (her saying that knowledge = $X+Y+Z$) is itself true. And is it? More pressingly, how will *this* be known, if indeed it can be? What epistemic guarantee does the epistemologist have that her own epistemological assurance to others (about their own epistemic achievements as philosophers) is giving voice to understanding or insight or knowledge on her part?

Those questions are not rhetorical. On the contrary, they are epistemological. More precisely, they are meta-epistemological – meta-*achievement* epistemological. Will we ever answer them? Who knows? (This is likewise a real epistemological question!)[3] Still, we possess even a chance of answering such questions only if we have ready to hand a representative range of candidate theories – ones that we can inspect, apply, test, reformulate, apply again, test again, and so on. Such theories are what you will find within this volume.

These theories are also representative of the wider philosophical *era* within which they have emerged as theories being discussed and evaluated. Each reflects ideas, preoccupations, and methods of thought that have enjoyed independent lives within the wider world of philosophy as a whole during this past century or so. Here are some of those further themes and influences that are explored in this volume.

1. *Science.* Throughout the history of philosophy, many philosophers have looked to science as the paradigm case of knowledge acquisition. This tendency is certainly visible – even dominant – in contemporary philosophy as well. But the beginning of the twentieth century famously saw major scientific upheavals, including two revolutions in fundamental physics: the theory of relativity and quantum physics. One result of this was that the philosophy of science rose to prominence as an independent subfield of philosophy. But a further result was to bring to prominence fundamental *epistemological* questions about science itself, through the work of foundational figures such as Rudolf Carnap, Carl Hempel, Karl Popper, and W. V. O. Quine. Science promises to give us knowledge that goes beyond ordinary experience. More specifically, scientific theories purport to explain observable phenomena, by means of describing their underlying causal structure. But how can science accomplish this feat? By what methods are scientists able to move rationally beyond the bounds of experience? Stathis Psillos explores this theme in Chapter 5.

2. *Probability*. One side effect of the renewed focus by philosophers on science and its methods has been the rise of probability as a central concept for epistemology, as well as for the study of rationality more broadly. Scientific tests rarely (if ever) absolutely confirm or refute any given hypothesis; they render it merely more or less probable. As a result, it seems, scientific rationality would rarely (if ever) allow us to accept any claims *fully*; we should give only *partial* confidence (or *credence*) to competing hypotheses, in proportion to how probable they are on our evidence.[4] But this idea appears to be at odds with traditional epistemology. The latter provides standards for the evaluation of *full* belief. But what standards should we use to evaluate states of partial belief? A *full* belief can be evaluated as true or false; but if I only have 60 per cent confidence in the hypothesis that it will rain tomorrow, what observable outcome can either confirm or falsify my prediction? Linking probabilistic thinking with more traditional epistemological concepts – and specifically the concept of knowledge – is an important theme in contemporary epistemology, as Weng Hong Tang explains in Chapter 10.

3. *Naturalism and knowledge*. In addition to revolutions in fundamental physics, the twentieth century saw the development and maturation of the *cognitive* sciences, including psychology, neuroscience, and research into artificial intelligence. This research has raised urgent questions about the status of epistemic concepts, including the concept of knowledge, in our picture of the world. Some philosophers have thought that epistemic concepts, such as those of justification and knowledge, are irreducibly *normative*. (Clayton Littlejohn explores this idea in Chapter 13.) If this claim is correct, then it may entail that epistemic concepts will resist integration into a purely naturalistic world view. Other philosophers, by contrast, have proposed naturalistic accounts of epistemic notions. Kourken Michaelian examines such issues in Chapter 4.

4. *Self-knowledge*. One area where the impact of empirical research deserves special mention is *self-knowledge*. As self-conscious thinkers, we are naturally inclined to think that there are certain aspects of ourselves – specifically, our conscious thoughts and experiences – to which we have special epistemic access: we can know our own minds – if not infallibly, then at least with an especially high degree of certainty. However, as is increasingly pointed out by many philosophers, psychology challenges this belief: our first-personal knowledge of ourselves turns out to be more limited and fragile than we might have expected. The extent and nature

of self-knowledge is a very contested area of contemporary philosophy, explored by Markos Valaris in Chapter 8.

5. *Is science the measure of all things?* While many contemporary philosophers have looked to science both as an ideal and as a source of insight for philosophical work, others remain unconvinced.[5] The natural home of epistemological concepts is the 'game of giving and asking for reasons' (Sellars 1956) – that is, our socially embedded practices of constructing, evaluating, and criticizing arguments and judgements. Seen from this broader point of view, science is but one of these practices (and so, of course, is philosophy itself). This wider social perspective is taken and examined by Julia Tanney (Chapter 3) and by Peter Graham (Chapter 6).

6. *Traditional themes: scepticism and the analysis of knowledge.* As explained above, interaction with the sciences has been one important spur for contemporary work in epistemology. At the same time, however, more traditional epistemological projects have continued to be pursued and to flourish, such as the projects of addressing scepticism[6] and of analysing knowledge. (Claudio de Almeida in Chapter 2 traces some of the origins of contemporary thought on these topics, in the work of Bertrand Russell and G. E. Moore.) The project of analysing knowledge, in particular, took on special urgency for contemporary philosophy in the wake of Edmund Gettier's (1963) argument that knowledge is not merely justified true belief. This project is examined in this volume by Duncan Pritchard (Chapter 11). Not only by him, though. For, even while contemporary epistemology has continued working on traditional themes, it has often made use of a wider range of philosophical tools. For one thing, epistemologists have drawn extensively and fruitfully on the philosophy of language (see Michael Blome-Tillman's discussion of contextualism, in Chapter 9) and metaphysics (see Stephen Hetherington on knowledge and modality, in Chapter 12). Furthermore (as we will explain next), contemporary epistemology has long enjoyed a fruitful interaction with ethics and the theory of action.

7. *Knowledge and action.* Several recent and contemporary philosophers have sought to address traditional epistemological questions about knowledge's nature and scope by asking *how epistemic agents ought to comport themselves,* if they are to achieve knowledge. What sorts of abilities, dispositions, or character traits are involved in the acquisition and retention of knowledge? Answering such questions might well be valuable in its own right. But it might also shed light on the *nature* of

knowledge. Despite important differences between the two traditions, both the *pragmatist* tradition (explored by Scott Aiken, in Chapter 1), and the *virtue epistemological* one (Heather Battaly, in Chapter 14) are animated by this cluster of ideas. But while work in the pragmatist and virtue epistemological traditions attempts to shed new light on traditional epistemological questions by highlighting the links between knowledge and agency, there is also a significant body of work exploring the role of knowledge *within* action. Concepts such as those of skill, expertise, and know-how have received much attention in recent years, as exemplified here by Berit Brogaard's Chapter 7.

So, this is a rich and involving group of themes. Their presence within this book is a clear mark of epistemology's present vibrancy, due in part to its persistent intermingling with so much else from the wider reaches – now and during the past century or so – of philosophy.

Notes

1 Or, at least, those that would be included *if* such an end-point is possible. Yet notice that the question of whether it *is* possible is itself meta-epistemological (in this sense of 'meta-epistemology').
2 The term 'epistemic' denotes such phenomena or attainments as knowledge, rational support, understanding, evidence, and the like. The term 'epistemological' denotes reflection upon some or all of whatever is epistemic.
3 For further discussion of meta-achievement epistemology, see Hetherington (1992, 2010).
4 For an introduction and defence of this project, see Howson and Urbach (1993).
5 An important source of doubt derives from the work of the later Wittgenstein, particularly his (1953) *Philosophical Investigations*.
6 We should note that this volume's chapters, though, do not include discussions of sceptical epistemology. For extensive treatment of that provocative and often perplexing segment – 'the other half' – of epistemology, see Machuca and Reed (2018).

References

Gettier, E. L. (1963), 'Is Justified True Belief Knowledge?' *Analysis* 23: 121–3.
Hetherington, S. (1992), *Epistemology's Paradox: Is a Theory of Knowledge Possible?* Savage, MD: Rowman & Littlefield.

Hetherington, S. (2010), 'Elusive Epistemological Justification', *Synthese*, 174: 315–30.

Howson, C. and Urbach, P. (1993), *Scientific Reasoning: The Bayesian Approach*, Chicago: Open Court.

Machuca, D. and Reed, B. (eds) (2018), *Skepticism: From Antiquity to the Present*, London: Bloomsbury.

Sellars, W. F. (1956), 'Empiricism and the Philosophy of Mind', *Minnesota Studies in the Philosophy of Science*, 1: 253–329.

Wittgenstein, L. (1953), *Philosophical Investigations*, (ed.) G. E. M. Anscombe, Oxford: Blackwell.

1

Pragmatism and Epistemology

Scott Aikin

1. Introduction

The pragmatist tradition is motivated primarily by the thought that the only differences that make a difference are those with distinct practical effects. This broad agreement that makes pragmatism a practical philosophy nevertheless yields disagreement in how to track these differences and what differences are relevant.[1] When pragmatists turn to epistemological issues such as what conditions must be met for knowledge, what the appropriate scope for doubts are, and how inquiry should proceed, their answers are focused on the differences in action and practical results yielded. Again, what differences are relevant or preferable distinguish these pragmatists from each other, but they are all focused on the practical upshot of their theoretical views.

In this short chapter, I will focus on the epistemological views of the three formative figures in pragmatism's classical period: Charles S. Peirce, William James, and John Dewey. Then I will turn to highlight two pragmatist themes in contemporary epistemology: questions of pragmatic encroachment in knowledge-attributions, and the neopragmatist view of knowledge and entitlement as instances of conferred social status.

2. The classical pragmatists: Peirce

Pragmatism's core commitment is to the deep connection between theory and practice, and the three pioneering figures of the tradition developed this view in particular fashions. Charles S. Peirce conceived of himself primarily as a scientist, and his views about knowledge are devised to reflect the realities of human cognition and to mesh with the best scientific practices of the day.

The most significant realities of human thought, Peirce held, are the mind's incapacities. Once we are clear about our limits, Peirce reasoned, we can responsibly proceed with inquiry. Failing to be clear about the mind's limitations leads to unrealistic research programs. Consequently, Peirce identified four incapacities that we must be aware of in order to properly theorize and expand our knowledge:

1. We have no power of Introspection, but all knowledge of the internal world is derived by hypothetical reasoning from our knowledge of external facts.
2. We have no power of Intuition, but every cognition is determined logically by previous cognitions.
3. We have no power of thinking without signs.
4. We have no conception of the absolutely incognizable.[2]

Peirce's reasons for holding these limits to obtain are all based on the thought that if a belief or claim means something, then it must be identifiable in terms of the differences in how one comes to hold it and what inferences about the world one makes in terms of holding it.[3] The first two incapacities clearly follow from this, as they would deny that one reasons to an intuition or to instances of introspection. They must function, as Peirce terms it, as *premises not themselves conclusions* (CP: 5.135). The third, then, is simply that such signs of an object of thought (what leads one to think it is, and what follows from it obtaining) are all that one can think about it. And the fourth follows from these, since if one is to have a conception of something, one must have some familiarity with the things that would lead one to think it exists and what would follow were it to exist. But to do so is precisely to have cognized it, and so the incognizable is something we cannot conceive.

Two significant consequences of these few incapacities are restrictions on relevant philosophical doubts and directives as how to clarify one's ideas. The first doubt restriction is that one's philosophical doubts must be within the bounds of other things known. 'Ignorance and error can only be conceived as relative to a real knowledge and truth' (CP: 5.257). Consequently, 'we cannot begin with complete doubt' (CP: 5.265). We must doubt only when we have identifiable reasons that lead us to doubt, which requires a background of knowledge to support the reasoning. Doubts should be understood as contrasting with beliefs, which are 'distinguished by the different modes of action to which they give rise' (CP: 5.398). So doubts, as occasions that beliefs and their correlate actions falter, must be occasioned by particular reasons – those that arise as particular failures of particular practice. Any philosophical program dependent on antecedent or universal doubt is itself without determinate content. Peirce pauses to note the contrast between this view and those that are in what he calls the 'Cartesian spirit', proceeding on a program of universal doubt in search of intuitive and certain knowledge.[4]

The second consequence of Peirce's program is that of clarifying what determinate content is. Peirce's view is well captured by the rule that 'our idea of anything *is* our idea of its sensible effects' (CP: 5.401). This rule is often termed the *Pragmatic Maxim*:[5] 'Consider what effects that might conceivably have practical bearings, we conceive the object of our conception to have. Then our conception of these effects is the whole of our conception of the object' (CP: 5.402). This criterion for meaning, Peirce acknowledges, is a form of 'prope-positivism', in that, like the positivists, those using the pragmatic maxim reveal a good deal of philosophical debate to be either 'meaningless gibberish' or 'downright absurd' (CP: 5.423). For example, the issue of the transubstantiation of the Eucharist in Catholic mass is clarified, since if wine becomes blood and bread becomes flesh, then there must be some detectable difference. If the wine after the ceremony still tastes, smells, and has the same bodily effects as wine, then it is 'senseless jargon' to say it has become something else (CP: 5.401). However, as distinct from the positivists, who aspire to eliminate all metaphysics, Peirce holds that the pragmatic maxim provides the means to 'extract from [some metaphysical claims] a precious essence', in particular, a distinct form of realism (CP: 5.424).

In light of the Pragmatic Maxim, Peirce holds that a significant change in how we talk about reality must be put into effect. Given that 'all the followers of science are fully persuaded that the process of investigation, if only pushed far enough, will give one certain solution to every question to which they can be applied', it follows that all questions have distinct, testable answers (CP: 5.407). Further, given that we cannot conceive of things independently of their effects and evidence, Peirce holds an inquiry-convergence theory of truth and reality: 'The opinion which is fated to be ultimately agreed to by all who investigate, is what we mean by truth, and the object represented in this opinion is the real' (CP: 5.407). The activity of thought in inquiry, then, is that of being carried not where we merely wish, but 'to a foreordained goal' (CP: 5.408). Truths are, in short, those views that are indefeasible.[6]

The final component of Peirce's epistemological program is that of formulating how such inquiry works – how we are to be carried by the facts instead of pushing things along as we please. In 'The Fixation of Belief', Peirce surveys four methods of coming to and maintaining one's beliefs:

1. The Method of Tenacity
2. The Method of Authority

3. The A Priori Method
4. The Method of Scientific Investigation

The first three of these methods have significant problems, primarily because they have no way, at least internally, to distinguish between properly and improperly following the methods. Only the scientific method 'presents any distinction of a right and a wrong way' (CP: 5.385). Tenacious believers cling to their opinions and shut out any outside influence. For sure, they have resoluteness, but 'the social impulse is against [the method]', since one must hold that others' opinions (however tenaciously held) are of no worth (CP: 5.378). The method of authority, which holds lists of particular opinions to be obligatory, suffers a similar shortcoming, since there is no non-question-begging reason one can give for why one follows any one authority over another. The *A Priori* method is defined as the method of inquiry that identifies reason's natural preferences, or what is 'agreeable to reason' (CP: 5.382). The problem, as one might expect, is that what is agreeable to one person's reason is not always agreeable to another's. Peirce analogizes the intellectual situation for the *A Priori* method to that of taste, and he notes that 'taste, unfortunately, is always more or less a matter of fashion' (CP: 5.383).

In contrast to all of these methods, the scientific method has as a core component a set of conditions for self-correction, because the method first identifies what the objects of inquiry are in terms of the differences in experience one would see if they are or are not. One then may go to experience, conduct an experiment, and find out one way or the other. And thereby, the facts make the determination.[7] The fundamental hypothesis, then, is that a method that can allow the realities that we want to get right about determine our beliefs is preferred to the alternate methods: 'There are real things, whose characters are entirely independent of our opinions about them; those realities affect our senses according to regular laws ... and any man, if he have sufficient experience and reason enough about it, will be led to the one true conclusion' (CP: 5.384). In light of this methodological commitment, inquirers must be willing to change their views when the evidence and reasoning about the evidence runs against their views. Peirce terms this orientation of intellectual modesty *fallibilism*: 'any scientific proposition whatever is always liable to be refuted and dropped at short notice.... The best hypothesis ... is the one which can be most easily refuted if it is false' (CP: 1.120). The fallibilist holds that 'our knowledge is never absolute, but always swims, as it were, in a continuum of uncertainty and indeterminacy' (CP: 1.170).

3. The classical pragmatists: James

William James, like Peirce, took pragmatism's focus to be that of reformulating questions in terms of the practical differences consequent of the various options. And, like Peirce, James took the practical differences to be scientifically detectable. The difference was that Peirce's model for scientific research was that of the laboratory sciences, but James' model was psychology. James (1977 [1898]: 348) held that this orientation 'broadened' the range of relevant practical differences: 'The ultimate test of what a truth means is indeed the conduct it dictates or inspires. But it inspires that conduct because it first foretells some particular turn to our experience which shall call for just that conduct from us.' James' psychological modification of Peirce's pragmatic maxim incudes not only the passive consequences for subjects (what experiences they undergo if the object of thought obtains), but also their active consequences (what holding the content true will impel the subject to do).

James' psychologized pragmatism is posited on the thought that there must be a reciprocity between the active and passive elements of experience.[8] A further contrast with Peirce is useful to clarify this. Recall that with Peirce's Pragmatic Maxim, the notion of transubstantiation is 'senseless jargon', because there are no detectable differences between the wine and bread before and after the proper ceremonies. James' criterion includes the actions and satisfactions of believers and disbelievers as relevant differences, and this yields a different result from Peirce's. As James (1991 [1907]: 40) puts it: 'But tho these [the properties of wine and bread] don't alter, a tremendous difference has been made ... that we who take the sacrament, now feed upon the very substance of divinity. The substance-notion breaks into life, then, with tremendous effect.' Because the difference in belief makes a practical difference, James holds, there is a meaning (and a kind of truth) to the notion of transubstantiation.

This broadened notion of practical difference yields a significant change to how one inquires about a variety of issues. James' signal contribution along these lines is about how to proceed with the question of belief in God. Central to his program is his notion of the will-to-believe, which puts the reciprocity of the active and passive consequences of belief at the centre. James' essay, 'The Will to Believe', is complex, but the core of his argument is that cases wherein one's beliefs may contribute to their being true are those wherein it may be appropriate to believe, even when one does not have evidence of the truth of that belief. James asks us to consider the activity of making friends. If one takes up with others in a way that assumes we are all friends, James holds, it is considerably more likely that one will win friends than if one does not. One will be, in a word, *friendlier*. The same goes, James (1979 [1897]) holds, for social cohesion, good performance, and brave action. And in many instances, without the confident belief, no such actions would be forthcoming, much less successful[9]: 'There are, then, cases where a fact cannot come at all unless a preliminary faith exists in its coming' (29). Rather, he holds, these are cases wherein 'faith in a fact can help create the fact' (ibid.). The consequence is that even belief in God is allowable when there is no evidence in its favour, because it, too, has a reciprocity between the active and passive consequences of the commitment: 'We feel ... as if the appeal of religion to us were made to our own active good-will, as if evidence might be forever withheld from us unless we meet the hypothesis half-way' (31). James holds that religious commitment entails feeling that 'by obstinately believing that there are gods, ... we are doing the universe the deepest service we can' (ibid.).[10]

The differences in experience that make a difference, James argues, are those to which believers contribute. This is not merely a function of what differences an action *can* make, as one could, as one does with defeatist attitudes, believe that everyone dislikes you or that you will fail at your job. These are bad self-fulfilling prophesies, and ones to be avoided. Rather, James holds, one should direct one's beliefs to those consequences one prefers. Glossing the friend-making example from earlier, James observes that 'the desire for a certain kind of truth here brings about that truth's existence' (28).

With this coordination of the actional side of the pragmatist view of meaning with one's desires, James (1991 [1907]: 28) has developed an *instrumentalist theory of truth*: 'Any idea upon which we can ride, so to speak; any idea that will carry us prosperously from anyone part of our experience to any other part, linking things satisfactorily, working securely, simplifying, saving labor; is true just so much, true insofar forth, true *instrumentally*' (emphasis in the original). On this instrumentalist view, James holds that 'on pragmatic principles we cannot reject any hypothesis if consequences useful to life flow from it' (119). Now, noting that the instrumentalist view requires that one coordinate satisfactions with beliefs, truths must be indexed to what kinds of things one desires and one does not.[11] And so James' instrumentalist view is also a *pluralist* view of truth: 'We say this theory solves it on the whole more satisfactorily than that theory; but that means more satisfactorily to ourselves, and individuals will emphasize their points of satisfaction differently. To a certain degree, therefore, everything here is plastic' (30). The pluralism James sees arising is one that indexes the term 'true' to the desires and satisfactions of those for whom the proposals are true (or not): 'Our account of truth is an account of truths in the plural, of the processes of leading, realized *in rebus*, and having only this quality in common, that they *pay*' (96). We do not know beforehand which hypothesis will pay for us or for others. We know these things only after having tried them, only after having taken the risk that things may not work out. James (1979 [1897]: 25), like Peirce, enjoins a kind of fallibilism as part of proper inquiry, and given that these truths must be indexed to our desires and proclivities, holds that we should have a 'lightness of heart' about many of our errors. They are occasions to learn, cases where we've risked getting a truth.

4. The classical pragmatists: Dewey

Like James beforehand, John Dewey took an instrumentalist view of knowledge. In fact, 'instrumentalism' was Dewey's preferred term for his philosophical program. Thought, on Dewey's view, is a response to the environment, a coping with or anticipation of some coming event or change. Knowledge is a form of biologically adaptive behaviour, and its ultimate purpose is that of keeping the organism properly coordinated with the things around it: 'The function of intelligence is ... not that of copying the objects in the environment, but rather of taking account of the ways in which more effective and profitable relations with these objects may be established in the future.'[12] A contrast is useful for understanding the Deweyan view. Consider the program of identifying cognition as distinct from and not in the service of the rest of a life's interests. The knower in these cases is a pure spectator. But once the spectator is removed from the scene as something that does not interact with its objects of interest, but only watches from a distance, a puzzle arises as to how it comes to know its objects. But the instrumentalist model puts the subject of knowledge amid the things it knows – testing, experimenting, trying, failing, and succeeding. For Dewey, 'knowing is one mode of doing' (LW 4:184).

Dewey is keen to diagnose the errors of those who take on the spectator theory of knowledge.[13] Why, if knowledge is practical, did so many in the history of philosophy take the purely theoretical line? Dewey's answer was that the theory-practice division and the quest for theoretical certainty that arose from that divide were themselves instruments appropriate for a particular situation. Certainty, even if it is with but a few things, offers comfort in the face of an uncertain world. And so, Dewey reasoned, it was natural to withdraw to precise but empty points of perfect intellection when faced with widespread ignorance and lack of control. '[I]nsecurity generates the quest for certainty' (LW 4:202), and in social and scientific conditions under which uncertainty rules the day, such a retreat is reasonable. But the modern world does not have such rampant insecurity. We have well-established laws and norms. The natural sciences have made meteorology, medicine, and engineering quite successful, so that we can manage storms, illnesses, and chasms. The material conditions that make one intellectual program fecund will make another otiose. And so it is with the quest for certainty – it is an instrument that has outlived its usefulness.

The upshot is that Dewey's instrumentalist view yields a form of historicism, as the conditions for knowledge change with what objectives knowers have and what projects are feasible at the time. Intellectual progress is only, then, that of our views keeping up with what practices are successful or not: 'We have seen how the cognitive quest for absolute certainty by purely mental means has been surrendered in behalf of a search for security, having a high degree of probability, by means of preliminary active regulation of conditions' (LW 4:231). Dewey's view is that we are always in the midst of managing some question, in the middle of a set of problems with a background of values and disvalues. Knowledge is one appellation for our successfully managing that practical complex, but because the conditions change, knowledge, too, will look different at different times and in different contexts.

Central to Dewey's view of cognition is his Darwinian take on the struggle for existence. In 'The Influence of Darwinism on Philosophy', Dewey takes on the evolutionary view that all adaptations (including intelligence) are 'due simply to constant variation and the elimination of those variations which are harmful in the struggle for existence' (MW 4:9). Darwin's influence, because the crucial element was that of variation, reorients 'interest from the permanent to the changing' (MW 4:7). Because cognition is primarily a form of problem-management, Dewey holds that 'awareness means attention, and attention means a crisis of some sort of existential situation' (MW 4:72). In one way, this seems an overstatement, as one may ask how peering out the window and seeing the neighbour's dog must be an existential crisis.[14] However, in another way, the instrumentalist view is one that yields content in terms of what kinds of questions, plans and answers one's experiences occasion: 'The conjunction of problematic and determinate character in nature renders every experience as well as every idea and human act, an experiment in fact, even though not in design' (LW 1:63). We are, as it were, always inquiring and problem-solving.

The theory of inquiry, on Dewey's model, is, again, biological. Inquiry is the cognitive action of an organism seeing either to regain or to maintain a homeostatic equilibrium. Doubts, then, are the intellectual products of problems for that organic objective: 'Reflection appears as the dominant trait of a situation where there is something seriously the matter, some trouble, due to active discordance, dissentiency, conflict among the factors of a prior non-intellectual experience' (MW 10:326). Such practical failures Dewey terms *problematic situations*, and the process of inquiry is set into motion by them.[15] In 'How We Think', Dewey explains that knowledge is the product of inquiry that resolves these indeterminate situations: '[Instrumentalism] starts from acts, functions, as primary data, functions both biological and social in character; from organic responses, adjustments. It treats the knowledge standpoint, in all its patterns, structures, and purposes as evolving out of, and operating in the interests of, the guidance and enrichment of these primary functions' (MW 6:88). With these redescriptions in place, Dewey hoped that his proposals would prompt a recovery of philosophy's 'vision, imagination, and reflection' (MW 10:46).

Eventually, Dewey came to think that terms such as 'knowledge' and 'truth' could not be retrieved from their intellectualist corruptions. They are ripe for the abuses of the 'industry of epistemology' (MW 7:49). In their stead, he proposed *warranted assertability* (LW 12:15). The term had a number of advantages the prior two did not. First, the connection to inquiry is clear with warranted assertion, as it is in the process of inquiry, its successes in answering the questions that problematic situations occasion, that warrant arises. Warrant for assertions comes from 'their pertinancy and efficacy in satisfying conditions that are rigorously set by the problem they are employed to resolve' (LW 14:183).

The second advantage Dewey sees to the term change to warranted assertability is that the focus is on the sociality of intelligence. 'Knowledge' and 'truth' have the potential to be private, singular. But if inquiry is the determinant, the results are shareable. And so assertion is the model for intellectual resolution, a public statement and proposal. Dewey saw philosophy (and other intellectual programs) as taking up with a broader culture of action and communication: '[I]nquiry grows out of a background of culture and takes effect in greater or less modification of the conditions out of which it arises. Merely physical contacts with physical surroundings occur. But in every interaction that involves intelligent direction, the physical environment is part of a more inclusive social or cultural environment' (LW 12:27). Inquirers, on Dewey's model, are not on a solitary journey, nor are their results incommunicable or cut off from their fellows. Rather, intellectual pursuits are continuous with our broader social lives.

5. Neopragmatism: knowledge and social entitlement

The first significant theme extending beyond the classical pragmatists is what might be termed the *social view of knowledge*, that the term 'knowledge' tracks a social standing, one that allows a person to make pronouncements, be part of planning further action, participate in ongoing conversation. A good deal of this program is inspired by Dewey's notion of warranted assertion as being rooted in a culture. In *Philosophy and the Mirror of Nature*, Richard Rorty (1979: 9) invokes Dewey when he proposes a development of the social model: 'If we have a Deweyan conception of knowledge, … we will not imagine that there are enduring constraints on what count as knowledge, since we will see all 'justification' as a social phenomenon.' Rorty (1985) terms his new model *epistemological behaviorism*. He introduces the view with the question, '[C]an we treat epistemology as the study of certain ways humans interact?' (99). Rorty frames the model as based on the thought that knowledge-attribution tracks social standing: 'Explaining rationality and epistemic authority by reference to what society lets you say, rather the latter by the former, is the essence of behaviorism when applied to human knowledge … Behaviorism claims that if you understand the rules of a language game, you understand all there is to understand about why moves in that language game are made' (98). In short, Rorty's view is that understanding knowledge is a matter of understanding how people use the relevant epistemic terms, and that is a function of their interests, projects, and histories. 'The only criterion we have for applying the word "true" is justification, and justification is always relative to an audience' (Rorty 1998: 4). Rorty's view, consequently, is a form of historicism, in that he holds that languages and terms are tools, indexed for their aptness to particular times and places. And instead of being designed to represent the world, they are designed as means for coordinating people in it: 'By "historicism" I mean the doctrine that there is no "closeness of fit" between language and the world: no image of the world projected by language is more or less representative of the world than any other' (294). Rorty (1989: xiii) holds that taking on such historicism and anti-representationalism as an outlook frees us from trying to 'escape from time and chance', but rather than pursuing Truth or Knowledge, we understand ourselves pursuing 'freedom … as the goal of thinking'.

Robert Brandom's work has extended and developed the sociality thesis. With what he terms *the default and challenge structure of entitlement*, Brandom's (2000: 11) program is a form of rationalized pragmatism, in that reason-exchange is central to the model for justification. Brandom (1994: 142) begins *Making It Explicit* by setting out what he calls *the game of giving and asking for reasons*, wherein 'competent linguistic practitioners keep track of each other's commitments and entitlements. They are deontic scorekeepers'. The basic move of the game is that of announcing and undertaking a commitment, making an assertion. Once one takes on a particular commitment, one is entitled to take on some others and barred from taking on yet others. That is, once one has commitments, one may make certain *inferences*. Brandom holds that inferring in these fashions is the 'key component linking semantic content and pragmatic significance' (190).

Commitments for which participants are entitled are those for whom their undertakings are permitted in the game. Entitlements can be inherited over permitted inferences, and disavowals of commitments can be licensed by being incompatible with other entitled commitments. However, not all entitlement is transmitted by inference. Such a requirement would, as Brandom reasons, yield a vicious regress. Instead, some commitments must be treated as *default entitled* when a speaker's mere undertaking them entitles them. However, this default entitlement comes with conditions, particularly that if the commitment is *challenged* by other participants and if the target speaker cannot bring forth other entitled commitments to answer the challenges, then the commitment is no longer entitled: 'If many claims are treated as innocent until proven guilty – taken to be entitled until and unless someone is in a position to raise a question about them …, then the global thread of regress dissolves' (177). Brandom's primary model for default entitlement is that of observation reports made by those an audience takes as reliable reporters: 'The default entitlement … of observation reports … is thought of as broadly inferred because the one who attributes such authority implicitly endorses the reliability of the reporter' (189). The upshot is that the default-and-challenge structure of entitlement arises from the game of giving and asking for reasons – a game wherein one takes on commitments and keeps track of others' commitments, and particularly, which ones they are entitled to and which ones they are not. Consequently, Brandom's model, like Rorty's before, takes the social give-and-take of critical discussion as the key to what epistemic evaluation is, namely that of testing and conferring a particular social standing. 'Entitlement is … a social status that a performance or commitment has in a community' (77).

Brandom's epistemic program is pragmatist at its core, since the model of entitlement transmission and generation is tied to intentional action. On the one hand, commitments and entitlements can be inherited through inference from those with default status, and so observation statements are *language-entry* acts of speech, bringing information into a linguistic community. On the other hand, entitlements may also license certain actions, so one may believe and act for reasons that are continuous. Such are what Brandom terms *language-exit* transitions, wherein one moves from a linguistic commitment to a non-linguistic performance. 'A scorekeeping account can pick out (non-linguistic) performances as intentional … insofar as they are expressions of doxastic attitudes' (223).

The pragmatist theory of knowledge Brandom's social model for entitlement yields is one that places the attribution of knowledge by other scorekeepers at the centre. Brandom (2009) takes the *justified true belief* analysis of knowledge as a case in point. He notes that when one attributes a piece of knowledge to another, one must first attribute that commitment to the other. Second, one must 'take it that you are entitled to that commitment' (157). Third, attributors must, themselves, endorse the commitment. This, we call the *truth* condition for knowledge, but Brandom holds that '*all* that condition is doing is marking the coincidence of belief across social perspectives: I only count as knowledge beliefs that I *share*' (158; emphasis in the original).

6. Neopragmatism: pragmatic encroachment

A second theme from the classical pragmatists extending into contemporary discussion is the variance of standards for scrutiny with the practical costs of error. The higher the error costs, the better one's reasons for belief must be – being careful with one's beliefs is important, since there are practical consequences for holding them. The question is whether this piece of practical wisdom means that knowledge, too, varies with stakes. Consider the following two cases.

> **Bank (Low Stakes):** It is Friday and Hannah plans to stop at the bank to deposit her paycheck. However, as she approaches, she finds the lines are very long. She has no impending bills and she remembers visiting the bank on a Saturday a few months back.
> **Bank (High Stakes):** It is Friday and Hannah plans to stop at the bank to deposit her paycheck. However, as she approaches, she finds the lines are very long. Her mortgage is due Sunday, and if she misses the payment, she incurs hefty

fines. She can pay the mortgage only if she is able to deposit the paycheck. She remembers visiting the bank on a Saturday a few months back. (Adapted from DeRose 1992)

It's clear that it would be unwise for Hannah to chance it that her memory was wrong or that the bank has changed schedules in the high stakes case, but it would be perfectly fine for her to wait for Saturday in the low stakes case. The question is whether the difference in our assessments of the different practically wise decisions makes a difference in whether Hannah knows (or justifiably believes) that the bank is open on Saturday in one, but not the other.

On the one hand, *evidentialism* is the view that whether one's belief is justified or is a case of knowledge depends entirely on the truth-related factors in the case. So, if two subjects have the same evidence for a proposition, then if one is justified so is the other. In both bank cases, Hannah has the same evidence, her memory of visiting the bank on a Saturday. If evidentialism is true, then Hannah's justification for believing that the bank will be open in the low stakes case will be the same as her justification in the high stakes case. Given that it seems she's epistemically justified to believe in the low stakes case, it should follow that she's justified in the high stakes case. The trouble is that with this outcome, theoretical and practical reason come apart – Hannah is epistemically justified in believing that the bank will be open on Saturday, but it is practically unwise for her to act in light of that belief. That seems deeply odd.

Pragmatism, on the other hand, is the view that practical and epistemic rationality should not diverge, and were they to, practical reasons trump or defeat the intellectual. And so in the high stakes case, it seems that because it would not be practically rational for Hannah to act on the belief that the bank will be open on Saturday, her epistemic justification for believing so evaporates. She may still have the same evidence as before, but the costs of error defeat that evidential support. Again, the pragmatist view is that there must be a continuity between theoretical and practical reason, and that practical reason has a prime of place. Practical differences are those that make the relevant differences.

This pragmatist constraint on knowledge is known as *pragmatic encroachment*, in that practical concerns may intervene on what may seem as purely intellectual matters. Jeremy Fantl and Matt McGrath (2000, 2002) have defended two versions of the view. They may be stated roughly as follows:

S knows that p only if S is rational to act as if p;

S is justified in believing that p only if S is rational to act as if p

Jason Stanley (2005: 2) proposes a version of pragmatism along similar lines: '[T]he factors that make true belief into knowledge include elements from practical rationality ... What makes true belief into knowledge is not entirely an epistemic matter.' The benefit of the pragmatist view is that the norms of knowledge-ascription help explain why we endorse or reject some actions.

Another face of the pragmatic encroachment model in epistemology is not only along the lines of knowledge- and justification-attribution, but along the lines of how to structure inquiry. Again, in cases where errors are costly, scrutiny is higher. Consequently, areas where research is foregone or taken on with high costs are also objectionable. Philip Kitcher has held that the pragmatist perspective may help craft research programs that can do the most good or at least not promote the worst possibilities. First, Kitcher holds that some research programs are obligatory, or at least our foregoing them is objectionable, because of the costs associated with not taking them up. For example, consider the fact that there is disproportionately more research on non-urgent medical issues than on ones that could easily do great good – particularly, mitigating the damage done by malaria (Flory and Kitcher 2004). Further, Kitcher argues that inquiry ought not be pursued in cases where the consequences of its pursuit are likely to affect negatively the lives of those in underprivileged groups. For example, Kitcher holds that it is imperative of researchers on intelligence not to connect any of their research to race, because no matter how the results come out, the consequences of the research endangers people in underprivileged groups. There are, then, cases wherein 'free inquiry may be too dangerous to be tolerated' (1997: 280; 2001: 96).[16]

Finally, on the matter of pragmatic views of inquiry's goals, Nicholas Rescher (2015: 146) has observed that the objectives of simplicity in theoretical explanation can be overridden when higher resolution is needed, but the variance between simplicity and high-detail is a matter of the purposes to which one plans on putting the information yielded by inquiry. 'To say that one fact or finding is more important than another within the problem-setting of a particular subject-matter is to make a judgment of worth or value. Accordingly, it merits a greater expenditure of intellectual resources ... Importance, that is to say, is a fundamentally economic concept.' As a consequence, Rescher holds that levels of detail will rise or fall in research programs dependent on values in the background that determine what the importance of a finding and its detail will be. Also, there is an inevitable and ineliminable risk of oversimplification in all of inquiry's products. And as a consequence, there is no in principle end to inquiry. Rescher terms this sanguine view the *Law of Imperfectability*: 'With any practicable human arrangement in this world there is a limit to the extent that errors can be eliminated on a systematic basis' (24). Fallibilism, then, is endemic to the pragmatist conception of inquiry.

Notes

1 A. O. Lovejoy noted in 1908 that there were already thirteen logically distinct trends within the pragmatist program. Surely that number is much greater now. Misak's (2013) history of the pragmatist movement traces many of these differences.

2 CP: 5.265. References to Peirce's writings will be keyed to *The Collected Papers of Charles Sanders Peirce*, employing the following formula: (CP: volume number, paragraph number).

3 Notice that this view sets Peirce's theory of cognition along an anti-foundationalist trajectory. See Aikin (2009).

4 The contrast between Peirce and Descartes is useful if only to highlight the pragmatist tradition's emphasis on the continuity between theory and practice. Those emphasizing this contrast are prominently Haack (1982), DeWaal (2005), and Bernstein (2010). Thomas Dabay (forthcoming) has challenged the depth of this contrast.

5 See Hookway (2012) for a systematic study of the consequences of and reasons for the pragmatic maxim.

6 See Misak (1991) for the indefeasibilist interpretation of Peirce's view of truth as the end of inquiry.

7 See Hookway (2002) for an overview of Peirce's program ensuring this outcome. Elizabeth Cooke (2007) observes that this must also involve a kind of hope about inquiry.

8 See DeWaal (2005) and Talisse and Aikin (2008) for an explication of the psychologized version of pragmatism. Smith (1992) argues for this broadened version as a significant improvement over Peirce's view.

9 Richard Gale (2005) terms this the *beliefs help make the fact* cases, and Aikin (2014) terms them *conditions of doxastic efficacy.*

10 For a defence of this Jamesian view as a form of religious realism, see Slater (2009).

11 In this regard, Jeff Kasser (2014) has held that James' view is a form of expressivism.

12 LW 2:17. References to Dewey's works will be to the thirty-seven volume *Collected Works* (1969–91), and will employ the following formula (Early/Middle/Later period's volume number: page number).

13 Joseph Margolis (1977: 120) remarks in 'The Relevance of Dewey's Epistemology', that the Deweyan program anthropomorphizes knowledge.

14 See Gale (2010) for the worry that this thesis of the universality of inquiry is hyperbolic.

15 See Hildebrand's (2008: 53–60) overview of Dewey's stages of inquiry.

16 See Talisse and Aikin (2007) for a critique of Kitcher's proposal along the lines that the alternatives are worse.

References

Aikin, S. F. (2009), 'Prospects for Peircean Epistemic Infinitism', *Contemporary Pragmatism*, 6: 71–87.

Aikin, S. F. (2014), *Evidentialism and the Will to Believe*, London: Bloomsbury.

Bernstein, R. (2010), *The Pragmatic Turn*, Cambridge: Polity Press.

Brandom, R. B. (1994), *Making It Explicit: Reasoning, Representing, and Discursive Commitment*, Cambridge, MA: Harvard University Press.

Brandom, R. B. (2000), *Articulating Reasons: An Introduction to Inferentialism*, Cambridge, MA: Harvard University Press.

Brandom, R. B. (2009), *Reason in Philosophy: Animating Ideas*, Cambridge, MA: Harvard University Press.

Cooke, E. (2007), *Peirce's Pragmatic Theory of Inquiry: Fallibilism and Indeterminacy*, London: Continuum.

Dabay, T. (forthcoming), 'Why Peirce's Anti-intuitionism is not Anti-Cartesian: The Diagnosis of a Pragmatist Dogma', *International Journal of Philosophical Studies*.

DeRose, K. (1992), 'Contextualism and Knowledge Attributions', *Philosophy and Phenomenological Research*, 52: 913–29.

DeWaal, C. (2005), *On Pragmatism*, Belmont, CA: Wadsworth Publishing.

Dewey, J. (1969–91), *The Collected Works of John Dewey: The Early Works, The Middle Works, and the Later Works*, 37 vols, ed. J. A. Boydston, Carbondale: Southern Illinois University Press.

Fantl, J. and McGrath, M. (2000), 'On Pragmatic Encroachment in Epistemology', *Philosophy and Phenomenological Research*, 75: 558–89.

Fantl, J. and McGrath, M. (2002), 'Evidence, Pragmatics, and Justification', *Philosophical Review*, 111: 67–94.

Flory, J. H. and Kitcher, P. (2004), 'Global Health and the Scientific Research Agenda', *Philosophy and Public Affairs*, 32: 36–65.

Gale, R. M. (2005), *The Philosophy of William James: An Introduction*, Cambridge: Cambridge University Press.

Gale, R. M. (2010), *John Dewey's Quest for Unity: The Journey of a Promethean Mystic*, Amherst, NY: Prometheus Books.

Haack, S. (1982), 'Descartes, Peirce, and the Cognitive Community', *The Monist*, 62: 156–81.

Hildebrand, D. (2008), *Dewey: A Beginner's Guide*, Oxford: One World Publications.

Hookway, C. (2002), *Truth, Rationality, and Pragmatism: Themes from Peirce*, Oxford: Clarendon Press.

Hookway, C. (2012), *The Pragmatic Maxim: Essays on Peirce and Pragmatism*, Oxford: Oxford University Press.

James, W. (1977 [1898]), 'Philosophical Conceptions and Practical Results', in J. J. McDermott (ed.), *The Will to Believe and Other Essays in Popular Philosophy: The Writings of William James*, Chicago: University of Chicago Press.

James, W. (1979 [1897]), *The Will to Believe and Other Essays in Popular Philosophy*, Cambridge: Harvard University Press.

James, W. (1991 [1907]), *Pragmatism*, Amherst, NY: Prometheus Books.

Kasser, J. (2014), 'Prospects for a Jamesian Expressivism', *William James Studies*, 10: 1–5.

Kitcher, P. (1997), 'An Argument about Free Inquiry', *Noûs*, 31: 297–306.

Kitcher, P. (2001), *Science, Truth, and Democracy*, New York: Oxford University Press.

Lovejoy, A. O. (1908), 'The Thirteen Pragmatisms', *The Journal of Philosophy, Psychology and Scientific Methods*, 5: 5–12.

Margolis, J. (1977), 'The Relevance of Dewey's Epistemology', in S. M. Cahn (ed.), *New Studies in the Philosophy of John Dewey*, Hanover, NH: University of Vermont Press.

Misak, C. (1991), *Truth and the End of Inquiry: A Peircean Account of Truth*, Oxford: Clarendon Press.

Misak, C. (2013), *The American Pragmatists*, Oxford: Oxford University Press.

Peirce, C. S. (1965), *The Collected Papers of Charles Sanders Peirce*, ed. C. Hartshorne and P. Weiss, Cambridge, MA: Belknap Press of Harvard University Press.

Rescher, N. (2015), *Cognitive Complications: Epistemology in Pragmatic Perspective*, Lanham, MD: Lexington Books.

Rorty, R. (1979), *Philosophy and the Mirror of Nature*, Princeton, NJ: Princeton University Press.

Rorty, R. (1985), 'Epistemological Behaviorism and the De-transcendentalization of Analytic Philosophy', in R. Hollinger (ed.), *Hermeneutics and Praxis*, Notre Dame, IN: Notre Dame University Press.

Rorty, R. (1989), *Contingency, Irony and Solidarity*, Cambridge: Cambridge University Press.

Rorty, R. (1998), *Truth and Progress: Philosophical Papers*, Vol. 3, Cambridge: Cambridge University Press.

Slater, M. R. (2009), *William James on Ethics and Faith*, Cambridge: Cambridge University Press.

Smith, J. E. (1992), *America's Philosophical Vision*, Chicago: University of Chicago Press.

Stanley, J. (2005), *Knowledge and Practical Interests*, Oxford: Clarendon Press.

Talisse, R. B. and Aikin, S. F. (2007), 'Kitcher on the Ethics of Inquiry', *The Journal of Social Philosophy*, 38: 654–65.

Talisse, R. B. and Aikin, S. (2008), *Pragmatism: A Guide for the Perplexed*, London: Continuum.

2

On Our Epistemological Debt to Moore and Russell

Claudio de Almeida

1. Introduction: the view from here

Writing in the late 1950s, Allen Wood (1959: 190) introduced his unfinished essay on Russell's philosophical work with the following words: 'I believe there is little of importance in present-day philosophizing which is not derived from [Russell]. The post-Russellians are all propter-Russellians … Any adequate commentary on Russell must take account of his influences on subsequent philosophy; which it means that it may be many centuries before it can be written.' And here's what Alice Ambrose and Morris Lazerowitz (1970: 11) wrote in their preface to a well-known *festschrift* honouring G. E. Moore's work: 'Philosophy after Moore can never again be what it was before Moore, because of the standards of exactness and refinement he brought to the doing of philosophy, but more importantly because of the direction he gave to philosophical investigation.' Several decades later, as well-equipped as any commentator can be to denounce hyperbole in Wood's words, or in Ambrose and Lazerowitz's, if there was hyperbole there to be denounced, Scott Soames (2014) describes Moore and Russell, alongside Frege, as 'founding giants' of analytic philosophy, no less.

Only a fool would argue with this kind of reverence. Our debt to Moore and Russell, in major areas of philosophy and in philosophical methodology, is, in a word, *immense*. But that is compatible with noting that, if we throw a cold, hard look at those bodies of work *from our post-Gettier epistemological angle exclusively*, it is tempting to conclude that, like most of what has been accomplished by overachievers since Sextus Empiricus, their contributions to *epistemology*, specifically, are dwarfed by what has been accomplished since Edmund Gettier triggered a radical revision to the field. No surprise here to those who are familiar with the history of epistemology.

The post-Gettier work in epistemology, especially the work done in the two decades following the publication of Gettier's paper, is so creative, when compared to what had been done in the preceding couple of millennia, that it seems to have come close to rebuilding the field from scratch. To those who are familiar with post-Gettier epistemology, the claim is not at all exciting. But, no, epistemology didn't quite start from scratch when Gettier published his paper. So much has, of course, been retained from tradition, and so much of what has been retained dates back to the luminaries in Plato's Academy and to their ancient critics. And, yet, it is not unfair to say that, in the period from Sextus to Gettier, we collected a number of *merely incremental* improvements to the ancient legacy, as important as some of those advances undoubtedly were. Writing just before Gettier's seismic impact could be registered, Roderick Chisholm (1964: 239), arguably the foremost authority in epistemology at the time, put the point as follows: 'Most of the problems and issues constituting the 'theory of knowledge' were discussed in detail by Plato and Aristotle and by the Greek skeptics. There is some justification, I am afraid, for saying that the subject has made very little progress in the past two thousand years.' '*Very little* progress', he wrote (and I add the emphasis). So, maybe, by the reasonable standards of a Chisholm, the contributions made to epistemology by these two 'founding giants', Moore and Russell, don't quite amount to revolutionary material. And those of us who are even superficially familiar with their works should know that epistemology was never front-and-centre in their philosophical agendas anyway – close to their hearts, yes, undoubtedly, but not a number-one priority to either of them. Both were deeply, and primarily, involved with issues in metaphysics throughout their careers. In Russell's case, only his early work in logic and the foundations of mathematics, up to the publication of *Principia Mathematica*, eclipses his involvement with metaphysics.[1] In Moore's case, ethical theory was, early on, a top priority, but one that was soon to be replaced with his metaphysical concerns. If you had to mention a single issue to which they made *groundbreaking* contributions in philosophy, it would have to be the idealism/realism debate.[2] They led the way to the discrediting of every major form of idealism in contemporary philosophy. That's their calling card, *if they must have only one*. Still, they were both fascinated by epistemological problems all along, and often enough applied themselves strenuously to major issues in the field.

This is a chapter on their contributions to epistemology. But you won't find the typical historian's voice here. I can't make it a priority to speculate on what either of them *really thought* about the epistemological issues on which they wrote. That task would require long-range engagement with what influential historians have claimed they *really thought*. Instead, I'll be more concerned with what *we think* (possibly unjustifiably) belongs in our agenda on account of their influence on us; more specifically, with what we think (possibly unjustifiably) may amount to *definitive* contributions they have made to our epistemological agenda, not just to *important* contributions they may have made to the *evolution* of our epistemological agenda. More precisely, the emphasis will be on what we *should think, by our current standards for epistemological significance,* we have learned from them once we have been alerted to the epistemological nuggets in their works. Maybe this is something of which we are in greater need at this stage of our involvement with both epistemology and their bodies of work, if we want to acknowledge our debts. Maybe this is something we haven't hitherto been offered by commentators, not for epistemology anyway.

Otherwise, there are the obvious space constraints. So many epistemological nuggets will remain ignored here! This short chapter is, as you may expect, much too short for an appraisal of all the contributions made by such imposing figures to such a lively philosophical field as contemporary epistemology, if the schematic presentation that follows must also be intelligible. But, hopefully, it's long enough to provide the reader with some useful reminders of our debt to two giants who toiled in the dimly lit terrain of pre-Gettier epistemology.

2. Acknowledging a Russellian milestone (or two, or three)

Why should the most merciless and impatient of our A+ students of post-Gettier epistemology welcome Russell as 'one of us' in the seminar room, if s/he looked carefully at his epistemological ideas? Which among those ideas might command respect from that irreverent student? This section provides an answer that you will not find elsewhere in its entirety. The part of my answer that I believe you will not find elsewhere follows a brief note on the part that is already familiar from the literature on our debt to Russell.

Russell has been credited with providing us with a proper understanding of 'the problem of induction', so-called – roughly, the problem of explaining why we deem rational beliefs which are produced by some of our episodes of non-deductive reasoning (while others are deemed irrational). As Sainsbury (1979: 165) notes, we owe it to Russell to have understood that the problem of induction is *not*, at bottom, the problem of why 'the [inductive] arguments we intuitively regard as strong are just those that project experienced phenomena on to the unobserved'. In other words, the problem is not, as pre-Russellian tradition would have us believe, the problem of justifying our reliance on a principle of the 'uniformity of nature'. The depth of the problem is clearly found in what became known as Nelson Goodman's 'New Riddle of Induction' (aka 'Grue Paradox'), which is sketchily anticipated by some of Russell's remarks in a 1912 paper 'On the Notion of Cause'. Goodman's problem remains a staple of the epistemological agenda to this day.

Another well-known Russellian contribution to our post-Gettier concerns – in fact, the one most obviously commanding reference to Russell in post-Gettier epistemology – is the set of Gettier-type examples he put into circulation beginning in 1912. In *The Problems of Philosophy*, Russell offers us two cases of true belief formed on the basis of good reasoning from a false premise that is evidentially essential to the conclusion. In the first case, the believer infers that *The late Prime Minister's last name began with a 'B'*. This is a true belief, but it is based on the false belief that *The late Prime Minister was Arthur Balfour*, whereas, in fact, the relevant late Prime Minister, so-described in 1912, was Balfour's successor, Henry Campbell Bannerman, who died in 1908.[3] In the second case – if we make Russell's very sketchy presentation a little more perspicuous – the believer, taking testimony from a newspaper, comes to believe that *The battle has been won* (by whichever side has won said battle). And the battle had, in fact, been won, but, uncharacteristically, the newspaper had not, at that point, been apprised of the fact by reputable channels. In both cases, according to Russell, there is no inferential knowledge, even though the relevant inferential beliefs are true.

In *Human Knowledge* (1948), Russell revisits the issue and gives us his most famous case, the case of the stopped clock. Here – again, adapting his extremely sketchy exposition of the case – the believer, looking at a clock in the afternoon, sees the hands showing 3 o'clock, believes that the clock is in perfect working order, and, on that basis, believes that *it's 3 p.m.* And it is 3 p.m. exactly. But, unbeknown to the believer, the clock had stopped working at 3 a.m. (or at 3 p.m. on a previous date).

Is it reasonable to think that Russell gave us Gettier cases long before we heard from Gettier? That would seem to depend on the surrounding text. What Russell *explicitly said* is that those are cases of true (inferential) belief that does not amount to knowledge: 'you cannot claim to have known merely because you turned out to be right' (140). But the crucial issue is: Did Russell *tacitly* assume that those were cases of true belief that was also *justified*? There is good textual evidence to think that he did. The Prime Minister case involves a confusion between a couple of PMs whose last names both begin with a 'B', one of those PMs having succeeded the other, which seems to suggest a minor slip by a generally well-informed believer. In the newspaper case, according to Russell (1912: 205), the newspaper announces the right result 'by an intelligent anticipation ... before any telegram giving the result has been received' – which makes it an even clearer case of a justified false premise acquired from a generally reliable source that turned out to have been, on that occasion, uncharacteristically hasty, or sloppy. In that case, we're enjoined to think that the false premise is something like *The newspaper has learned that the battle has been won*. (The believer would then be in a position validly to infer that *The battle has been won*, if we assume, as Russell clearly did, that knowledge is factive.) But the 'intelligent anticipation' is not supposed to justify the announcement to the degree required for knowledge. So, it's false that the newspaper had already *learned* about the victory (since the newspaper would then not have *known* about it). And the stopped clock case is, very straightforwardly, generally regarded as an obvious Gettier-type case, with all the right ingredients thrown in (for an inferential Gettier-type case). In that case, we naturally assume that the believer's inference is based on the well-justified premise that the clock is in perfect working order.

Unfortunately, that is not all we find in the surrounding text. In the 1948 discussion, the stopped clock and Prime Minister cases are followed by the case of 'the lucky optimist who, having bought a ticket for a lottery, has an unshakeable conviction that he will win, and, being lucky, does win' (Russell 1948: 140). And that's the fly in the ointment right there! The lucky optimist is no Gettier-type believer. He epitomizes that charming form of doxastic pathology we call 'optimism'. But Russell's diagnosis does not distinguish between that irrational believer and the rational ones in the other cases.

Roy Sorensen (1992: 272) may have expressed a majority view when he wrote, in reference to the stopped clock case, that 'Russell did not notice he had a counterexample to JTB [i.e. the justified-true-belief analysis of knowledge] because he was not looking for one'. That is the point exactly: He failed to see the fundamental feature of the Gettier Problem as that feature was being paraded by Russell himself before his own eyes. So, how close was Russell to anticipating Gettier? Maybe not as close as we'd like to believe, given our tendency to discount what he *explicitly said*, namely, that he was showing us that knowledge is not merely true belief. In any case, this much seems certain: There might well not have been a Gettier had Russell not given us his Gettier-type cases. The pressure Russell put on the epistemological community to think about those cases must have been a decisive factor in our evolution on that front. Arguably, no other influence on early-1960s epistemological thought could have been any greater than his.

Those two instances of our epistemological debt to Russell – his anticipation of Goodman's 'New Riddle of Induction' and his Gettier-type cases – have been amply acknowledged in the literature. In the remainder of this section, I will concentrate on another of his contributions to the field that is not nearly as well advertised as the ones mentioned above.

Russell's 1912 response to (improperly so-called) Cartesian scepticism packs considerable punch, whatever its ultimate fate by our estimation. We're still chewing on it, though we may not know we are. Much of that early reaction to the sceptical problem is kept throughout his philosophical career. While holding an anti-sceptical view in *My Philosophical Development* (1959), Russell remained, as he was at the opposite end of his involvement with epistemology, in 1912, ready to concede all of the premises on which the sceptical voice in Descartes' first 'meditation' would have based its attack on the possibility of empirical knowledge. It was a tortured reaction throughout his career, as the following passage reveals:

> A very great deal of what we all unquestioningly accept as knowledge depends upon testimony, and testimony, in turn, depends upon the belief that there are other minds besides our own. To common sense, the existence of other minds does not appear open to doubt, and I do not myself see any reason to disagree with common sense on this point. But, undoubtedly, it is through experiences of my own that I am led to believe in the minds of others; and, undoubtedly, as a matter of pure logic, it would be possible for me to have these experiences even if other minds did not exist. (144–5)

To which, that irreverent A+ student of post-Gettier epistemology might reply: 'So, you do see *some* reason to disagree with common sense after all – namely, the very anti-common-sense observation that, *undoubtedly*, your experiences may be misleading you into falsely believing that the world you're in is as common sense would take it to be.' The critic would be on strong grounds, as the post-Gettier emergence of *contextualism* in epistemology amply shows: once you so much as *consider* a sceptical hypothesis that is incompatible with what you ordinarily claim to know, the tenability of common-sense beliefs should be under the gun *from your own perspective*.

But, as it turns out, the Russell of 1912 did a whole lot better on that front than the Russell of 1959! He did have, in 1912, a surprisingly elaborate answer to that challenge. Unfortunately, only the most superficial part of that answer is recalled in 1959, when he addresses it as follows:

> You might have experiences in a dream which would be equally convincing while you still slept, but which you would regard as misleading when you woke. Such facts warrant a certain degree of doubtfulness, but usually only a very small degree. In the immense majority of cases, they justify you in accepting testimony if there is no evidence to the contrary. (145)

In the later work, only the most superficial form of epistemological *conservatism* is apparent – in a way that does so much less than what is hoped for by a full-blooded conservative response, since Russell acknowledges that a 'very small degree of doubtfulness' will still attach to common-sense beliefs.[4] This makes us ponder the dilemma: either adopt a graded view of belief, in conjunction with the familiar graded view of justification, and admit that knowledge requires less than full belief, or else admit that knowledge requires justified full belief and face the sceptical challenge of removing every little ground for doubt.[5] So, there will be no clear road past scepticism at the level of superficiality which characterized Russell's 1959 review of the issue.

But the earlier work supplied us with a much more elaborate response to scepticism. That response rested on epistemological ideas that are very much under scrutiny in post-Gettier epistemology. Here, I can only mention them briefly and, also very quickly, compare the Russellian conceptual mix with a contemporary alternative that is put forward as an improvement on the Russellian recipe.

Russell's epistemology, in 1912, had all of the following elements: it was internalist; it rejected forms of global scepticism that seem to imply (a kind of) ineffability (such as certain versions of Pyrrhonism); it accepted the premises of Cartesian-style scepticism; it combined elements of both foundationalism and coherentism (into what may have been the clearest form of 'foundherentism' on record at that point in time); it championed the view that justification is truth-conducive; it upheld fallibilism as regards the justification of superstructure beliefs; it was infallibilistic for foundational beliefs; and it claimed that Cartesian-style scepticism could be defeated by a combination of the aforementioned elements. Let us see some evidence for the mix in Russell's own words, followed by a brief review of his anti-sceptical strategy.

Internalism and justificational truth-conduciveness:

> We must, … if possible, find, in our own purely private experiences, characteristics which show, or tend to show, that there are in the world things other than ourselves and our private experiences. (Russell 1912: 34)[6]

'Ineffability', global scepticism discredited:

When we speak of philosophy as a *criticism* of knowledge, it is necessary to impose a certain limitation. If we adopt the attitude of the complete sceptic, placing ourselves wholly outside all knowledge, and asking, from this outside position, to be compelled to return within the circle of knowledge, we are demanding what is impossible ... [F]rom blank doubt, no argument can begin ... [I]t is not difficult to see that scepticism of this kind is unreasonable. Descartes' 'methodical doubt', with which modern philosophy began, is not of this kind. (234; emphasis in the original)[7]

The premises of Cartesian-style scepticism granted:

No logical absurdity results from the hypothesis that the world consists of myself and my thoughts and feelings and sensations, and that everything else is mere fancy. (34)

Justificational infallibility for foundational beliefs:

Some knowledge, such as knowledge of the existence of our sense-data, appears quite indubitable, however calmly and thoroughly we reflect upon it. (235)[8]

Fallible justification for superstructure beliefs:

[W]hen we are trying to show that there must be objects independent of our own sense-data, we cannot appeal to the testimony of other people, since this testimony does not reveal other people's experiences unless our own sense-data are signs of things existing independently of us ... In one sense it must be admitted that we can never *prove* the existence of things other than ourselves and our experiences. (33)

Coherence as a justification-enhancing feature of a doxastic system:

Of course it is not by argument that we originally come by our belief in an independent external world. We find this belief ready in ourselves as soon as we begin to reflect: it is what may be called an *instinctive* belief [such as the belief that there is a table over there, or a book over here] ... There can never be any reason for rejecting one instinctive belief except that it clashes with others; thus, if they are found to harmonize, the whole system becomes worthy of acceptance ... [B]y organizing our instinctive beliefs and their consequences ... we can arrive, on the basis of accepting as our sole data what we instinctively believe, at an orderly systematic organization of our knowledge, in which, though the possibility of error remains, its likelihood is diminished by the interrelation of the parts and by the critical scrutiny which has preceded acquiescence. (37–40; emphasis in the original)[9]

Such are the core elements of Russell's epistemology in 1912, and it should be clear to that A+ student of post-Gettier epistemology that each of them has been extensively discussed in recent literature. Here, we don't have the space to comment on the tenability of all of these Russellian views in light of recent developments. Our central issue will simply be this: How might this combination of elements yield a response to scepticism?

Russell's *explicit* response suggests a very superficial approach to the sceptical challenge. Here is the passage of *The Problems of Philosophy* most readily recalled by commentators in that connection:

> There is no logical impossibility in the supposition that the whole of life is a dream … But … there is no reason whatever to suppose that it is true; and it is, in fact, a less simple hypothesis, viewed as a means of accounting for the facts of our own life, than the common-sense hypothesis that there really are objects independent of us, whose action on us causes our sensations. (35)

Here, the part that most readily attracts attention is the *simplicity* claim.[10] But why should we think that a real-world hypothesis is simpler than, say, a demon-world hypothesis? Why is the hypothesis that our beliefs about, say, dinosaurs, black holes, and Maria Callas are made true by facts involving dinosaurs, black holes, and Callas any simpler than a world where there are, say, a powerful demon, the doxastic agent, and the agent's fanciful beliefs about dinosaurs, black holes, and Callas? Is the real-world hypothesis the one that is *ontologically* simpler? Does it provide for a *formally* simpler explanation of the data? What is supposed to make the simplicity claim appealing? The simplicity claim looks puzzling even before we ponder the harder problem of why simplicity should be thought of as truth-conducive.[11]

Russell was in a position to look beyond the mere simplicity claim and explain it with the help of the coherentist element in his epistemology. There should be no doubt that the real-world hypothesis is *more coherent* with any ordinary system of beliefs than any demon-world, massive-error hypothesis. Plainly, any hypothesis according to which our beliefs turn out *true* is more coherent with our beliefs than one according to which they turn out *false*. Coherence is what results from inferential relations between beliefs. So, the coherentist element alone suffices to explain the appeal of a simplicity claim. On close inspection, what looks abhorrent in scepticism is not that it fails by some (possibly elusive) standard for simplicity, but the fact that it fails to cohere well with our 'instinctive beliefs', assuming we are already saddled with a sizeable supply of those. So, once the sceptical hypothesis arises, it would seem (prima facie, at any rate) warranted for us to dismiss it as one for which there is no epistemic support in our doxastic system. (*Well* ... again, as the contextualist would urge, not obviously if you are actively pondering a sceptical threat. But, what if you are not? Would deflecting the sceptical threat on coherentist grounds reward the incurious, the unimaginative, with knowledge, while denying it to the more reflective among us?)

Is that enough for a victory over scepticism? When we look closely at the post-Gettier literature on the sceptical challenge, the answer would seem to be: the jury is still out on what the satisfactory answer to this question might be (and I cannot pursue it here any further).[12] Be that as it may, here's a Russellian view that our A+ student clearly should welcome in the seminar room.

I conclude this brief review of Russell's 1912 epistemology – again, arguably, his greatest contribution to the field – with the following observation. Russell's epistemology is best seen as a form of neoclassical foundationalism of the kind developed by Richard Fumerton (1995) and Laurence BonJour (2003). It is not of the classical kind because it acknowledges inductive support between foundations (beliefs about 'private experiences' and necessary truths) and superstructure ('instinctive beliefs' and scientific generalization) as justification-conferring. It is neoclassical, however, as opposed to 'moderate', or 'modest', because it holds that foundational beliefs are infallibly justified by private experiences and rational intuition. The hope for such a project is that an acceptable account of justification transmission between foundations and superstructure will be found. But it is somewhat misleading for us to put much stock on the coherentist element of Russellian 'foundherentism'.[13] Unless we think of justification as a 'two-way street', with superstructure beliefs somehow affecting the justification of foundational beliefs – no reason to think that Russell would have subscribed to that – some measure of coherentism *trivially* comes with the justification-conferring inferential relations between foundations and superstructure. But why is the justification supplied to superstructure beliefs by the foundations not enough to justify those superstructure beliefs to the degree required for knowledge, if that's what a foundherentist must hold? Might Russell's coherentist talk be just a clumsy way of promoting the need for a *defeasibility* condition, one according to which justification can be lost to non-overridden counter-evidence for a given belief in one's doxastic system?[14] We can surely understand the motivation for the coherentist (as opposed to a merely defeasibilist) element in foundherentism: the availability of reasons to ward off sceptical challenges to one's beliefs. And we can also clearly see the need for infallible justification at the bottom of the edifice, so to speak: to account for justificational truth-conduciveness. But the epistemic division of labour between foundationalist and coherentist elements, especially the *justification-enhancing* powers of coherence at superstructure level, remains blurry.

Interestingly, Russell's neoclassical foundationalism in 'foundherentist' guise seems quite a bit more promising than Susan Haack's (1993) version of the view. On a superficial look, Russell led the way to a form of foundherentism that was developed in detail by Haack.[15] The superficial look is deceiving, however. One of Haack's main theoretical contentions is that her brand of foundherentism is 'pervasively fallibilistic' (7). But the problem for any *internalist* view on which foundational beliefs are only fallibly justified is that truth-conducive justification becomes a chimera. For an internalist, like Russell, who rejects a coherentist account of *truth*, as he forcefully did, pervasive fallibilism would deprive him of theoretical reasons to think that there is *any* true belief in one's belief system. Where does foundational truth come from? If foundational beliefs are justified solely by one's 'purely private experiences', but only *fallibly* so, there's no accounting for the assumption that *there will be* foundational truths in the system. (Fallibilist externalism, by contrast, ensures the conceptual tie between justification and truth by making foundational justification depend on the objective reliability of the process causing a given belief.) So, on 'pervasive fallibilism', there would be no theoretical reason for thinking that foundational beliefs make non-foundational beliefs at least likely to be true, simply because there'd be no theoretical assurance that truth has 'entered the building', so to speak. But, on Russell's neoclassical foundationalism (as on BonJour's and on Fumerton's), justificational truth-conduciveness for non-foundational beliefs is at least in-principle attainable, which gives him some leverage against the sceptic – momentary as the advantage may ultimately prove to be. (Superficially, that kind of leverage may be expressed in coherentist terms, as when Russell claims that there is no reason to believe the sceptic.) Haack is aware of the problem for one, like her, who is not happy about surrendering truth-conduciveness.[16] She tries to tackle it in various ways, from seeking refuge in metaphysics, in the kind of pragmatist theory of truth that Russell advised against in 1912, to embracing 'evolutionary epistemology', and, finally, at the 'evolutionary' stage of the discussion, to conceding defeat to Cartesian-style scepticism while suggesting that that is okay after all: '[M]y sights are set *much* lower than Descartes's; I have aspired only to give reasons for thinking that, if any truth-indication is available to us, satisfaction of the foundherentist criteria of justification is as good an indication of truth as we could have' (220). Russell's sights, by contrast, were set to providing us with a *non*-pragmatist way out of scepticism that is at least conceptually intriguing. When we contrast their views from our vantage point, it's hard to avoid the conclusion that Russell's brand of foundationalism, as developed in the works of BonJour and Fumerton, is quite a bit more insightful than Haack's – or, at any rate, quite a bit more ambitious than hers.[17]

3. Moore's Paradox

When we read Russell with post-Gettier epistemological concerns in mind, it seems inevitable to conclude that, for the most part in any case, his epistemological views go by at breakneck speed, and we're left picking up the pieces of views that, on close inspection, seem a whole lot more complex than he made them look in his haste. Russell was a philosopher of *gigantic* scope. It is hard to even imagine that kind of scope if the topics in it were tackled at Moore's pace! The expository styles of the two philosophers – and whatever gave rise to the contrasting styles in each man's psychological profile – couldn't have been more different. As we look at Moore's work from our post-Gettier perspective, two issues stand out very clearly as screaming for our attention. He made sure they would, in his inimitable meticulous way. And both of them, largely in his own terms, are as entrenched in our post-Gettier agenda as anything we have discussed since Gettier. (So, Moore is routinely acknowledged 'as one of us' by irreverent A+ students in our seminar rooms.[18])

One of those issues is the form of 'absurdity' that Wittgenstein (1953) labelled 'Moore's Paradox'. This is the kernel of the paradox in Moore's (1993: 207–208) own words:

> [I]t's perfectly absurd or nonsensical to say such things as 'I don't believe it's raining, but as a matter of fact it is'... And [Wittgenstein, in response to my observations on the problem,] pointed out (I think) that there's nothing nonsensical in saying ... 'If I don't believe it's raining, but as a matter of fact it really is, then I am mistaken in my belief' ... To say [the aforementioned conjunction] in an assertive way really is absurd ... [T]here's no absurdity whatever in saying of a past occasion 'I didn't believe it was raining, but as a matter of fact it was'. This is in itself paradoxical: ... though it's absurd for me to say this of myself *in the present*, it's not the least absurd for another person

to say *what seems to express exactly the same proposition* either *to* me or *of* me. (Emphases in the original)

Moore's emphasis was on the oddity of asserted instances of the following propositional form:

(i)   p & I don't believe that p.

But even cursory inspection of the fragments in which he discusses the problem reveals that the following propositional form is thought to be equally odd, but taken as logically equivalent to (i):

(ii) p & I believe that ~p.[19]

Propositional form (i) ended up getting the lion's share of the attention in the literature, with many calling it alone 'Moore's Paradox'.[20]

It was John N. Williams (1979, 1994) who gave us the simplest, most compelling explanation of why both (i) and (ii) are paradoxical. His explanation ostensibly assumes only the following principle of belief-distribution (aka 'belief conjunction-elimination'):

> (BD) If S believes that p&q at a given time t, then S believes that p at t and S believes that q at t.

With that in mind, we can follow Williams and conclude, by two very simple arguments, that, in both cases, *S must harbour false belief in her doxastic system* – the claim on which Williams builds his account of why both (i) and (ii) are paradoxical. Notice: In the case of (i), by BD, if S believes the Moorean conjunction, S believes that p at t. But that falsifies the right-hand conjunct, according to which S doesn't believe that p at t. So, a belief of the form (i) is *self-refuting*.

In the case of form (ii), by BD, if S believes the Moorean conjunction, S believes that p at t. And, if the conjunction is true, S also believes that ~p at t. So, if the conjunction is both believed and true, S believes contradictories at the relevant time t. And, trivially, if the conjunction is believed and false, S has a false belief at t. So, belief in an instance of form (ii) guarantees that the believer is *logically inconsistent*.

We must be looking at a paradox. Although every instance of propositional forms (i) and (ii) is *contingent*, the fact that they are conjunctions one of the conjuncts of which contains a singular term given self-referring use in subject position, a present-tense occurrence of the verb 'to believe' in its higher clause, and the other conjunct as its lower clause suffices to ensure that the Moorean believer holds a false belief – by self-refutation in the case of (i) and by logical inconsistency in the case of (ii).

Interestingly, the problem is even harder than it looks on Williams' formulation of it, as clear and precise as that formulation already is. In fact, we can see the paradox emerge on the basis of *BD alone* (plus classical logic). No need even to deploy the concepts of self-refutation and inconsistency! To see that, notice that the proposition expressed by 'All of a's beliefs (at the relevant time) are true' is naturally symbolized by the following formula: '$(\forall q)(B_t a q \supset q)$', where '$a$' names our believer, '$t$' is the time to which the Moorean belief is indexed, 'B' is the belief operator, and 'q' is a propositional variable. Given that, here's a simple proof that a's belief in an instance of Moorean form (i) guarantees the presence of falsehood in her belief system:

(1) $B_t a(p \;\&\; \sim B_t a p)$	[Contingent fact]
(2) $(\forall q)(B_t a q \supset q)$	[Assumption for RAA]
(3) $B_t a p$	[1, BD]
(4) $B_t a(p \;\&\; \sim B_t a p) \supset (p \;\&\; \sim B_t a p)$	[2, $\forall$E]
(5) $p \;\&\; \sim B_t a p$	[1, 4, MP]
(6) $\sim B_t a p$	[5, &E]
(7) $\sim(\forall q)(B_t a q \supset q)$	[2–6, RAA]

And here's a proof that belief in an instance of form (ii) is incompatible with the believer's having only true beliefs:

(1) $B_t a(p \;\&\; B_t a \sim p)$	[Contingent fact]
(2) $(\forall q)(B_t a q \supset q)$	[Assumption for RAA]
(3) $B_t a p$	[1, BD]
(4) $B_t a p \supset p$	[2, $\forall$E]
(5) p	[3, 4, MP]
(6) $B_t a(p \;\&\; B_t a \sim p) \supset (p \;\&\; B_t a \sim p)$	[2, $\forall$E]
(7) $p \;\&\; B_t a \sim p$	[1, 6, MP]
(8) $B_t a \sim p$	[7, &E]
(9) $B_t a \sim p \supset \sim p$	[2, $\forall$E]
(10) $\sim p$	[8, 9, MP]
(11) $\sim(\forall q)(B_t a q \supset q)$	[2–10, RAA]

We've come a long way since Moore impressionistically characterized instances of propositional forms (i) and (ii) as those 'perfectly absurd or nonsensical [things] to say'. Based on the seemingly benign BD alone (plus classical logic), we have now *proven* Williams' claim that *the Moorean believer must hold a false belief*. This is paradoxical because the Moorean forms are *contingent*. And, of course, this is not what we should expect from belief the content of which is a contingent proposition.

Have we just seen a proof that BD is false? Hardly. Most of us would lay the blame for the paradox elsewhere. Where, then? How have we managed to get ourselves into this kind of conceptual trouble? And why does it matter? That's what we are presently debating in the literature on the problem.[21]

4. Mooreanism and scepticism

It is hard to exaggerate Moore's importance to the current debate about Cartesian scepticism. In fact, the whole field of anti-sceptical epistemologists can be informatively divided into two factions, the 'Mooreans' (or 'neo-Mooreans') and the anti-Mooreans. You'll find clear expressions of Mooreanism (not always identified by that label) in the works of Ernest Sosa (1999), Steven Luper (2003), Peter Klein (2004), Roger White (2006), Noah Lemos (2008), and Matthew McGrath (2015a,b), among many others.[22] Anti-Mooreans include all contextualists and some 'invariantists', most notably, Fred Dretske (1970) and Robert Nozick (1981), among a few others (this writer included).[23] What did Moore do to become as important to our post-Gettier concerns as the debate about Cartesian scepticism itself? I confess that the task of giving you a precise answer at the tail end of this short chapter is overwhelming to me. But maybe I can give you a precise idea of what, in most circles, should count as the distinctive mark of a Moorean.

To be sure, Moore put forward at least three arguments against scepticism, and adherence to any one of those arguments, or to essential features of any one of them, may suffice to make you a Moorean of some kind.[24] But, to most of us, the distinctive mark of Mooreanism is to be found in the elements of Moore's 1939 paper on a 'Proof of an External World'. Mooreanism is *clearly* outlined in that paper, in spite of the important differences you'll find in contemporary Moorean proposals.

To see how one becomes a Moorean, consider the inferences in the following bits of dialogue:

> 'You're saying I can't accuse him of giving me the finger because I don't even know if he has fingers? Look, here: a photo of the incident ... See? He has hands. So, he has fingers!'

'I'm sorry, sir: You have hands. So, you're not eligible for the procedure reserved for handless people.'

'Here's what I have to say to my opponent: I have groping hands, Hillary. So, I'm not just a checkbook with a loud mouth!'

I trust that, to *all* of the non-sceptics among us, in each of those cases, if the speaker knows that the relevant character has hands, the speaker has a bit of inferential knowledge in the conclusion of each argument. Call those cases of inferential knowledge 'ordinary'. Now, contrast the above cases of (presumably valid) inference, with the following case:

H: I have hands (now).
~SH: So, I'm not (now) a disembodied brain in a high-tech lab being manipulated to falsely believe I have hands.

You're a Moorean epistemologist if you think the anti-Mooreans – sceptics and non-sceptics alike – are wrong in their claim that you can't know that ~SH on the basis of H. To the Moorean, the non-sceptical anti-Moorean has helped dignify one of the grandest illusions in the history of epistemology: the view that inferential knowledge of ~SH is somehow different from the instances of inferential knowledge in the ordinary cases. The Moorean regards the non-sceptical anti-Moorean as one who concedes too much to the sceptic. To the sceptic, we know that you can't know that H *because* we know that you can't know that ~SH. Mooreans acknowledge, of course, that sceptics have an elaborate explanation for why this is supposed to be the case. Still, to the Moorean, we know that you *can* know that ~SH *because* we know that you can know that H. Here, both Mooreans and sceptics assume what we have called 'knowledge-closure': the view that *valid deductive reasoning infallibly transmits knowledge from premises to conclusions.*[25] The most influential 'invariantists' among non-sceptical anti-Mooreans, for their part, claim that knowledge-closure is a false principle. Contextualist anti-Mooreans defend the principle.

Now, and last, notice this striking feature of Mooreanism: Unlike modest anti-sceptics (like the aforementioned anti-Mooreans) – who must fight against each and every sceptical argument that's put in their way, with no prima facie assurance that the next sceptical argument will be vanquished – the Moorean purports to offer us *conclusive evidence* that we can have empirical knowledge. In fact, like Moore himself, most Mooreans hold that we *do have* empirical knowledge (for instance, perceptual knowledge that a given individual has hands). To the Mooreans, given any piece of empirical knowledge, plus the philosophical knowledge that Mooreanism itself affords us, *we know that we have knowledge*. That is, Mooreanism is supposed to give us *metaknowledge*. From this, it clearly follows that the Moorean can know that *every* anti-Moorean argument, regardless of whether it comes from sceptics or from fellow non-sceptical anti-Mooreans, is fallacious, *just by knowing that the argument is anti-Moorean*. No need to even look at the opposing argument! If you know that you know that p, you're entitled to infer that all evidence against your knowledge that p is misleading, and you will then know that it is based on the inference. Anybody who gives you a proof *and defends the proof as really proving what it purports to prove*, represents herself as knowing that s/he knows through the proof. The study of both scepticism and non-sceptical anti-Mooreanism becomes, at best, a merely academic exercise. Well, isn't that the kind of joy we're supposed to derive from a good proof?!²⁶

I don't have the space to tell you about all the steps by which Mooreans may seem to become entitled to their very ambitious conclusion. The full story has enough steps for a whole book, or two, or three … But I trust you'll agree that we're looking at an exciting view.

5. Concluding remarks: reverence renewed?

Russell is often taken for granted by epistemologists nowadays – in that many of us seem to think that several decades of reverent scrutiny have left no surprises for epistemology in his body of work. That may well be unfair to his legacy, however. Maybe there really aren't any earth-shattering discoveries to be made in Russellian epistemology. But there is, if I'm not much mistaken, quite a bit more sophistication in his epistemological work than we have been led to believe by even the best among our historians. Maybe the work in Section 2 above helps shed some new light on epistemological ideas in Russell's work that may have seemed more familiar than they really were.

And there's quite a bit more, amid Russell's epistemological ideas, than this short chapter could have reported on. For instance, we haven't been able to look into Stephen Hetherington's (2011: 227) recent claim that Russell anticipated much of Nozick's tracking account of knowledge in his 1921 book on *The Analysis of Mind* – a claim that seems entirely reasonable to this writer.

The story of how we, post-Gettier epistemologists, relate to Moore's work is a very different one. He's never been thought of as any less than 'one of us'. While those two issues canvassed in Sections 3 and 4 above stand out as obvious highlights among his epistemological ideas, there is quite a bit more where that comes from. For instance, we haven't had the space to look into his pioneering work on epistemic modality.[27] We'd need a lot more space for that as well.

As you may have noticed, this has been the recurring theme of this chapter: In epistemology, too, these two giants deserve gigantic space.[28]

Notes

1 Notice: Russell (1959) identified his most important contribution to epistemology as comprising three of his books, two of which are titled *The Analysis of Mind* (1921) and *An Inquiry into Meaning and Truth*! (1980). Only one of those three, *Human Knowledge* (1948), is properly titled for an essay in epistemology. But Russell has misled us in this regard. Arguably, his greatest contribution to the field was put forward, in programmatic form, in *The Problems of Philosophy* (1912), as we shall see in Section 2. As so much in the Russellian corpus, however, the depth of the ideas in that early work may have been underestimated by their own author.

2 For insightful commentary on their involvement with idealism, of both Hegelian and Kantian varieties, see Baldwin (1990), Hylton (1990), Griffin (1991), and Candlish (2007).

3 When the case reappears in Russell (1948: 140), the believer mistakes Bannerman for Balfour when identifying the British PM in 1906. Bannerman had then just been elected. This is a relevant feature of the case for our purposes, as noted below.

4 *Very roughly*, your epistemology is a case of conservatism if you hold that a given belief is justified, to whichever degree, unless the believer is in possession of non-neutralized counter-evidence for the belief. For a very helpful look at conservatism and its shortcomings, see Vahid (2004).

5 If you go the graded belief route, expect trouble for the belief/justification alignment from the Lottery Paradox, as explained by Kaplan (1996: 89–103). If you go the full belief route, expect trouble in accounting for the data of ordinary linguistic practice, as explained by Christensen (2004: 12–68), plus the challenge posed by the Preface Paradox. This is not the place to pursue the dilemma in any great detail. But do notice, in any case, that fallibilistic, anti-sceptical options are available in epistemology to the full-belief route. See Section 4 below for a little more on the issue.

6 The view is well-represented in Fumerton (1995: 73–9) and in BonJour and Sosa (2003: 60–96).

7 See Amico (1993: 17–43) for an introduction to the problems of Pyrrhonian scepticism.

8 As the reference to reflective stability shows, Russell is here concerned with infallible *justification*, not just with infallible *beliefs*. The distinction looms large in contemporary epistemology. See Fumerton (1995) for discussion of the point.

9   Russell was clear about the fact that *epistemological premises* must be distinguished
    from *psychological premises*. The justification for common-sense beliefs comes from
    foundational beliefs by reasoning that uncovers those premises (in the typical case).
    The explanation for the distinction, in slightly different guise, was given by Russell
    (1973: 272–83) in a 1907 lecture on 'The Regressive Method of Discovering the
    Premises of Mathematics'.

10 For the emphasis on simplicity, see Huemer (2002: 31). Vogel (2008: 545) goes
    farther and emphasizes explanatory power. The historical Russell goes still farther
    than that with the coherentist element in his epistemology.

11 Most of us would deny that there is any good reason to deem simplicity truth-
    conducive. The majority view is represented by Newton-Smith (1981: 230–2). The
    dissenting view, according to which simplicity *is* truth-conducive, is championed
    by Swinburne (2001: 83–102).

12 But we shall briefly return to the issue in Section 4 below.

13 BonJour (1985: 28) deems Russell's (1912) view a form of 'weak foundationalism',
    another label for foundherentism.

14 For more on epistemic defeasibility, see Klein (1981) and de Almeida (2017).

15 She does not acknowledge Russell as one of her sources for the view.

16 See Haack (1993: 214–22).

17 I have been describing Russell's early foundationalism as the sketchy inspiration
    for the neoclassical form of the view that's fully developed in the works of
    BonJour and Fumerton. But it should be noted that the fallibilist element in
    Russell's 1912 epistemology takes a hit in 1914, when it becomes subordinate to
    the set of metaphysical and semantic views designed to defend his new claim that
    propositions about material objects are 'logical constructions' out of propositions
    about sense data. His early epistemology was then significantly *blurred* by the
    case for that new claim. For an introduction to the 1914 views, see Soames
    (2014: 535–67).

18 Due to space constraints and because these two items from Moore's epistemological
    agenda are so entrenched in post-Gettier epistemology, only the briefest
    commentary will be offered in what follows, with a view to indicating that the
    issues are in no imminent danger of becoming negligible.

19 Did Moore really overlook the difference between forms (i) and (ii)? Green and
    Williams (2007: 5) cautiously hypothesize that he did. I'd say he unquestionably
    did, as did Wittgenstein, Hintikka (1962: 64–71), and many others. (I thank John
    Williams for correspondence on the point.)

20 For more on the history of the paradox and on the problems with Moore's and
    Wittgenstein's reactions to forms (i) and (ii), see Green and Williams (2007).

21 In forthcoming work, I put forward a new set of answers to these questions. For the
    widest panorama of proposed solutions to the problem, see Green and Williams
    (2007).

22 This is not to suggest that some of these authors (e.g. White) have not expressed misgivings about aspects of Mooreanism, or sought to distance themselves somewhat from the historical Moore.

23 You'll find a form of anti-Mooreanism that is neither Dretskean nor Nozickian in de Almeida (2012). For an intriguing defence of the Dretskean line, see Adams, Barker, and Figurelli (2012). For an intriguing defence of the Nozickian line, see Becker (2007).

24 One of Moore's arguments is effectively criticized in Steup (1996: 207–10). Another is briefly described in de Almeida (2015).

25 I choose to ignore Crispin Wright's distinction between closure and 'transmission'. All closure deniers (like me) will surely find something to like in Wright's and Martin Davies's works on the issue, as exemplified in Wright (2002) and Davies (2003), but they may also find much to dislike in their works (as I do). The issue cannot be pursued here.

26 If this is right, Luper (2003: 189) may seem downright incoherent when he writes that, '[o]n the view I have offered, we know we are not brains in vats' while also claiming that 'I do not have a knockdown case against [anti-Moorean] tracking theorists [such as Dretske and Nozick]'.

27 Moore's leading role in the study of epistemic modals is acknowledged in MacFarlane (2011: 145).

28 I'm indebted to John N. Williams and to the editors, Stephen Hetherington and Markos Valaris, for helpful comments on a draft of this chapter.

References

Adams, F., Barker, J. A., and Figurelli, J. (2012), 'Towards Closure on Closure', *Synthese*, 188: 179–96.

Ambrose, A. and Lazerowitz, M. (1970), 'Preface', in A. Ambrose and M. Lazerowitz (eds), *G.E. Moore: Essays in Retrospect*, London: George Allen & Unwin.

Amico, R. P (1993), *The Problem of the Criterion*, Lanham, MD: Rowman & Littlefield.

Baldwin, T. (1990), *G.E. Moore*, London: Routledge.

Becker, K. (2007), *Epistemology Modalized*, New York: Routledge.

BonJour, L. (1985), *The Structure of Empirical Knowledge*, Cambridge, MA: Harvard University Press.

BonJour, L. and Sosa, E. (2003), *Epistemic Justification: Internalism vs. Externalism, Foundations vs. Virtues*, Oxford: Blackwell.

Candlish, S. (2007), *The Russell/Bradley Dispute and Its Significance for Twentieth-Century Philosophy*, Basingstoke: Palgrave Macmillan.

Chisholm, R. M. (1964), 'Theory of Knowledge', in R. M. Chisholm, H. Feigl, W. K. Frankena, J. Passmore, and M. Thompson (eds), *Philosophy (The Princeton Studies of Humanistic Scholarship in America)*, Englewood Cliffs, NJ: Prentice-Hall.

Christensen, D. (2004), *Putting Logic in Its Place: Formal Constraints on Rational Belief*, Oxford: Clarendon Press.

Davies, M. (2003), 'The Problem of Armchair Knowledge', in S. Nuccetelli (ed.), *New Essays on Semantic Externalism and Self-Knowledge*, Cambridge: The MIT Press.

de Almeida, C. (2012), 'Epistemic Closure, Skepticism and Defeasibility', *Synthese*, 188: 197–215.

de Almeida, C. (2015), 'G.E. Moore Shift', in R. Audi (ed.), *The Cambridge Dictionary of Philosophy*, 3rd edn, New York: Cambridge University Press.

de Almeida, C. (2017), 'Knowledge, Benign Falsehoods, and the Gettier Problem', in R. Borges, C. de Almeida, and P. Klein (eds), *Explaining Knowledge: New Essays on the Gettier Problem*, Oxford: Oxford University Press.

Dretske, F. (1970), 'Epistemic Operators', *The Journal of Philosophy*, 67: 1007–23.

Fumerton, R. (1995), *Metaepistemology and Skepticism*, Lanham, MD: Rowman & Littlefield.

Green, M. S. and Williams, J. N. (2007), 'Introduction', in M. S. Green and J. N. Williams (eds), *Moore's Paradox: New Essays on Belief, Rationality, and the First Person*, Oxford: Oxford University Press.

Griffin, N. (1991), *Russell's Idealist Apprenticeship*, Oxford: Clarendon Press.

Haack, S. (1993), *Evidence and Inquiry: Towards Reconstruction in Epistemology*, Oxford: Blackwell.

Hetherington, S. (2011), *How to Know: A Practicalist Conception of Knowledge*, Malden, MA: Wiley-Blackwell.

Hintikka, J. (1962), *Knowledge and Belief: An Introduction to the Logic of the Two Notions*, Ithaca, NY: Cornell University Press.

Huemer, M. (2002), 'Perception', in M. Huemer (ed.), *Epistemology: Contemporary Readings*, London: Routledge.

Hylton, P. (1990), *Russell, Idealism, and the Emergence of Analytic Philosophy*, Oxford: Clarendon Press.

Kaplan, M. (1996), *Decision Theory as Philosophy*, Cambridge: Cambridge University Press.

Klein, P. (1981), *Certainty: A Refutation of Scepticism*, Minneapolis: University of Minnesota Press.

Klein, P. (2004), 'Closure Matters: Academic Skepticism and Easy Knowledge', in E. Sosa and E. Villanueva (eds), *Epistemology, Philosophical Issues*, Volume 14, Oxford: Blackwell.

Lemos, N. (2008), 'Moore and Skepticism', in J. Greco (ed.), *The Oxford Handbook of Skepticism*, New York: Oxford University Press.

Luper, S. (2003), 'Indiscernibility Skepticism', in S. Luper (ed.), *The Skeptics: Contemporary Essays*, Aldershot: Ashgate.

MacFarlane, J. (2011), 'Epistemic Modals Are Assessment-Sensitive', in A. Egan and B. Weatherson (eds), *Epistemic Modality*, Oxford: Oxford University Press.

McGrath, M. (2015a), 'Skepticism about Knowledge', in A. I. Goldman and M. McGrath (eds), *Epistemology: A Contemporary Introduction*, New York: Oxford University Press.

McGrath, M. (2015b), 'Perceptual Justification', in A. I. Goldman and M. McGrath (eds), *Epistemology: A Contemporary Introduction*, New York: Oxford University Press.

Moore, G. E. (1993), 'Moore's Paradox', in T. Baldwin (ed.), *G.E. Moore: Selected Writings*, Abingdon: Routledge.

Moore, G. E. (1993 [1939]), 'Proof of an External World', in T. Baldwin (ed.), *G.E. Moore: Selected Writings*, Abingdon: Routledge.

Newton-Smith, W. H. (1981), *The Rationality of Science*, London: Routledge & Kegan Paul.

Nozick, R. (1981), *Philosophical Explanations*, Cambridge, MA: Harvard University Press.

Russell, B. (1912), *The Problems of Philosophy*, London: Williams and Norgate.

Russell, B. (1912a), 'On the Notion of Cause', *Proceedings of the Aristotelian Society*, New Series, 13: 1–26.

Russell, B. (1921), *The Analysis of Mind*, London: George Allen & Unwin.

Russell, B. (1948), *Human Knowledge: Its Scope and Limits*, London: George Allen & Unwin.

Russell, B. (1959), *My Philosophical Development*, London: George Allen & Unwin.

Russell, B. (1973 [1907]), 'The Regressive Method of Discovering the Premises of Mathematics', in B. Russell (ed.), *Essays in Analysis*, London: George Allen & Unwin.

Russell, B. (1980 [1940]), *An Inquiry into Meaning and Truth*, London: George Allen & Unwin.

Sainsbury, R. M. (1979), *Russell*, London: Routledge & Kegan Paul.

Soames, S. (2014), *The Analytic Tradition in Philosophy, Volume 1: The Founding Giants*, Princeton: Princeton University Press.

Sorensen, R. (1992), *Thought Experiments*, New York: Oxford University Press.

Sosa, E. (1999), 'How to Defeat Opposition to Moore', in J. Tomberlin (ed.), *Philosophical Perspectives 13: Epistemology, 1999*, Oxford: Blackwell.

Steup, M. (1996), *An Introduction to Contemporary Epistemology*, Upper Saddle River, NJ: Prentice-Hall.

Swinburne, R. (2001), *Epistemic Justification*, Oxford: Clarendon Press.

Vahid, H. (2004), 'Varieties of Epistemic Conservatism', *Synthese*, 141: 97–122.

Vogel, J. (2008), 'Internalist Responses to Skepticism', in J. Greco (ed.), *The Oxford Handbook of Skepticism*, New York: Oxford University Press.

White, R. (2006), 'More Praise for Moore's Proof', in S. Hetherington (ed.), *Aspects of Knowing: Epistemological Essays*, Oxford: Elsevier.

Williams, J. N. (1979), 'Moore's Paradox: One or Two?' *Analysis*, 39: 141–2.

Williams, J. N. (1994), 'Moorean Absurdity and the Intentional "Structure" of Assertion', *Analysis*, 54: 160–6.

Wittgenstein, L. (1953), *Philosophical Investigations*, trans. G. E. M. Anscombe, Oxford: Basil Blackwell.

Wood, A. (1959), 'Russell's Philosophy: A Study of Its Development', in B. Russell (ed.), *My Philosophical Development*, London: George Allen & Unwin.

Wright, C. (2002), '(Anti-)Sceptics Simple and Subtle: G.E. Moore and John McDowell', *Philosophy and Phenomenological Research*, 65: 330–48.

3

What Knowledge Is Not: Reflections on Some Uses of the Verb 'To Know'

Julia Tanney

1. Introduction

Midway through the novel *Harry Potter and the Order of the Phoenix*, Harry suffers a searing pain in the scar on his head. Ron, alarmed, wonders if Voldemort is near. Harry's response is immediate (Rowling 2003: 338): 'He's probably miles away. It hurt because ... he is angry.' The narrator then continues: 'Harry had not meant to say that at all, and heard the words as though a stranger had spoken them – yet knew at once that they were true. He did not know how he knew it but he did; Voldemort, wherever he was, whatever he was doing, was in a towering temper' (ibid.). What are we to gather from the narrator's comments? We may, I submit, conclude that Voldemort was indeed very angry, that Harry was spot on in saying so, and that if he were asked how he knew, he would not be able to tell us. We may also infer – can we not? – that Harry was on solid ground when he said that Voldemort was angry, even if neither he nor we are able to elaborate. Harry was not, that is, merely guessing: the narrator is crediting him with some kind of recognitional capacity.[1] *This is an example of the way 'S/he knows ...' is used.* And the logical implications of the narrator's claim are part of what we learn and understand when we master natural language – in this case, English.[2]

The scene continues when Harry, again quite suddenly, blurts out an explanation why Voldemort is angry (ibid.): 'He wants something done, and it's not happening fast enough', he said. The narrator explains: 'Again, he felt surprised to hear the words coming out of his mouth, and yet was quite certain they were true' (ibid.). Harry was convinced that Voldemort wanted something done and that it was not happening fast enough. Can we conclude, with as much confidence as before, that Harry was right: that Voldemort did, indeed, want something done and that it was not happening fast enough? Probably. But by claiming that Harry was certain, the narrator is not committing herself, as she did above, to the truth of what he said. *This is an example of the way 'S/he is certain...' is used.*

This simple scene illustrates a number of features of well-established, core uses of the expressions 'S/he knows' and 'S/he is certain', some of which can be extended to the first-person singular uses of 'I know' and 'I am sure'. It provides a lever with which to pry apart traditional doctrines of epistemology: namely, that knowledge is a type of mental state; in particular, a belief that is true and justified.

2. The relevance of expressions

Before continuing, it will be worth addressing a preliminary question. If a philosopher is interested in the nature of knowledge, then why should she pay attention to the use of the natural language (here, English) expressions in which, for example, various forms of the verb 'to know' and its cognates figure? Why, that is, should she concern herself, as I shall do here, with the logical ties of central, established uses of 'S/he knows' or 'I know'?[3]

This question divides into two. First, what does the nature of knowledge have to do with the established uses of expressions? And, second, why should we not restrict our study to those which are ripe for theoretical or formal purposes and ignore the others? I shall say something about the second question when we discuss scepticism below, but will address the first here.

'Ideas', Ryle (1945: 217) reminds us, 'like *spaniel, dog, ache, thunder* in their original use are instances of concrete concepts ... Their "logical geography" is taught by one's daily walks. Such concepts are formed by noticing similarities in the real world'. Abstractions, by contrast, are those to which a person cannot be introduced by being presented with the 'corresponding realities'; for there is nothing in the world we can put a finger on that exemplifies *knowledge, belief, certainty, perception, justice, truth, time, causation, mind, meaning, good,* and so forth. Since the kinds of items we file under 'knowledge' cannot be indicated in the same way as those we file under 'dog' or 'spaniel', how are we supposed to proceed with a philosophical investigation?

G. E. Moore (1903) appears to answer this (early on) when, in asking 'What, then, is good? How is good to be defined?', he explicitly denies looking for an answer to a verbal question. He claims not to be interested in how people generally use the word 'good' or with its proper usage as established by custom. Rather, he says: 'My business is solely with that object or idea, which I hold, rightly or wrongly, that the word is generally used to stand for' (sec. 6). The supposition – like that of Plato's Socrates – seems to be that there is an object or idea for which the word in question stands that can be discerned by revealing what is common among its 'instances': what, that is, they all share with respect to which they are called the same. Even if this were so, whether an investigation of this object or idea were to result in a definitional analysis of a composite concept, or were to show it to be simple or sui generis and thus indefinable, it could only proceed by looking at the kinds of things we call, or count as, *good*.[4]

Gettier's (1963) famous counterexamples convinced generations of philosophers that the answer to his title question 'Is Justified True Belief Knowledge?' is negative on the grounds that the conditions originally proposed by Ayer and Chisholm are not sufficient to credit an individual, Smith, with knowledge. He does this by securing our agreement that we should not accept as true 'Smith knows that *such-and-such*' for the several fillings-in of *such-and-such* and the various circumstances in which he describes Smith to be. His rebuttal of the standard analysis, that is, is intimately tied to what his readers (presumed to be fluent in English) agree to be acceptable conditions for the third-person singular application of the verb 'to know'.

Thus, in spite of some philosophers' protests not to be interested in how the relevant expressions are used, their own analyses of what they assume to be designated by the abstract noun under consideration are carried out precisely by examining the application conditions for at least some of the core, well-established uses of related expressions in, if not their nominal, their verbal, adjectival, or adverbial forms. I emphasize this historical practice in response to today's philosophers who claim to see no connection between 'the nature of the thing' on the one hand and the way we speak and – crucially – understand each other on the other.

A further question, and one I shall be disputing here, is whether it is reasonable to suppose, with Plato, Moore, and Gettier – as well as most today – that there is a thing (an object, a property, or state) for which the abstract noun 'knowledge' stands or even that it 'expresses a concept' in the traditional sense, from which pre-established, stable, timeless, and communication- and other circumstance-independent rules (such as truth-conditions) for the use of its cognate expressions can be extracted.

3. Reflections on first-person and third-person (singular) uses of 'to know', 'to be certain', and 'to believe'

Harry was certain of all manner of things in *The Order of the Phoenix*. Some of these, such as his thought that something magical had been near him as he lay among his Aunt Petunia's dying begonias, turned out to be true, even though he found that as his frustration mounted, 'his certainty leaked away' (Rowling 2003: 12). Other ideas about which Harry remained convinced, for example, that Dumbledore was snubbing him, turned out to be entirely wrong.

Claims to be certain, like those to believe, can be contrasted with claims to know, even if 'I know' and 'I am certain' are sometimes used interchangeably and both are thought in the general case – mistakenly – to describe a mental state. For, as Austin (1946: 170) famously noted, 'When I say "S is P", I imply at least that I believe it, and, if I have been strictly brought up, that I am (quite) sure of it.' By contrast, when I say 'I know', a 'new plunge' is taken (171): 'I give others my word: I give others my authority for saying that "S is P".' Here we see a difference in the logical ties or implication threads between the claim that something is the case, the claim to be certain of it, and the claim to know it to be so. These pronouncements fall on a sliding scale of liability which is reflected both in terms of the grounds we are expected to produce for our assertions, if demanded, and the degree to which we are held accountable if we turn out to be mistaken.

My declaration that such and such is so, that I think it to be so, or even that I am certain or sure of it can stand even if I am neither able to give persuasive grounds for my belief or conviction nor appeal to my reliability or experience. Perhaps I just feel it in my bones. Correspondingly, such assurances of mine make no particular claim on your judgement. As Austin notes, 'I am sure for my part, you can take it or leave it: accept it if you think I'm an acute and careful person, that's your responsibility' (ibid.). But there is a stark contrast with my claim to know, for 'I don't know "for my part", and when I say "I know" I don't mean you can take it or leave it (though of course you can take it or leave it)' (ibid.). With the added level of commitment that our claims to knowledge bring comes further responsibility, and thus a higher degree to which we lay ourselves open to blame: 'When I have said only that I am sure, and prove to have been mistaken, I am not liable to be rounded on by others in the same way as when I have said "I know"' (ibid.). There are, naturally, uses of 'I know' that do not function to give one's imprimatur to take what one says to be so.[5] But when 'I know' does constitute an endorsement, or functions as a signal about the evidential backing I have in making a claim,[6] it invites a satisfactory answer to the question 'How do you know?'[7] We might say, borrowing Anscombe's (1957) terminology, that this question is refused application by the response 'I don't know how I know, but I do.' It represents a standoff in the game of giving and asking for reasons. In the general case, others should not be expected to accept our endorsement unless we have established our authority or reliability on the matter or we can offer reasons or grounds for that which we claim to know.

Let us take a look at how these logico-grammatical remarks apply to our case. Harry was certain – he was convinced – that Dumbledore was treating him badly. He misinterpreted Dumbledore's apparent diffidence, however, and is obliged later to admit that he had been wrong. But he is not obliged to retract his claim to have been certain. Upon discovering why Dumbledore had been – or as he would later admit – had *seemed* to have been unkind, he can nonetheless retrospectively maintain to have been certain of it. Although he had been convinced or sure of it, he now was able to see that he had been wrong. By contrast, had he claimed to know that Dumbledore was snubbing him, and found out subsequently this was not the case, he can no longer use the verb 'to know' to characterize his conviction, even retrospectively. Here he would be obliged to correct or recant with 'I thought I knew'. This exemplifies what is right about the idea that (as it might be said) knowledge implies truth. But it undermines the idea that 'I know' describes a state of affairs which guarantees what is known as a fact.[8] Indeed it casts into doubt the thought that the standards that govern the use of 'I know' do so, as truth-conditions are traditionally conceived to do, 'outside time'.

We can develop this further by looking at two different ways in which our claims to knowledge might go wrong.[9] On the one hand, we might have been irresponsible in claiming to know that something is so and (in so doing) being taken to impart, with such a high level of assurance, our recommendation to others. Perhaps we passed ourselves off as experts; perhaps we gave the false impression that we checked our results, or perhaps we checked them irresponsibly given what was at stake in the particular circumstances. For 'I know', as distinct from 'I believe' or 'I am guessing', implies in the particular context 'that there is all the evidence one could need' (Urmson 1952 [1960]: 199).

On the other hand, we might have had impeccable grounds for passing on our endorsement to others and nonetheless turn out to be wrong. In acknowledging our mistake with the self-correction 'I thought I knew', we need not, in this case, be admitting any irresponsibility in claiming to have known. As Austin (1946: 169) points out: 'Surely ... we are often right to say we know even in cases where we turn out subsequently to have been mistaken – and indeed we seem always, or practically always, liable to be mistaken.' We may have been well within our rights – or justified – in any number of ways: we are reliable in these matters; we saw it with our own eyes; we performed the calculations; but in spite of this and against the odds we were wrong. Like making predictions, declaring intentions, and making promises, we are not deemed to have been irresponsible, or to have spoken wrongly, simply because the future does not unfold the way we anticipated. However, unlike the expression of certainty, the making of a promise, or the expression of an intention which permits 'Although I was certain of it, I was nonetheless wrong' or 'Although I in good faith intended, or promised, it was not to be', the logic or grammar of knowledge requires not 'I knew that it was so but it turned out not to be the case' but rather 'I thought I knew'.

These considerations apply to third-person uses of 'to know' as well. When Harry uttered the words 'It hurt because he is angry' as if a stranger had spoken them and yet knew them right away to be true, he was not in a position to give Ron his full endorsement by claiming to know about Voldemort's wrath, for he had no grounds to give. Instead, as we saw, the extra assurance that his words were true and the implication that he was on solid ground (in this case, as it turns out, by exercising a recognitional capacity) was passed on to us by the narrator, who was in the position to 'take the plunge'.[10] The narrator's claim that 'Harry knew his words were true' commits her in this context to the truth of those words and constitutes an endorsement of them to her readers.[11]

Suppose, contrary to fiction-fact, Harry had announced to Ron not only that Voldemort was angry but that he knew he was. Unable to provide grounds or even to contemplate the mechanism by which he could empathize with a distant Voldemort, he would not be able to reassure Ron that what he said was true. In such a case, how should Ron describe the situation to Hermione? In the circumstances I am trying to bring into focus, Ron is not, we are supposing, in the position to report 'Harry knows that Voldemort is angry' since to do so would not only commit him to agreeing with Harry but, in addition, to invite Hermione to accept that Voldemort is angry on his authority. Because of this, it leaves him open not only to the question 'What grounds have you for claiming that Harry thinks so?' but for the different question 'What grounds do you have for thinking that Voldemort is angry?' If Ron does not want to 'take the plunge' or stick his neck out and risk being rounded on by Hermione should he turn out to be mistaken, he shields himself by reporting to Hermione that Harry says that, or thinks that, Voldemort is angry. In saying so, he is signalling to Hermione his own reluctance to endorse, or at least his own neutrality with respect to, what Harry has said.

Perhaps we can generalize these particular features as follows. From another's claim to know that such-and-such is the case, we may safely, without sticking our neck out (and if we have no reason to suspect deception) reason that she believes it to be so. From my own claim 'I know that it is so' or 'She knows that it is so' I am committed – if my claims are to be understood – to assenting to so-and-so's being the case. Of course, from my own claim to know that such-and-such, I would not immediately be inclined to agree with your inference 'She believes that such-and-such', said about myself. On the contrary, I may protest strongly, since for me to assent to 'I believe that such-and such' would be, in the circumstances I am considering, to *take away* or to *back off from* my endorsement and the implication that I have grounds to offer. And yet if there were a question as to whether I hold what I have stated to be true in the first place, then the correct rejoinder on my part would be 'Of course I believe it! I know it!'[12] 'Believe', like 'know', is a tool with various functions and thus with different logical powers.

As I have indicated throughout, there are deviations from these well-established, core uses of 'S/he knows' and 'I know' which do not fit the pattern described. But such is to be anticipated, for reasons we will discuss subsequently. My purpose here has been to highlight some central features of *what we say and what we understand* by these expressions. This has been sufficient – even without an examination of other (second-person or plural verbal, adverbial, or adjectival) forms – to indicate that the logical relations between knowledge, truth, justification, and belief are far more complicated than is suggested by the simple formula: knowledge is true, justified belief. The notion of 'being on solid ground' is wide enough to encompass a range of justification-possibilities and the question of whether or not the ascriber of knowledge or the one to whom it is ascribed is liable to produce grounds or to appeal to the solid footing upon which her claim rests depends on a variety of considerations. The fact that 'I believe' cannot be inferred from 'I know' in, for example, just those situations in which the evidential support for the speaker's claim is signalled, impugns the too coarse characterization of knowledge as a type of belief. And that *both* 'to know' and 'to believe' may function to indicate the speaker's evidential support for her claim or her willingness or reluctance to endorse it to others is devastating to the general claim that ascriptions of knowledge, like those of belief, function as descriptions. When employed in such ways, neither of them does so. There thus seems no hope for the simple formula – often put forward as a priori and obvious – that knowledge, or indeed belief, is a type of mental state.[13]

4. Scepticism

We saw that we may be on strong ground for making a claim and giving it our full endorsement, and yet still turn out to be mistaken. We distinguished this kind of mistake – which requires the subsequent retraction 'I thought I knew' – from the mistake we make when we speak irresponsibly in saying 'I know' – for example, when we were not on solid ground to begin with and our retraction would be better framed as 'I should not have claimed to have known'.

Should the fact that we might, in any particular circumstance, get it wrong in the first sense – no matter how impeccable our grounds or reasons in the particular circumstances – exert pressure on us to refrain from claiming to know in the first place? If so, perhaps we have been misguided in focusing attention on what we say and understand by these expressions if they are to be dismissed as insufficiently sophisticated from a philosophical point of view. Indeed, this would be one way of construing the practical ramifications of the extreme demands imposed by the philosophical sceptic.

Suppose we construe our claims – whether qualified with 'probably' or 'possibly' or put forward tentatively with a parenthetical 'I believe' or an authoritative 'I know' – as being grounded by an argument which we are ready to produce on demand. How are we to construe the logical relations or the kind of support that exists between the backing we can produce, if demanded, and the claims, however qualified, we wish to make?[14]

We normally have no hesitation in drawing conclusions, making inferences, or even insisting that, given the backing together with the relevant circumstances, our claim *must* hold true, for an indefinite range of moral, legal, aesthetic, medical, prudential, pedagogical, biological, physiological, and so on possibilities or senses of 'must'. This kind of everyday reasoning (exemplified by the inferences and conclusions drawn in the opening paragraphs of this chapter) relies on presuppositions that are relevant to the subject matter and the particular circumstances in which we are considering it. They fall well short, however, of the standard of argument typically demanded by the sceptic. As one philosopher has put it,

> The striking feature about philosophical skepticism is that once one is in its grasp, one's most unquestioned certainties appear to be shaky and without justification. It has this result, not because it finds that particular judgments have not been fulfilling accepted standards, but because it finds a weakness in those standards themselves. And the weaknesses it finds are so judged, not because they have led to erroneous judgments, but because they do not meet other,

> stricter, standards, ones that often seem incapable of realization. The result is
> that entire areas of knowledge claims become relegated to the realm of opinion
> and guesswork. (Vander Veer 1978: 7)

What are these 'other, stricter' standards that often seem incapable of
realization? Presumably, that we must rule out all conceivable circumstances
that would defeat our claims before we can give them our full endorsement.
This seems to be what Descartes had in mind when he suggested that, even in
favourable circumstances (sitting by the fire in his dressing gown, a piece of
paper in his hand), he could not trust his senses unless he could rule out the
possibility that he was dreaming. One way of obtaining these stricter standards
would be to require that a claim to knowledge follows, as a matter of analytic
entailment, from the grounds that are available for its support; that is, if and
only if its contradictory is formally inconsistent with its premises and their
backing.

This is a formidable demand. Is it reasonable? Philosophers such as Ryle,
Wisdom, and Toulmin have insisted that 'substantial' arguments, as distinct
from 'analytic' ones, involve by their very nature a difference of kind between
the type of claim put forward and that of those used for its backing and support.
We cannot avoid these type-jumps between our conclusions and their backing
without begging the question, changing the subject, or, I would add, utterly
distorting the logical power of the expressions in use. We encounter these
'jumps' in a wide variety of domains, not only, as suggested above, in claims
about physical objects or the external world, typically backed up, for example,
by what we see and hear; but also about other minds, often grounded on claims
about what others say and do; or about the goodness of an action, sometimes
justified by a reckoning of its effects or by the good or bad intentions of the
agent; as well as in a myriad of other domains of philosophical interest.

We find, however, that in much analytic philosophy today, instead of
recognizing the inevitability and inescapability of these categorical differences
between the kind of justifications that are available within different fields of
argumentation and the purposes of the moment,

> pride of place has been given to arguments backed by entailments; wherever
> claims to knowledge have been seen to be based on evidence not entailing
> analytically the correctness of the claim, a 'logical gulf' has been felt to exist
> which the philosopher must find some way either of bridging or of conjuring
> away, and as a result a whole array of epistemological problems have grown
> up around scientific, ethical, aesthetic, and theological claims alike. (Toulmin
> 1958: 9)

The standard responses are as disturbing as the sceptic's challenge, for their proponents proceed as if they *accept* there is a logical gap to be filled and thus implicitly acquiesce in the demand for analytic entailments. Thus the analytic-reductionist, exemplified by the phenomenalist, behaviourist, and consequentialist, in our examples above, tries to bridge the logical gap by offering a definition or translation of the type of predicate to be reduced (material object, mental, moral) into a type that belongs to the proposed reduction-base. Ironically, today's 'theoretical reductionist' who eschews a priori analysis (thus conceived) seems nonetheless committed to a similar enterprise when her naturalistically conceived theorems or theoretical identities attempt to ford the logical gulf between the target theory and its reductive base through the postulation of a posteriori bridge laws.[15]

The typical response to the reductionist is supplied by the realist, who sidesteps the gap by avoiding the need to provide grounds for her claim. No grounds, no gap. In her traditional guise as Platonist or Cartesian, the realist appeals to a special faculty (intuition, empathy, direct perception) by which she claims to discern the thing in itself – physical objects, other minds, the good. Today's realist is exemplified at the two extremes by the one who claims special logical insight at one end and by the scientific naturalist at the other. Both profess to espy 'real properties' which answer to 'facts'; the first exercises her capacity to scrutinize possible worlds and the second by subcontracting the epistemological work to our 'best scientific practices'. (The common-sense realist, who falls in between, just uses her senses.)

The interminable dispute between the reductionist and realist, which Ryle (1979) parodies as between those whose battle cry is 'Nothing But ...' and 'Something Else as Well', is hopeless, for although both sides are right in their criticism of each other their own solutions fail. We can agree with the realist that the reductionist errs in attempting to bridge the logical gap by forging either conceptual equivalences or theoretical identities between the terms in the class to be analysed or reduced and its definitional or reductive base. But so can we agree with the reductionist that the realist dismantles the logical/justificatory relations that obtain between utterances in which the proprietary predicates of the two classes figure. The reductionist is wrong to suppose that these relations – upon which the soundness and acceptability of our arguments depend – can be cast as definitional or a posteriori equivalences which hold outside time and in all conceivable circumstances. The realist, however, in supposing that objects, properties, events, states, or relations are the genuine *designata* of our (e.g.) physical, mental, or moral predicates – whether they be sui generis or composite – sunders these predicates from their time-bound and circumstance-dependent conditions of application. This leaves an utter mystery of their correct employment.

It might be helpful to look at this dispute from a particular angle. The sceptic holds up analytic entailment as the standard to which our claims to knowledge must aspire. This requires not only that the sentences in which a given argument is framed be frozen into propositions whose truth, like the statements of mathematics, are independent of time, context, or purpose. It also requires that the logical relations upon which the acceptability of our arguments depend be cast in a similar timeless, context, and purpose-free mould. But anybody can make an argument analytically valid, simply by introducing a warrant (a major premise) that bridges the type-jump between that which is put forward as the claim and that which is put forward as its grounds. The problem, which *had* been one that questioned the right to travel between premise and conclusion, now becomes a question about the 'truth-maker' of the hypothetical that (allegedly) expresses the warrant permitting the travel.[16] Puzzling about the nature of this truth-maker, we eventually arrive at insoluble, but completely avoidable, ontological puzzles about 'normative properties' and 'meaning facts'.

In other words, what had been a question about our right to put forward assertions, for example, about other minds based on claims about what is said and done, turns – hopelessly – into a dispute about the definability of mental predicates by behavioural ones or about the theoretical identity of mental properties with physical ones. In understandable despair, the realist (here, the Cartesian) responds: 'Forget about definability!', 'Forget about theoretical identities!' Disastrously, however, she continues, 'Mental predicates pick out real properties, states, and events! Their relation, if any, to descriptions of behaviour or speech are merely contingent at best!' And, even more deplorably, 'My formal training gives me special logical insight!' or 'Scientists are in the best position to enlighten us about their real nature!' But the questions 'Which phenomena are the logical-intuitionist and the philosopher-scientist *counting* as exemplifying, say, knowledge?' and 'With what right are they doing so?' have simply dropped out of the picture. Needless to say, neither can do the job advertised without satisfactory answers to these unacknowledged yet fundamental questions.

With this battle smouldering in the background, it is no wonder that well-established, even core or central uses of the relevant predicates seem utterly beside the point. But both the reductionist and the realist go wrong in bowing to the sceptic's charge that only analytic entailments can provide the appropriate standard of justification required. The backing or grounds for our claims to knowledge about the external world, other minds, or the goodness of an action are to be found in *various* and often *competing* considerations from those of a different logical type. To say that they are of a different logical type is to say that they cannot, without gross distortion, be assimilated in the way *either* phenomenalists-versus-direct realists, behaviourists-versus-identity theorists, or consequentialists-versus-moral realists have attempted to do. Both the realist and the reductionist, as I understand it, are committing a type-error or category mistake in attempting to elide the differences in the logical powers – including, importantly, their force – between the claims we make in these domains and the grounds or backing we produce for them. What will count as conclusive in certain situations may well be ruled out in others. Some considerations will, as we saw, not be strong enough to be put forward on our highest authority, but only with varying degrees of tentativeness. There will also be arguments which do not amount to a chain of demonstrative reasoning, but rather, as Wisdom (1963: 191–2) describes it, 'a presenting and representing of those features of the case which severally co-operate in favour of the conclusion, in favour of saying what the reasoner wishes said, in favour of calling the situation by the name by which he wishes to call it. The reasons are like the legs of a chair not the links of a chain'.

Earlier, we asked why a philosopher interested in the nature of knowledge should concern herself with the logical commitments of core, well-established uses of, for example, 'She knows' and 'I know'. We postponed a version of the question that asks why we, as philosophers, should not restrict our study to those that are ripe for theoretical or formal purposes and ignore the others. 'Who cares', we might say, 'what we say or should say when we are not, or not even attempting to speak strictly? What matter are not the standards we accept outside our theoretical or formal practices but rather those that these practices would require.'

The suggestion, however, that the philosopher's demands should not be construed either as being constrained by or as constraining what we say and understand outside our discipline is disingenuous. This can be seen from asking what they – whether sceptics or not – wish to conclude from their epistemological investigations. Let us turn again to the quotation above representing the sceptic's position. From the concern that our judgements do not meet the highest standards of justification, it is argued, 'the result is that entire areas of knowledge claims become relegated to the realm of opinion and guesswork'. In other words, we do not know what we claim to know. This is a conclusion about what we can claim to know *point final*. It is not one restricted to philosophical enquiry.

There have been a number of attempts to dismiss the sceptic's challenge on the grounds that it engenders absurdities.[17] We might, instead, simply make explicit the disguised invitation to change the standards of what is to count as appropriate grounds for our claims to knowledge and reject it. The propriety of our knowledge claims depends upon the kind of support and backing that is relevant both to the particular subject and the situation at hand. We would have no use for knowledge-claims if our right to make them depended – *per impossibile* – on their contradictories being logically ruled out.[18]

5. Conclusion

Trouble begins, as Wittgenstein, Ryle, and others have insisted, when we attempt to abstract from expressions using a live verb such as 'to know' an imagined common factor which we designate with an abstract noun. For there is no such common factor. Instead, *knowledge* and its philosophical cousins are better construed as abstractions from sayings or utterances in which their correlative live verbs, adjectives, and adverbs perform their roles. We discern their features, as Ryle insisted, not by inspecting them 'in isolated splendour' as we would coins in a museum, withdrawn from their native transactions, but by comparing and contrasting the logical powers of live sentences at work; for it is these situated utterances or sayings that reveal the logical powers of their constituents.

That individual words are not 'the atoms which combine to give sense to the sentence-molecules to which they contribute' becomes clear when we examine our live sentences at work. For, as the later Wittgenstein showed with numerous examples and Ryle (2009b: 206) made explicit: 'A given word will [like complex expressions and grammatical constructions], in different sorts of context, express ideas of an indefinite range of differing logical types and, therefore, with different logical powers.' In these different sorts of contexts, that is, the same word or expression will contribute differently to what is said, as revealed, for example, in the implications licensed and forbidden; the tests for truth or falsehood required; and the compatibility or incompatibility with, or being evidence for or against, other related sayings and doings.[19]

To understand the nature of knowledge, then, requires, among other things, discerning the logical powers of the verb 'to know', which in turn requires examining the different sorts of contexts in which its various (e.g. first-peson and third-person) forms contribute to what is said, as this is revealed in the implications licensed and forbidden (e.g. from 'I know it' or 'S/he knows it' to 'it is so'), to the compatibility or incompatibility with, or being evidence for or against, each other and other related sayings (e.g. 'believes' or 'is certain') or doings (e.g. endorsing, hedging, signalling). It is these ever-changing differences in the logical ties – the elasticities of significance – of, for example, 'to know' in its various forms and in its various uses – even those that are core and well-established – that make an analytic definition, a general account or theory, or the idea that the abstract noun 'knowledge' functions to designate something, a non-starter.

This view constitutes a rejection of the idea that there is something in virtue of which we call a thing by the same name and stands in opposition to the view that the meaning of an expression (such as a sentence) is determined by the independently and antecedently fixed meanings of its constituent elements (such as words or phrases) and the rules used to combine them. It is nevertheless compatible with the fact that we are able to understand an indefinite number of utterances. This view does not render mysterious our ability to understand any particular expression's use in different grammatical contexts; for example, in negations or conditionals, or embeddings in more complex expressions, or its role in inferences and arguments. On the contrary, it is in virtue of our ability to ascertain which inferences, embeddings, and transformations are mandated, licensed, or forbidden on any particular occasion that we are able to understand the employment of the sentence or utterance.

This is bad news for those who hanker after an idealization of natural language expressions that is suited to the aims of mathematical logic. It is not an encroachment, understood as a tentative foray, but rather a full-blown attack: not only on the aspirations of semantic theory, but on any philosophical position – such as those described in the previous section – which, for one reason or another, strive to force our expressions into the 'too few dockets' that formal logicians have to offer. For, as Toulmin (1958: 180) reminds us,[20]

> Certainly language as we know it consists, not of timeless propositions, but of utterances dependent in all sorts of ways on the context or occasion on which they are uttered. Statements are made in particular situations, and the interpretation to be put upon them is bound up with their relation to these situations: they are in this respect like fireworks, signals or Very lights. The ways in which statements and utterances require to be criticised and assessed reflect this fact ... Only in pure mathematics can our assessments be entirely context-free.

Notes

1 'He is separated from one who doesn't know not just by a difference in conviction, but in understanding' (Wittgenstein 1969: sec. 563).

2 'And the concept of knowing consists in these various uses' (ibid.: sec. 560).

3 'We are asking ourselves: what do we do with a statement "I know ..."? For it is not a question of mental processes or mental states ... And that is how one must decide whether something is knowledge or not' (ibid.: sec. 230).

4 It is worth noting that, notwithstanding Moore's characterization of his practice, his contribution to analytic philosophy is lauded precisely because '[h]e taught us to try to assess and how to assess the forces of expressions on which philosophical issues hinge' (Ryle 1963: 280).

5 There is the 'I know' of 'Don't remind me!' or 'Leave me alone!' and there is the 'I know' said to reassure myself or defend myself against something that has been called into doubt ('But I know I put the keys on the table!'). (Wittgenstein [1969] considers several examples such as these, as well as the 'I know' that appears to be grounded in a 'mental state' such as a feeling of conviction – a use which he gleans, and criticizes, in Moore's response to the sceptic. See, e.g., secs 6, 42, 86, 90, 230, 308, 356.) It can also function as a joke. Luna Lovegood to Harry, upon their first encounter: '*You're* Harry Potter.' Harry's response: 'I know I am' (Rowling 2003: 168).

6 Urmson (1952) takes pains to distinguish what he calls the 'parenthetical' use of verbs which functions as a signalling device with a 'performatory' use. The distinction is not relevant here. For whether 'I know' functions as a signalling device about the evidential context of my claim or as an endorsement or both, these uses serve to call into question the idea that the function of these expressions is to describe mental states or indeed, as Urmson points out, dispositions to behave.

7 Wittgenstein (1969) offers a book-length treatment on why Moore's declarations 'I know these are my hands' and 'I know the earth existed long before I was born' sound so odd to him as a repudiation of the sceptic's position. One reason for their oddness, in addition to that mentioned in note 5 above, is that there are no grounds to offer in response to the question 'How do you know?' which can (logically speaking) be put upon solider footing than the claim itself since the obvious appeal 'I see them with my own eyes' is precisely of the type that the sceptic is calling into question. For passages that touch on this, see ibid., secs 18–19, 125, 201–2, 445.

8 See ibid., secs 12, 90.

9 I am indebted here to Toulmin's (1958) discussion of predictive statements.

10 We do of course say 'I have no idea how she knows, but she knows!', and our grounds for saying this may be her confident (as opposed to tentative) assertions and other actions, or perhaps the delight on her face or air of superiority. In so

doing, we are cushioning ourselves from the implications of the 'plunge': though admitting we are not in a position to elaborate, we are nonetheless implying not only that she is convinced and correct, but that she is on solid ground.

11   We are not blessed with omniscient narrators outside certain literary practices, but we nonetheless receive testimony upon which we rely. Perhaps the one to whom we grant authority has mastered a technique or is an expert in a particular domain. Perhaps she has witnessed an event, has heard from someone who has, or has read the relevant report. Indeed it is part of the backdrop of our linguistic practices that we rely on the authority of others, including in circumstances in which it makes no sense to demand their grounds or reasons. Assertions or judgements may function, on occasion, like hinges that are kept stable or in place while other assertions or judgements are tested (Wittgenstein 1969: secs 341–3). Which, of course, is not to say that these hinges are forever immune to revision.

12   See Wittgenstein (1969: secs 12–13, 424; also 177).

13   This signalling function can be discerned for a host of so-called psychological verbs, including verbs of perception ('to see', 'to hear', 'to descry' which may contrast with 'to look', 'to listen', 'to search'), verbs of cognition ('to understand', 'to grasp', 'to deduce', sometimes but not always used to contrast with 'to infer'), as well as modal qualifications on assertions ('probably', 'certainly', 'possibly'), and, I imagine, plenty of other examples, in which the speaker's and interlocutor's tentativeness or firmness in putting forward her claim is marked. Like the use of 'I imagine' in the previous sentence, such 'parenthetical' uses of psychological verbs and modal qualifications on assertions function not to describe possibilities, probabilities, or certainties, nor to describe imaginings, reflectings, or cogitatings, but to signal the strength or tentativeness with which their assertion is to be taken. This sort of contrast is kindred to the one often marked between 'achievement' or 'factive' verbs and their more neutral, less committal, 'seeming' or 'trying' verbs which often serve to signal neutrality, reluctance, or refusal to commit to the implied success. Language is fluid and these uses evolve. As Ryle (2009c: 195) notes, we often borrow 'achievement' verbs to signify the performance of corresponding task activities, where the hope of success is good (a runner's winning the race from the start; a doctor's curing his patient as the treatment begins). 'Hear' is sometimes used as a synonym of 'listen' and 'mend' as a synonym of 'try to mend'. The context will make clear the signalling function of the contrasting claims. But even with these borrowings or stretches in significance, it is interesting to note how the role or function of the speaker's commitment or endorsement – and her interlocutor's acceptance or scepticism – survives (Rowling 2003: 133):

> 'They went for the boys', said Mrs. Figg, her voice stronger and more confident now, the pink flush ebbing away from her face. 'One of them had fallen. The other was backing away, trying to repel the Dementor. That was

Harry. He tried twice and produced only silver vapour. On the third attempt, he produced a Patronus, which charged down the first Dementor and then, with his encouragement, chased the second one away from his cousin. And that … that is what happened', Mrs. Figg finished, somewhat lamely.

Madam Bones looked down at Mrs Figg in silence. Fudge was not looking at her at all, but fidgeting with his papers. Finally, he raised his eyes and said, rather aggressively, 'That's what you saw, is it?'

'That is what happened', Mrs Figg repeated.

14 This discussion follows Toulmin's (1958) main theme. He, in turn, acknowledges (among others) Ryle (1950) and Urmson (1953), as well as Wisdom's Gifford Lectures (unpublished). See also Ryle (1946).

15 I argue for this in more detail in Tanney (2013).

16 See Ryle (1946, 1950), Toulmin (1958), and Wisdom (1991).

17 Even the sceptic cannot doubt everything – for example, the meaning of words. And if the sceptic cannot rule out dreaming, then she cannot rule out that she is dreaming that she is dreaming. See Wittgenstein (1969: secs 114, 383, 506, 676).

18 Wisdom, commenting on Russell's and McTaggart's scepticism, notes that these philosophers do not merely point out that conclusions about, for example, the external world do not follow as a matter of deductive entailment from premises about, for example, sensations. They go further in suggesting that there is no real reason to believe in, for example, matter or physical objects. Their attitudes – 'Human folly, human folly, and really if you'd only had the proper logical training you'd see the whole thing is folly!' – support this suggestion. But, Wisdom (1991: 176–7) counters, 'McTaggart and Russell seem to have no grasp of the fact that 'know' and 'have real reason' have been so considerably modified as they use them that the sceptical statements they make are necessary truisms … they bring it out as true without bringing it out as something which couldn't have been false.'

19 See Ryle (1962: 442–3).

20 The expression is Ryle's. See Ryle (1949) for more discussion.

References

Anscombe, G. E. M. (1957), *Intention*, Oxford: Basil Blackwell.

Austin, J. L. (1946), 'Other Minds', *Proceedings of the Aristotelian Society*, S20: 148–87.

Gettier, E. L. (1963), 'Is Justified True Belief Knowledge?', *Analysis*, 23: 121–3.

Moore, G. E. (1903), *Principia Ethica*, Cambridge: Cambridge University Press.

Plato, (1875), *Meno*, trans. B. Jowett: http://www.gutenberg.org/files/1643/1643-h/1643-h.htm.

Rowling, J. K. (2003), *Harry Potter and the Order of the Phoenix*, London: Bloomsbury.

Ryle, G. (1945), 'Philosophical Arguments', in Ryle (2009b).

Ryle, G. (1946), 'Why Are the Calculus of Logic and Arithmetic Applicable to Reality?', in Ryle (2009b).

Ryle, G. (1949), 'Discussion of Rudolf Carnap: "Meaning and Necessity"', in Ryle (2009a).

Ryle, G. (1950), ' "If", "So", and "Because" ', in Ryle (2009b).

Ryle, G. (1962), 'Abstractions', in Ryle (2009b).

Ryle, G. (1963), 'G.E. Moore', in Ryle (2009a).

Ryle, G. (1979), 'Adverbial Verbs and Verbs of Thinking', in K. Kolenda (ed.), *On Thinking*, Oxford: Basil Blackwell.

Ryle, G. (2009a [1971]), *Collected Papers, Volume 1: Critical Essays*, London: Routledge.

Ryle, G. (2009b [1971]), *Collected Papers, Volume 2: Collected Essays 1929–1968*, London: Routledge.

Ryle, G. (2009c [1949]), *The Concept of Mind*, London: Routledge.

Tanney, J. (2013), 'Conceptual Analysis, Theory Construction, and Philosophical Elucidation', in J. Tanney, *Rules, Reason, and Self-Knowledge*, Cambridge, MA: Harvard University Press.

Toulmin, S. E. (1958), *The Uses of Argument*, Cambridge: Cambridge University Press.

Urmson, J. O. (1952 [1960]), 'Parenthetical Verbs', in A. Flew (ed.), *Essays in Conceptual Analysis*, London: MacMillan.

Urmson, J. O. (1953 [1960]), 'Some Questions Concerning Validity', in A. Flew (ed.), *Essays in Conceptual Analysis*, London: MacMillan.

Vander Veer, G. L. (1978), *Philosophical Skepticism and Ordinary-Language Analysis*, Lawrence: The Regents Press of Kansas.

Wisdom, J. (1963 [1944/5]), 'Gods', in A. Flew (ed.), *Logic and Language: First Series*, Oxford: Basil Blackwell.

Wisdom, J. (1991), *Proof and Explanation: The Virginia Lectures*, ed. S. Barker, Lanham, MD: University Press of America.

Wittgenstein, L. (1969), *On Certainty*, ed. G. E. M. Anscombe and G. H. von Wright, trans. D. Paul and G. E. M. Anscombe, Oxford: Basil Blackwell.

4

Naturalistic Descriptions of Knowledge

Kourken Michaelian

1. Introduction

Is knowledge naturalistically describable? Can and should epistemology become a naturalistic field? To a non-epistemologist, the answer to these questions might seem to be obvious. For epistemology to become *naturalistic* would be for it to become *empirical*. The central goals of epistemology are to tell us what knowledge is and how to go about acquiring it, and, surely, if we are to have any hope of attaining those goals, then we will have to investigate knowledge empirically. How else might we hope to formulate an adequate description of something as complex as human knowledge? How else might we hope to give useful advice about how to acquire knowledge?

There is, as we will see, certainly something to this line of thought. Among epistemologists, however, these questions have been highly controversial. Depending on their interpretations of the goals of epistemology, epistemologists have endorsed radically different answers to them, with some taking the naturalization of epistemology to be the only hope for the field, even as others have taken it to be impossible even in principle to naturalize epistemology. The debate over the possibility and desirability of naturalizing epistemology has thus been intense. This chapter aims, first, to describe the basic outlines of that debate and, second, to provide a feel for some of the work done under the banner of naturalistic epistemology. The overall aim is to provide the reader with a sense both of what naturalistic epistemologists have hoped to accomplish in principle and of what they have done in practice.

The positions that epistemologists have adopted in the debate over naturalism have depended not only on their interpretations of the goals of epistemology but also on how, exactly, they have understood the idea of naturalism itself.

Section 2 therefore introduces different forms of naturalism, focusing on the methodological form deriving from Quine. It then describes three (somewhat notional) waves of naturalistic epistemology, each of which goes further in the direction of methodological naturalism than its predecessor does. Sections 3 through 5 look at each of these waves in detail, and Section 6 briefly sums up.

2. What is naturalistic epistemology?

Discussions of naturalistic epistemology inevitably begin with a reference to Quine, but it is worth noting that, from an historical point of view, naturalistic approaches to epistemology are arguably nothing new. Reid (1997), for example, can be seen as a precursor of contemporary naturalistic epistemology (Rysiew 2002), and there are numerous other historical figures that might be cited to make the same point. Nevertheless, it is indisputable that it was only in the latter half of the twentieth century that some epistemologists self-consciously began to describe themselves as naturalists. Quine (1969b) is generally regarded as the founding father of contemporary naturalism and his 'Epistemology Naturalized' as its founding text.

2.1 Quine's impact

The dominant approach to epistemology when Quine wrote was thoroughly a priori, in the sense that it eschewed a posteriori empirical investigation. The guiding thought of this approach was that, because the aims of epistemology are normative rather than descriptive – because epistemology aims to tell us not how we *do* form our beliefs but rather how we *should* form our beliefs – its method is properly a priori rather than empirical. The relevant contrast is with psychology, which, because it aims to tell us how we do form our beliefs, can and must employ empirical methods. The thought is vividly expressed by Reichenbach (1938: 5; qtd by Rysiew 2016):

> Epistemology does not regard the processes of thinking in their actual occurrence; this task is entirely left to psychology. What epistemology intends is to construct thinking processes in a way in which they ought to occur if they are to be ranged in a consistent system; or to construct justifiable sets of operations which can be intercalated between the starting-point and the issue of thought-processes, replacing the real intermediate links. Epistemology thus considers a logical substitute rather than real processes.

The idea here is that whether a subject has knowledge – as opposed to mere belief, or mere true belief – has to do with whether the way in which he does form his beliefs corresponds to the way in which he should form his beliefs. Empirical methods can tell us about how subjects do form their beliefs. But they cannot tell us how subjects ought to form their beliefs. Hence, while empirical methods are appropriate for psychology, they are inappropriate for epistemology. The latter must rely instead on a priori methods – roughly, reflection on how an epistemically ideal subject would go about forming his beliefs.

Against the dominant rejection of psychology as irrelevant to epistemology, Quine (1969b: 75) advocated 'a surrender of the epistemological burden to psychology'. Epistemology, he maintained, ought to become an empirical field, a part of psychology:

> [E]pistemology still goes on, though in a new setting and a clarified status. Epistemology, or something like it, simply falls into place as a chapter of psychology and hence of natural science. It studies a natural phenomenon, viz., a physical human subject. This human subject is accorded a certain experimentally controlled input – certain patterns of irradiation in assorted frequencies, for instance – and in the fullness of time the subject delivers as output a description of the three dimensional world and its history. The relation between the meager input and the torrential output is a relation that we are prompted to study for somewhat the same reasons that always prompted epistemology; namely, in order to see how evidence relates to theory, and in what ways one's theory of nature transcends any available evidence. (82–3)

Interpreting Quine's argument for the surrender of the epistemological burden to psychology is no mean task. This is due in part to the nature of the text itself, which, while inspiring, is in many places somewhat opaque. But it is also due in part to the fact that the intellectual context in which Quine produced the text is decidedly not our own. In particular, 'Epistemology Naturalized' is devoted in large part to critiquing Carnap's (2003) version of the project of rational reconstruction, and adopts a behaviourist vision of psychology which now seems decidedly outdated. Fortunately, many detailed discussions of the text are available – see, for example, Fogelin (2004), Gregory (2008), and, for brief discussions of naturalism in the context of Quine's broader epistemological project, Creath (2011) and Kelly (2014) – and we need not concern ourselves here with the difficult task of interpreting Quine, for his importance to epistemology is attributable less to the details of his argument than to the impact that his basic vision of an empirical epistemology has had on the field.

That impact has been dramatic. The possibility and the desirability of naturalizing epistemology were debated throughout the 1970s and 1980s – when the first edition of the important edited collection *Naturalizing Epistemology* (Kornblith 1994b) appeared – and into the 1990s. The debate, which was concerned, among other issues, with the ability of naturalistic epistemology to accommodate epistemic normativity, began to subside in the late 1990s and today appears to have more or less run its course. But if the debate has run its course, it is not immediately obvious what its outcome has been. As Creath (2011: 792) puts it, some epistemologists have 'marched proudly under [the banner of naturalistic epistemology], and others bemoaned it'. Thus, on the one hand, the naturalistic program has been explicitly endorsed by many influential epistemologists: for example, Goldman (1986), Kitcher (1992), and Kornblith (2002). On the other hand, it has been explicitly rejected by many others: for example, BonJour (1994), Feldman (1999), and Stroud (2000). Chisholm, for example, writing in 1989, remained dismissive: 'For the most part, the facts with which [empirical investigations of knowledge] are concerned are not relevant to the traditional philosophical questions. Unfortunately, however, this relevance has been exaggerated by many writers who do not seem to have grasped the traditional problems' (vii). Moreover, even among those who have endorsed empirical methods in principle, many have continued to rely primarily on traditional a priori methods in practice. As Kornblith (2007) observes, for example, the method of the first, epistemological, part of Goldman's influential *Epistemology and Cognition* (1986) consists entirely of a priori conceptual analysis, despite his explicit endorsement of naturalism. We will come back to Goldman's naturalistic justification of conceptual analysis in Section 3. The point, for now, is that, if Quine's argument has been successful, it has been successful only to some extent and in some respects.

2.2 Forms of naturalistic epistemology

The details of Quine's argument may be difficult to interpret, but the gist of its conclusion is not: Quine is explicit about wanting to link epistemology tightly with psychology. Many subsequent proponents of naturalistic epistemology have shared this goal, but, as Goldman (1994) emphasizes, the goal itself is subject to multiple interpretations. 'Naturalistic epistemology' has thus come to refer to a broad family of interconnected views.

The family tree has three branches, which Goldman refers to as meta-epistemic, substantive, and methodological naturalism. *Meta-epistemic* naturalism should be understood on the model of meta-ethical naturalism. Just as meta-ethical naturalism is a metaphysical thesis about the nature of ethical properties, meta-epistemic naturalism is a metaphysical thesis about the nature of epistemic properties. On this view, epistemic properties are natural properties, in the sense that they reduce to, supervene on, or stand in some other appropriately tight relationship to uncontroversially natural properties.

This is a variety of naturalism so bland that most epistemologists endorse it (though some, e.g., Chisholm [1989], may have rejected it), and meta-epistemic naturalism is quite distant from Quine's methodological concerns. Somewhat closer to the latter, but still distinct from them, is *substantive* naturalism. Substantively naturalistic views 'invoke physico-causal processes of the epistemic agent, or perhaps relations that obtain between the cognitive agent and its environment' (Goldman 1994: 302). Reliabilism, for example, which analyses knowledge in terms of the reliability of belief-producing processes, is substantively naturalistic (Goldman 2012). Theories that analyse knowledge in terms of normative notions such as 'evidence', in contrast, are incompatible with substantive naturalism (Conee and Feldman 2004).

Methodological naturalism, finally, is what Quine had in mind by naturalized epistemology. The core claim of methodological naturalism is that epistemology should be intimately linked to psychology. The precise nature of the appropriate relationship between epistemology and psychology has been one point of contention among methodological naturalists, but Quine himself was explicit on this point as well: in his view, epistemology was to become *part* of psychology.

2.3 Waves of naturalistic epistemology

To what extent has Quine's argument for methodological naturalism had an impact? A survey conducted by Turri (2016) to measure perceptions of traditional areas of philosophy and their relationship to science may shed some light on this question. For each of a number of areas, respondents were asked to rate their agreement, on a scale from 1 to 7, with the following three statements. (1) *This area is currently central to the discipline of philosophy.* (2) *To the extent that this area is currently central to philosophy, it depends on being integrated with the relevant natural, cognitive, or social sciences.* (3) *Current work in this area is sufficiently integrated with the relevant natural, cognitive, or social sciences.* The focus of Turri's own discussion is not on epistemology, but it is instructive to compare his findings on perceptions of epistemology and on perceptions of philosophy of mind, arguably the area of philosophy most closely related to epistemology. (Respondents tended to view both mind and epistemology as central to philosophy: mean agreement with the relevant statement was 5.89 for mind and 6.18 for epistemology.) Respondents, most of whom were philosophers, tended to view philosophy of mind's centrality as depending more on its integration with science: mean agreement with the relevant statement was 5.6 for mind versus 4.45 for epistemology. And they had a slightly stronger tendency to view philosophy of mind as being sufficiently integrated with science: mean agreement with the relevant statement was 4.78 for mind versus 4.18 for epistemology.

Taking 'integrated with science' as being roughly equivalent to 'naturalistic', these responses suggest two observations. First, arguments for naturalizing epistemology have had considerable influence. Nevertheless, naturalistic approaches to philosophy of mind are more widely accepted than are naturalistic approaches to epistemology. Second, to the extent that philosophers have been convinced by arguments for naturalizing epistemology, many judge that contemporary epistemology is insufficiently naturalistic. While many philosophers likewise judge that contemporary philosophy of mind is insufficiently naturalistic, the tendency here is slightly less pronounced than in the case of epistemology.

Turri's findings are interesting but provide little insight into the extent to which Quine's argument has actually led to an empirical turn in epistemology. A comparison with philosophy of mind is again instructive. Despite the absence of an explicit debate over the naturalization of philosophy of mind comparable to the debate that took place over the naturalization of epistemology, there has been a clear trend towards greater integration with psychology (and the cognitive sciences more broadly) in philosophy of mind. Knobe (2015) studied this trend by comparing two samples of philosophy of mind papers from leading journals, covering the years 1960–99 and 2009–13, respectively. With respect to topical focus, he found a decline of interest in traditional philosophy of mind topics (such as the mind-body problem) and an increase of interest in 'specific aspects of cognition'. With respect to method – the dimension of greatest interest here – he found a decline in purely a priori approaches and an increase in approaches that either rely on empirical research or themselves conduct empirical research. In the 1960–99 sample, a majority of papers (62.4 per cent) were purely a priori, a substantial minority (37.6 per cent) relied on empirical research, and none (0 per cent) reported original empirical research. In the 2009–13 sample, a small minority of papers (11.5 per cent) were purely a priori, a majority (61.8 per cent) relied on empirical research, and a substantial minority (26.8 per cent) reported original empirical research.

Knobe's findings suggest that there have been two dramatic shifts in the practice of philosophy of mind. First, philosophers of mind now standardly rely on empirical research. Previously, this was unusual. Second, philosophers of mind now themselves often conduct empirical research. Previously, this was unheard of. Have there been comparable shifts in epistemology? No one has conducted a quantitative study of method in epistemology analogous to Knobe's study of method in philosophy of mind. But an informal qualitative survey of the literature suggests the following observations. First, there *has* been a shift in epistemology comparable to the first shift in philosophy of mind: that is, epistemologists increasingly rely on empirical research. Second, there has *not* been a shift in epistemology comparable to the second shift in philosophy of mind: that is, epistemologists do not yet generally conduct empirical research.

These observations suggest a division of work on naturalistic epistemology into three 'waves'. The *first wave* of naturalistic epistemology was programmatic in character, concerned largely with arguments for naturalization. The *second wave* of naturalistic epistemology has moved, to varying extents, beyond programmatic discussions to attempt to base theories of knowledge on relevant empirical research. And a hypothetical *third wave* of naturalistic epistemology would move beyond reliance on relevant empirical research to itself conducting empirical research. While the reality is of course messier than this simple picture would suggest, the idea of waves will nonetheless provide a convenient means of organizing our discussion.

3. The first wave of naturalistic epistemology: programmatic debates

The first, programmatic, wave of naturalistic epistemology was concerned primarily with determining the feasibility and the implications of the methodological naturalism advocated by Quine. Reactions to his argument were varied. Some epistemologists accused him of attacking a straw man. As noted above, Quine was concerned in large part to respond to the Carnapian project of rational reconstruction, but, by the time he wrote, that project had largely been abandoned in favour of the project, with which we are now more familiar, of attempting to analyse knowledge (Almeder 1990; Kelly 2014) – that is, to produce a set of necessary and sufficient conditions for knowledge (Shope 2004). Space does not permit an in-depth examination of this debate or of many of the others that were occasioned by Quine's argument (see Rysiew 2016). We will therefore restrict our attention to two debates. First, we will consider the question of the role of *intuition* in epistemology, a question which, under the impact of experimental philosophy, has recently resurfaced in a form that is of direct relevance to naturalism. Second, we will consider the question of *normativity*, which was undoubtedly the key issue in first-wave naturalistic epistemology.

3.1 The intuition debate

While some accused Quine of attacking a straw man, others accused him of incoherence, on the ground that his argument relied on a tacit – and illegitimate – appeal to a priori intuition. As we have seen, Quine's argument was directed in part against the a priori methods of traditional epistemology. Traditional epistemology, as embodied in Carnap's rational reconstruction or, earlier, in Descartes' attempt to provide secure foundations for knowledge, relies on a priori intuition, in the sense that it relies on intuitions – spontaneous judgements – to justify claims about epistemic norms or principles. For example, most discussions of the Gettier (1963) problem (see Section 5 below) proceeded by constructing hypothetical cases, asking for our intuitions about whether the beliefs involved in those cases qualified as knowledge, and then proposing general principles designed to capture those intuitions. In fact, though there are some who deny the centrality of intuition to epistemology and to philosophy more generally (Cappelen 2012), much epistemology still proceeds in essentially this manner. The problem is that the means by which Quine argued against a priori methods in epistemology itself appears to employ precisely this a priori method (Siegel 1984; Bealer 1992; Kaplan 1994). Quine does not appeal to any empirical data. Instead, he offers an argument which presupposes general principles of the very sort that can only be established by appeal to intuition.

Naturalistic epistemologists have employed various strategies when responding to this objection (see Rysiew 2016). One strategy is to attempt to provide an account of the use of intuition which does not treat it as an a priori source of understanding. Kornblith (2002), for example, argues that our intuitions about whether hypothetical cases of belief qualify as instances of knowledge do not reflect a priori understanding. Instead, on his view, they reflect an understanding of the phenomenon of knowledge that has been acquired in an empirical manner. We will return to Kornblith's account in Section 4, but not everyone, of course, has been convinced by the account (BonJour 2006). Another strategy is to attempt to make room for a priori intuition within a recognizably naturalistic epistemology. Goldman (1988, 1993, 2007), for example, argues that our intuitions about whether hypothetical cases of belief qualify as instances of knowledge reflect the features of our own concept of knowledge. On his view, our concept of knowledge is the source of our intuitions about whether hypothetical beliefs qualify as knowledge, so that consulting our intuitions about such cases in effect amounts to performing a small-scale psychological experiment (Kornblith 2007). This understanding of the role of intuition foreshadows the recent experimental approaches to epistemology to which we will return in Section 5.

3.2 The normativity debate

While the question of intuition is important, much of the early debate around naturalistic epistemology was concerned with the distinct issue of normativity. Epistemology is a normative field: it seeks both to tell us what knowledge is and how we ought to go about acquiring it. This leads to the worry that, because psychology is purely descriptive, turning epistemology into a chapter of psychology is bound to deprive it of its normative character: 'Quine seems to have abandoned normative epistemology in favor of simply describing our present practices. And this will not be at all surprising if we believe that science is a purely descriptive endeavor. If that is so, then a naturalized epistemology must also be purely descriptive' (Gregory 2008: 20). Kim (1988: 389), for example, pointing out that much traditional epistemology is in fact naturalistic in meta-epistemic or substantive terms, argues that Quine's rejection of traditional epistemology on methodological grounds commits him to rejecting epistemic normativity entirely: for Quine, '[e]pistemology is to go out of the business of justification'.

Quine himself, however, argued that methodological naturalists are able to countenance a certain degree of normativity. As he wrote later,

> [n]aturalization of epistemology does not jettison the normative and settle for the indiscriminate description of ongoing procedures. For me normative epistemology is a branch of engineering. It is the technology of truth-seeking, or, in a more cautiously epistemological term, prediction ... There is no question here of ultimate value, as in morals; it is a matter of efficacy for an ulterior end, truth or prediction. (1986: 664–5)

Quine's suggestion here is that naturalistic epistemology remains normative in the sense that it can provide us with guidance about how to go about forming our beliefs, where the guidance in question is *hypothetical* in nature. Just as engineering might advise us, for example, to avoid using certain materials when building bridges, naturalistic epistemology might advise us to avoid relying on visual perception in circumstances which are likely to give rise to visual illusions. The normativity in the engineering case is of an unmysterious kind: what engineering tells us is that, *if* we want to build a bridge that will not collapse in the first strong wind, *then* we should avoid using certain building materials. The same thing goes for the normativity in the epistemology case: *if* we want accurate beliefs, *then* we should be aware of circumstances in which vision is likely to be unreliable. What engineering does not tell us is that we must want sturdy rather than fragile bridges. Similarly, epistemology cannot tell us that we must want accurate rather than inaccurate beliefs.

How should we react to this suggestion? A first reaction is to take the fact that naturalism can provide us only with hypothetical normativity to be fatal to the naturalistic project. Hypothetical normativity is considerably weaker than the *categorical* normativity that epistemologists have traditionally sought to provide. Kelly (2003), for example, argues that epistemic norms are categorical, in the sense that they are binding on agents regardless of their aims or goals. There is no apparent way in which naturalistic epistemology can ground such categorical norms – how might they be discovered empirically? – and those who are committed to them seem to be bound to reject methodological naturalism. Another reaction is to attempt to provide a substitute for categorical norms. In particular, one might argue that the norms grounded by naturalism are *hypothetical but universal*. Kornblith (2002), for example, argues that we are bound to value having accurate beliefs, no matter what else we happen to value, since our ability to secure the other things that we value presupposes our having accurate beliefs. Yet another reaction is to argue that we should be content with *hypothetical and non-universal* norms. In contrast to Kornblith, Stich (1993), for example, argues that we are not in fact bound to value having accurate beliefs, with the result that epistemic norms are not universally binding (see Kappel 2011).

Depending on where one stands on the nature of epistemic norms, then, the issue of normativity may or may not prevent one from endorsing naturalism. But it is important to note that even the weaker hypothetical norms that can be provided by naturalistic epistemology may in an important sense be more robust than the norms that traditional epistemology has been able to provide.

Kornblith has argued that naturalistic epistemology need not give up on the normative concerns of traditional epistemology, in the sense that it can give useful epistemic *guidance*. Indeed, the naturalist is in an important sense better positioned than the traditional epistemologist to give such advice, for he is free to avail himself of the findings of our best psychology: 'If we wish to offer constructive advice for improving our epistemic situation, we need to begin with an accurate assessment of our epistemic strengths and weaknesses' (Kornblith 1994a: 47). It is, in contrast, unclear how an epistemology that lacks the sort of solid empirical basis that naturalists aim to give it might be capable of providing normative guidance worthy of being taken seriously (Grandy 1994). In Section 5 we will return to the issue of epistemic guidance.

4. The second wave of naturalistic epistemology: building on empirical research

It is one thing to *endorse* naturalistic epistemology; it is another thing to *do* it. If the first wave of naturalistic epistemology was largely concerned with programmatic arguments for naturalism, the second wave involved attempts to put methodological naturalism into practice by basing theories of knowledge directly on relevant empirical research. There is no way, in a chapter of this length, to survey everything that might be included under the heading of second-wave naturalistic epistemology. We will therefore look at two representative examples. First, some naturalists have argued that knowledge is a *natural kind* and that the general phenomenon of knowledge can and must therefore be investigated empirically. Second, some have argued that empirical research on *constructive memory* forces us to abandon received views of memory's epistemic role.

4.1 Knowledge as a natural kind

Picking up on another theme from Quine (1969a), Kornblith (2002) has claimed that knowledge is a natural kind. Natural kinds are kinds that 'carve nature at their joints'. Because they reflect the objective structure of the world, natural kinds ground reliable inductive inferences, in the sense that determining the features of one instance of a kind enables us to infer that other instances of the kind have similar features. They thus play a crucial role in the empirical sciences. The case of jade is often used to illustrate the notion of a natural kind. The term 'jade' has been applied to two different minerals – namely, jadeite and nephrite. While superficially similar, jadeite and nephrite differ in terms of their underlying structure. Inferences from features of jadeite to features of nephrite, and vice versa, will therefore often go wrong. Thus jade, if it includes both jadeite and nephrite, is not a natural kind. In contrast, all instances of jadeite share an underlying structure, as do all instances of nephrite, allowing them to support inductive inferences. Thus, jadeite and nephrite are natural kinds.

Knowledge, Kornblith claims, is, like jadeite and nephrite, a natural kind. His argument for this claim is somewhat involved but appeals crucially to the causal-explanatory role that attributions of knowledge – as opposed to mere true belief – play in empirical disciplines such as cognitive ethology, which studies the role of cognition in animal behaviour. The core idea is that knowledge attributions could not play this role, were knowledge not a natural kind. The claim that knowledge is a natural kind, if true, has a pair of important implications. First, it implies that Quine was right in suggesting that knowledge cannot be investigated by means of a priori intuitions. Consider how absurd it would be to attempt to investigate jadeite or nephrite by means of a priori intuitions. If Kornblith is right, it is similarly absurd to attempt to investigate knowledge by means of such intuitions. Second, it implies that Quine was right in suggesting that knowledge can be investigated by empirical means. Empirical investigation of samples of jadeite or nephrite enables us to understand what all instances of jadeite or nephrite have in common. If Kornblith is right, empirical investigation of samples of knowledge will similarly enable us to understand what all instances of knowledge have in common.

While intriguing, Kornblith's view is subject to a number of challenges. In particular, it is telling that, in two key respects, knowledge does not look much like paradigmatic natural kinds. On the one hand, in the case of paradigmatic natural kinds, such as jadeite and nephrite, 'illuminating necessary and sufficient conditions for kind membership are identified at the level of underlying microstructure' (Horvath 2016: 175): that is, there is typically a low-level explanation available of what all instances of a given kind have in common. Knowledge does not seem to be like this: no one has yet proposed a low-level explanation of what all instances of knowledge have in common, and the fact that belief, a necessary constituent of knowledge on any account, is multiply realizable suggests that no such explanation is available even in principle. Second, Kornblith's own high-level proposal for what all instances of knowledge have in common – namely, that they are cases of reliably produced true belief (Goldman 2012) – is not the result of empirical investigation of samples of knowledge. On

Naturalistic Descriptions of Knowledge 81

the contrary, reliabilism is the product of precisely the sort of a priori intuitions that methodological naturalism seeks to dismiss (Horvath 2016).

4.2 Memory as a source of knowledge

A possibility worth considering is that knowledge might be, like jade, not itself a natural kind but rather a merely nominal kind that includes more than one natural kind. If so, epistemologists would do well to focus not on understanding knowledge as such but instead on understanding particular kinds of knowledge. One kind of knowledge that epistemologists, in their attempts to analyse knowledge as such, have tended to neglect is memory knowledge. In psychology, memory has long been a major area of research, and we have a great deal of empirical understanding of its workings. In epistemology, in contrast, detailed treatments of memory have been few and far between, and those treatments that epistemologists have offered have usually been almost entirely empirically uninformed. This is beginning to change, however, and the psychology of memory has the potential to transform traditional views in the epistemology of memory. Let us briefly consider two examples.

First, it has traditionally been assumed that memory is capable of generating but not preserving knowledge. Just as testimony cannot give the hearer knowledge that the speaker did not have, the thought goes, memory cannot give a subject at a later time knowledge that he did not have at an earlier time (e.g. Dummett 1994). This preservationist view has been challenged by Lackey (2005), who argues that, because defeaters for a belief – factors that counteract its justification – can come and go while the belief is preserved in memory, memory can indeed generate knowledge, in the sense that memory can give a subject knowledge that he did not have at an earlier time. Though it is interesting, Lackey's argument is entirely compatible with a traditional preservationist picture of the workings of memory, since it does not require memory to generate new beliefs. The psychology of constructive memory, however, suggests that memory does in fact routinely generate new beliefs. If so, and if memory functions reliably when it does so, then it may indeed generate new knowledge in a way that departs radically from the traditional preservationist picture (Michaelian 2011).

Second, if memory routinely generates new beliefs, there is a worry about whether it does in fact function reliably when it does so. If it does not, then we might have far less memory knowledge than we ordinarily take ourselves to have. The result would be a sort of empirically grounded scepticism about memory knowledge (Shanton 2011), in contrast to the sort of a priori scepticism about memory knowledge traditionally discussed by philosophers (Russell 1921). Whereas a priori scepticism about memory knowledge arises because we cannot with certainty rule out propositions such as 'the world, including my apparent memories, came into existence five minutes ago', empirically grounded scepticism arises because it is difficult to imagine how new beliefs generated by memory might be accurate. While this may be difficult to imagine, there is in fact reason for optimism here. Consider, for example, the phenomenon of boundary extension, in which a subject remembers more of a scene than he originally saw (Intraub, Bender, and Mangels 1992). If the principles that determine the ways in which portions of a scene that were beyond the subject's field of view are filled in by memory ensure that those portions of the scene are usually filled in accurately, then memory may indeed function reliably in cases of boundary extension (Michaelian 2016).

5. A third wave of naturalistic epistemology? Conducting empirical research

If the second wave of naturalistic epistemology has built on existing empirical research, a third wave might involve original empirical research. In this section, we will look briefly at two forms that third-wave naturalistic epistemology might take. First, we will consider the possibility that recent work on knowledge in *experimental philosophy* qualifies as third-wave naturalistic epistemology. Second, we will consider the possibility that some work conducted in *experimental psychology* itself qualifies as third-wave naturalistic epistemology.

5.1 Experimental philosophy as experimental epistemology

One might argue that third-wave naturalistic epistemology has already emerged in the form of 'experimental philosophy' – in particular, the part of experimental philosophy that concerns itself with knowledge. Experimental philosophy (Knobe and Nichols 2008, 2014) is a recent methodological innovation that arose from a novel take on the idea (discussed in Section 3 above) that our intuitions reveal the contours of our concepts. If our intuitions reveal our concepts, the thought goes, then the traditional project of conceptual analysis has much going for it. But if philosophers want to map the contours of our concepts in a reliable manner, the thought continues, they should not be content to rely on their own, possibly idiosyncratic, intuitions. Instead, they should perform experiments designed to elicit the intuitions of a representative range of people. Doing so might confirm existing analyses of certain concepts, but it might also overturn these, suggesting novel analyses. In the case of epistemology, of course, the key concept is knowledge, and experimental philosophers have indeed claimed to have discovered novel features of the concept of knowledge.

There is no need to attempt to survey the full range of work on experimental epistemology here (see Weinberg 2011), but let us consider one representative line of inquiry. An early study claimed to find that judgements about Gettier (1963) cases varied across cultures. Consider the following case:

> Bob has a friend, Jill, who has a driven a Buick for many years. Bob therefore thinks that Jill drives an American car. He is not aware, however, that her Buick has recently been stolen, and he is also not aware that Jill has replaced it with a Pontiac, which is a different kind of American car. Does Bob really know that Jill drives an American car, or does he only believe it? (Weinberg, Nichols, and Stich 2001)

Epistemologists usually have the intuition that Bob does not know that Jill drives an American car. It is difficult to say *why* Bob should not know that Jill drives an American car, since his belief is both true (Jill really does drive an American car) and justified (Bob has good reason to think that Jill drives an American car), and a whole industry within epistemology has been devoted to solving the resulting 'Gettier problem' (Shope 2004).

What Weinberg, Nichols, and Stich (2001) claimed to find when they surveyed American subjects of European and Asian descent was that, while the former tended to share the epistemologists' intuition, the latter did not. This result has been challenged (e.g. Machery et al. forthcoming), but, if it is right, it would threaten to undermine one of the core projects of contemporary epistemology – namely, the attempt to formulate an account of knowledge that captures the incompatibility of knowledge and Gettierization. Even if the result is wrong, moreover, we must – unless we are prepared to deny that cross-cultural or other variations in intuitions are irrelevant even in principle to the analysis of epistemic concepts – concede that, to the extent that epistemology is concerned with the analysis of epistemic concepts, the naturalists were right: epistemology must become an empirical field. A thoroughgoing naturalism (of the sort endorsed by Kornblith, for example), however, which takes the appropriate target of epistemology to be not our concept of knowledge but rather knowledge itself, will nevertheless view experimental epistemology with scepticism. The experiments conducted by experimental philosophers may reveal something interesting about our concept of knowledge; but they cannot reveal (because they are not designed to reveal) anything interesting about knowledge itself (Nanay 2015).

5.2 Experimental psychology as experimental epistemology

If the experiments conducted by experimental philosophers are of relatively little interest to naturalistic epistemology, there may nevertheless be experiments in other domains that are of direct epistemological interest. So far, such experiments have not generally been done by epistemologists themselves. But we can look to relevant work done by psychologists to get a general idea of what an experimental epistemology concerned with knowledge itself, as opposed to our concept of knowledge, might look like. Recall the idea, introduced in Section 3, that one task of epistemology is to provide us with epistemic guidance – roughly, to tell us how to go about forming beliefs in an epistemically adequate manner. Epistemologists have traditionally sought to provide highly general advice (along the lines of the *Rules for the Direction of the Mind*, in which Descartes advises us to investigate only those matters that we are competent to know with certainty). But such rules are of questionable utility, and we may do better to seek to formulate domain-specific guidelines. There is a good deal of work in psychology which, in combination with a substantively naturalistic epistemology such as reliabilism, may ground such guidelines.

Thus Bishop and Trout (2005), for example, adopting what they refer to as 'strategic reliabilism' – a form of reliabilism on which good reasoning consists in reasoning that produces significant true beliefs in a robustly reliable manner – appeal to psychological research to recommend certain heuristics as guides for reasoning about a wide variety of matters. Consider, for example, the planning fallacy, which refers to the tendency to underestimate how much time it will take to complete a task, such as packing to move to a new apartment (Bishop and Trout 2008). They argue that the planning fallacy occurs because we rely on an 'internal' approach to estimating the necessary time: roughly, we break the task down into steps, estimate how long each step will take, and then judge that the task as a whole will take the resulting total amount of time. Instead of relying on an internal approach, they suggest, there is research that suggests that we would do better to rely on an 'external' approach (Kahneman and Tversky 1979) in which we determine how long it has taken us to complete similar tasks in the past and judge that the task as a whole will take a similar amount of time in the future. Such an approach does not give us certainty, but, if they are right, it is more reliable than the internal approach that we naturally tend to adopt.

6. Conclusion

As we saw in Section 2, there has been a shift in philosophy of mind from a situation in which philosophers did not themselves perform empirical research to one in which they perform such research on a fairly regular basis. A comparable shift has not yet occurred in epistemology. The empirical research to which Bishop and Trout appeal is conducted by psychologists rather than epistemologists, and the third wave of naturalistic epistemology thus remains largely hypothetical. But there is no reason in principle why a genuine third wave of naturalistic epistemology might not emerge in the future. Some have worried that, should such a shift emerge, it would deprive epistemology of its philosophical character. On one version of this worry, epistemology is meant to be normative, while empirical research can only be descriptive. We have already seen that the naturalist has ways of responding to this worry. On another version, the questions with which epistemology is meant to be concerned are, if not purely conceptual, too highly general to be empirically tractable. Here we might suggest applying naturalistic epistemology to itself: rather than trying to determine a priori whether it is possible to develop an empirical epistemology, we ought to determine this empirically – by trying to develop an empirical epistemology and seeing whether we succeed.

References

Almeder, R. (1990), 'On Naturalizing Epistemology', *American Philosophical Quarterly*, 27: 263–79.

Bealer, G. (1992), 'The Incoherence of Empiricism', *Proceedings of the Aristotelian Society, Supp. Vol.*, 66: 99–138.

Bishop, M. A. and Trout, J. D. (2005), *Epistemology and the Psychology of Human Judgment*, New York: Oxford University Press.

Bishop, M. A. and Trout, J. D. (2008), 'Strategic Reliabilism: A Naturalistic Approach to Epistemology', *Philosophy Compass*, 3: 1049–65.

BonJour, L. (1994), 'Against Naturalized Epistemology', *Midwest Studies in Philosophy*, 19: 283–300.

BonJour, L. (2006), 'Kornblith on Knowledge and Epistemology', *Philosophical Studies*, 127: 317–35.

Cappelen, H. (2012), *Philosophy without Intuitions*, Oxford: Oxford University Press.

Carnap, R. (2003 [1928]), *The Logical Structure of the World*, La Salle, IL: Open Court.

Chisholm, R. M. (1989), *Theory of Knowledge*, 3rd edn, Englewood Cliffs, NJ: Prentice-Hall.

Conee, E. and Feldman, R. (2004), *Evidentialism: Essays in Epistemology*, Oxford: Clarendon Press.

Creath, R. (2011), 'Willard Van Orman Quine', in S. Bernecker and D. Pritchard (eds), *The Routledge Companion to Epistemology*, New York: Routledge.

Dummett, M. (1994), 'Testimony and Memory', in B. K. Matilal and A. Chakrabarti (eds), *Knowing from Words: Western and Indian Philosophical Analysis of Understanding and Testimony*, Dordrecht: Kluwer.

Feldman, R. (1999), 'Methodological Naturalism in Epistemology', in J. Greco and A. Sosa (eds), *The Blackwell Guide to Epistemology*, Oxford: Blackwell.

Fogelin, R. J. (2004), 'Aspects of Quine's Naturalized Epistemology', in R. F. Gibson (ed.), *The Cambridge Companion to Quine*, Cambridge: Cambridge University Press.

Gettier, E. L. (1963), 'Is Knowledge Justified True Belief?' *Analysis*, 23: 121–3.

Goldman, A. I. (1986), *Epistemology and Cognition*, Cambridge, MA: Harvard University Press.

Goldman, A. I. (1988), 'Psychology and Philosophical Analysis', *Proceedings of the Aristotelian Society*, 89: 195–209.

Goldman, A. I. (1993), 'Epistemic Folkways and Scientific Epistemology', *Philosophical Issues*, 3: 271–85.

Goldman, A. I. (1994), 'Naturalistic Epistemology and Reliabilism', *Midwest Studies in Philosophy*, 19: 301–20.

Goldman, A. I. (2007), 'Philosophical Intuitions: Their Target, Their Source, and Their Epistemic Status', *Grazer Philosophische Studien*, 74: 1–26.

Goldman, A. I. (2012), *Reliabilism and Contemporary Epistemology: Essays*, New York: Oxford University Press.

Grandy, R. E. (1994), 'Epistemology Naturalized and "Epistemology Naturalized"', *Midwest Studies in Philosophy*, 19: 341–9.

Gregory, P. A. (2008), *Quine's Naturalism: Language, Theory, and Knowing the Subject*, London: Bloomsbury.

Horvath, J. (2016), 'Conceptual Analysis and Natural Kinds: The Case of Knowledge', *Synthese*, 193: 167–84.

Intraub, H., Bender, R. S., and Mangels, J. A. (1992), 'Looking at Pictures but Remembering Scenes', *Journal of Experimental Psychology: Learning, Memory, and Cognition*, 18: 180–91.

Kahneman, D. and Tversky, A. (1979), 'Intuitive Prediction: Biases and Corrective Procedures', in D. Kahneman, P. Slovic, and A. Tversky (eds), *Judgement under Uncertainty: Heuristics and Biases*, Cambridge: Cambridge University Press.

Kaplan, M. (1994), 'Epistemology Denatured', *Midwest Studies in Philosophy*, 19: 350–65.

Kappel, K. (2011), 'Naturalistic Epistemology', in S. Bernecker and D. Pritchard (eds), *The Routledge Companion to Epistemology*, New York: Routledge.

Kelly, T. (2003), 'Epistemic Rationality as Instrumental Rationality: A Critique', *Philosophy and Phenomenological Research*, 66: 612–40.

Kelly, T. (2014), 'Quine and Epistemology', in G. Harman and E. Lepore (eds), *A Companion to W.V.O. Quine*, Malden, MA: Wiley Blackwell.

Kim, J. (1988), 'What Is "Naturalized Epistemology?"', *Philosophical Perspectives*, 2: 381–405.

Kitcher, P. (1992), 'The Naturalists Return', *Philosophical Review*, 101: 53–114.

Knobe, J. (2015), 'Philosophers Are Doing Something Different Now: Quantitative Data', *Cognition*, 135: 36–8.

Knobe, J. and Nichols, S. (eds) (2008), *Experimental Philosophy, Volume 1*, Oxford: Oxford University Press.

Knobe, J. and Nichols, S. (eds) (2014), *Experimental Philosophy, Volume 2*, Oxford: Oxford University Press.

Kornblith, H. (1994a), 'Naturalism: Both Metaphysical and Epistemological', *Midwest Studies in Philosophy*, 19: 39–52.

Kornblith, H. (ed.) (1994b), *Naturalizing Epistemology*, Cambridge: The MIT Press.

Kornblith, H. (2002), *Knowledge and Its Place in Nature*, Oxford: Clarendon Press.

Kornblith, H. (2007), 'The Naturalistic Project in Epistemology: Where Do We Go from Here?', in C. M. Mi and R. Chen (eds), *Naturalized Epistemology and Philosophy of Science*, Amsterdam: Rodopi.

Lackey, J. (2005), 'Memory as a Generative Epistemic Source', *Philosophy and Phenomenological Research*, 70: 636–58.

Machery, E., Stich, S., Rose, D., Chatterjee, A., Karasawa, K., Struchiner, N., Sirker, S., Usui, N., and Hashimoto, T. (forthcoming), 'Gettier across Cultures', *Noûs*.

Michaelian, K. (2011), 'Generative Memory', *Philosophical Psychology*, 24: 323–42.

Michaelian, K. (2016), *Mental Time Travel: Episodic Memory and Our Knowledge of the Personal Past*, Cambridge: The MIT Press.

Nanay, B. (2015), 'Experimental Philosophy and Naturalism', in E. Fischer and J. Collins (eds), *Experimental Philosophy, Rationalism and Naturalism: Rethinking Philosophical Method*, London: Routledge.

Quine, W. V. O. (1969a), 'Natural Kinds', in N. Rescher (ed.), *Essays in Honor of Carl G. Hempel: A Tribute on the Occasion of his Sixty-Fifth Birthday*, Dordrecht: Springer.

Quine, W. V. O. (1969b), *Ontological Relativity and Other Essays*, New York: Columbia University Press.

Quine, W. V. O. (1986), 'Reply to Morton White', in L. E. Hahn and P. A. Schilpp (eds), *The Philosophy of W.V. Quine*, La Salle, IL: Open Court.

Reichenbach, H. (1938), *Experience and Prediction*, Chicago: University of Chicago Press.

Reid, T. (1997 [1764]), *An Inquiry into the Human Mind on the Principles of Common Sense*, Edinburgh: Edinburgh University Press.

Russell, B. (1921), *The Analysis of Mind*, London: George Allen & Unwin.

Rysiew, P. (2002), 'Reid and Epistemic Naturalism', *The Philosophical Quarterly*, 52: 437–56.

Rysiew, P. (2016), 'Naturalism in Epistemology', in E. N. Zalta (ed.), *Stanford Encyclopedia of Philosophy*, Summer 2016 edition: http://plato.stanford.edu/archives/sum2016/entries/epistemology-naturalized.

Shanton, K. (2011), 'Memory, Knowledge and Epistemic Competence', *Review of Philosophy and Psychology*, 2: 89–104.

Shope, R. K. (2004), 'The Analysis of Knowing', in I. Niiniluoto, M. Sintonen, and J. Woleński (eds), *Handbook of Epistemology*, Dordrecht: Springer.

Siegel, H. (1984), 'Empirical Psychology, Naturalized Epistemology, and First Philosophy', *Philosophy of Science*, 51: 667–76.

Stich, S. P. (1993), 'Naturalizing Epistemology: Quine, Simon, and the Prospects for Pragmatism', in C. Hookway and D. Peterson (eds), *Philosophy and Cognitive Science*, Cambridge: Cambridge University Press.

Stroud, B. (2000), *Understanding Human Knowledge: Philosophical Essays*, Oxford: Oxford University Press.

Turri, J. (2016), 'Perceptions of Philosophical Inquiry: A Survey', *Review of Philosophy and Psychology*, 7: 805–16.

Weinberg, J. M (2011), 'Experimental Epistemology', in S. Bernecker and D. Pritchard (eds), *The Routledge Companion to Epistemology*, New York: Routledge.

Weinberg, J. M., Nichols, S., and Stich, S. (2001), 'Normativity and Epistemic Intuitions', *Philosophical Topics*, 29: 429–60.

5

Knowing the Unobservable: Confirmation and Theoretical Virtues

Stathis Psillos

1. Introduction

What's peculiar about science, from an epistemological point of view, is that it makes a claim about extending our knowledge of the world beyond whatever can be observed by the naked eye, or perceived by the senses. The epistemological question then is: how are scientific claims that extend beyond what is, or can be, observed justified? If we take knowledge to be justified true belief, then the focus of the epistemology of science should be on justification and not on truth. There are, of course, theories of truth that tie truth to justification or related epistemic notions such as warranted assertibility, superassertibility, and so on (cf. Dummett 1991; Wright 1992). But I will assume throughout a non-epistemic account of truth, which as I have argued elsewhere (2012a; 2017) is the hallmark of realism, and of scientific realism in particular. This is mainly because if we were to accept an epistemic account of truth, truth would be what is delivered, perhaps ultimately or in the ideal end of inquiry, by the persistent and consistent application of best scientific method. Hence, insofar as scientific truth is conceptually tied to justification, scientific knowledge is, in principle at least, possible. But if truth is non-epistemic, then it is possible that justified beliefs, even ideally justified beliefs, are false. Where anti-realists see a gap between truth and its knowledge that has to be closed by making truth connected to epistemic conditions that are tied to justification (or verification), realists see the possibility of a gap between truth and justification as *securing* that the world that science tries to map out is independent of the cognitive and epistemic means that are used to acquire knowledge of it. Still, justified beliefs should be true to count as knowledge, but truth is something external to them; if they are true, they constitute knowledge; if they are not, they do not.

Some care is needed here, however. It is well known and readily admitted that scientific assertions are rarely, if ever, *strictly* true. This is because of the very nature of scientific representation and theorizing which involves, constitutively, idealizations, abstractions, simplifications, and the like. So even when they are representationally accurate, scientific assertions can at best be approximately true, or truthlike, or partially true and the like. But a truthlike belief is, *strictly speaking*, a false belief; if strict truth is required for knowledge, then there is virtually no scientific knowledge, period. This would be too quick though. Science can offer knowledge of the world even when its claims are approximately true, if only because the world, or the particular target system, might well resemble the theoretical model or satisfy the relevant theoretical description to a good approximation. I am not going to discuss this issue in any detail here (cf. Psillos 1999: ch. 11). I just flag it as worth exploring further.

Care is also needed when it comes to the demand for justification itself. What's significant about science is that it relies on ampliative methods. But ampliative methods face a constitutive problem. Being ampliative, they are such that the output of the method has more content than the input (this is to say, ampliative methods are non-deductive). And without this being so, it's hard to see how science could even in principle promise to offer knowledge beyond what is observed and given to us in direct experience. Yet, if it is knowledge that is being gained, or at least justified belief, then the method should be such that it is also epistemically probative: the excess content produced by the application of the ampliative method (viz. hypotheses and theories) should be epistemically warranted. Now, the constitutive problem of scientific method is precisely that ampliation and epistemic warrant are not obviously and automatically satisfied together. The tension between them arises from the fact that ampliation does not carry its epistemically probative character on its sleeves. The following question then arises: what makes it the case that the method conveys epistemic warrant to the intended output of the method rather than to any other output which is *consistent* with the input? Sceptics argue that the foregoing question cannot be answered in a non-question-begging way. It follows that a full investigation of the issue of scientific knowledge should include in it the discussion of the philosophical problem of the justification of the scientific method (perhaps starting with the well-known problem of induction). This cannot be done here, but I have dealt with it extensively elsewhere (cf. Psillos 2002). An intricate issue is whether rule-circular justifications of a rule of inference are epistemologically admissible and probative. I have argued that they are and have tried to show that if they are not admitted as such, our basic inferential practices fall prey to the sceptic (1999: ch. 4; 2011a).

Now that I have flagged the issues of (approximate) truth and of the justification of scientific method, I can say that the main point that I want to drive home in this chapter is relatively modest. Suppose someone is not a sceptic about ordinary scientific (and common-sensical) knowledge that is issued by observations and experience. Then, it's hard for them to be sceptics about more exotic scientific claims, which posit unobservable entities and processes. I will argue that the epistemological question I started with, namely, 'how are scientific claims that extend beyond what is, or can be, observed justified?' should be answered thus: in the very same way and for the same reasons that ordinary observational claims are justified.

2. Foundationalist conceptions of scientific knowledge

We live in the post-foundationalist era in epistemology, but it was not always like this. In the early days of Logical Positivism the general attitude towards scientific knowledge was foundationalist, and for a reason: a foundationalist theory of justification makes justification a transferrable property of the foundational beliefs insofar as the non-foundational beliefs are suitably connected with the foundational. The basic beliefs were taken to be beliefs based on perceptual experience (or perceptual episodes *simpliciter*), and the criterion for justification of scientific knowledge-claims (non-foundational beliefs) was verification: a scientific assertion constitutes knowledge if and only if it can be verified or decided by perceptual experience. The unit of verification was provided by protocol sentences which expressed the immediately 'given' in someone's perceptual experience. They were taken to be the basis for knowledge and the task was to show that all other knowledge claims should and could be justified by being verified by elements of this basis. For Moritz Schlick (1959: 221, 213), for instance, it was 'self-evident that the problem of the basis of knowledge is nothing other than the question of the criterion of truth' and verification was taken as the criterion of truth.

Protocol sentences came to be understood in two different ways: either as expressible in a sense-data language, or as expressible in a thing-language. For instance, a protocol sentence can have the form 'here now blue', or 'A red cube is on the table'. Both forms had in common their being, *in some sense*, immediately (i.e. non-inferentially) given to the knower, one referring to the 'immediately perceived', the other referring to the 'immediately observed' (Carnap 1932: 45–7). However, as Karl Popper and Otto Neurath observed, protocol sentences with propositional content cast in an observation-language or thing-language, such as 'I remember I saw a fox yesterday night', or 'I see that the pointer of the ammeter moves', are defeasible and revisable, if only because the perceptual processes that yield the relevant contents are fallible and subject to correction. Therefore no certainty can be attributed to them; if known at all, they are not known with certainty (cf. Neurath 1959; Hempel 1935). Carnap (1932: 45) toyed with the idea that protocol sentences 'need no justification' for they constitute 'the simplest states of which knowledge can be had'. But he was soon convinced by Neurath's (1959: 5) arguments that 'there are neither primitive protocol sentences nor sentences which are not subject to verification'. As Carnap (1932: 49) argued, *no* collection of protocol sentences logically implies a singular statement expressed in a scientific language; which means that any singular statement, for example, 'the density of this particular piece of iron is thus-and-so', is always a *hypothesis* in relation to protocol statements.

This was a significant twofold departure from foundationalism. On the one hand, protocol sentences, cast in intersubjective thing-language, are not certain. On the other hand, no scientific hypothesis (no matter how elementary) can be logically implied by any collection of protocol sentences. Hence *no* collection of protocol sentences would be of any help in building up scientific knowledge upon secure foundations.

Fifty or so years later, this point was remade by Bogen and Woodward (1988) who emphasized that when scientists go from the data to a phenomenon, they are engaged in a network of theory-guided inferences. Scientists collect data and use methods such as controlling for possible confounding factors, data-reduction, and statistical analysis to evaluate them. They make assumptions about, and try to check, the reliability of the equipment involved in the experiment. They make assumptions about the possible sources of systematic error and try to eliminate them (or correct the data in their light). They also make assumptions about the causes of variation in the data points they collect. Only when all this is in place can there be a reliable *inference* from the data (or a subset of them) to the phenomenon. And even then, the inference is as reliable as the background assumptions relied upon. Hence, whatever authority accrues to an observable phenomenon (e.g. that the melting point of lead is thus-and-so) is a function of background assumptions and theory (though perhaps not of the theory under test, if any). If all these assumptions fail to be adequate (or well-confirmed), the observed phenomenon is called into question.

Could a *stricter* understanding of protocol sentences be of any help? Schlick (1959: 220–1, 226), it should be noted, did not deny that protocol sentences – understood as standing observational statements, registered in scientific protocols – are short of epistemic security. However, he thought that there was a special class of sentences, what he called 'konstatierungen' ('confirmations' or 'reports'), which constituted the 'absolute end' of scientific knowledge (223). He suggested that *konstatierungen* must be understood as *occasion* sentences, of the form 'here now blue' or 'here yellow borders on blue'. But *konstatierungen* were not proper sentences; they were not written down or memorized; they had 'no duration'; for, as Schlick put it, 'the moment they are gone one has at one's disposal in their place inscriptions, or memory traces, that can play only the role of hypotheses and thereby lack ultimate certainty' (222). They were more akin to direct perceptual episodes. In particular, Schlick thought that *konstatierungen* are immediately present in one's mind: 'the occasion of understanding them is at the same time that of verifying them' (225). It seems that unlike standing observational sentences, *konstatierungen* are not hypotheses because one cannot possibly be deceived regarding their truth, once – for a fraction of time – one possesses them.

It's not hard to see that these fleeting perceptual episodes cannot constitute the basis of scientific knowledge. And Schlick saw that clearly too. Knowledge claims are *not* reducible to them; nor are they verified on their basis. In fact, as soon as they are explicitly uttered or written down, they become ordinary protocol sentences 'which as such [have] a wholly different nature', being hypotheses (226). What then could the role of these perceptual episodes be? Schlick's answer to this question was rather strange. He thought that the essential function of science is to make predictions that are tested by experience. When one's prediction is fulfilled, one obtains 'a feeling of fulfilment', a 'quite characteristic satisfaction' which takes place the very moment in which an occasion sentence verifies one's expectations (222–3). *Konstatierungen* were the reports of episodes that, as it were, were in one's own mind when a prediction was verified. They constituted the 'absolute fixed points of contact' between one's own mind and reality (229). Schlick thought that the verification of a hypothesis, or prediction, consisted, ultimately, in the psychological state one was in at the very moment when a relevant *konstatierung* appeared in one's own mind. The fleeting state expressed by a report of the form 'blue and red side by side here and now' is certain since one cannot be in error when one thinks it. Certainty, Schlick thought, is ultimately the state of satisfaction 'with which verification fills us' (223).

Whatever the psychological value of Schlick's *konstatierungen* may be for oneself, intersubjective scientific knowledge cannot *possibly* be based on them. The knowledge they warrant (if this is knowledge at all, given Wittgenstein's argument against private language) is, ultimately, the *solipsistic knowledge* of one's own private experiences, which once they are memorized or become public, that is, are written down or communicated, become hypotheses and lose their infallibility and certainty. Schlick thought that 'it gives us joy to reach them [*konstatierungen*], even if we cannot stand upon them' (223). But this has little or no value since 'science does not rest on them', from an objective (or intersubjective) point of view.

The point of this analysis is not to flog a dead horse. Rather, it is to drive home the claim that foundationalism in the epistemology of science faces an insurmountable dilemma. If it goes for an infallible basis for scientific knowledge, such as Schlick's *konstatierungen*, it renders itself simply irrelevant to scientific knowledge, even if we were to make sense of this infallible basis of perceptual episodes. If it goes for a fallible basis for scientific knowledge, such as Carnap's 'observation reports', then it undermines itself since it relies on hypotheses to verify hypotheses.

More, actually, can be said, since fallible foundationalism leads to a regress. An observation report, unlike a *konstatierung*, is subject to doubt. Hence, to be used as a basis for knowledge, it has to be *itself* verified. One, for instance, has to exclude that there have been observational errors and the like. If *any* protocol sentence has to be verified, since verification is a process that includes *other* sentences, there cannot be any privileged sentence which can be verified in the absence of other sentences. There is simply no set of epistemically authoritative protocol statements.

The problems with verificationism become more visible if we take into account that strict verification is not possible in the case of universally quantified statements, which normally express laws of nature, as was quickly observed by Carnap and other empiricists, especially after Popper's (1935) *Logik der Forschung*. If verification on the basis of observational statements is the gold standard for scientific knowledge, then simply there is no such knowledge.

3. Holistic confirmation

Foundationalism, in both of its forms, is far from securing a sense of scientific knowledge which is directly verified on the basis of true observational reports.

Still science is full of observational reports, even though they do not have absolute epistemic authority. In fact the very testing of scientific theories, and more specifically the very idea of a comparative testing of competing theories, requires that there is a kind of observational report, even if this is not epistemically secure. All it requires is that observation, though fallible and inference-laden, is not theory-laden to such an extent that each theory 'produces' its own observations. I think this is broadly right and that the theory-ladenness of observation debates in the 1960s have obscured this fact. In fact, this was first called into attention by Pierre Duhem (1906: 159), when he noted that there is always some room to interpret an observation in light of commonly accepted background theories or some room for finding some common sub-language (not necessarily observational, even in the loose sense discussed above) between competing theories, which can describe the phenomenon at hand.

We can then expand on Carnap's (1936: 445–6) account, and characterize a predicate P in-the-language-of-a-theory as observational if a person can, under suitable circumstances, decide with the aid of observations alone (and commonly accepted background theories) whether or not an object belongs to the extension of this predicate. In other words, a (monadic) predicate P is observational if for a given object b, observations can decide (with some elements of conventional decision as to when the testing should stop and what theories to count as background) between the atomic sentences 'Pb' and '¬Pb'. Analogously, a theoretical predicate is one that does not satisfy the foregoing condition. This account of observational terms and predicates is not foundational; yet it does allow us to ask the following question: how could the rest of scientific knowledge be justified on the basis of claims expressed in observational language, if verificationism fails?

The natural way forward is to replace the notion of verification with the weaker notion of *confirmation*. Indeed, offering accounts of the relation of confirmation (*piece of evidence e confirms hypothesis H*) has been a major preoccupation in the epistemology of science. Though the project of formalizing confirmation has acquired a life of its own, I want to stress that the key function of confirmation is justificatory: 'e confirms H' should be taken to be licencing the claim 'e justifies, or contributes to the justification of, (believing in) H'.[1]

A key thought about confirmation that emerged after the collapse of verificationism was that confirmation is holistic: hypotheses hunt in packs for confirmation or disconfirmation. It might come as a surprise to non-Carnap scholars that Carnap himself preached holistic confirmation. With due acknowledgement to Duhem and Henri Poincaré, already in 1934, he noted that confirmation is holistic because it is whole theories, or at least clusters of theoretical assertions, that issue in observations. Here is how Carnap (1937: sec. 82) put it:

> It is, in general, impossible to test even a single hypothetical sentence. In the case of a single sentence of this kind, there are in general no L-consequences of the form of protocol sentences; hence for the deduction of sentences having the form of protocol-sentences the remaining hypotheses must also be used. Thus the test applies, at bottom, not to a single hypothesis but to the whole system of physics as a system of hypotheses (Duhem, Poincaré).

Holism goes back to Duhem (1906) but became prominent in the work of Quine. What's important for our purposes is that for Quine, once it is accepted that the content of scientists' talk of unobservables cannot be reduced to talk about observables and their actual, and possible behaviour and once it is acknowledged that confirmation is holistic, then there is no principled reason to think that theoretical assertions referring to unobservables are not confirmable and confirmed. Given that the issue of how we know what there is should be subsumed under the issue of 'the evidence for truth about the world', the 'last arbiter' of which 'is so-called scientific method, however amorphous' (Quine 1960: 23), there is evidence for the reality of all kinds of unobservables posited by scientific theories, since there is evidence for theories.

What kind of evidence is this? The crucial point made by Quine is that whatever evidence it is, it is no different from the evidence there is for middle-sized observable objects. Hence, Quine's master argument for accepting the reality of unobservables is that 'they are on a par with the most ordinary physical objects' (22). As he explains: 'The positing of those extraordinary things [molecules and their extraordinary ilk] is just a vivid analogue of the positing or acknowledging of ordinary things: vivid in that the physicist audibly posits them for recognised reasons, whereas the hypothesis of ordinary things is shrouded in prehistory' (ibid.). Time is not of the essence here. We might have lost track of why we believe in the existence of middle-sized material objects; this is an 'archaic and unconscious hypothesis'. But on reflection, we realize that this too is a hypothesis relative to what is given to us immediately through our senses; what Quine aptly calls 'surface irritations'. Since whatever evidence there is is couched in terms of 'surface irritations', molecules and chairs are on a par, epistemically speaking. As he put it:

> Considered relative to our surface irritations, which exhaust our clues to an external world, the molecules and their extraordinary ilk are thus much on a par with the most ordinary physical objects ... If we have evidence for the existence

of the bodies of common sense, we have it only in the way in which we may be said to have evidence for the existence of molecules. The positing of either sort of body is good science insofar merely as it helps us to formulate laws – laws whose ultimate evidence lies in the sense data of the past, and whose ultimate vindication lies in anticipation of sense data of the future. (22)

If we deny the reality of molecules, we will have to deny the reality of ordinary objects too. But this 'double verdict of unreality leaves us nothing, evidently, but the raw sense data themselves'. We end up, as it were, with Schlick's *konstatierungen* which are worth nothing epistemically, since even the existence of other persons 'has no better support than has the assumption of there being any other sorts of external objects'.

Would it be a relevant objection to Quine's argument that there are no sense-data? Or that sense-data themselves are theoretical entities? Not quite! For his point should be seen in context. No matter what one thinks of Quine's behaviourism, he made a valid point against all those who thought that there is a privileged epistemic observational basis for science, namely, that the objects which this basis is about (middle-sized material objects) are no less conjectural and hypothetical than theoretical entities, given that the evidence there is for them is not in any way unmediated but based on what is given to us immediately in experience, namely, surface irritations. The latter might or might not be sense data but whatever else they are, they are the means by which we commit ourselves to middle-sized material objects.

Note that holistic confirmation plays a key role in Quine's argument precisely because, for Quine (1966: 241), positing common-sense objects is just as much a matter of coming to accept a theory as positing theoretical entities: 'Statements about bodies, common-sense or recondite, thus commonly make little or no empirical sense except as bits *of a collectively significant containing system*" (emphasis added). Both systems (common-sense theory; scientific theory) are networks of hypotheses which are holistically confirmed by the evidence and they are both confirmed *in the same way*, namely, on the basis of the fact that they are indispensable for simplifying our world-picture. Simplicity for Quine (1960: 20–2, 250) is not only a guide for reasoning and extrapolation; it is also sufficient reason for accepting or rejecting entities, advancing and testing theories, but also 'the best evidence for truth we can ask' for a theory which squares with observations.

The point then is that if someone is committed to the existence of observable entities, she must also be committed to the existence of unobservables posited by science since claims about them are confirmed in the same way. Then, as Quine put it, 'so much the better for the molecules' (22).

4. Theoretical virtues

What's important to stress is that a holistic theory of confirmation relies on, and requires, what have come to be known as 'theoretical virtues'. This is important because there may be two or more theories for which there is exactly the same empirical evidence. If the evidence is to confirm one more than the other, there must be factors such that, if they are taken into account, different degrees of confirmation can accrue to the theories.

Now, both Quine *and* Duhem, who favoured confirmational holism, advanced arguments that support the so-called underdetermination of theories by evidence. The underdetermination thesis is that two or more empirically equivalent rivals are equally well confirmed by the available evidence. But it should be noted that this conclusion requires two premises. The first is that for any theory there are nontrivial empirically equivalent rivals, namely, theories which entail exactly the same observational consequences. But this premise, in and of itself, does not entail that the rival theories are equally supported (well-confirmed) by the evidence. This would follow only if the only constraint on empirical support (or confirmation) was deductive entailment of the evidence. It is this view of evidential support which generates the potential problem that no theory is confirmed by the evidence, since every theory has (conceived or unconceived) empirically equivalent rivals (see Psillos 1999: ch. 8; 2015).

The perceived tension here is that, on the one hand, confirmational holism promises to justify belief in theories or hypotheses about unobservables on the basis of the evidence but, on the other, unless the underdetermination thesis is blocked, it leads to the conclusion that no hypothesis or theory about unobservables is ever warranted on the basis of the evidence.

I am not going to deal here with the thesis that for each and every theory there are (conceived or hitherto unconceived) incompatible empirically equivalent rivals (see Psillos [2015] for a thorough discussion). Let us assume (for the sake of the argument) that this is proven – though it is not. Still, as we saw, what is required for underdetermination is the *further* claim that two empirically equivalent rivals are equally well-confirmed by the evidence. This further claim follows only if the sole constraint on confirmation of a theory T by evidence e is that T entails e. That's exactly where the theoretical virtues get in. They add more factors to the relation of confirmation between theory and evidence, which make confirmation go beyond mere deductive entailment.

Note, for a start, that both Duhem and Quine did admit the role of theoretical virtues in theory confirmation. Duhem, to be sure, focused his attention mostly on when it reasonable to *abandon* a theory which is in conflict with experience. This, actually, is the mirror-image of the problem we have been discussing. As is well known, Duhem (1906: 188) forcefully argued that there are no crucial experiments in science. Based on the thought that theories entail predictions holistically (as clusters of hypotheses and only with the aid of auxiliary assumptions), he argued that no experiment can lead to a conclusive refutation of a theory. A theory that is in conflict with some experimental results can always be saved from refutation by making suitable changes to some auxiliary hypotheses. Yet Duhem was one of the first to recognize that though experience cannot, strictly speaking, contradict a theory, it can *condemn* it, even though experience on its own cannot dictate how to revise theories in the face of recalcitrant evidence. What kinds of considerations, then, lead to the abandonment of a theory? Duhem employs other *theoretical* criteria of assessment. Here are some that he suggests: the scope of the theory, the number of hypotheses, the nature of hypotheses, novel predictions (28, 195), compatibility with other theories (221, 255), unification into a single system of hypotheses (293). These criteria are the so-called theoretical *virtues*. As such they transcend the bounds of logic. Their employment is not algorithmic; and yet, it is indispensable if choice of theories is to be possible.

Theoretical virtues permit scientists to 'decide' among competing and rival hypotheses. Quine (1960) generalized Duhem's point and talked of five virtues of a scientific theory: simplicity, familiarity, scope, fecundity, and success under testing. Referring to the virtues of the molecular hypothesis, he said:

> One is simplicity: empirical laws concerning seemingly dissimilar phenomena are integrated into a compact and unitary theory. Another is familiarity of principle: the already familiar laws of motion are made to serve where independent laws would otherwise have been needed. A third is scope: the resulting unitary theory implies a wider array of testable consequences than any likely accumulation of separate laws would have implied. A fourth is fecundity: successful further extensions of theory are expedited. The fifth goes without saying: such testable consequences of the theory as have been tested have turned out well, aside from such sparse exceptions as may in good conscience be chalked up to unexplained interferences. (234)

When it comes to simplicity, in particular, Quine noted: 'Now simplicity, in a theory that squares with observation sentences so far as its contacts with them go, is the best evidence of truth we can ask; no better can be claimed for the doctrines of molecules and electrons' (249).

It is certainly legitimate for an epistemologist to wonder whence these virtues acquire their epistemic force. That is, why should they be taken to be factors that contribute to the probability of a theory that possesses them to be true? But it is doubtful, to say the least, that these virtues altogether lack epistemic force. Consider how Quine (1966: 234) introduces 'familiarity' as a virtue: 'the already familiar laws of motion are made to serve where independent laws would otherwise have been needed'. It's not hard to see that a way to read this virtue is that familiarity increases the degree of confirmation of a theory, since the so-called familiar laws are already well-confirmed ones. Or consider 'fecundity': 'successful further extensions of the theory are expedited'. Here again, the connection with an increase in the degree of confirmation is not far away. We have noted that to say that a factor x has epistemic force for a belief (or theory) y is to say that x raises the probability of y's being true. This can be argued for independently of the Quinean framework, though it is true that for Quine too the virtues do have this force. Recall what Quine (1960: 250) said about simplicity as a virtue of a theory that squares with observation sentences: 'it is the best evidence of truth we can ask'. There should be no doubt then that Quinean virtues have epistemic force.

Be that as it may, the theoretical virtues need more defence qua *epistemic* factors. For the time being, let me just make a note of this issue and get back to it in Section 6 after we have discussed the role of virtues in *non-holistic confirmation*.

5. Probabilistic confirmation

If Quine went for confirmational holism in the wake of the collapse of verificationism, Reichenbach (1938) went for probabilistic confirmation. He introduced the probability theory of meaning, which allows statements that are not directly verifiable to be meaningful, and confirmable on the basis of experience.

Probability, then, is the new element that Reichenbach brings to confirmation. The key idea, if you like, is that probabilistic relations can capture the content-increasing, or ampliative, character of scientific inference. Observational statements can be the premises of (probabilistic) inferences to theoretical statements and yet the latter can have excess content over the former.

To motivate his theory of confirmation, Reichenbach introduced the example of the shadows cast by birds (108). Imagine some birds flying over us. The shadows of the birds are projected along two perpendicular axes. The birds are then *inferred* to be located at the point where the coordinates meet. This is clearly a non-demonstrative inference *from* the shadows *to* the birds: the shadows are *marks* of the presence of birds. What is important in this example is that there are *two distinct kinds of existents*, which are however coordinated with each other. It is precisely because of this that we can use the marks (viz. the effects) to infer something about the causes, though the inference is clearly non-deductive.

Note that the birds are observable. It is part of the initial point of Reichenbach's strategy that their presence can be identified *independently* of their being inferred on the basis of the shadows. This move aims to render plausible an inference from the effects to their causes. The fact that the inferred entity is observable turns out to be a, perhaps pleasant, add-on, which does not affect the status of the inference. But one might wonder: how can we possibly infer the existence of something which we cannot have an independent epistemic access to?

Reichenbach's answer to this question is motivated by a modification of the example of the birds and their shadows – the example of the cubical world (C-world) (sec.14). In this modified story, the inhabitants of the C-world are confined within a huge cube, whose walls are made of white cloth. It is soon observed that there are shadows dancing around the walls. Unbeknown to the inhabitants, these are the shadows of birds flying outside the cubical world. A 'friendly ghost' (a benevolent demon?) has set up a complex set of mirrors that project shadows of the birds on the walls. The birds (causes of the shadows) are, by hypothesis, unobservable – in fact, the laws of nature are presumed to be such that the birds cannot be seen. Is it possible for the inhabitants to come legitimately to believe that there are birds outside the C-world?

Reichenbach points out that the inhabitants of the C-world are in the *same epistemic situation* as those involved in the initial example of the birds. To bring this out, he introduces a local Copernicus who uses a telescope and finds out that the marks on the walls fall under regular patterns: the movements on the side wall are coordinated with movements on the top wall. The local Copernicus is pictured as engaging in an inference from the marks on the walls to their causes, *inferring* the existence of unobservable birds as causes of the marks on the walls. Here is how Reichenbach puts it:

> He [the local Copernicus] will maintain that the strange correspondence between the two shades of one pair cannot be a matter or chance but that these

two shades are nothing but effects caused by one individual thing situated outside the cube within free space. He calls these things 'birds' and says that these are animals flying outside the cube, different from the shadow-figures, having an existence of their own, and that the black spots are nothing but shadows. (118)

Let us try to dig a bit deeper into the way the local Copernicus reasoned, since Reichenbach does not say much about it. Here is how I would put the matter. He observes the patterns on the walls, and he forms a hypothesis that purports to explain them. This is a causal hypothesis: it posits a cause of the observed pattern in virtue of which this pattern is rendered intelligible. Copernicus, in other words, posits an entity (better: a type of entity) that brings some causal-nomological order in the world view of the inhabitants of the C-world. Instead of taking a certain pattern as a brute fact, he offers an explanation of it – an explanation by postulation (of unobservable entities). As is stressed in the quotation above, the call for explanation is motivated by the thought that surprising coincidences should not be attributed to chance – there must be a reason for them to hold and hence an explanation. It is this explanatory hypothesis which is confirmed by the available evidence.

After presenting the brief summary of Copernicus' reasoning, Reichenbach went on to claim that the hypothesis of the local Copernicus is 'highly probable' when 'judged from the facts observed'. For, as he put it, it is 'highly improbable that the strange coincidences observed for one pair of dots are an effect of pure chance' (120). Faced with improbable coincidences, he added, scientists will not believe that they are a matter of chance but instead they will look for a causal explanation (or for 'causal connection', as he put it).

This suggests that Reichenbach saw his argument as a straightforward probabilistic argument with a highly likely conclusion. Reichenbach has invited us to compare the likelihoods of two competing hypotheses, namely, H: the existence of unobservable birds; and not-H: there are no birds outside the cubical world (and hence that the observed coincidences are a matter of chance). More generally put, Reichenbach's argument so far is this: there is an effect e (the strange coincidences) observed; e would be very unlikely if not-H were the case, but e would be very likely if H were the case; hence, H is very likely (or much more likely that not-H). Indeed, he says quite clearly: 'Reflections like this would incline the physicists to believe in the hypothesis of Copernicus' (121). But, stated thus, this kind of argument faces a problem: the likelihoods are not enough to fix the posterior probability of H, let alone to make it high.

In order to deal with this problem, we need to take into account prior probabilities.[2] The form of the argument, then, would be like this – call it argument (A):

prob(e/H) is high.
prob(e/-H) is very low.
e is the case.
prob(H) is not very low.
Therefore, prob(H/e) is high.

(A) is a sound probabilistic argument. In fact, even with relatively low prob(H), the posterior probability prob(H/e) can be quite high. In any case, assuming prior probabilities, the degree of confirmation of hypotheses in light of evidence becomes quite definite.

Reichenbach was clearly aware that the probabilistic inference he has in mind requires another element, namely, the prior probabilities of the competing hypotheses. Curiously, however, he relegated this important point to a brief and obscure footnote (under the pretentious heading 'Remark for the mathematician') (124). There he notes that the probabilistic inference he has in mind relies on 'Bayes' rule' (which, however, he never states). All he says is that one can use Bayes' rule to specify the posterior ('backward') probability of a hypothesis given the evidence as a function of the likelihood ('forward probability') and the 'initial probability' of a hypothesis. More importantly, different prior probabilities make a difference to the posterior probabilities of competing hypotheses, even if the likelihoods are equal. Towards the end of the book, Reichenbach notes that Bayes' theorem is a rule 'for inferring from given observations the probabilities of their causes' (390).

Surprisingly little is said about the status of prior probabilities: 'It is these initial probabilities that are involved in the reflections of the physicist about causal connections' (124n4). What Reichenbach has in mind is this. The two competing hypotheses H (the existence of unobservable birds) and not-H (the observed coincidences are a matter of chance) can legitimately be given different prior probabilities on the basis of *analogy* and *past experience*. Even if a persistent positivist contrived a hypothesis such that a strange coincidence is the outcome of a (strange) causal law that did not involve unobservable causes, one could point to the fact that in many other similar cases where strange coincidences were present, there had been a causal connection among them that involved unobservable (simply put, there had been a common cause) (123).

By bringing prior probabilities into play, Reichenbach is able to show that hypotheses about unobservables are confirmable on the basis of the evidence – provided of course they are allowed some nonzero initial probability. Besides, he is able to argue that the difference between forming beliefs about observables and forming beliefs about the unobservable on the basis of the evidence is one of degree. Both kinds of belief are ampliative; they concern causes; their degree of confirmation is based on the same type of probabilistic reasoning. So probabilistic inference is 'overreaching': it allows the justification of hypotheses (by showing how they are confirmed by the evidence) irrespective of whether or not their content is observationally accessible. For him, this type of probabilistic inference 'is the basic method of the knowledge of nature' (127).[3]

6. Prior probabilities and plausibility

The tricky point, in this kind of argument, is the status of prior probabilities. Where do they get their epistemic force? Reichenbach (1938: sec. 30) was naturally sensitive to this issue. He came back to this quite late in the book and treated prior probabilities as initial weights (or posits), and hence as estimates of how likely a hypothesis is prior to the incoming evidence. The overall tone of Reichenbach's discussion (as well as his frequentist theory of probability) suggests that for him the assignment of prior probabilities to competing hypotheses is not a matter of subjective preferences. But it is not quite clear how they are fixed. Importantly, Reichenbach's conception of probabilities as limiting relative frequencies creates a number of problems; for instance, it is not clear how relative frequencies can be specified for advanced hypotheses, namely, hypotheses for which analogy and past experience cannot be relied upon.

How then are prior probabilities fixed? There are various answers to this question. The subjective Bayesian answer is that they are free choices of the scientists, expressing their subjective degree of belief in the hypothesis they test (cf. Howson and Urbach 1989). Hence, there is no room for being right or wrong in assigning priors to hypotheses: if two scientists disagree about prior probabilities, there is no further issue to be dealt with as to who is right and who is wrong. To remove the sting of extreme subjectivism, Bayesians appeal to the convergence-of-opinion theorems to argue that in the long run, the prior probabilities wash out: even widely different prior probabilities will converge, in the limit, to the same posterior probability, if agents conditionalize on the same evidence. But, though true, this move offers little consolation in the present context because the convergence-of-opinion theorem holds only under limited and very well-defined circumstances, which can hardly be met in ordinary scientific cases (Earman 1992: 149ff). In any case, this kind of argument, insofar as is it can be relied upon, is fine for anyone who conditionalizes on the evidence irrespective of how exactly the prior probabilities are fixed.

Another answer comes from what Jon Williamson (2010: 15) has called 'empirically based subjective Bayesianism'. In this case, Calibration is added as a requirement for prior probabilities: priors should be calibrated with known frequencies.[4] Yet another answer comes from 'objective Bayesianism' (Williamson 2010), according to which to the sound requirement of calibration further factors such as evidential symmetry can be added in fixing the priors.

Once we move away from subjective versions, what transpires is that there is room for a *theory* of what fixes prior probabilities. This theory concerns what goes into the various judgements of initial plausibility that, undoubtedly, scientists make when they adopt a hypothesis before they look for (further) evidence for it. This theory has as its subject-matter the theoretical virtues that inform or determine plausibility judgements. Hence, the two approaches we have been discussing as ways to justify belief in unobservable entities (*holistic confirmation* and *probabilistic confirmation*) converge on the need to appeal to theoretical virtues in the theory of confirmation. Thus, theoretical virtues become indispensable.

Wesley Salmon (1990) was one of the first to make the connection when he took theoretical virtues (such as those espoused by Quine or Kuhn, too) to be confirmational virtues and to inform plausibility judgements that fix or aid fixing prior probabilities. Take, for instance, consistency with background theories. This is a confirmational virtue since a hypothesis which is consistent with what is currently accepted accrues some of the probability assigned to currently accepted theories. Or take analogy. This virtue is confirmational because it suggests extending to other areas what has worked well – and hence has been confirmed – in analogous situations.

It is true that the application of theoretical virtues and the concomitant plausibility judgements based on them is not algorithmic. There is simply no set of universally applicable rules which can and should be followed in fixing the plausibility of a hypothesis or theory. But all this shows is that there is more to the 'logic' of confirmation than logic. Plausibility judgements may well express rational degrees of belief even though they are not fixed by strict rules. Rationality need not involve universally applicable and mechanically executable recipes for belief-formation and justification. Now, to start taking seriously this last point requires that a broader conception of rational belief is adopted, and in particular one that does not rely on a topic-neutral logic of induction, which is supposedly based on a priori principles of rationality. Such principles are hard to find, and even harder to justify. Still, there are rational grounds for assigning initial degrees of plausibility to competing theories: relying, for instance, on theoretical virtues such as simplicity, explanatory power, coherence with other theories, fecundity. These kinds of virtues are typically of the sort that make scientists take a theory seriously as subject to further exploration and test.

As we have seen, both kinds of confirmation discussed cut across the distinction between observables and unobservables. The distinction is simply irrelevant to coming to have a justified belief in the reality of an entity. What matters is only whether this belief is confirmed by the relevant evidence, and the indispensably relevant theoretical virtues. And that's how it should be. There is no reason for double standards in confirmation. The typical strategy of those who deny knowing the unobservable is this: the content of a theory is split into two parts – let's call them the OK-assertions and the not-OK-assertions respectively. This partition can be made on several grounds, but typically it is made along the lines of empirical versus theoretical or observable versus unobservable. The OK-assertions are confirmable and confirmed by the evidence. But then the claim is made (or implied) that the principles of confirmation that concern the OK-assertions are *not* transferable to the not-OK-assertions. What we have shown is that the allegedly OK-assertions are confirmed in the very same ways in which the allegedly not-OK assertions confront the relevant evidence. So the distinction between OK-assertions and not-OK ones is confirmationally spurious.

There is no way to put this better than the following by Quine (1960: 21):

> Actually the truths that can be said even in common-sense terms about ordinary things are themselves, in turn, far in excess of any available data. The incompleteness of determination of molecular behavior by the behavior of ordinary things is hence only incidental to this more basic indeterminacy: both sorts of events are less than determined by our surface irritations. This remains true even if we include all past, present, and future irritations of all the far-flung surfaces of mankind, and probably even if we throw in an in fact unachieved ideal organon of scientific method besides.

Given what was said in the *Introduction*, one may ask: even if scientific assertions are confirmed by the evidence, do they constitute knowledge of the world? The answer is: it depends on the way the world is. A full discussion of this issue would require delving into the issue of the pessimistic induction and the supposed argument that well-confirmed past theoretical hypotheses have turned out to be radically false, and abandoned. I have discussed this issue in great detail elsewhere (1999, 2009). For now, suffice it to say that that the discontinuity in theory-change has not been as radical as the advocates of pessimism have claimed. And it should be added that there is defeasible historical evidence that the world is such that theories with the relevant theoretical virtues are more likely to be true than those that lack them (cf. Psillos 1999: 165–6).

7. Concluding thoughts

The prospects of knowing anything about reality relies on coming to justifiably believe hypotheses about what reality is like. Coming to justifiably believe such hypotheses requires confirming them on the basis of available evidence. Confirming them on the basis of available evidence requires the employment of theoretical virtues that inform plausibility judgements concerning the hypothesis under test and its rivals. This cuts across the board, as the failures of verificationism has shown. It applies both to what is visible and what is invisible. And it holds for both of the two major ways to view confirmation. Moreover, if one does not doubt that we can have (non-verificationally) justified beliefs about the visible, one cannot doubt that we can have justified beliefs about the unobservable. All of this requires that the theoretical virtues have epistemic force. But taking them to have epistemic force is taking a stand on the issue of rationality: there is more to rationality than strict empirical evidence and algorithmic and universally applicable rules. (For more on this, see Psillos [2012b].)[5]

Notes

1   There are notable complications, of course. A single positive instance of a hypothesis (a single black raven) does not justify believing the hypothesis (that all ravens are black); but it is certainly a contributing factor to its justification. There is also the problem of how likely the hypothesis must be in light of the evidence, for the evidence to justify belief in it. Should the probability of the hypothesis given the evidence be higher than a threshold close to one? Or is it enough that its probability is higher than ½? Moreover, there is the problem of full belief versus degrees of

belief and the problem of detachment: can a probability, no matter how high, ever be detached and be replaced by certainty? These are issues worth exploring in detail but I will refrain from treating them here, since they are not absolutely relevant to the central point I want to make. For a thorough discussion, see Achinstein (2001).

2   One can always adopt likelihoodism, which uses the *likelihood ratio* to capture the strength by which the evidence supports a hypothesis over another, but does not issue in judgements as to what the probability of a hypothesis in light of the evidence is (cf. Sober 2002). But this is clearly not the way in which Reichenbach proceeded.

3   For more on Reichenbach's argument, see Psillos (2011b). As I have shown in my work (2011c), a similar kind of argument was used by the famous physicist Jean Perrin to show that there are molecules – that is, that matter is discrete and non-continuous.

4   Calibration is a norm according to which the degrees of belief of a subject X at a particular time should be calibrated with physical probability (expressed in objective chances or actual relative frequencies). A weather forecaster, for instance, is well-calibrated if when her judgement is that the chance of rain today is 0.8, it turns out that 80 per cent of the days like today (in relevant respects) were rainy.

5   A notable absence of my discussion has been constructive empiricism (CE). But as van Fraassen has insisted, CE is a philosophy of science and not an epistemology of science. As such, CE is compatible with *any* epistemology of science, and in particular with one that claims that science does succeed in delivering true theories – though it might aim only for empirically adequate ones. As van Fraassen (1998) also says, it's more natural that the advocate of CE is a *scientific agnostic*, namely, someone who believes that the theories they accept are empirically adequate but suspend their judgement as to their truth or falsity. In any case, for reasons to resist CE as a philosophy of science, see Psillos (2012a).

References

Achinstein, P. (2001), *The Book of Evidence*, New York: Oxford University Press.

Bogen, J. and Woodward, J. (1988), 'Saving the Phenomena', *The Philosophical Review*, 97: 303–52.

Carnap, R. (1932), *The Unity of Science*, trans. M. Black, London: Kegan Paul, Trench, Trubner and Company.

Carnap, R. (1936), 'Testability and Meaning', *Philosophy of Science*, 3: 419–71.

Carnap, R. (1937), *The Logical Syntax of Language*, London: Kegan Paul, Trench, Trubner and Company.

Duhem, P. (1906), *The Aim and Structure of Physical Theory* [(1914) 2nd edn; (1954) trans. P. P. Wiener, Princeton: Princeton University Press].

Dummett, M. (1991), *The Logical Basis of Metaphysics*, Cambridge, MA: Harvard University Press.

Earman, J. (1992), *Bayes or Bust? A Critical Examination of Bayesian Confirmation Theory*, Cambridge: The MIT Press.

Hempel, C. (1935), 'On the Logical Positivists' Theory of Truth', *Analysis*, 2: 49–59.

Howson, C. and Urbach, P. (1989), *Scientific Reasoning: The Bayesian Approach*, La Salle, IL: Open Court.

Neurath, O. (1959 [1932/33]), 'Protokollsatze', (trans. as) 'Protocol Sentences', in A. J. Ayer (ed.), *Logical Positivism*, Glencoe, IL: The Free Press.

Popper, K. R. (1935), *Logic der Forschung: zur Erkenntnistheorie der Modernen Naturwissenschaft*, Vienna: J. Springer.

Psillos, S. (1999), *Scientific Realism: How Science Tracks Truth*, London: Routledge.

Psillos, S. (2002), 'Simply the Best: A Case for Abduction', in A. C. Kakas and F. Sadri (eds), *Computational Logic: Logic Programming and Beyond*, *(LNAI 2408)*, Berlin-Heidelberg: Springer-Verlag.

Psillos, S. (2009), *Knowing the Structure of Nature: Essays on Realism and Explanation*, London: Palgrave MacMillan.

Psillos, S. (2011a), 'The Scope and Limits of the No-Miracles Argument', in D. Dieks, W. J. Gonzalez, S. Hartmann, T. Uebel, and M. Weber (eds), *Explanation, Prediction, and Confirmation*, Dordrecht: Springer.

Psillos, S. (2011b), 'On Reichenbach's Argument for Scientific Realism', *Synthese*, 181: 23–40.

Psillos, S. (2011c), 'Moving Molecules above the Scientific Horizon: On Perrin's Case for Realism', *Journal for General Philosophy of Science*, 42: 339–63.

Psillos, S. (2012a), 'One Cannot Be Just a Little Bit Realist: Putnam and van Fraassen', in J. R. Brown (ed.), *Philosophy of Science: The Key Thinkers*, London: Continuum.

Psillos, S. (2012b), 'Reason and Science', in M. C. Amoretti and N. Vassallo (eds), *Reason and Rationality*, Frankfurt: Ontos Verlag.

Psillos, S. (2015), 'Evidence: Wanted, Alive or Dead', *Canadian Journal of Philosophy*, 45: 357–81.

Psillos, S. (2017), 'Scientific Realism and the Mind-Independence of the World', in E. Agazzi (ed.), *Varieties of Scientific Realism*, Dordrecht: Springer, 209–26.

Quine, W. V. (1960), *Word and Object*, Cambridge: The MIT Press.

Quine, W. V. (1966), 'Posits and Reality', in his *The Ways of Paradox and Other Essays*, Cambridge, MA: Harvard University Press.

Reichenbach, H. (1938), *Experience and Prediction*, Chicago, IL: The University of Chicago Press.

Salmon, W. C. (1990), 'Rationality and Objectivity in Science or Tom Kuhn Meets Tom Bayes', in C. W. Savage (ed.), *Scientific Theories, (Minnesota Studies in the Philosophy of Science, Volume XIV)*, Minneapolis: University of Minnesota Press.

Schlick, M. (1959 [1934]), 'The Foundation of Knowledge', in A. J. Ayer (ed.), *Logical Positivism*, Glencoe, IL: The Free Press.

Sober, E. (2002), 'Bayesianism – Its Scope and Limits', *Proceedings of the British Academy*, 113: 21–38.

Van Fraassen, B. C. (1998), 'The Agnostic Subtly Probabilified', *Analysis*, 58: 212–20.

Williamson, J. (2010), *In Defence of Objective Bayesianism*, Oxford: Oxford University Press.

Wright C. (1992), *Truth and Objectivity*, Cambridge, MA: Harvard University Press.

6

Social Knowledge and Social Norms

Peter J. Graham

1. Introduction

Many philosophers in the twentieth century argued that knowledge was social, for belief was social, for belief was impossible without language. A weaker view was also popular: although perhaps belief does not depend on other minds, knowledge does, for knowledge requires the ability to justify one's belief to others according to social standards of justified belief. By the end of the twentieth century, however, both views fell on hard times. The current wisdom holds that neither belief nor knowledge is essentially social.

Nevertheless, a good deal (if not most) of what we know we know because we believe what other people tell us. The extent of our knowledge owes a great deal to what we learn from others. Epistemology would be far from complete if it did not thoroughly address testimony. Although discussed during the Modern Period, it was not until the late twentieth century that testimony came to the fore.[1] In this chapter I focus on testimony as a central source of knowledge.[2]

2. Justification versus knowledge (the anti-luck condition)

I begin with the distinction between justification and the anti-Gettier or 'anti-luck' condition on propositional knowledge. I will rely on this distinction to frame our discussion.

On the traditional analysis of propositional knowledge, a subject's knowledge that P is comprised of (1) S's belief that P, (2) the fact that P (so that S's belief that P is true), and (3) S's having a justification for believing that P. Gettier (1963) showed that there are cases of justified true belief that P that fall short of knowledge. Here is an example from Bertrand Russell (1948): an individual may look at a clock and as a result truly believe, with justification, that the time is 2 p.m. But what if the clock is stopped and the individual only looked at just the 'right' time? Then the individual does not know it is 2 p.m. (despite having a justified true belief): you can't learn the time by looking at a stopped clock. The 'Gettier problem' led most epistemologists to conclude that propositional knowledge includes an additional 'anti-luck' condition.[3] Let's then assume that justification is one thing and the anti-luck condition is another, for you can meet one without meeting the other.

3. What is testimony?

This is a question not about the speech act per se – namely, what is testimony as one speech act among others? – but rather about the *process* that leads to so-called testimony-based beliefs. The question 'What is testimony?' (for our purposes) is the question 'What makes a belief a testimony-based belief?' Testimonial knowledge is then testimony-based belief that meets the conditions for knowledge: testimonial knowledge is justified true testimony-based belief that satisfies the fourth, anti-luck condition, just as perceptual knowledge is justified true perceptual-belief that satisfied the fourth, anti-luck condition.

Here are three easy examples of testimony-based belief. You want to know the time, so you ask a passer-by. '2 p.m.' she says. You believe her. You want to know the best time to visit Shanghai, so you do a web search. The top hits tell you that the second week of October has the best weather and the fewest tourists. You decide that you want to know a little chemistry, so you buy a textbook. When you read about the elements, you form a series of testimony-based beliefs.

These examples have the following three ingredients in common.

(1) Someone's testimony that P is the *distal cause*. A belief is testimony-based because it is causally based or sustained (in part) on someone else's testimony, where 'someone's testimony that P' includes assertions, sayings, tellings, even assertive conversational implicatures.

(2) A hearer's representation as of a speaker's testimony that P is (part of) the *proximal cause*. The hearer must represent the speaker's speech act *as* a telling or saying that P – the hearer must comprehend the speaker's testimony as a part of the process of forming a testimony-based belief. No comprehension *as of* a speaker asserting that P as a normal part of the formation of a testimony-based belief, no testimony-based belief that P.

(3) The psychological transition from comprehension to belief involves *deference* or *epistemic dependence* to the epistemic authority of the speaker. The hearer is 'turning to' the speaker (to the passer-by, to informants on the internet, to chemistry as a science) for information (for knowledge), and deferring to, or depending upon, the speaker (the sender) for the facts the hearer wants to know. Testimony-based beliefs are 'second-hand' beliefs, beliefs formed through deference to, or dependence on, the word – the testimony – of another.[4]

Given our distinction between justification and the anti-luck condition, I divide the epistemology of testimony into two questions:

(i) What is testimonial justification? When and why are testimony-based beliefs justified?
(ii) What is testimonial knowledge? When a hearer forms a justified true testimony-based belief, when and why does the hearer satisfy the anti-luck condition?[5]

But before discussing those questions, we should first decide whether testimonial knowledge is even possible.

4. The possibility of knowledge transmission

John Locke is frequently quoted as claiming that testimonial knowledge is not even possible:

> For, I think, we may as rationally hope to see with other men's eyes as to know by other men's understandings. So much as we ourselves consider and comprehend of truth and reason, so much we possess of real and true knowledge. The floating of other men's opinions in our brains makes us not one jot the more knowing, thought they happen to be true … In the sciences, every one has so much as he really knows and comprehends. What he believes only, and takes upon trust, are but shreds; which, however well in the whole piece, make no considerable addition to his stock who gathers them. Such borrowed wealth, like fairy money, though it were gold in the hand from which he received it, will be but leaves and dust when it comes to use. (*Essay Concerning Human Understanding*, Bk I, ch. III, sec. 24)

People read this as denying the very possibility of testimonial knowledge, of the transmission of knowledge – gold – from one mind to another; all that results from deference and dependence is shreds and dust.

This strikes nearly everyone as incredible; we are deeply social creatures after all, living lives of massive mutual interdependence. Surely we learn (come to know) enormous amounts from relying on others. Locke's British intellectual heir, David Hume, famously remarked that 'there is no species of reasoning more common, more useful, and even necessary to human life, than that which is derived from the testimony of men, and the reports of eye-witnesses and spectators' (*Inquiry Concerning Human Understanding*, sec. 10, para. 5). As opposed to Locke and in line with Hume, common sense, it seems, asserts that knowledge from one mind to another can be, and often is, transmitted through testimony. C. A. J. Coady (1992: 389) agrees: 'If S knows that P ... then S can bring his listeners to know that P by telling them that P.' Elizabeth Fricker (1987: 57) claims: 'If S's belief is knowledge, then we may allow that title to H's belief too.' And Tyler Burge (1993: 477) asserts: 'If one has acquired one's belief from others in the normal way, and if the others know the proposition, then one acquires knowledge.' A cursory review of the literature on this question will result in a score of similar passages. Indeed, the agreement is so widespread on this issue that it must form a piece of our folk epistemology.

Although it goes without saying, these passages require qualification: the knowledge is transferred only if the hearer is also justified in forming the corresponding testimony-based belief. If someone knows that P and tells you that P, but you have every reason to believe that they are either lying or mistaken, then it is far from obvious, and probably false, that you would come to know that P by believing them.

Is the speaker's knowledge that P also necessary for a hearer's testimonial knowledge that P? The answer here, too, seems to be in the affirmative: a hearer can acquire testimonial knowledge that P only if the speaker has knowledge that P to transmit. If the speaker doesn't have the knowledge to transmit, how could the hearer, in depending on the speaker, acquire knowledge? Magic?

Commentators agree. Robert Audi (1997: 410) says: 'My testimony cannot give you testimonially grounded knowledge that P without my knowing that P.' Tyler Burge (1993: 486) writes: 'If a recipient depends upon interlocution for knowledge, the recipient's knowledge depends on the source's knowledge as well.' Angus Ross (1986: 62) asserts: 'Your telling me that P can only be said to provide me with knowledge if you know that P.' And Michael Welbourne (1986: 302) says: 'It is necessary, if there is to be a successful process of testimonial transmission, that the speaker have knowledge to communicate.'

Philosophical reflection, in line with common sense, reveals that (*pace* Locke) testimony transfers knowledge from one mind to another.[6]

5. Testimonial justification: reductionism versus anti-reductionism

This brings us back to our two questions: what is testimonial justification, and what is testimonial knowledge? In this section I discuss the first question; I discuss the second in the subsequent two sections.

Why are we justified, when we are, in believing another's testimony? There are two opposing perspectives on this question. The so-called anti-reductionist believes that we enjoy a default epistemic right to take the assertions and testimonies of others at face value. If someone tells you that P, you have a default defeasible epistemic right or entitlement to believe that P; testimony-based beliefs are default defeasibly justified. Tyler Burge (1993, 2013) calls this the 'Acceptance Principle':

> A person is entitled to accept a proposition that is presented as true and that is intelligible to him or her, unless there are stronger reasons not to.

When Burge advances this principle, he is working within a broadly reliabilist view of justification (or 'warrant'), where entitlement (his word for justification or warrant that does not rely on having a reason or reasons) entails the reliability of the belief-forming competence in normal conditions when functioning normally (Burge 1993, 2013; Graham forthcoming). Very roughly, his idea is that, when you take someone to have told you that P, you enjoy a prima facie defeasible epistemic entitlement to believe what they tell you, for your ability to comprehend others reliably leads to true beliefs in normal conditions when functioning normally: relying on others (in normal conditions) is a good route to truth.

Thomas Reid advanced a similar view in the eighteenth century. In section 24 of chapter 6 of his *Inquiry into the Human Mind* (1764), he argued that there were two principles of human social psychology that tallied with one another – the principles of veracity and of credulity.

> The wise and beneficent Author of Nature, who intended that we should be social creatures, and that we should receive the greatest and most important part of our knowledge by the information of others, hath, for these purposes, implanted in our natures two principles that tally ... The first ... is a propensity to speak truth ... so as to convey our real sentiments. This principle has a powerful operation, even in the greatest liars; for where they lie once, they speak truth a hundred times. Truth is always uppermost, and is the natural issue of the mind. It requires no art or training, no inducement or temptation, but only

> that we yield to a natural impulse. Lying, on the contrary, is doing violence
> to our nature; and is never practised, even by the worst men, without some
> temptation.... Another original principle implanted in us by the Supreme Being,
> is a disposition to confide in the veracity of others, and to believe what they tell
> us ... [T]he former ... may be called the principle of veracity [and the latter] we
> shall ... call this the principle of credulity. It is unlimited in children, until they
> meet with instances of deceit and falsehood: and it retains a very considerable
> degree of strength through life.

The result of these paired principles of human psychology is that true information, for the most part, flows reliably from one mind to another. Or so Reid believes.

Although Reid attributes this fortunate epistemic situation to the wisdom and good will of the Supreme Being, most contemporary followers of this broadly Reidian view would ground our social psychologies in our evolutionary and cultural history, cultivated in different ways by our varying social norms and traditions. I'll touch again on this issue.

Burge, however, ambitiously argues that the ground of the reliability of assertive communication lies not in our social psychologies, but rather in the very nature of reason. Famously, he argued that the Acceptance Principle is a priori true, for the reliability of assertive communication in normal conditions when functioning normally follows from the very nature of the expression of propositional content as a sign of reason, and the very nature of reason as a sign of truth. Regrettably, space does not allow for discussion of Burge's ambitious argument for this surprising conclusion.[7]

Without assuming that anti-reductionists are 'simple' reliabilists about epistemic justification (generally they're not), let's assume that behind the spirit of anti-reductionism is the assumption that our default defeasible entitlement involves the reliability of assertive communication in normal conditions.

Not everyone agrees that the Acceptance Principle is true. Those who reject the Principle are often called reductionists. They deny that we can take for granted, in the absence of defeating evidence, that other people are trustworthy. Reductionists believe that, in order to be justified in believing what another tells you, you need independent, non-essentially testimony-based, positive reasons for believing that the person is sincere and competent on the occasion, either because *testimony* is generally trustworthy, or because *they* are generally trustworthy, or because they are apt to be trustworthy *on this occasion*. The reductionist believes another's report that P as such is epistemically neutral on the question whether P; on its own, it provides no support to believe that P.

Their main intuitive motivation seems to be this: you just can't trust other people to be as reliable as you need them to be. There is too much mendacity and honest error, too many sources for error in the chain of communication, to simply risk believing what other people tell you. Indeed, for all that you know, most testimony may be misleading. To avoid being duped, either intentionally or accidentally, you need to sort out the good from the bad, and that requires positive non-testimonial grounds for thinking that your source is sincere or reliable or both. Not doing so is a recipe for objectionable gullibility (Fricker 1994: 144–5).[8]

The structure of this debate between the reductionist and the anti-reductionist parallels an older debate over perceptual justification. The classical foundationalist held that beliefs formed through perception about the external world were not prima facie justified (experiences as such were neutral guides to external reality), but instead required for their justification background support from more 'basic' or 'fundamental' beliefs about the characteristic patterns of our own consciously known inner sensations and perceptual experiences. From beliefs about the patterns of inner experience, we would then infer the characteristics and existence of objects in the external world, presumably via an inference to the best explanation. The justification for beliefs about the external world then 'reduced' to the justification for beliefs about our own minds and what we can in turn infer about the external world from those. The classical foundationalist's opponent (often called 'moderate' foundationalism) insisted instead that perceptual beliefs about the external world are justified 'directly' by the perceptual experiences (perceptual representations) that cause them. There was then no need to 'reduce' perceptual justification to any other form of justification; we enjoy default entitlement to take perceptual experience at face value.

You should now see the parallel, and the point of the labels. Reductionists about testimony think that testimonial justification reduces to first-hand justification through perception, stored in memory, and extended through reasoning (for testimony as such is epistemically neutral; the fact that someone told you that P is no right on its own to believe that P), just as reductionists about perception think that perceptual justification reduces to other sources (for perceptual experience as such is epistemically neutral; the fact that it perceptually appears to you as if P is not right on its own to believe that P). Anti-reductionists about testimony think that testimonial justification doesn't so reduce, but instead stands on its own two feet, just as anti-reductionists about perception think that perceptual justification doesn't reduce to other more 'basic' sources of justification.[9]

What is the main motivation for anti-reductionism? Here is the standard argument. First, most of our testimony-based beliefs are justified. Second, as a matter of fact we lack the reductive non-testimonial reasons required to reductively justify the extent of our reliance on testimony. The full extent of the justification for our testimony-based beliefs thus does not 'reduce' to a non-testimonial basis (see, especially, Coady [1992]). The anti-reductionist sees the reductionist alternative as overly demanding.[10]

Although many people find this point against the reductionist compelling, it has its detractors.[11] Instead of pausing to evaluate these replies, let me rehearse instead its most plausible instance: childhood testimony. Children form justified testimony-based beliefs, even before the age of two. From two years onwards, they are deeply dependent for information on what other people tell them, especially on topics they cannot observe for themselves (Harris 2012; Harris and Lane 2014). Infants and young children have a strong and adaptive tendency to rely on testimony (Cole, Harris, and Koenig 2012). But children lack some of the conceptual resources to formulate meta-arguments about the reliability of their interlocutors. They also lack sufficient first-hand evidence to justify the premises in those arguments, even if they can formulate them. And, last, even if they have the evidence and can formulate the arguments, it is unlikely that they rely on that evidence and formulate those arguments; they seem to lack the executive ability. Thus, if children have justified testimony-based beliefs, but they cannot 'reduce' that justification to justification from other sources, then testimony-based beliefs do not require positive non-testimonial reasons for their justification.[12]

There have been two main responses to this argument in the literature. The first denies that children have justified testimony-based beliefs; since they lack the positive reasons, they lack justified beliefs (e.g. van Cleve 2006). The second denies that children lack the positive reasons – recent developmental psychology has shown us that children are smarter than we think they are. I simply reject the first reply. As for the second, too much time would be needed to review it. Suffice it to say that the recent evidence from developmental psychology, in my view, shows no such thing.[13]

Fricker (1995) offers a unique and telling reply. She grants the case for children but then goes coherentist for adults. That is, an Acceptance Principle is true for justified testimony-based beliefs when the hearer has little to go on by way of background support (the childhood case), but then coherentism is true when the hearer has a coherent set of beliefs to deploy to justify her reliance on testimony (the adult case). By my lights, this is just to grant anti-reductionism. First, it grants the case where background belief is insufficient. Second, it grants the anti-reductionist argument against the distinctively *reductionist* requirement on background reasons. Third, the existence and relevance of coherent background beliefs is fully compatible with anti-reductionism (Graham 2006c). Fourth, without embracing coherentism, the anti-reductionist can even explain why so many of those background beliefs are justified, and thus relevant to new testimony-based beliefs: those background beliefs were themselves justified by testimony, not by further reductive background beliefs (Graham 2006b; Burge 2013). A main concern of Fricker's, it seems to me, is not the abstract issue of the structure of testimonial justification, but instead the feared laziness or epistemic irresponsibility that might result if a believer took the Acceptance Principle as a license to ignore relevant background beliefs, or to ignore evidence of untrustworthiness on the speaker's part. And that concern is shared equally by the anti-reductionist.

The reductionist thinks that the Acceptance Principle is too permissive; the anti-reductionist thinks that the alternative is just too demanding. Is there a way to settle this debate?[14] Let me offer three points in favour of anti-reductionism. First, as I just remarked, the Acceptance Principle is not a recommendation to ignore counterevidence: it's not a policy or a license to hand over all of your thinking to what other people tell you, willy-nilly. Second (and relatedly), the Acceptance Principle is fully compatible with hearer's possessing, developing, and deploying filters and countermeasures. Various forms of monitoring and epistemic vigilance are not only compatible with the Acceptance Principle (compare analogous filters and monitors for perceptual justification), but are often recommended by anti-reductionists (Goldberg and Henderson 2006; Henderson 2008; Graham 2010; Sperber et al. 2010). Third, reductionist anxiety is nearly always driven by armchair considerations. Although this is not objectionable as such, one might naturally wonder what the empirical evidence suggests. Surprisingly, empirical studies suggest that 'gullibility' isn't such a bad thing, especially if our goal is to promote truth and avoid error (Michaelian 2010; Shieber 2014; Ahlstrom-Vij 2016). Some initial computer modelling reaches a similar conclusion (Zollman 2015). I think these three points, individually and collectively, squarely place the burden of proof on the reductionist. This conclusion should not be surprising, once we recognize not only the *extent* of our reliance on other people for information, but the extent of our *nature* as social beings.

6. Counterexamples to transmission

I now turn to our question about testimonial knowledge: when and why does a hearer satisfy the anti-luck condition? You might think that the answer to this question is easy. Since the speaker knows and thereby satisfies the anti-luck condition, the hearer has only to satisfy the justification condition to come to know. The neat thing about testimonial knowledge is that the speaker (in possessing knowledge) does the work for the hearer. Problem solved. Hence, we don't need an independent treatment for the hearer, beyond an account of the hearer's justification. This seems to be the point behind the common-sense view that testimony *transfers* knowledge.

Unfortunately, the issue isn't so easily resolved. Even if the speaker has knowledge, that may not be enough for the hearer to satisfy the anti-luck condition. Here's an example of just that possibility (modified from Nozick [1981]):

> HOSPITAL. A father knows his son is fine today, even though his son suffers serious health problems. The father's mother (the son's grandmother) is sick in the hospital. When the father visits, he tells her that her grandson is fine. But if his son were sick (or even dead), he would not tell her, so as not to upset her. Although the father knows his son his well, his mother does not learn from him, for he would easily tell her that her grandson is fine even when that is not so. Relying on his testimony about her grandson's well-being, she would easily form a false belief.[15]

The hearer forms a justified true testimony-based belief, but the hearer doesn't acquire knowledge, for in a sense the hearer's true belief is just luckily true. Although the speaker has knowledge to transmit, and the hearer (we assume) has every right to believe the speaker (and so forms a justified belief), something goes wrong.

Matters get even worse for the simple common-sense answer, for it may be possible for a hearer's justified testimony-based belief to satisfy the anti-luck condition, even though the speaker does not have knowledge to transmit, so it cannot be that the speaker's knowledge that secures the hearer's knowledge. Here is a variant of a much discussed case (Graham 2000b, 2006a, 2016b):

> FOSSIL. A devout creationist teaches at a public school where she must teach a section on evolutionary theory. She does not believe a word of it, but is a dedicated and responsible teacher. She develops a near-expert understanding based on deep reading of books and articles on evolutionary science. She

even develops a deep understanding of fossils that parallels highly skilled scientifically trained expertise. On a field trip, she discovers a fossil that proves that ancient humans once lived in this area (itself a surprising discovery that no one previously knew). Although she does not believe it, when she tells this to her students, they believe her. Because of her commitment to teaching, her exposure to evolutionary science, and her mastery of fossils, she would not say what she did unless it were true. Relying on their teacher, the schoolchildren would not easily be mistaken when coming to believe what she tells them. The children come to know something that no one has ever previously known.

As I said, variants have been much discussed (Lackey 1999; Carter and Nickel 2014).[16] Although many people are willing to accept that knowledge transmission does not always succeed (as in HOSPITAL), people find FOSSIL much harder to accept. How can children acquire knowledge from relying on another, if the sender doesn't have knowledge to pass along? That's like borrowing money from someone who doesn't have any to lend. How can someone give you something that they themselves don't have? So, how can the speaker ensure that the hearer meets the anti-luck condition for knowledge, if the speaker doesn't have knowledge herself?

Digging in their heels against the intuitive force of the example, people have tried three different replies. First, people have argued that, even though it looks like the children acquire knowledge, they really don't, for on closer inspection the teacher has a flaw that prevents her from inducing knowledge in her pupils: she doesn't always tell them what she believes (when it comes to evolutionary science, she tells them what the science would say, and not what she believes). But this isn't very persuasive. It would mean that they never learn from their teacher (and that you can never learn anything from someone who isn't completely honest with you about everything). And, after all, isn't it intuitive that, because she relies *on the science*, the children are clearly positioned to acquire knowledge from her (Burge 2013)?

Second, people have argued that, although it looks like the children form testimony-based beliefs, they are really relying on their background beliefs about the reliability of their schoolteachers and their first-hand, independently acquired knowledge of this teacher's track-record for telling the truth. Their beliefs are more 'first-hand' than 'second-hand', and so they are not really deferring to their teacher or epistemically depending on her expertise as opposed to their own, and so they are not really forming testimony-*based* beliefs, and so their knowledge isn't *testimonial* knowledge after all (Audi 2006; Fricker 2006). But this isn't very persuasive. The children are young children; they are not nascent critical reasoners sorting out which teacher to trust and which to ignore. They are schoolchildren, after all, there to learn from their teachers. If anyone learns from deferring to others, to depending on the expertise of their informants, small children do.

Third, people have argued that, even though the children acquire knowledge from the teacher and form genuinely testimony-based beliefs, they don't acquire *testimonial* knowledge. 'Testimonial knowledge', they say,

> is essentially knowledge from another person's knowledge through testimony. If the speaker doesn't have knowledge to transmit, it is *a priori* analytically impossible for the hearer to acquire *testimonial* knowledge; testimonial knowledge is knowledge *secured from someone else's knowledge*. It's just a part of the very concept, or the very idea, of *testimonial* knowledge. It is what the phrase 'testimonial knowledge' *means*.

So, even though the children acquire knowledge through epistemic dependence on their teacher's assertion (they form a testimony-based belief that is knowledge), they don't acquire *testimonial* knowledge.

I've never found this reply very persuasive, but I'm happy to grant it. I shall not, that is, dispute about a word. The children then acquire *testimonial knowledge** (testimony-based belief that is knowledge) but not *testimonial* knowledge (knowledge that a priori analytically entails knowledge from a speaker's knowledge). Although all *testimonial* knowledge is also testimonial knowledge*, not all testimonial knowledge* is *testimonial* knowledge.

But, having made this linguistic concession, I shall ignore it. For the interesting and worthwhile category of inquiry is not the narrower category of testimonial knowledge, but is instead the broader category of testimonial knowledge*. That, I believe, is the category we should strive to understand. I'll give a brief argument for this at the end of the next section.

We still need an answer to our second question: how and why do hearers satisfy the anti-luck condition when forming justified true testimony-based beliefs? The answer from reflection on common sense – that the speaker knows, and so the speaker, in satisfying the anti-luck condition, takes care of for the hearer – didn't work. We need to dig a little deeper.

7. A safe-basis account of testimonial knowledge

Maybe we should choose a proposed anti-luck condition, and see where that leads. Since Gettier published his short article in 1963, there has been no shortage of attempts to articulate the correct 'fourth' or 'anti-luck' condition on propositional knowledge. The issue is still a matter of controversy, well over fifty years later. Even so, a handful of leading contenders have emerged: the 'no-essential falsehoods' account, the 'defeasibility' account, the Dretske-Nozick 'sensitivity' account (Dretske 1971; Nozick 1981), and the 'safety' account (proposed by Luper-Foy [1984] and Sosa [1999]; taken up by Pritchard [2005], among others). Although the points I am about to make are compatible with both the sensitivity and the safety accounts, for reasons that need not detain us I prefer to work with the safety account over the sensitivity one. And the other accounts, to my mind, tend to over-intellectualize propositional knowledge: they start at the wrong end of the spectrum. But that's a debate for another day. In the rest of this section I will explain the safety account, and then put it to work in answering our question, to see where it leads.

According to the safety account, propositional knowledge that P is (justified, true) belief that P held on a *safe* basis. When is a true belief that P held on a safe basis? When holding the belief that P on that basis, you would not easily be mistaken. When would you not easily be mistaken? This is usually glossed in terms of possible worlds: a true belief that P is held on a safe basis just in case, in each nearby possible world, if one forms a belief within that world on the same basis as in the actual world, then one forms a true belief in that world.[17]

How does the safe-basis account apply to our cases? Take HOSPITAL. The father knows that his son is healthy; he believes on a safe-basis (perception, testimony, background knowledge, etc.), so he would not easily be mistaken. But his mother's belief that her grandson is healthy (from her son's testimony) is not formed on a safe basis, for there is a nearby world where she relies on her son's testimony to the effect that her grandson is fine but she forms a false belief. That's why she doesn't acquire knowledge from him, even though he knows that his son (her grandson) is fine.[18]

Now take FOSSIL. The schoolteacher relies on a safe-basis (careful observation, a sophisticated understanding of the contents of evolutionary theory and the fossil record, etc.) to reach the conclusion – a conclusion she 'accepts' but, because of her personal convictions, does not believe – that ancient humans once lived in this area: she relies on a safe-basis to reach a cognitive state of 'acceptance' but not of belief (cf. Bratman [1992]). 'Accepting' that conclusion, she tells the children that ancient humans once lived in the area. Being young schoolchildren, they believe her. Her 'acceptance' results from a safe-basis, and she wouldn't say what she does unless it was formed on such a basis, and so her testimony, too, is a safe-basis for the schoolchildren.

When they believe her, they, too, form a belief on a safe-basis. Relying on her testimony, the schoolchildren would not easily be mistaken. That's why they come to know something, something that (as the example goes) no one has previously known.[19]

The safe-basis account also allows us to argue that ordinary cases (where a speaker transfers knowledge) and unusual cases (like FOSSIL) fall within the same epistemic kind. Imagine an ordinary case where knowledge transfers. Why did that happen? Because the speaker believed on a safe basis, which partly explains why her assertion is a safe basis for the hearer, which partly explains why the hearer forms a belief on a safe basis. What happened in the FOSSIL case? The speaker did not believe on a safe basis, but she did 'accept' on a safe basis, which then partly explains why she asserts on a safe basis, and so on. The underlying 'epistemic mechanics' is the same in both so-called *testimonial* knowledge cases and what I called testimonial knowledge* cases. But if the epistemic mechanics are the same, the epistemic kinds are the same. I conclude that the 'broader' category of testimonial knowledge* is the category that we want to understand if we want to understand the epistemology of testimony, especially the transmission of knowledge from one mind to another.

After all, knowledge per se does not transfer from one mind to another. Suppose that I have some perceptual knowledge. Then I have knowledge on a safe-basis, where the basis involves perception and perceptual experience. Then I tell you, and you learn from me. Did I transfer my perceptual experience to you? Do you now have exactly what I have? No, not at all. You have neither my *perceptual* knowledge nor my *perceptual* warrant. But you do have knowledge, *testimonial* knowledge. Why? Because you formed a belief on a safe basis, because the epistemic force (the safety) of my perceptual belief was transferred through testimony to your belief. Testimony transmits *epistemic force* – it transmits the safety of one basis (perception) to the safety of another basis (comprehension and belief) through the safety of a medium (assertion, telling). Testimony doesn't *transmit* my knowledge to you per se. That's why the motivation for the so-called narrower category '*testimonial* knowledge' (as knowledge essentially derived from someone else's knowledge) puts the wrong foot forward.[20] It is not the speaker's knowledge that secures knowledge for the hearer; it is the epistemic force supporting the speaker's belief that secures the epistemic force supporting the hearer's belief. The same story explains unusual cases like FOSSIL: same epistemic mechanism, same epistemic kind.

8. The reliability of testimony and social norms

But why, you might ask, is testimony reliable enough for justified uptake and knowledge? Consistent with everything else that we know about ourselves, what explains the reliability of testimony?

There is so much to say about this topic that I can barely begin to scratch the surface. I'll make three quick remarks, and then discuss one answer in a little more detail, just to take a stab at this important issue.

First, there's always the possibility, consistent with Reid, that it is a part of our God-given nature. Second, there's the parallel possibility, consistent with the growing literature on the evolution of cooperation, that we're born to be helpful, especially in communication. Young children are especially helpful at providing information, unprompted, to adults in apparent need (Tomasello 2009). For a similar reason, parents tell their children the truth out of parental concern. Third, it is obviously frequently the case that, to coordinate with others, we need to tell the truth (I'll need to tell you the correct time that my flight arrives if you are going to pick me up). Another answer, consistent with these three, is that human life is governed by socially shared prescriptions – social norms – for telling the truth and providing useful information. It's this last answer I'll discuss in a little more detail.

What's a social norm? According to Cristina Bicchieri (2006, 2014, 2017), a social norm is not merely a collective pattern of behaviour in a group. Everyone may want to stay warm when they go out, and so everyone may wear a coat during the winter, so we are all behaving the same way. But that's not a social norm; that is a social custom, a pattern of behaviour in a group where everyone acts the same way because we all have the same needs and we've all discovered the same solution. A social norm is not a trend or a fashion either, where people imitate a crowd or follow the leader to go along or to simply rely on what probably works. Nor is a social norm a convention, where people act the same way in a recurrent situation to coordinate their behaviour, such as driving on the right-hand side of the road in the United States.

According to Bicchieri, social norms are patterns of behaviour that are collectively approved or disapproved in a group or population, and enforced by informal sanctions, positive and negative. Social norms arise from (1) (second-order) beliefs we have that other people believe we ought – normatively and not just prudentially – to behave a certain way (these are normative social expectations), and (2) a conditional preference to behave a certain way, provided we believe that other people believe we ought to believe that way (a preference to meet normative social expectations). The conditional preference exists because of the sanctions, often external but also internal. Positive sanctions include tangible rewards, praise, status, reputation, and so on. Negative sanctions for censured behaviour include punishments, shaming, ostracism, ridicule, and so on. Often just thinking that others would disapprove can stop us in our tracks. Likewise, just thinking that others would approve might lead us to conform (Pettit 1990; Graham 2015b).[21]

Social norms – our normative expectations and conditional preferences to conform – then strongly motivate compliance. 'With social norms', Bicchieri (2017: 34–5) explains, 'the normative influence is strong and plays a crucial role in driving compliance. It matters to us that most people in our reference network believe we ought to conform to a certain behavioural pattern. This point must be emphasized … [T]he social pressure to conform, expressed in social expectation that one ought to conform, is a powerful motivator.' And it is the pressure to conform, enforced by sanctions, that really does a good deal of the motivational work. For, left to ourselves, we often prefer not to conform. Indeed, many social norms emerge as solutions to social dilemmas, where narrow individual self-interest might lead us to behave in non-cooperative ways, such as prisoner's dilemmas and public goods games. 'With a [social] norm, there is often the temptation to transgress it – this is precisely why norms must be socially enforced' (39).

However, sometimes we internalize the norm, so that we positively value the behaviour, and we might conform, regardless of social expectations. 'Especially with norms that are well established, norm followers tend to value what the norm stands for. An external observer may be induced to think that, since people have a positive attitude toward a norm, they may obey it regardless of what others around them do' (40). Even so, personal values – our personal normative attitudes – often fall short of motivating behaviour (Fishbein 1967; Eagly and Chaiken 1993), so that social expectations and conditional preferences often play a much stronger role than meets the eye.

What if truth-telling is a social norm? What if we believe that other people believe that we ought to tell the truth, and what if we also believe that there are rewards for conformity and costs for noncompliance? Then we'll be motivated, in addition to any other motivations that might already be in place, to tell the truth. The social pressure to conform would then be a powerful motivator. We might even positively value telling the truth.

Is it? Yes, indeed. It's a textbook case of a social norm: open any textbook discussion of social norms, and *tell the truth* will surely be on the shortlist of examples. In her contribution to a recent introductory anthology of social science, Bicchieri (2014: 208) proclaims that '[e]ach group has its own norms, and some, like reciprocity or truth telling, [are] very general, spanning all groups'. When providing examples of social norms in his book *Social Action*, Seumas Miller (2001) lists refraining from violence, remaining faithful to one's spouse, avoiding incest, keeping promises, telling the truth. Bowles and Gintis (2011) emphasize a number of times the social norm that one ought to tell the truth. Philip Pettit (1990) treats truth-telling as the central case in his work on social norms. As I said, it's a textbook case.

Social norms are surely a part of the story – a very complex story – as to why testimony is as reliable as it is, not just in general but in varying domains and in different situations. Although maybe the Supreme Being didn't implant the principle of veracity in our hearts, it has a powerful operation in our lives, even so.[22]

Notes

1   Testimony was discussed by Locke, Hume, Reid, and Kant (among others), but then was for the most part marginalized until the late twentieth century. Michael Welbourne (1986) was often a lone voice in the 1970s, later joined by Elizabeth Fricker, among others, in the 1980s. Then Coady's (1992) book and Burge's (1993) essay stirred considerable interest in the early 1990s, which led to a handful of dissertations completed by the end of the 1990s and then a flowering of interest that continues unabated, including the recent publication of two excellent textbooks (Gelfert 2014; Shieber 2015).

2   I won't pretend to be as exhaustive or even-handed as possible – I'll be opinionated, for sure – but I'll do my best in the space available. For other ways of orienting the literature, I recommend Fricker (2004), Lackey (2011), Adler (2012), Greco (2012), Gelfert (2014), Goldman and Blanchard (2015), and Shieber (2015). There are issues that I will sideline, including disagreement, epistemic injustice, group knowledge, and group testimony, whether the reliability of a process, or even the cognitive process itself, somehow interestingly 'extends' to the speaker (Goldberg 2010), among other issues. And the assurance view, regrettably, will receive only the barest mention. For the assurance view, see Ross (1986), Moran (2005), McMyler (2011), and Hinchman (2014); against it, see Lackey (2008), Schmitt (2010), and Owens (2017).

3   For an up-to-date discussion, see Hetherington (2016).

4 For discussion of testimony as a speech act, see Graham (1997, 2015a). For more discussion of testimony-based beliefs, see Graham (2015a, 2016).

5 Not every participant to the literature sharply distinguishes these two questions, sometimes resulting in unnecessary confusion. Robert Audi (1997), however, sharply distinguishes these two, arguing that a hearer can acquire testimonial knowledge without simultaneously acquiring a justified testimony-based belief. Audi relies on a general framework where knowledge is belief based on a reliable indicator, and justified belief is belief based on accessible justifiers that can be cited when justifying the belief.

6 For the record, I think that this representation of Locke is far from the truth. For one, in context this passage is targeting an almost blind deference to the so-called 'authority of others' on matters of theological and abstract philosophical affairs, exactly the kind of topic where Locke, as a spokesperson of the Enlightenment, believed that we can, and should, think for ourselves. For another, Locke also had a very different *conception* of knowledge than we have today. On his *conception* of knowledge, knowledge is the perceived agreement or disagreement among ideas (roughly, but not entirely, what we would consider knowledge of self-evident truths and what can be self-evidently deduced from self-evident truths). Given that conception of *knowledge*, you cannot just acquire knowledge from relying on someone who knows, for even though they have perceived the relevant agreements among ideas to reach a conclusion, it does not follow that by believing their testimony you will ipso facto perceive the relevant agreement among ideas yourself. Hume probably would have agreed with Locke, for they probably shared this conception of knowledge. So even the quotation from Hume is, for the opposite reason, also a little misleading. Furthermore, in line with the quotation from Hume, in Book IV of the *Essay* Locke includes testimony as a 'ground of probability': namely, a ground for reasonable belief – what in many cases *we* would count as knowledge. In sum, Locke probably did not mean what most people who cite this passage take him to mean (see Shieber [2009] for more discussion). Regardless, this representation of Locke is a useful foil for common sense, which is why I started with it.

7 See Graham (forthcoming) for critical exposition and discussion of Burge's argumentation. There's a tendency to equate Burge's a priori defence of the Principle with the truth of the Principle, so that if the Principle isn't a priori necessary then it isn't even true (van Cleve 1996; Faulkner 2011). Burge assumes the Principle and then asks for its basis. The Principle, as we've just implied, might have more than one basis: God, evolution by natural selection, human psychology, social psychology, social structures, the nature of promising and the institutions of promising, and so on, or the very nature of reason itself. Burge opts for the last option. His account of its basis may fall short without the Principle falling short in any way.

8   For other arguments, see Fricker (1987, 2004, 2016) and Lackey (2008). Lackey
thinks that she has a persuasive counterexample to anti-reductionism. Imagine
stumbling across an apparent diary written apparently in English, where it is clear
to you that it was written by an alien from another planet. You possess no positive
reasons for what it says, and simultaneously you possess, she says, no defeating
reasons not to believe what it says. But intuitively, she thinks, you are not justified
in believing what it says. Generalizing, every testimony-based belief requires non-
testimonial support. I don't agree. By my lights, a mature adult will be puzzled by
the fact that it was an alien, and so is surely to have defeaters. Perrine (2014: 3236)
argues along these lines: the adult in Lackey's case 'has a wealth of background
knowledge that ought to make him skeptical in this case' (cf. Burge 2013). However,
it the recipient were a young child who could read but had few thoughts, if any,
about the consequences of the author's alien status, then we'd have a case of no
reasons on either side. But then it seems fine to say that child has a prima facie
justified testimony-based belief.

9   I provide more detailed formulations of some of these issues elsewhere (2006,
forthcoming). For testimony aficionados, there are two possible ways to frame the
reductionism/anti-reductionism debate. One is about justification (that is how I see
it); the other is about knowledge (about converting true belief into knowledge).
If you see it the latter way, then you see the reductionist as saying that a true
testimony-based belief, provided that it is reductively justified (usually inductively
by a track-record), is then knowledge: to really 'reduce' the hearer's *knowledge*
to perception, memory, and induction, everything required *for knowledge* must
'reduce' to the hearer's track-record. Seen this way, the 'reductionist' rejects the
common-sense idea that the hearer gets what she needs for knowledge from the
speaker, and thus rejects testimonial knowledge as involving knowledge transfer
of either knowledge or justification from the speaker. This 'reductionist' view is
then easy to dismiss with Gettier counterexamples. Lackey (2008: 142–59) does
so. Imagine that the speaker is right just by luck, but that the hearer has a pretty
good track-record of evidence to justify reliance. Then intuitively the hearer, too,
despite the track-record, has a Gettierized justified true belief. The hearer's track-
record is then not enough to convert a true belief into knowledge. Lackey argues
that a further, anti-Gettier, condition is required, involving the reliability of the
speaker's testimony. Paralleling her formulation of reductionism, she formulates
'non-'reductionism as the view that a true testimony-based belief, provided that the
hearer has no defeaters, is knowledge. This view also suffers the same fate: Gettier
counterexamples are easy to formulate. She concludes that both reductionism
(about knowledge) and anti-reductionism (about knowledge) are wrong, for the
same reason. She then formulates a 'hybrid' theory, neither 'reductionist' nor
'non-reductionist', for testimonial knowledge. (By these lights, any theory that
sees the speaker as playing some role in meeting the anti-luck condition is a

'hybrid' theory – which includes nearly everyone working on the topic, including our common-sense view that the hearer's knowledge depends on the speaker's knowledge.) Putting all of this to one side, Lackey ends up advancing a reductionist account of testimonial *justification* (she would call this the 'rationality dimension' of justification), for she adopts a 'positive reasons requirement' on testimonial knowledge, where 'for each report R, the positive reasons justifying R cannot ultimately be testimonially grounded, where this means that the justificatory or epistemic chain leading up to R cannot "bottom out" in testimony' (186). Although Lackey spends some time in her book arguing that adults have plenty of positive reasons supporting testimony, she spends little time addressing whether adults satisfy this reductive requirement, which is just the requirement at issue.

10   For other arguments, see Coady (1992) and Rysiew (2007). For some discussion of these arguments, see Fricker (1995) and Graham (2000c).

11   For detractors, see Lyons (1997), Shogenji (2006), van Cleve (2006), Lackey (2008), and Kenyon (2013). Fricker (1995, 2018) is well known for the distinction between 'local' and 'global' reductionism. She grants that testimonial justification does not 'globally' reduce (individuals do not possess a reductive justification for the proposition that testimony is generally reliable), but she insists that it 'locally' reduces (individuals possess reductive justification for propositions of the form that this speaker on this occasion is trustworthy on this topic). Many commentators, including myself, doubt that this move succeeds, for they doubt that individuals possess adequate *reductive* local justifications, never mind adequate reductive global justifications. See Insole (2000), Gelfert (2009), and Graham (2016a).

12   Selective trust in special cases some of the time is one thing; reductive trust in every case is another altogether. I discuss this argument in considerable detail elsewhere (2016a).

13   See Graham (2016a, sec. 5) for a review of the literature and references. See also Harris (2012), Cole, Harris, and Koenig (2012), and Harris and Lane (2014).

14   Paul Faulkner (2011) claims to occupy a middle ground. He argues that the anti-reductionist is wrong – we don't enjoy a prima facie default right to testimony – but the reductionist is wrong, too – we don't need a reductive justification showing that testimony in general, or in the particular 'local' case, is reliable. Because of the 'problem of communication' – because hearers want the truth, but because speakers, as rational self-interested agents, want the freedom to lie when that serves their interests – hearers need a reason in each and every case (even small children) to justifiably believe the speaker's report; it would be epistemically irrational otherwise to believe testimony without such a reason. But if the reason is not a reductive argument showing the reliability of the speaker, what is it? The reason is the hearer's affective trust that the speaker will prove trustworthy, where that is the normative expectation that the speaker should prove trustworthy, for

the speaker and the hearer are both subject to, and have internalized, the social norm of trustworthiness (of truth telling). (More on social norms in the final section.) The speaker, then aware of the hearer's normative expectation, will prove trustworthy (will fulfil the expectation). The hearer then possesses a mini-argument rationalizing acceptance of the speaker's assertion: (1) I normatively expect truth telling; (2) the speaker knows this; (3) the speaker has also internalized the norm, and so will prove trustworthy; (4) so, the speaker is telling the truth; (5) so, it is rational to believe the speaker's assertion. Although I agree with Faulkner about the important role that social norms play in the overall epistemology of testimony, I do not agree they tell the whole story: they are one mechanism among others underwriting the reliability of testimony, not the only one. (More on this in the final section.) Also, I think that he has conflated two issues. One issue is that of whether hearers need to represent, in their psychology, a rationalizing argument justifying their reliance. Another issue is that of whether there is a problem of communication, whether the possibility of deceit shows that the anti-reductionist cannot be right. Once social norms of truth-telling enter the picture, the problem of communication goes away. So, the case against the anti-reductionist dissolves. Why then think that everyone (even small children), in each and every case, needs a mini-argument to rationalize trust? Well, if you were an internalist with a tendency to intellectualize (some would say hyper-intellectualize) the epistemology of testimony, then you'd go for that conclusion. But since I don't, I won't. Faulkner thinks that the problem of cooperation motivates an internalist result, but it is (I believe) his internalist convictions that are doing the work, not the problem of cooperation. The structural problem of communication is one thing; the case for internalism is another. For discussion of Faulkner in more detail, see Graham (2012, 2013).

15 Here is another: ASTROLOGIST. Mary sometimes believes that it is raining in her village because she pulls the drapes and looks outside, and sometimes because she consults an astrological table with the drapes closed. Today, Mary looks outside and sees that it is raining. But when she takes your phone call and tells you that it is raining, you do not come to know that it is, for she would just as easily tell you that it is raining when it is not. Relying on her testimony about the weather, you would easily be mistaken (Peacocke 1986). For discussion of the issue and additional counterexamples, see Graham (2000a, 2016b) and Lackey (2008).

16 The difference between FOSSIL and Lackey's (1999, 2008) SCHOOLTEACHER example is that FOSSIL involves testimonial knowledge of a proposition that no one has ever previously known. In Lackey's example, the schoolteacher is passing on knowledge of evolutionary theory, well-known throughout the science. FOSSIL seems to illustrate the possibility that testimony can 'generate' knowledge, namely,

be the very first source of a new piece of knowledge, something that typically only occurs in perception, introspection, a priori understanding, and reasoning from those three sources. Those who think that testimony cannot 'generate' knowledge allow such cases like Lackey's (they only insist on knowledge in the chain of sources), hence the need to create a case that avoids the qualification. For further discussion of these and related cases, see Audi (2006), Fricker (2006, 2015, 2016), Graham (2006a, 2016b), Faulkner (2010), Burge (2013), Carter and Nickel (2014), Wright (2016), and Bachman and Graham (forthcoming).

17 'Basis' safety is not to be confused with 'belief' safety. A basis is safe just in case it leads you to a true belief in the actual world and doesn't lead you astray in any nearby possible world. A belief is safe just in case it is true in the actual world and true in all nearby worlds. The standard example to illustrate this difference involves flipping a coin to form the belief that $14 + 23 = 37$. If you believe because you flipped a coin, then you didn't believe on a safe basis. In a nearby world the coin flip will come up the other way, and you'll end up believing a falsehood. But the belief that $14 + 23 = 37$ (on the other hand) is true in all nearby worlds where you believe it, because it is true in any world where you believe it, because (as a necessary truth) it is true in all worlds! Forming a belief on a coin flip is not a safe basis, but the belief in the mathematical proposition is a safe belief. The safety account of knowledge is a safe-basis account, not a safe-belief account: there are safe beliefs that fail to measure up to knowledge, but no belief is knowledge without being held on a safe basis.

18 Mary in ASTROLOGY works the same way. By looking out the window through the drapes, Mary forms the belief, on a safe basis, that it is raining outside. That's why she knows that it is raining. But when she tells you that it is raining, you do not form a belief on a safe basis. She would easily tell you that it is raining outside when it is not; relying on her testimony about the weather would then easily lead you astray. That's why you don't acquire knowledge from her, even though she knows it is raining today.

19 For more discussion, detail, and defence of – and further references for – the safe-basis account of testimonial knowledge, see Graham (2016b).

20 For additional arguments for a further broadening of the epistemology of testimony, see Graham (2000a, 2015a, 2016b).

21 Among our social practices – our shared patterns of behaviour – there are many kinds: customs, descriptive norms, conventions, and social norms. Thus, it is not trivially true that some of our epistemic norms are social norms (or habits, or customs), just because we have a social practice of asking for and giving reasons. For that practice might be a custom, a descriptive norm, a convention, or a social norm. The case must be made.

22 For a longer discussion of some of these issues, see Graham (2015b). For more exploration of Bicchieri's framework for epistemic norms as social

norms, see Henderson and Graham (2017a,b). Faulkner's (2010, 2011) work is clearly relevant here, too (as discussed previously). The social norms account is an important alternative to both the constitutive norms account of the epistemology of testimony (e.g. see Goldberg [2015]; for critical discussion, see Johnson [2015]) and the assurance view, for each is sensitive to the normative dimension of testimony, but each locates it in other kinds of normativity, kinds that do not directly address the motivational basis for the reliability of testimony.

References

Adler, J. (2012), 'Epistemological Problems of Testimony', in E. N. Zalta (ed.), Stanford Encyclopedia of Philosophy, https://plato.stanford.edu/entries/testimony-episprob.

Ahlstrom-Vij, K. (2016), 'Is There a Problem with Cognitive Outsourcing?', *Philosophical Issues*, 26: 7–24.

Audi, R. (1997), 'The Place of Testimony in the Fabric of Justification and Knowledge', *American Philosophical Quarterly*, 34: 405–22.

Audi, R. (2006), 'Testimony, Veracity, Credulity', in J. Lackey and E. Sosa (eds), *The Epistemology of Testimony*, Oxford: Clarendon Press.

Bachman, Z. and Graham, P. J. (forthcoming), 'Counterexamples to Transmission', in M. Fricker, P. Graham, D. Henderson, and N. Pederson (eds), *The Routledge Handbook of Social Epistemology*, Routledge.

Bicchieri, C. (2006), *The Grammar of Society: The Nature and Dynamics of Social Norms*, New York: Cambridge University Press.

Bicchieri, C. (2014), 'Norms, Conventions, and the Power of Expectations', in N. Cartwright and E. Montuschi (eds), *The Philosophy of Social Science: A New Introduction*, Oxford: Oxford University Press.

Bicchieri, C. (2017), *Norms in the Wild: How to Diagnose, Measure, and Change Social Norms*, New York: Oxford University Press.

Bowles, S. and Gintis, H. (2011), *A Cooperative Species: Human Reciprocity and Its Evolution*, Princeton: Princeton University Press.

Bratman, M. E. (1992), 'Practical Reasoning and Acceptance in a Context', *Mind*, 101: 1–16.

Burge, T. (1993), 'Content Preservation', *The Philosophical Review*, 102: 457–88.

Burge, T. (2013), 'Postscript: Content Preservation', in his *Cognition through Understanding: Philosophical Papers, Volume 3*, Oxford: Oxford University Press.

Carter, J. A. and Nickel, P. J. (2014), 'On Testimony and Transmission', *Episteme*, 11: 145–55.

Coady, C. A. J. (1992), *Testimony: A Philosophical Study*, Oxford: Clarendon Press.

Cole, C. A., Harris, P. L., and Koenig, M. A. (2012), 'Entitled to Trust? Philosophical Frameworks and the Evidence from Children', *Analyse & Kritik*, 34: 195–216.

Dretske, F. (1971), 'Conclusive Reasons', *Australasian Journal of Philosophy*, 49: 1–22.

Eagly, A. H. and Chaiken, S. (1993), *The Psychology of Attitudes*, Orlando, FL: Harcourt Brace Jovanovich College.

Faulkner, P. (2010), 'Norms of Trust', in A. Haddock, A. Millar, and D. Pritchard (eds), *Social Epistemology*, Oxford: Oxford University Press.

Faulkner, P. (2011), *Knowledge on Trust*, Oxford: Oxford University Press.

Fishbein, M. (1967), 'A Consideration of Beliefs and Their Role in Attitude Measurement', in M. Fishbein (ed.), *Readings in Attitude Theory and Measurement*, New York: Wiley.

Fricker, E. (1987), 'The Epistemology of Testimony', *Aristotelian Society Supplementary Volume*, 61: 57–106.

Fricker, E. (1994), 'Against Gullibility', in A. Chakrabarti and B. K. Matilal (eds), *Knowing from Words: Western and Indian Philosophical Analysis of Understanding and Testimony*, Dordrecht: Kluwer Academic.

Fricker, E. (1995), 'Telling and Trusting: Reductionism and Anti-reductionism in the Epistemology of Testimony', *Mind*, 104: 393–411.

Fricker, E. (2004), 'Testimony: Knowing through Being Told', in I. Niiniluoto, M. Sintonen, and J. Woleński (eds), *Handbook of Epistemology*, Dordrecht: Kluwer Academic.

Fricker, E. (2006), 'Second-Hand Knowledge', *Philosophy and Phenomenological Research*, 73: 592–618.

Fricker, E. (2015), 'How to Make Invidious Distinctions amongst Reliable Testifiers', *Episteme*, 12: 173–202.

Fricker, E. (2016), 'Unreliable Testimony', in B. P. Mclaughlin and H. Kornblith (eds), *Alvin Goldman and His Critics*, Oxford: Blackwell.

Fricker, E. (2018), 'Inference to the Best Explanation and the Receipt of Testimony: Testimonial Reductionism Vindicated', in T. Poston and K. McCain (eds), *Best Explanations: New Essays on Inference to the Best Explanation*, Oxford: Oxford University Press.

Gelfert, A. (2009), 'Indefensible Middle Ground for Local Reductionism about Testimony', *Ratio*, 22: 170–90.

Gelfert, A. (2014), *A Critical Introduction to Testimony*, London: Bloomsbury.

Gettier, E. (1963), 'Is Knowledge Justified True Belief?' *Analysis*, 23: 121–3.

Goldberg, S. (2010), *Relying on Others: An Essay in Epistemology*, Oxford: Oxford University Press.

Goldberg, S. (2015), *Assertion: The Philosophical Significance of Assertoric Speech*, Oxford: Oxford University Press.

Goldberg, S. and Henderson, D. (2006), 'Monitoring and Anti-reductionism in the Epistemology of Testimony', *Philosophy and Phenomenological Research*, 72: 600–17.

Goldman, A. and Blanchard, T. (2015), 'Social Epistemology', in E. N. Zalta (ed.), Stanford Encyclopedia of Philosophy: https://plato.stanford.edu/entries/epistemology-social.

Graham, P. J. (1997), 'What Is Testimony?' *The Philosophical Quarterly*, 47: 227–32.

Graham, P. J. (2000a), 'Conveying Information', *Synthese*, 123: 365–92.

Graham, P. J. (2000b), 'Transferring Knowledge', *Noûs*, 34: 132–52.

Graham, P. J. (2000c), 'The Reliability of Testimony', *Philosophy and Phenomenological Research*, 61: 695–709.

Graham, P. J. (2006a), 'Can Testimony Generate Knowledge?' *Philosophica*, 78: 105–27.

Graham, P. J. (2006b), 'Liberal Fundamentalism and Its Rivals', in J. Lackey and E. Sosa (eds), *The Epistemology of Testimony*, Oxford: Clarendon Press.

Graham, P. J. (2006c), 'Testimonial Justification: Inferential or Non-inferential?' *The Philosophical Quarterly*, 56: 84–95.

Graham, P. J. (2010), 'Testimonial Entitlement and the Function of Comprehension', in A. Haddock, A. Millar, and D. Pritchard (eds), *Social Epistemology*, Oxford: Oxford University Press.

Graham, P. J. (2012), 'Testimony, Trust and Social Norms', *Abstracta*, 6: 92–116.

Graham, P. J. (2013), 'Review of Faulkner, *Knowledge on Trust*', *Notre Dame Philosophical Reviews*, http://ndpr.nd.edu/news/knowledge-on-trust.

Graham, P. J. (2015a), 'Testimony as Speech Act, Testimony as Source', in C. Mi, M. Slote, and E. Sosa (eds), *Moral and Intellectual Virtues in Western and Chinese Philosophy*, New York: Routledge.

Graham, P. J. (2015b), 'Epistemic Normativity and Social Norms', in J. Greco and D. Henderson (eds), *Epistemic Evaluation: Purposeful Epistemology*, Oxford: Oxford University Press.

Graham, P. J. (2016a), 'Formulating Reductionism about Testimonial Warrant and the Challenge from Childhood Testimony', *Synthese*, online 16 June 2016: http://dx.doi.org/10.1007/s11229-016-1140-y.

Graham, P. J. (2016b), 'Testimonial Knowledge: A Unified Account', *Philosophical Issues*, 28: 172–86.

Graham, P. J. (forthcoming), 'Sincerity and the Reliability of Testimony: Burge on the A Priori Basis of Testimonial Warrant', in E. Michaelson and A. Stokke (eds), *Lying: Language, Knowledge and Ethics*, Oxford: Oxford University Press.

Greco, J. (2012), 'Recent Work on Testimonial Knowledge', *American Philosophical Quarterly*, 49: 15–28.

Harris, P. (2012), *Trusting What You Are Told: How Children Learn from Others*, Cambridge, MA: Harvard University Press.

Harris, P. L. and Lane, J. D. (2014), 'Infants Understand How Testimony Works', *Topoi*, 33: 443–58.

Henderson, D. (2008), 'Testimonial Belief and Epistemic Competence', *Noûs*, 42: 190–221.

Henderson, D. and Graham, P. (2017a), 'Epistemic Norms and the "Epistemic Game" They Regulate: The Basic Structured Epistemic Costs and Benefits', *American Philosophical Quarterly*.

Henderson, D. and Graham, P. (2017b), 'A Refined Account of the "Epistemic Game": Epistemic Norms, Temptations and Epistemic Cooperation', *American Philosophical Quarterly*.

Hetherington, S. (2016), *Knowledge and the Gettier Problem*, Cambridge: Cambridge University Press.

Hinchman, E. (2014), 'Assurance and Warrant', *Philosophers' Imprint*, 14: 1–58.

Insole, C. J. (2000), 'Seeing Off the Local Threat to Irreducible Knowledge by Testimony', *The Philosophical Quarterly*, 50: 44–56.

Johnson, C. R. (2015), 'Testimony and the Constitutive Norm of Assertion', *International Journal of Philosophical Studies*, 23: 356–75.

Kelp, C. (2016), 'Assertion: A Function First Account', *Noûs*, online first: http://dx.doi. org/10.1111/nous.12153.

Kenyon, T. (2013), 'The Informational Richness of Testimonial Contexts', *The Philosophical Quarterly*, 63: 58–80.

Lackey, J. (1999), 'Testimonial Knowledge and Transmission', *The Philosophical Quarterly*, 49: 471–90.

Lackey, J. (2011), 'Testimonial Knowledge', in S. Bernecker and D. Pritchard (eds), *The Routledge Companion to Epistemology*, New York: Routledge.

Lyons, J. (1997), 'Testimony, Induction, and Folk Psychology', *Australasian Journal of Philosophy*, 75: 163–78.

Luper-Foy, S. (1984), 'The Epistemic Predicament: Knowledge, Nozickian Tracking, and Skepticism', *Australasian Journal of Philosophy*, 62: 26–49.

McDowell, J. (1994), 'Knowledge by Hearsay', in A. Chakrabarti and B. K. Matilal (eds), *Knowing from Words: Western and Indian Philosophical Analysis of Understanding and Testimony*, Dordrecht: Kluwer Academic.

McMyler, B. (2011), *Testimony, Trust, and Authority*, New York: Oxford University Press.

Mercier, H. and Sperber, D. (2011), 'Why Do Humans Reason? Arguments for an Argumentative Theory', *Behavioral and Brain Sciences*, 34: 57–74.

Michaelian, K. (2010), 'In Defence of Gullibility: The Epistemology of Testimony and the Psychology of Deception Detection', *Synthese*, 176: 399–427.

Miller, S. (2001), *Social Action: A Teleological Account*, Cambridge: Cambridge University Press.

Moran, R. (2005), 'Getting Told and Being Believed', *Philosopher's Imprint*, 5: 1–29.

Nozick, R. (1981), *Philosophical Explanations*, Cambridge, MA: Harvard University Press.

Owens, D. (2017), 'Human Testimony', in his *Normativity and Control*, Oxford: Oxford University Press.

Perrine, T. (2014), 'In Defense of Non-Reductionism in the Epistemology of Testimony', *Synthese*, 191: 3227–3237.

Pettit, P. (1990), 'Virtus Normativa: Rational Choice Perspectives', *Ethics*, 100: 725–755.

Pritchard, D. (2005), *Epistemic Luck*, Oxford: Clarendon Press.

Ross, A. (1986), 'Why Do We Believe What We Are Told?' *Ratio*, 1: 69–88.

Russell, B. (1948). *Human Knowledge: Its Scope and Limits*, London: George Allen & Unwin.

Rysiew, P. (2007), 'Beyond Words: Communication, Truthfulness, and Understanding', *Episteme*, 4: 285–304.

Schmitt, F. (2010), 'The Assurance View of Testimony', in A. Haddock, A. Millar, and D. Pritchard (eds), *Social Epistemology*, Oxford: Oxford University Press.

Shieber, J. (2009), 'Locke on Testimony: A Reexamination', *History of Philosophy Quarterly*, 26: 21–41.

Shieber, J. (2014), 'Against Credibility', *Australasian Journal of Philosophy*, 90: 1–18.

Shieber, J. (2015), *Testimony: A Philosophical Introduction*, New York: Routledge.

Shogenji, T. (2006), 'A Defense of Reductionism about Testimonial Justification', *Noûs*, 40: 331–46.

Sosa, E. (1999), 'How to Defeat Opposition to Moore', *Philosophical Perspectives*, 13: 141–53.

Sperber, D. (2013), 'Speakers Are Honest Because Hearers Are Vigilant: Reply to Kourken Michaelian', *Episteme*, 10: 61–71.

Sperber, D., Clement, F., Heintz, C., Mascaro, O., Mercier, H., Origgi, G., and Wilson, D. (2010), 'Epistemic Vigilance', *Mind and Language*, 25: 359–93.

Tomasello, M. (2009), *Why We Cooperate*, Cambridge: The MIT Press.

van Cleve, J. (2006), 'Reid on the Credit of Human Testimony', in J. Lackey and E. Sosa (eds), *The Epistemology of Testimony*, Oxford: Clarendon Press.

Welbourne, M. (1986), *The Community of Knowledge*, Aberdeen: Aberdeen University Press.

Wright, S. (2016), 'The Transmission of Knowledge and Justification', *Synthese*, 193: 293–311.

Zollman, K. J. S. (2015), 'Modeling the Social Consequences of Testimonial Norms', *Philosophical Studies*, 172: 2371–83.

7

Knowledge-How and Perceptual Learning

Berit Brogaard

1. Introduction

Following Gilbert Ryle, it has been common in the contemporary literature on knowledge-how to distinguish between intellectualism and anti-intellectualism. According to the reductionist varieties of intellectualism defended by Jason Stanley and Timothy Williamson (2001) and Berit Brogaard (2007, 2008, 2009), knowledge-how simply reduces to knowledge-that. To a first approximation, s knows how to A iff there is a w such that s knows that w is a way to A. For example, Bartek knows how to ride a bicycle if and only if there is a way w such that Bartek knows that w is a way to ride a bicycle. John Bengson and Marc Moffett (2007) defend an anti-reductionist version of intellectualism which takes knowledge-how to require, in addition, that s understand the concepts involved in her belief.

According to the anti-intellectualist accounts originally defended by Gilbert Ryle (1971 [1946]) and many others after him (see, e.g., Carter and Pritchard 2015a), knowledge how to do something requires the possession of a practical ability the exercise of which will bring about the desired end result and need not involve knowing that a particular procedure is a way to reach the outcome. For example, Bartek knows how to ride a bicycle only if he has the ability to ride it. Furthermore, on the anti-intellectualist view, having this knowledge does not require that Bartek knows that w (for some w) is a way to ride a bicycle.

Here I start out by arguing that the standard way of differentiating intellectualism and anti-intellectualism rests on a mistake. It is not the possession of practical abilities that sets the two views apart. Nor is it their take on the issue of whether knowledge-how simply reduces to knowledge-that. Rather, the two positions are better seen as providing different answers to the question of whether knowledge-how requires implicit or explicit (personal-level) beliefs about a particular procedure that can lead to the desired outcome. Intellectualism is best understood as the view that knowledge-how *does* require a personal level mental state about a particular procedure, whereas anti-intellectualism is best understood as the view that it does not.

After articulating this alternative distinction between intellectualism and anti-intellectualism, I will argue that both views have currency but with respect to different types of knowledge-how. Some types of knowledge-how require having the ability to consciously access information about a procedure that will achieve a desired goal, for instance, knowing how to make Chana Masala by following a recipe, knowing how to make Google the default search engine in Safari, and knowing how to get from Coral Gables to Miami Beach by using a map. Another type of knowledge-how to do something does not require this type of conscious accessibility but is instead the result of expertise acquired through perceptual or proprioceptive learning. Examples of the latter include knowing how to ride a bicycle, knowing how to speak Spanish, knowing how to play chess at an expert level, and knowing how to determine the sex of a day-old chick.

2. Belief-based knowledge-how

There is a marginal use of 'know-how' which I will briefly mention only to set it aside. We might say about a former Olympic gymnast who is no longer performing but who is now teaching her own students that she knows how to perform a quadruple salchow, even if she can no longer do it herself. Likewise, we might say of someone who is bedridden but who has a good sense of directions that he knows how to complete a run from Brickell Key to South Beach, even though he cannot do it himself. These sorts of cases are not the main instances of knowledge-how at the centre of dispute between intellectualists and anti-intellectualists. In fact, one could sensitively maintain that without the relevant practical abilities, the individuals in question do not possess knowledge of how to perform the relevant activities.

There are other forms of knowledge-how that are not at the centre of dispute between intellectualists and anti-intellectualists. These are instances of knowledge-how, none of which require practical abilities to do anything but refers to the fact that the subject knows a fact without mentioning what the fact is, for instance, the knowledge referred to by claims such as 'Bartek knows how hot it is', 'Sebastian knows how old Anna is', and 'Michael knows how far Miami is from Orlando'. When we make these kinds of claims, we are not aiming to pick out instances of *knowledge how to do things*. Rather, we are making claims that are semantically on a par with statements such as 'Sarah Beth knows where the meeting is', 'Peter knows what Alex had for lunch', and 'Lisa knows who stole the Macbook Air'. Sarah Beth knows where the meeting is, just in case there is a location such that Sarah Beth knows that the meeting is at that location. Likewise, Sebastian knows how old Anna is, just in case there is an age such that Sebastian knows that Anna is that age. I shall not be concerned with this other type of knowledge-how here but shall focus exclusively on knowledge of how to do things.

We are left, then, with a type of knowledge-how that does indeed require the possession of practical abilities.[1] This may suggest that anti-intellectualism is correct and that intellectualism is not. This conclusion, however, is premature. Although the distinction between intellectualism and anti-intellectualism is typically articulated in terms of whether knowledge-how just is a form of knowledge-that and hence appears to depend on whether the knowledge state in question requires the possession of practical abilities or not, this is not in fact what distinguishes the two views. Stanley and Williamson (2001), for instance, hold that knowledge-how typically requires knowing that there is a way w such that w will lead to the desired end result under a certain practical mode that requires the possession of the relevant practical abilities. So, if the focus is on whether knowledge-how requires the possession of practical abilities, then there is no real dispute between intellectualism and anti-intellectualism (Levy forthcoming).

A more fruitful way to draw the distinction between intellectualism and anti-intellectualism is in terms of whether knowledge of how to do things requires belief-based knowledge. Intellectualism is best understood as the view that it does, whereas anti-intellectualism is best understood as the view that it does not.

Here, 'belief' should not be understood as referring only to the explicit belief that, for some procedure w, w is a way to do A. For the reductive intellectualist, a dispositional or implicit (true) belief that a certain procedure will lead to A, together with a justificatory ground for the belief and the relevant practical abilities, suffices for knowing how to do A. Note, however, that, in order for a mental state to count as a belief (whether dispositional, implicit, or explicit), the subject must be able to consciously access it. If a mental state or dispositional structure is inaccessible to consciousness, then it subsists only on a sub-personal level and hence does not count as a belief.

Following Daniel Dennett (1969: 93), the distinction between the personal level and sub-personal level is grounded in distinct kinds of explanations that one can provide for why people behave the way they do. The distinction is that between 'the explanatory level of people and their sensations and activities and the sub-personal level of brains and events in the nervous system' (ibid.). Personal-level explanations are distinctive kinds of explanation for persons:

> When we've said that a person's in pain, that she knows which bit of her hurts and that this is what's made her react in a certain way, we've said all that there is to say within the scope of the personal vocabulary ... If we look for alternative modes of explanation, we must abandon the explanatory level of people and their sensations and activities and turn to the sub-personal level of brains and events in the nervous system. (ibid.)

Although personal-level explanations may refer to a-rational mental states, like pain, they can also refer to mental states that are assessable for rationality, such as 'needs, desires, intentions and beliefs' (164). Sub-personal-level explanations, by contrast, are not concerned with normative properties such as that of being rational; they merely make reference to causal relations and mechanisms. As belief is a type of state that contributes to making behaviour intelligible in terms of norms of rationality, mental states or dispositional structures that are inaccessible to consciousness do not and cannot count as belief states. So, the intellectualist position, as originally stated, is best understood as maintaining that, in order for a subject to have knowledge of how to do A, a (personal-level) belief that a particular procedure can lead to *A* is required.

Some types of knowledge-how seem to satisfy this criterion. Consider a culinary novice *s* who is successfully cooking a potful of Chicken Tikka Masala for the first time by following a recipe that he believes will result in a potful of the famous Indian dish. It makes perfect sense to say that *s* knows how to cook Chicken Tikka Masala, even if he is no master chef and has to pay close attention to each step of the recipe in order to reach the desired outcome. In this case, *s* can be said to possess knowledge of how to cook the Indian dish only insofar as he is able to consciously access true information about a particular procedure that will lead to the desired end result. Although *s* would not be able to cook the Indian dish without having certain pre-existing practical abilities, such as following the recipe and adding ingredients to the pot, his knowledge of how to cook the dish is not the result of exercising enhanced perceptual or proprioceptive skills specific for the task at hand. A satisfactory explanation of why *s* added onion, tomato paste, cardamom, and chillies to the heated ghee in the pot would not need to cite any new ways that *s* is perceiving the world or is controlling various parts of his body. A personal-level explanation to the effect that *s* wanted to cook a potful of Chicken Tikka Masala and believed that following the steps in the recipe would lead to the desired outcome would be quite good enough.

As another example of a case where the intellectualist has the upper hand, consider Paul Snowdon's (2003: 11) example of a man in a room who lacks knowledge of how to get out, despite apparently having the ability to get out: A man is in a room, which, because he has not explored it in the least, he does, as yet, not know how to get out of. In fact, there is an obvious exit which he can easily open. He is perfectly able to get out, he can get out, but does not know how to (as yet). It seems perfectly all right to say that the man has the ability to get out of the room (he just has to look around) and yet it seems highly plausible that he doesn't know how to get out. He doesn't know how to get out because there presently is no way *w* such that he believes that *w* is a way to get out.

Snowdon uses the example to illustrate that the possession of practical abilities is not sufficient for knowledge-how. However, when Snowdon points out that the man 'is perfectly able to get out', he is using the expression 'ability' loosely. Snowdon is right that the man in question does not know how to get out but, while there is a sense in which he is able to get out (he has the practical abilities to complete the steps), there is another sense in which he is unable to get out. If asked by his mate whether he is able to get out, the man would be wise to answer 'no'. 'Ability' can thus be used in two different ways (Brogaard 2011). In one sense of the word, *s* has the ability to *A* just in case *s* has a true belief that represents a certain procedure that will lead to *A*, and *s* has the bodily capacities needed to carry out the procedure. In another sense, *s* has the ability to *A* just in case *s* has the bodily capacities to carry out a procedure, even though the procedure is unknown to him. The man in Snowdon's example does not have a belief that a particular procedure will allow him to get out; he merely has the bodily capacities. Only the first kind of ability suffices for knowledge-how in the intellectualist sense.

'Ability', of course, is frequently used in the second way in ordinary language. For example, we might say: 'Of course, you can swim, everyone can swim, you just have to learn it first' or 'Of course, she is perfectly able to walk, she just doesn't know how to yet, she is only eleven months old'. Or consider a variation on the man-in-the-room example. To get out, one must press a button behind the bookshelves, step on a particular floor plank, and yell 'out' three times. Even so, saying the following seems perfectly fine: 'Of course, the man is perfectly able to get out. He just has to press a button behind the bookshelves, step on a particular floor plank, and yell "out" three times.' However, in neither the original case nor the variation can we attribute to the agent a true belief that a particular procedure will lead to the desired outcome. Hence, the agents in these scenarios do not know how to get out (as yet). They have not yet internalized the relatively simple procedures which will lead to their escape.

Snowdon is thus right for some cases of knowledge-how: there are cases in which pre-existing bodily capacities do not suffice for know-how. In those cases, pre-existing bodily capacities must be combined with procedures that have been internalized by the agent on a personal level. But this internalization of a procedure is just another way of referring to the formation of an implicit or explicit belief concerning a procedure that can lead to the desired end result.

In cases like these where the knowledge-how requires internalizing a procedure on a personal level and where the knowledge-how therefore is belief-based, intellectualism seems to offer an adequate description of the acquired knowledge-how. This is not to say that knowledge-how, in these cases, straightforwardly reduces to knowledge-that (plus practical abilities) (see Bengson and Moffett 2011; Brogaard 2011; Cath 2011, 2015; Carter and Pritchard 2015a,b,c). As I have argued in previous work (Brogaard 2011), the justificatory ground needed to turn a true belief that carrying out a particular procedure will lead to the desired outcome into knowledge how to reach the desired outcome may simply consist in having the practical abilities required to successfully follow the particular procedure.[2]

There are other cases of knowledge-how, however, in which we know how to do things, not as a result of being able to consciously access information about a procedure that will lead to a desired end result but rather as a result of exercising practical abilities acquired through perceptual or proprioceptive learning. I will turn to this type of knowledge-how next.

3. Perceptual and proprioceptive learning

Knowledge-how that ensues from perceptual learning does not consist in having conscious access to a belief that a set of steps can lead to a desired outcome. Perceptual learning, unlike other forms of learning, can be defined as 'experience-induced changes in the way perceivers pick up information' (Kellman and Garrigan 2009) or as extracting perceptual information that was previously unused (Gibson and Gibson 1955). In the case of perceptual learning, repeated exposure to a particular task makes us more attuned to the relevant features and structural relations that characterize the task in question.

The heightened attunement to features and structural relations in perceptual learning can virtually never be articulated by the learner. This suggests that the knowledge-how in question is not accompanied by any belief-like states to the effect that a particular procedure will lead to a desired end result. In fact, the processes that drives the knowledge-how seem best characterized as perceptual processes that occur on a sub-personal level (Dennett 1969) but that nonetheless can yield a reportable outcome.

Three mechanisms have been identified as responsible for perceptual learning (Goldstone 1998). One way that knowledge-how is acquired through perceptual learning is through imprinting. Through imprinting, detectors (also known as 'receptors') are developed that are specialized for stimuli or parts of stimuli. The receptive fields of the neurons that initially encode the stimulus adapt to become more sensitive to important features and structural relations. There is evidence for both perceptual learning via whole stimulus storage and perceptual learning via imprinting on specific features within a stimulus. Evidence for the former comes from cases where people's performance in perceptual tasks improves with increased exposure to a particular stimulus. It has been shown, for instance, that people can identify spoken words more accurately when they are spoken by familiar voices (Palmeri, Goldinger, and Pisoni 1993), and that doctors' diagnoses of skin disorders become more accurate when they are similar to previously presented cases (Brooks, Norman, and Allen 1991). There is also evidence of imprinting on parts of, or features of, a perceptual stimulus, leading to the generation of new building blocks for recognizing and describing stimuli (Schyns and Murphy 1994; Schyns et al. 1998).

A second way that knowledge is acquired through perceptual learning is through a development of the ability to differentiate low-features of a stimulus that once were perceived as fused together. Painters and vision scientists, for instance, have been shown to be better able to selectively attend to features of colour, such as hue, brightness, and saturation compared to non-experts (Burns and Shepp 1988). Presumably, what happens is that the learner learns to increase the attention paid to important perceptual features and to decrease attention paid to irrelevant features (Ahissar and Hochstein 1993). So, while the changes in perceptual abilities that take place in perceptual learning occur at stages of low-level processing in the brain, high-level attentional mechanisms are crucial in controlling these changes at the level of early processing. Perceptual learning effects of this kind thus reflect top-down influences on early vision (or other sensory systems), consisting in learning to attend to relevant stimuli (Saarinen and Levi 1995).

An oft-discussed example of knowledge-how that results from this latter type of perceptual learning is that of knowing how to determine the sex of chicks. Professional chicken sexers can classify 1,000 chicks per hour at over 98 per cent accuracy (Biederman and Shiffrar 1987). This means that they spend less than a second looking at each chick. Chicken sexers typically cannot articulate how they determine the sex of a chick. There is, indeed, a rough procedure that can be identified as underlying the perceptual abilities of chicken sexers. In typical cases, chicks, only a few hours old, are brought to the sexer in trays of 100. The chicken sexer holds the chick in the left hand and squirts its faecal contents in a container to clear the cloaca. He or she then exerts pressure to spread the surface of the cloaca upwards to expose what is called the 'bead'. The bead is the size of a pinhead. In typical cases, the male genitals look round and full, whereas the female genitalia look either pointed or flat.

There are, however, lots of exceptions to the typical cases; so chicken sexers implicitly use a number of different rules for determining the sex of chicks. For instance, male chicks sometimes (but not always) have larger genitalia than female chicks. Sometimes, additional pressure needs to be applied to obtain the critical contour information needed to determine the sex of the chick. This may explain why the success rate of experts who have only pictures to go by drops to 72 per cent.

A third way that knowledge-how is acquired through perceptual learning is through unitization, which may seem to be the opposite of differentiation. Whereas differentiation divides wholes into more differentiated features, unitization integrates parts into single units or chunks. This is typically what happens when people become expert chess players. Whereas novices are only able to encode the position of the individual chess pieces in long-term memory, expert chess players encode chess configurations. The basic unit encoded in long-term memory is the 'chunk', which consists of a configuration of pieces that are frequently encountered together and that are related by type, colour, role, and position (Chase and Simon 1973a,b). The number of figurations that the expert player have stored in long-term memory can be as high as 300,000 (Gobet and Simon 2000). The chunks can also be encoded in a combined form known as 'templates' (Gobet and Simon 1996).

Knowledge-how that is the result of expertise based on perceptual learning is not belief-based. It is grounded in cellular changes to areas of low-level sensory processing in the brain. This has been studied, for instance, in the case of Vernier acuity (Kellman and Garrigan 2009). In a standard Vernier task, two vertical lines, one above the other, are shown on each trial, and the participant is supposed to determine whether the upper line is to the left or to the right of the lower line. Vernier acuity is incredibly precise even without training. Some individuals can accurately detect misalignments smaller than ten arc secs, which is less than the diameter and spacing of retinal cone receptors (Westheimer and McKee 1978). It is believed that these individuals detect the misalignment by relying on cortical processing (Hennig et al. 2002). This ability is also known as 'hyperacuity' (Westheimer 1975). Radically enhanced Vernier acuity, and even hyperacuity, can be achieved through perceptual learning trials. Eight thousand trials have been shown to lead to up to a sixfold decrease in detection threshold (Saarinen and Levi 1995; Kellman and Garrigan 2009).

In these visual learning tasks, training appears to yield a kind of 'fine tuning' at the early stages of visual processing underlying the tasks (McKee and Westheimer 1978; Saarinen and Levi 1995). These changes in the neural structure of visual processing likely owes in part to top-down influences on early vision, consisting in learning to attend to relevant stimuli (Saarinen and Levi 1995).

As these processes are grounded in structural changes in early visual processing that are inaccessible to consciousness, the knowledge-how acquired in this way is not belief-based but is based primarily on expertise acquired through perceptual learning. This type of knowledge-how contrasts with the type discussed in the previous section. Recall that, if we were to ask why the novice *s* added onion, tomato paste, cardamom, and chillies to the heated ghee in the pot, it would suffice to provide a personal-level explanation to the effect that he did this because he wanted to cook a potful of Chicken Tikka Masala and he believed that these step were necessary to reach the desired outcome. But were we to ask why the chicken sexer squeezed the chick in the way he did, we could not offer the personal-level explanation that he wanted to determine its sex and he believed that squeezing it just as little or as much as he did was necessary in order to reach the desired outcome. What drives the acquisition of know-how in cases of perceptual learning is the exercise of enhanced perceptual abilities, not the subject's beliefs about which steps will lead to the desired outcome. So, for cases of knowledge-how that are based on perceptual learning, anti-intellectualism provides a better model than intellectualism of the acquired knowledge-how.

A special case of perceptual learning is proprioceptive learning (Bilodeau and Bilodeau 1961; Krakauer, Ghilardi, and Ghez 1999; Dayan and Cohen 2011; Avraamides, Sarrou, and Kelly 2014). Proprioception is a perceptual sense of the relative position of different parts of one's body and the effort required in order to perform certain movements. It is 'perceptual' in the sense that it consists of sensory signals about body parts and their movements provided by receptors in muscles, tendons, and joints. Knowing how to walk, write, ride a bicycle, or perform a quadruple salchow is the result of expertise obtained through extensive proprioceptive learning and muscle memory. So is the ability to enter your password to unlock your computer without having to think about it, and indeed sometimes even without possessing the ability to verbally reproduce the password.

Once proprioceptive knowledge has been acquired, it can be retained over extended periods of time or forgotten (Dayan and Cohen 2011). Retention typically owes to changes in the brain's grey and white matter. An increase in grey matter has been found in the occipital and parietal lobes of the brain following six weeks of juggling practice (Scholz et al. 2009), in the bilateral occipito-temporal cortex after seven days of juggling practice (Driemeyer et al. 2008), and in parieto-frontal regions following two weekly practice sessions in a whole-body balancing task (Taubert et al. 2010).

As processes that are grounded in structural changes in the brain's grey matter are inaccessible to consciousness, the knowledge-how acquired on the basis of these changes is not belief-based. Rather, this type of knowledge-how is acquired as a result of proprioceptive learning and related motor skill learning. What drives the acquisition of know-how in these cases is the acquisition of new proprioceptive abilities as well as new motor abilities. So, for these cases of know-how, anti-intellectualism provides a better model than intellectualism does of the knowledge how to do things.

4. Conclusion

There has been a lot of recent debate about whether knowledge how to do things is best accounted for on an intellectualist or an anti-intellectualist model. On the standard way of distinguishing between the two views, intellectualism is the view that knowledge how to do something requires knowing that a particular procedure will bring about the desired outcome, whereas anti-intellectualism is the view that knowledge-how to do something requires practical abilities, the exercise of which will bring about the desired outcome. In this chapter I have argued that there is a better way of drawing the distinction between intellectualism and anti-intellectualism. A closer look at different types of knowledge-how reveals that there are two types of knowledge-how, and that different models are required to account for them. One type of knowledge-how requires the acquisition of an explicit or implicit (true) belief that a particular procedure will lead to the desired end result, together with pre-existing practical abilities to follow the procedure. The other type of knowledge-how does not require any belief that a particular procedure will lead to the desired outcome but requires the ability to exercise skills grounded in perceptual or proprioceptive learning.

A culinary novice may correctly be said to know how to cook a potful of Chicken Tikka Masala if he is able to successfully follow a recipe that he correctly believes will lead to the desired end result. In addition to the belief that following the recipe will result in a potful of Chicken Tikka Masala, he will also need to rely on pre-existing practical abilities to follow each step (e.g. the ability to add opinion to the pot). Intellectualism offers a good account of this type of knowledge-how.

In order for someone to possess the knowledge of how to determine the sex of a chick, on the other hand, one need not know each step of the procedure that can lead to this outcome. A chicken sexer merely needs to have the expert vision and touch that can lead him to conclude with high accuracy that the chick is male or that it is female. For the latter type of knowledge-how, having the ability to consciously access information about the procedure that needs to be employed in order for the desired outcome to be brought about isn't required. So, anti-intellectualism provides a fair account of this type of knowledge-how.

It should be noted that, while one can differentiate two types of knowledge-how, most cases of knowledge-how presumably are mixed cases. Consider the case of riding a bicycle from Coconut Grove to Key Biscayne. In addition to the knowledge-how that ensues from proprioceptive learning, this feat might require, for instance, knowledge of how to retrieve the bike from the bike cellar and knowledge of how to use Google Maps to retrieve directions from Coconut Grove to Key Biscayne. The latter two pieces of knowledge-how may very well be a kind of belief-based knowledge-how rather than the result of utilizing information that stems from perceptual or proprioceptive learning.[3]

Notes

1   Following the literature in psychology, we can also refer to this as 'procedural knowledge' (Stadler 1989). Some limit the notion of procedural knowledge to the second type of knowledge-how, which I will deal with in the next section.

2 Consider the following case (Brogaard 2011). The faucet in Jason's apartment leaks. Jason finds a faucet manual in the kitchen drawer and fixes it. However, unbeknown to him, the manual was created by the previous owner's parrot who liked to step dance on the keyboard of the owner's old typewriter. Over the fifty years of step dancing the parrot had created a lot of nonsense but there was this one time where the parrot happened to hit the right keys and created something that made sense: 'the faucet manual'. The owner never looked at it but had left it in the kitchen drawer where Jason found it. Although Jason believes that there is a procedure that, if successfully followed, will lead him to fix the faucet, this belief is acquired via a faulty method. So Jason's knowledge is not based on warranted belief. Even so, it seems all right to say that Jason knows how to fix the faucet. In this case, the justificatory ground for Jason's belief that following the manual will fix the faucet consists in having the ability to follow the steps in the manual. As I have argued elsewhere (ibid.), having the ability to follow the steps in the manual can count as a justificatory ground because the true belief together with the abilities constitute a reliable way of reaching the desired outcome.

3 For helpful discussion of various older unpublished versions of this chapter as well as presentations of material herein, I am grateful to Yuri Cath, Brendan Balcerak Jackson, Otávio Bueno, Bartek Chomanski, Elijah Chudnoff, Dimitria Gatzia, Stephen Hetherington, Risto Hilpinen, Casey Landers, Azenet Lopez, Joshua Myers, Michael Slote, and Amie Thomasson as well as the students in an epistemology graduate seminar I co-taught with Elijah Chudnoff in the spring of 2016 at the University of Miami.

References

Ahissar, M. and Hochstein, S. (1993), 'Attentional Control of Early Perceptual Learning', *Proceedings of the National Academy of Sciences*, 90: 5718–22.

Avraamides, M. N., Sarrou, M., and Kelly, J. W. (2014), 'Cross-Sensory Reference Frame Transfer in Spatial Memory: The Case of Proprioceptive Learning', *Memory & Cognition*, 42: 496–507.

Bengson, J. and Moffett, M. A. (2007), 'Know-How and Concept-Possession', *Philosophical Studies*, 136: 31–57.

Bengson, J. and Moffett, M. A. (2011), 'Non-propositional Intellectualism', in J. Bengson and M. A. Moffett (eds), *Knowing How: Essays on Knowledge, Mind, and Action*, New York: Oxford University Press.

Biederman, I. and Shiffrar, M. M. (1987), 'Sexing Day-Old Chicks: A Case Study and Expert Systems Analysis of a Difficult Perceptual-Learning Task', *Journal of Experimental Psychology: Learning, Memory, and Cognition*, 13: 640–5.

Bilodeau, E. A. and Bilodeau, I. McD. (1961), 'Motor-Skills Learning', *Annual Review of Psychology*, 12: 243–80.

Brogaard, B. (2007), 'Attitude Reports: Do You Mind the Gap?' *Philosophy Compass*, 3: 93–118.

Brogaard, B. (2008), 'Knowledge-*The* and Propositional Attitude Ascriptions', *Grazer Philosophische Studien*, 77/1: 147–90.

Brogaard, B. (2009), 'What Mary Did Yesterday: Reflections on Knowledge-*Wh*', *Philosophy and Phenomenological Research*, 78: 439–67.

Brogaard, B. (2011), 'Knowledge-How: A Unified Account', in J. Bengson and M. A. Moffett (eds), *Knowing How: Essays on Knowledge, Mind, and Action*, New York: Oxford University Press.

Brooks, L. R., Norman, G. R., and Allen, S. W. (1991), 'Role of Specific Similarity in a Medical Diagnostic Task', *Journal of Experimental Psychology: General*, 120: 278–87.

Burns, B. and Shepp, B. E. (1988), 'Dimensional Interactions and the Structure of Psychological Space: The Representation of Hue, Saturation, and Brightness', *Perception & Psychophysics*, 43: 494–507.

Carter, J. A. and Pritchard, D. (2015a), 'Knowledge-How and Cognitive Achievement', *Philosophy and Phenomenological Research*, 91: 181–99.

Carter, J. A. and Pritchard, D. (2015b), 'Knowledge-How and Epistemic Value', *Australasian Journal of Philosophy*, 93: 799–816.

Carter, J. A. and Pritchard, D. (2015c), 'Knowledge-How and Epistemic Luck', *Noûs*, 49: 440–53.

Cath, Y. (2011), 'Knowing How without Knowing That', in J. Bengson and M. A. Moffett (eds), *Knowing How: Essays on Knowledge, Mind, and Action*, New York: Oxford University Press.

Cath, Y. (2015), 'Revisionary Intellectualism and Gettier', *Philosophical Studies*, 172: 7–27.

Chase, W. G. and Simon, H. A. (1973a), 'The Mind's Eye in Chess', in W. G. Chase (ed.), *Visual Information Processing: Proceedings of the Eighth Annual Carnegie Symposium on Cognition, Held at the Carnegie-Mellon University, Pittsburgh, Pennsylvania, May 19, 1972*, New York: Academic Press.

Chase, W. G. and Simon, H. A. (1973b), 'Perception in Chess', *Cognitive Psychology*, 4: 55–81.

Dayan, E. and Cohen, L. G. (2011), 'Neuroplasticity Subserving Motor Skill Learning', *Neuron*, 72: 443–54.

Dennett, D. C. (1969), *Content and Consciousness*, London: Routledge & Kegan Paul.

Driemeyer, J., Boyke, J., Gaser, C., Büchel, C., and May A. (2008), 'Changes in Gray Matter Induced by Learning – Revisited', *PLoS ONE*, 3: e2669.

Gibson, J. J. and Gibson, E. J. (1955), 'Perceptual Learning: Differentiation or Enrichment?' *Psychological Review*, 62: 32–41.

Gobet, F. and Simon, H. A. (1996), 'Templates in Chess Memory: A Mechanism for Recalling Several Boards', *Cognitive Psychology*, 31: 1–40.

Gobet, F. and Simon, H. A. (2000), 'Five Seconds or Sixty? Presentation Time in Expert Memory', *Cognitive Science*, 24: 651–82.

Goldstone, R. L. (1998), 'Perceptual Learning', *Annual Review of Psychology*, 49: 585–612.

Hennig, M. H., Kerscher, N. J., Funke, K., and Wörgötter, F. (2002), 'Stochastic Resonance in Visual Cortical Neurons: Does the Eye Tremor actually Improve Visual Acuity?' *Neurocomputing*, 44: 115–20.

Kellman, P. J. and Garrigan, P. (2009), 'Perceptual Learning and Human Expertise', *Physics of Life Reviews*, 6: 53–84.

Krakauer, J. W., Ghilardi, M.-F., and Ghez, C. (1999), 'Independent Learning of Internal Models for Kinematic and Dynamic Control of Reaching', *Nature Neuroscience*, 2: 1026–31.

Levy, N. (forthcoming), 'Embodied Savoir-Faire: Knowledge-How Requires Motor Representations', *Synthese*.

McKee, S. P. and Westheimer, G. (1978), 'Improvement in Vernier Acuity with Practice', *Perception & Psychophysics*, 24, 258–62.

Palmeri, T. J., Goldinger, S. D., and Pisoni, D. B. (1993), 'Episodic Encoding of Voice Attributes and Recognition Memory for Spoken Words', *Journal of Experimental Psychology: Learning, Memory, and Cognition*, 19: 309–28.

Ryle, G. (1971 [1946]). 'Knowing How and Knowing That', reprinted in his *Gilbert Ryle: Collected Papers (vol. 2)*, 212–25, New York: Barnes & Noble.

Saarinen, J. and Levi, D. M. (1995), 'Perceptual Learning in Vernier Acuity: What Is Learned?' *Vision Research*, 35: 519–27.

Scholz, J., Klein, M. C., Behrens, T. E. J., and Johansen-Berg, H. (2009), 'Training Induces Changes in White-Matter Architecture', *Nature Neuroscience*, 12: 1370–1.

Schyns, P. G. and Murphy, G. L. (1994), 'The Ontogeny of Part Representation in Object Concepts', in D. L. Medin (ed.), *The Psychology of Learning and Motivation, Volume 31: Advances in Research and Theory*, San Diego: Academic Press.

Schyns, P. G., Goldstone, R. L., and Thibaut, J. P. (1998), 'The Development of Features in Object Concepts', *Behavioral and Brain Sciences*, 21: 1–17.

Snowdon, P. (2003), 'Knowing How and Knowing That: A Distinction Reconsidered', *Proceedings of the Aristotelian Society*, 104: 1–29.

Stadler, M. A. (1989), 'On Learning Complex Procedural Knowledge', *Journal of Experimental Psychology: Learning, Memory, and Cognition*, 15: 1061–9.

Stanley, J. and Williamson, T. (2001), 'Knowing How', *The Journal of Philosophy*, 98: 411–44.

Taubert, M., Draganski, B., Anwander, A., Müller, K., Horstmann, A., Villringer, A., and Ragert, P. (2010), 'Dynamic Properties of Human Brain Structure: Learning-Related

Changes in Cortical Areas and Associated Fiber Connections', *Journal of Neuroscience*, 30: 11670–7.

Westheimer, G. (1975), 'Visual Acuity and Hyperacuity', *Investigative Ophthalmology and Visual Science*, 14: 570–2.

Westheimer, G. and McKee, S. P. (1978), 'Stereoscopic Acuity for Moving Retinal Images', *Journal of the Optical Society of America*, 68: 450–5.

8

Self-Knowledge

Markos Valaris

1. Introduction

Self-knowledge is a perennial concern of philosophers – indeed, Socrates in the *Phaedrus* claimed to be so busy complying with the Delphic command to 'know thyself' (γνῶθι σεαυτόν) that he had no time to spare for more remote subject matters (229e). Contemporary philosophers have been less concerned with *acquiring* self-knowledge (perhaps to their discipline's detriment!), but they have been very concerned with understanding the apparently uniquely human capacity for self-knowledge. By the end of this chapter, we will hopefully have some understanding of *why* the topic of self-knowledge has been so central to philosophy's concerns, and of how to approach it.

One useful way into these questions is by considering an increasingly influential *scepticism* about self-knowledge. Most philosophers believe that we possess a kind of knowledge about some parts of our minds which is different in kind from other kinds of knowledge, including our knowledge of the minds of others. However, there are also those who deny that our knowledge of our own minds is distinctive in any fundamental way. The ranks of these sceptics include Ryle (1949), Wittgenstein (1958), Dennett (1992), Schwitzgebel (2008, 2011), Carruthers (2009, 2011), Lawlor (2009), and Cassam (2011, 2014).[1] In Section 2, I introduce the sceptic's challenge, by contrasting it to a more optimistic – and, at least until recently, more widespread – view. In Section 3 I discuss some of the sceptical arguments in some depth. I do not think that the sceptics succeed in showing that we lack a distinctive capacity for self-knowledge; nevertheless, they may succeed in significantly narrowing down the range of live theoretical options for an account of self-knowledge.

2. A rough consensus, and a challenge

Let us begin by trying to home in on the kind of self-knowledge that is in question in contemporary philosophical debates. I clearly have a lot of knowledge about myself that philosophers would not find especially interesting. For example, there is nothing especially interesting about my knowledge that I have brown hair and weigh sixty-five kilograms – nothing interesting, that is, which is not shared by my knowledge of other contingent matters of fact. But both common sense and philosophical lore have it that *some* self-knowledge is not like that. For example, my knowledge

- that right now I am thinking about self-knowledge;
- that I am doing so because of a looming deadline;
- that at the same time I am wondering when it will be time to take a break for lunch;
- and that I have an annoying itch at the back of my neck

seem intuitively rather different. More generally, many have thought that each of us has a kind of epistemic access to certain facts about herself that is special along the following dimensions:

1 It is **privileged**, in the sense that it is epistemically *more secure* than other types of knowledge, including in particular the knowledge other people can have of those same facts about her.
2 It is **distinctive**, in that acquiring such knowledge does not involve the usual methods that we use to find out about contingent facts about our environment or about other people, such as perception and inference.

While the precise scope of special self-knowledge is itself a contested issue, our knowledge of *present mental states* figures centrally in most accounts of the specialness of self-knowledge.

Philosophers have ascribed different degrees and types of epistemic privilege to our knowledge of our own minds (see Alston 1971). These days, few philosophers think that there is any area of contingent matter of fact, including our own mental lives, regarding which we are *infallible*, that is, such that our judgements about it are guaranteed never to be mistaken.[2] And neither would many insist that there is any area of contingent matter of fact which is *luminous* (to use Williamson's [2000] term): that is, such that all facts in that area are knowable by us.[3] Even so, many do think that our access to facts about our present states of mind is *closer to* those ideals than our access to facts of other sorts.

Perhaps more central to contemporary debate, however, has been the idea that (some) self-knowledge is epistemically *distinctive*. Humans, even compared with other social primates, appear to be uniquely skilled at interpreting the behaviour of others in psychological terms, that is, by ascribing to them mental states such as beliefs, desires, and so on. Despite our excellent 'mindreading' skills, however, philosophers have generally thought that at least some of our knowledge of our own minds results from capacities that are different in kind from those involved in our knowledge of the minds of other people. While in order to know that *you* are in pain I need to interpret your behaviour, it looks like I can know that *I* am in pain *directly*, without interpretation. Some theorists seek to explain this (alleged) fact through a special 'self-scanning' mechanism, along the lines of Locke's (1690) 'inner sense' (Armstrong 1968; Lycan 1996; Nichols and Stich 2003); others appeal to a special quasi-perceptual relation of 'acquaintance' (Russell 1912; Gertler 2001, 2011b; BonJour 2003; Chalmers 2003; Pitt 2004). Still others tie self-knowledge more closely to our capacity for judgement or reasoning (Shoemaker 1996; Burge 1996, 1998; Peacocke 1996, 1998; Moran 2001, 2003; Boyle 2009; Fernández 2013; Valaris 2013). These differences will matter later on; for now, note that each of these views attempts, in its own way, to capture the thought that some of our self-knowledge is *distinctive*.[4]

But why should we accept that we have distinctive and privileged self-knowledge? While sceptical voices have been around for a while, they have been gaining ground in recent years. Sceptics tend to argue their case in two steps. The first step, meant to 'level the playing field' (as Carruthers [2011: 42] puts it), consists in highlighting the *limits* of self-knowledge. As sceptics point out, it is easy to find examples where our attempts at self-knowledge apparently fail, sometimes badly and pervasively. Here is a small selection, which could easily be expanded:

- We may be ignorant of, or mistaken about, our standing beliefs or other propositional attitudes. Peacocke (1998) (not himself a sceptic) describes the case of a university professor who sincerely claims not to believe that degrees from countries other than her own are inferior, and yet whose behaviour on the admissions committee shows systematic bias against applicants from other countries. And it may seem natural to describe the agent as, despite her protestations, really *believing that* degrees from countries other than her own are inferior.
- We may be ignorant of, or mistaken about, our *emotional states*. Schwitzgebel (2008: 252) describes a case in which his wife takes him

to be angry. He starts out by denying it, but upon reflection he comes to acknowledge that he is, indeed, angry. It is natural to say that Schwitzgebel's wife was *right* and he was *wrong* all along. But this implies that Schwitzgebel failed to recognize his own anger.

- We may be ignorant of, or mistaken about, the *motives* of our actions. Common sense has long recognized that people can be good at disguising the deeper motives of their actions from themselves – Bob may honestly believe he is acting out of a simple desire to help his daughter overcome a challenge, when in fact he is undermining her self-confidence, and ensuring her continuing dependence on him. Moreover, as in the earlier cases, external observers may be better placed to recognize Bob's true motives than he is.

- Perhaps more surprisingly, there is evidence that we can be wrong about our motives even in trivial cases. In a famous experiment, Nisbett and Wilson (1977) had subjects choose among what were, unbeknown to them, identical pairs of stockings. The best predictor of the subjects' choices was the relative position of each pair in the display (the more to the right an item was, the likelier it was to be chosen). However, when asked for their reason for choosing as they did, subjects sought to give substantive, and apparently spurious, explanations (e.g. in terms of apparent sheen or quality). Subjects, in other words, not only failed to recognize the factors really influencing their choice, they *invented* confabulatory explanations.[5]

- We may even be massively and pervasively mistaken about the subjective character of our own experience. Well-documented phenomena such as inattentional and change blindness show that it is easy to miss even prominent features of the visual scene (Mack and Rock 1998; Simons and Chabris 1999). Moreover, outside of a small central area, our eyes have very poor spatial resolution and are colour-blind. Taken on their own, of course, such facts do not undermine our claims to self-knowledge. However, as Dennett (2002) points out, people are *surprised* when those facts are demonstrated to them. And this does suggest a lack self-knowledge: we naively believe that our visual experiences are more detailed than they actually are.[6]

Now, merely demonstrating cases where we lack self-knowledge is not by itself a serious blow against the consensus view since, as we saw, contemporary philosophers are careful to circumscribe the ways in which our epistemic access to our own mind is supposed to be privileged. Thus the consensus view is compatible with even widespread lack of self-knowledge. But this is where the second step in the sceptic's argument comes in. A theory of our capacity for self-knowledge must *explain* both its successes *and* its failures. And, the sceptics argue, the best explanation of the particular patterns of success and failure we observe is inconsistent with the consensus view. More specifically, they argue for rejecting any deep distinction between the way in which we know our own minds and the way in which we know the minds of others. In both cases, our knowledge rests on an inferential process of *interpretation* (Dennett 1992; Carruthers 2011; Cassam 2014).[7]

Obviously, it is the second step in the sceptics' argument that is the contentious one. In the next section we will consider some of the ways in which it has recently been defended.

3. Assessing the case for scepticism

As pointed out above, everyone – sceptic and non-sceptic alike – needs to accept that our capacity for self-knowledge can fail. The question is whether those failures show that our capacity for self-knowledge is no different from our capacity to know things in other domains (including the minds of others), or whether they are compatible with (and perhaps even support) the consensus view that our capacity for self-knowledge is distinctive and privileged. In this section I will consider three recent attempts to put failures of our capacity for self-knowledge to use in support of scepticism. Although there are ways to resist each of these arguments, there are still important lessons to be learned from them.

3.1 Knowledge of the attitudes

Carruthers' (2011) book *The Opacity of Mind* is a sustained attack on the consensus view on self-knowledge. Carruthers does not deny that we have special access to *some* of our mental states; indeed, he thinks that some version of the consensus view is true of our knowledge of our sensory (perceptual, memory-based, or spontaneously generated) states (52–4, 80), and perhaps for certain affective states (135). But, he argues, our access to our own attitudinal states – including beliefs, desires, intentions, and the like – is not in principle different from our access to other people's attitudes, and is based on interpretation.

Carruthers' argument draws on empirical work on 'global workspace' models of cognitive architecture, in the tradition of Baars (1993). On such models there is a central cognitive resource, the global workspace, whose contents are globally 'broadcast' to a variety of more specialized systems – for example, systems for judging, planning, and decision-making. Among those 'consumer systems' is the 'mindreading' system which, on Carruthers' approach, is the system responsible for all mental state attributions.

Given this setup, how could we determine whether we have a capacity for distinctive knowledge of our own attitudes? Carruthers (2011) answers as follows. First, he argues that current evidence suggests that all information broadcast in the global workspace must be in sensory form, or at least 'bound up with' representations that are in such form (73–6). Second, since most of our beliefs and other attitudes are not obviously related to any sensory representations (e.g. no sensory state normally accompanies my belief that first-order logic is complete), Carruthers claims that this bars them from being globally broadcast. In the absence of any reason to think that the mindreading system has massive side-connectivity to all our attitudinal systems (52–4), this implies that the mindreading system has *no direct access* to most of our attitudes. Finally, Carruthers argues, if the mindreading system has no direct access to our attitudes, we do not have direct, non-interpretive access to our own attitudes.

But the argument can be questioned. Many have argued that a core characteristic of beliefs and other attitudes is their 'inferential promiscuity', that is, the ability of each of them to combine arbitrarily with virtually any other in reasoning (Stich 1978; Evans 1982; Fodor 2001). This raises two distinct challenges for Carruthers' approach. To begin with, there is a challenge to the first step of his argument: given that beliefs and other attitudes are inferentially promiscuous in the sense indicated, why isn't this evidence that, contrary to what Carruthers maintains, non-sensory states can *also* be globally broadcast?[8]

Carruthers (2011: 167–8) anticipates this challenge. He does not deny that beliefs and other attitudes are inferentially promiscuous. Instead, he responds to the challenge by suggesting a particular *mechanism* by means of which they could be so, while maintaining the constraint of a sensory-only global broadcast system. Specifically, he suggests that attitudes can be globally broadcast only to the extent that they are 'clothed in' sensory garb, for example, in inner speech (a form of auditory imagery). We globally broadcast our attitudes by *talking* to ourselves. This explains, according to Carruthers, how our attitudes can be inferentially promiscuous, consistently with an exclusively sensory global workspace.

But even granting this point, inferential promiscuity remains a problem for the *second* step in Carruthers' argument. For, even if attitudes are only globally broadcast in sensory garb, it remains the case that *they are globally broadcast*; so what would block their direct, non-interpretive self-attribution?

It is to the point here to consider Carruthers' concession that what he calls 'perceptually embedded judgments' can be non-interpretively self-ascribed (75). These are judgements that are 'bound up' with perceptions – for example, in a situation where it is true of me that I saw that my mother had entered the store, Carruthers suggests that my perceptual state incorporates something like a judgement to the effect that my mother entered the store (76). And, crucially, although such judgements are globally broadcast only in virtue of their sensory garb, this does not prevent them from being available for non-interpretive self-knowledge. What would stop other attitudes, then, clothed in sensory garb via inner speech, from being similarly non-interpretively self-ascribed?

Carruthers considers a proposal somewhat along these lines, in his discussion of 'expressivist' accounts of self-knowledge. His response is that speech, whether inner or outer, needs to be *interpreted* before it can be used as a basis for mental state attribution (84–96). We need, for example, to resolve ambiguities (given an utterance that contains the word 'bank', we need to decide whether the speaker is referring to a financial institution or the bank of a river), and to assess what attitude a given utterance expresses (is the speaker expressing a belief that the bank is open, or merely a hope?). The problem with this response, however, is that it undermines the attempt to use inner speech to explain the inferential promiscuity of the attitudes. When I form the intention to stop at the bank on my way home because I believe that I need to go to the bank today, my reasoning depends crucially both on the disambiguated propositional content of that belief and on the attitude I have to that content (merely *wondering* whether I need to go to the bank today would not lead me to form the intention). Does our ability to recover propositional content and attitude type from inner speech in the case of reasoning always involve interpretation, then? But if recovering content and attitude type from inner speech does not always involve interpretation, then Carruthers' attack on the consensus view of self-knowledge may be possible to resist.

There is an important point that deserves to be highlighted here. The reason why Carruthers' attack is less than conclusive is that our capacity for self-knowledge seems intimately connected to our capacity for *reasoning* – a point, as noted earlier, developed in different ways by a number of philosophers. Within this broad spectrum of views, one that has proven especially influential is the so-called *transparency* approach, often traced back to a famous passage by Evans (1982: 225):

> [I]n making a self-ascription of belief, one's eyes are, so to speak, or occasionally literally, directed outward – upon the world. If someone asks me 'Do you think there is going to be a third world war?', I must attend, in answering him, to precisely the same outward phenomena as I would attend to if I were answering the question 'Will there be a third world war?'

Different authors differ over important details, but the core idea is that I can treat a certain question about *myself* (viz. whether I believe that *P*) as 'transparent to' a question about the world – namely, whether *P*.[9] If I answer the *world*-directed question by judging that *P*, I am thereby entitled to answer the *self*-directed question by self-ascribing the belief that *P* (for versions of this story, see Gallois [1996]; Moran [2001]; Byrne [2005]; Fernández [2013]; Valaris [2013]). There is no further epistemic work (e.g. self-observation or interpretation) I need to engage in in order to be entitled to this self-ascription. In the terms we have been using in this section, we can put the point like this: whatever mechanisms make the judgement that *P* available for the purposes of world-directed reasoning also make it available for *self-ascription*. It is not clear that anything in Carruthers' model undermines this claim.

3.2 Knowledge of conscious experience

While Carruthers targets claims about our capacity to know our own attitudinal states, Schwitzgebel (2008, 2011) targets our capacity to know our own current conscious experiences. Schwitzgebel is less concerned with proposing a specific mechanism for our knowledge of conscious experience than with demonstrating that we are not nearly as reliable about them as we might have thought. In our earlier terminology, he targets *privilege* rather than distinctiveness. But while contemporary philosophers do not insist on the absolute privilege of self-knowledge, the claim that we are seriously unreliable with regard to our own conscious experiences may still seem extreme: even radical sceptics have tended to make an exception for our knowledge of our own conscious experiences. And yet, according to Schwitzgebel (2008: 247):

> Most people are poor introspectors of their own ongoing conscious experience. We fail not just in assessing the causes of our mental states or the processes underwriting them; and not just in our judgments about non phenomenal mental states like traits, motives, and skills; and not only when we are

distracted, or passionate, or inattentive, or self-deceived, or pathologically deluded, or when we're reflecting about minor matters, or about the past, or only for a moment, or where fine discrimination is required … There are major lacunae in our self-knowledge that are not easily filled in, and we make gross, enduring mistakes about even the most basic features of our currently ongoing conscious experience … even in favourable circumstances of careful reflection.

In support of this claim Schwitzgebel offers a wealth of examples where our attempts to know the identity, structure, or character of our own conscious experiences appear to fail, often in surprising and dramatic ways. These include the colour of dreams (Schwitzgebel 2011: 1–16), the 'flatness' or otherwise of visual experience (17–34), and the character of experiences of thinking (Schwitzgebel 2008: 257–9).

Schwitzgebel's examples deserve much more discussion than I can give them here. However, even granting the correctness of his characterization of them, there are reasons to doubt that Schwitzgebel succeeds in establishing his conclusion. Here is Schwitzgebel again, wrapping up his discussion:

> Descartes, I think, had it quite backwards when he said the mind – including especially current conscious experience – was better known than the outside world. The teetering stacks of paper around me, I'm quite sure of. My *visual experience* as I look at those papers, my *emotional experience* as I contemplate the mess, my *cognitive phenomenology* as I drift in thought, staring at them – of these, I'm much less certain.
>
> …
>
> The tomato is stable. My visual experience as I look at the tomato shifts with each saccade, each blink, each observation of a blemish, each alteration of attention, with the adaptation of my eyes to lighting and colour. (267; emphases in the original)

But if *this* is the lesson of Schwitzgebel's argument, then it falls short of showing that we are 'poor introspectors of our own ongoing conscious experience'.

The issue has to do with what exactly is meant when we talk about knowing our own conscious experience. 'Experience' is just a term for certain events in the lives of complex organisms such as ourselves. But one striking feature of such events – and part of what makes them philosophically interesting – is that they are events of the organism's *being aware of* something or other. Visual experiences, for example, make us aware of visible features of environment, while kinaesthetic experiences of the disposition and motion of our own limbs.

This is known as the 'intentionality' of experience. And, as philosophers have explicitly recognized at least since Moore (1903), it is generally much easier for us to access the *intentional* features of our experience than the non-intentional ones. Moore himself considers the example of having a sensation of blue, and writes: 'When we try to introspect the sensation of blue, all we can see is the blue: the other element [i.e. the sensation itself] is as if it were diaphanous' (41). Following Moore, this phenomenon has been dubbed the 'diaphanousness' or 'transparency' of experience (and is related to, though distinct from, the 'transparency' approach to self-knowledge mentioned above). It has received much discussion in recent work. Here is Tye (1995: 30), for instance, discussing an experience of a blue square:

> Intuitively, you are directly aware of blueness and squareness as features of an external surface. Now shift your gaze inward and try to become aware of your experience itself, inside you, apart from its objects ... The task seems impossible: one's awareness seems always to slip through the experience to blueness and squareness, as instantiated together in an external object. In turning one's mind inward to attend to the experience, one seems to end up concentrating on what is outside again, on external features or properties.

The thought that both Moore and Tye are expressing is that it is much easier for us to access the *intentional* features of our visual experiences – that is, the way they represent the world as being – than their non-intentional or 'intrinsic' features. Moreover, the same thing is true even in the case of pains and other bodily feelings (Harman 1990: 40):

> Consider the experience of having a pain in your right leg. It is very tempting to confuse features of what you experience as happening in your leg with intrinsic features of your experience. But the happening in your leg that you are presented with is the intentional object of your experience; it is not the experience itself. The experience itself is not located in your right leg. If the experience is anywhere specific, it is somewhere in your brain.

Now, Harman and Tye (but not Moore) think that we have no first-personal access at all to the non-intentional features of experience. Many have found this claim too strong (Block 2003; Kind 2003). For present purposes, however, the crucial point is that even this claim is compatible with recognizing a robust and reliable capacity for knowing *the intentional* features of own conscious experiences: it may be hard for you to focus on your *sensation* of blue, for example, but it is not similarly hard for you to know that you are *visually aware* of something blue.

Furthermore, it is not clear that Schwitzgebel's argument can take him further than this. The intrinsic features of Schwitzgebel's experience of the tomato may be constantly shifting and unstable, but Schwitzgebel is, throughout, in a position to know that he is visually aware of the tomato. (Indeed, if Schwitzgebel were to doubt that he is visually aware of the tomato, he would likely have to doubt the presence of the tomato as well.) And the point of course generalizes: subjects thinking about the Prince of Wales (Schwitzgebel 2008: 258) may find it hard to introspect the intrinsic features of their events of thinking, but they will *not* find it hard to know *that they are thinking about the Prince of Wales*. There is no general threat of scepticism here.

There are, I think, two important points that emerge from this discussion. The first concerns the role of introspection in psychology and philosophy of mind. Sometimes introspection is marshalled to adjudicate debates regarding the *structure* of experience. Schwitzgebel mentions the debate on 'cognitive phenomenology'. Almost everyone agrees that there is such a thing as the *experience of thinking* that, for example, the sky is blue. But does this experience consist merely in inwardly rehearsing the sentence 'the sky is blue'? Or is there another, non-sensory component to the experience? Now, if introspection *were* a reliable guide to the structural features of experience, we would expect that – setting aside the possibility of massive variability across different human subjects – this debate would be easy to resolve: we would just have to introspect our own experiences of thinking. As Schwitzgebel points out, however, there is no agreement on this question (257–9). But, of course, this is exactly what we should have expected, given the diaphanousness of experience: when we try to focus on our experience of thinking that the sky is blue, we end up focusing on *the sky's being blue* – the event of thinking itself proves elusive. Similar difficulties can be expected to attend other attempts to use introspection to settle disputes about structural features of experience.

The second point, which is more germane to present concerns, has to do with what we should expect from a theory of self-knowledge. Our considerations suggest that we should expect it to be *outward-looking*, in a sense that parallels our earlier discussion of the transparency approach to our knowledge of our own attitudes. We are creatures with a subjective point of view on the world. We take the world to be a certain way, and this in turn helps explain how we reason and act. What the diaphanousness of experience suggests is that our capacity to know our own conscious experience is, in the first instance, just a capacity to reflectively access those features of our experience that contribute to our subjective take on the world – that is, its *intentional* features.[10] Indeed, following in the spirit of the transparency approach discussed in the previous section, we may suggest that it is *because* those features of our experience contribute to our take on the world (and so to reasoning and action) that they are also available for self-knowledge.

3.3 Knowledge of causes and dispositions

A different source of scepticism may be reflection on the metaphysics of mental states. According to mainstream views in contemporary philosophy of mind, many (perhaps all) mental states are to be understood in broadly functional terms, that is, in terms of their typical causes and effects. For example, a partial characterization of what it is to believe that there is beer in the fridge would involve a disposition to walk to the fridge, given that one wants a beer. But this, one might think, poses problems for the idea that we can have non-interpretive knowledge of our own minds, for the standard ways we have for coming to know the causal properties of things is through inference and theorizing. For example, while I may directly *see* the colour and shape of a vase, I cannot similarly just see its fragility – I can only *infer* that the vase is fragile, on the basis of past experience and background knowledge. Similarly, one might argue, we can only know our own functional and dispositional states through some sort of theorizing.[11]

An argument of this sort is developed by Gertler (2011a: 70–9), who links it to the Humean claim that causal relations (and, by extension, causal properties) are not directly observed. The Humean claim can, of course, be questioned. But even setting this aside, it seems that the present argument only applies to approaches that treat our capacity for self-knowledge as relevantly similar to *observation*. Perhaps this is true of some inner sense and acquaintance theories; but there are, as we have already seen, other theories that do not treat self-knowledge as similar to observation in any relevant sense. On the transparency approach, as we saw, it is the capacities that make the belief that *P* available for use in reasoning that also make it available for the purposes of self-ascription. Nothing analogous to observation plays a role here. Gertler's argument does not seem to get purchase.

Authors such as Schwitzgebel (2010) and Cassam (2011) have argued that the dispositional nature of mental states poses a different sort of problem for transparency, however. As we saw, the basic idea of the transparency approach is that if I answer the world-directed question whether *P* by judging that *P*, I am thereby entitled to answer the *self*-directed question whether I believe that *P* by self-ascribing the belief that *P*. But, one might worry, this method is not guaranteed to give correct results, because *judging* that *P* does not guarantee *believing* that *P*. To adapt the example given earlier, a professor may judge that degrees from universities in countries other than her own are not inferior – and so, following transparency, self-ascribe the corresponding belief – while her behavioural dispositions point the other way. Cassam calls this the 'sticking problem'. Beliefs, as complex dispositional states, are habits of thought and action; and just as a smoking habit may be very hard to give up despite your judgement that you should give it up, beliefs may 'stick' and be unresponsive to our judgements.

Now, Cassam's (2011) point is not that the sticking problem shows that transparency is *unreliable*. He just takes it to show that self-ascribing attitudes through transparency involves the substantive theoretical assumption that, on any given occasion, my belief aligns with my judgement (557–61). More specifically, if I self-ascribe the belief that *P* on the basis of answering the question whether *P* in the affirmative, Cassam suggests that this is the result of (possibly unconscious) reasoning of the form 'I judge that *P*, and my beliefs generally align with my judgements; therefore, I believe that *P*'. But I think there is room to question this conclusion.

The first thing to note is that it is not actually so clear that the result that transparency gives in our example is false. Is it so clear the professor in our example does *not* believe that degrees from countries other than her own are not inferior? By hypothesis, she does not lack *all* dispositions associated with that belief – for instance, she is disposed to answer a direct question by asserting that such degrees are not inferior. It also seems plausible that she would use this claim as a premise for explicit reasoning, at least in some contexts. So perhaps the right description of the situation is that the professor harbours contradictory beliefs: perhaps she believes *both* that degrees from foreign universities are not inferior *and* that they are. Indeed, this interpretation would seem to be better able to capture our intuitive sense that the professor is conflicted. In that case the verdict delivered by transparency would be *true*, not false (though it would not constitute the whole truth of the matter).

The purpose of reinterpreting the example is not to insist that transparency will always give the right result: even its proponents do not claim that transparency is *infallible*. (And, as noted above, Cassam's claim is not that transparency is unreliable, but only that it relies on substantive presuppositions.) It is, rather, to highlight the possibility of an alternative diagnosis of the cases where transparency is contentious: they are cases in which the subject's take on the topic in question is *genuinely unsettled*. The problem is not that the subject has a settled belief which fails to align with her explicit judgement, but rather that she does not have a single settled belief to begin with (Schwitzgebel [2010] emphasizes the 'in-between' character of such cases as well). But then, perhaps the right conclusion to draw from Cassam's 'sticking problem' may be not that self-ascriptions via transparency rely on substantive presuppositions, but rather that they are liable to prove contentious in cases of internal conflict. This is plausible, but not especially threatening to proponents of transparency: after all, *all* ascriptions of belief to a subject in such a conflicted state are going to be contentious.

4. Conclusion

My aim in this chapter has been to introduce some central contemporary debates about self-knowledge, and to indicate what directions I think future research should pursue. As we have seen, sceptical voices have, in recent years, challenged the consensus view that humans possess a capacity for distinctive and privileged self-knowledge. I do not think that the sceptics succeed in establishing that we do not have such a capacity. But they do, I think, succeed in raising some important questions about what we should expect from a theory of self-knowledge. As I have tried to argue, sceptical arguments are most threatening against views that portray our capacity for self-knowledge as a special-purpose faculty for *observing* or *detecting* happenings inside ourselves. They seem to leave open, however, a rather different approach to self-knowledge.

On this approach, we start with the idea that humans are creatures with *subjective points of view* on the world, comprising our beliefs, desires, perceptions, and so on. Such points of view are clearly 'subjective' in one sense: namely, that they reflect only *our own* take on the world, which may be as mistaken as you like. But they are also 'subjective' in a *different* sense: they *matter* to us, because they are what we draw upon in reasoning, decision-making, and action. As I understand the transparency approach, its main suggestion is that we do not need to look further than the set of capacities involved in this second sense of 'subjectivity' – essentially, our capacity to do things for reasons – in order to understand the kind of self-knowledge philosophers have been so interested in. The thought here is that, at least in creatures (such as ourselves) capable of using the first person and concepts of mental states, possession of a subjective point of view is *inseparable from* a capacity to reflect upon that very point of view itself, *as* one's own point of view. Our capacity for self-knowledge is not something extra, over and above our world-directed cognitive capacities; it is just a *reflective use* of those same cognitive capacities.

This is the thread I have tried to follow throughout the discussion of the various sceptical arguments. Carruthers, as we saw, owes us an argument for the claim that the capacities that make our attitudes non-interpretively available for inference do not suffice for making them available for self-ascription. Similarly, Schwitzgebel fails to show that our judgements regarding the intentional features of our experiences – those, that is, that contribute to our point of view on our environment – are massively unreliable. And, finally, this was the conclusion of our discussion of Cassam's argument as well: transparency is liable to fail just on those occasions where one's first-order view about a certain matter is unsettled as well. There is, of course, much more to say, and challenges remain in developing such an approach to self-knowledge. But the fact that it can accommodate these recent sceptical challenges would seem to be an important point in its favour.

Finally, there is a further point that deserves mention here. The sceptics, as we have seen, are quite right to highlight the *limits* of privileged and distinctive self-knowledge. The transparency approach is not a way to *overcome* those limits, but rather to learn to live within them. But the existence of these limits means that there is a lot about ourselves, both as individual persons and as members of the species *homo sapiens*, that we cannot know 'from the inside', in the privileged and distinctive way suggested by transparency. In those areas, our knowledge of ourselves will need to rely on self-interpretation, the testimony of others, and the sciences of the mind.

Notes

1 The label of 'sceptic' requires qualification. None of these authors are sceptics in the sense of *denying that we know* quite a bit about ourselves. They are only sceptical of the idea that our capacity for self-knowledge is *epistemologically privileged* or *distinctive*.

2 There are views according to which self-knowledge is constitutively linked to the states it is about. For instance, according to Shoemaker (1990), believing something metaphysically *includes* believing that you believe that thing, while Gertler (2001) and Chalmers (2003) both claim that we have certain ways of thinking about our own experiences that require that we *actually undergo* those experiences. Such views may support restricted versions of infallibility. Sometimes it is suggested that we treat each other's introspective reports as *incorrigible*, that is, as not amenable to correction (Shoemaker 1963; Rorty 1979; Dennett 2002). This seems false as an

empirical matter ('come on, it doesn't *really* hurt!' is something parents of small
children frequently say, and not because they suspect their children of dishonesty), but
even if it were true, the inference from incorrigibility to infallibility is not a valid one.

3 Williamson (2000) himself argues that the limitations of our capacities for
discrimination entail that no domain of fact is luminous for us. This argument has
been challenged by a number of philosophers, including Brueckner and Fiocco
(2002), Neta and Rohrbaugh (2004), Weatherson (2004), Berker (2008), Wong
(2008), Cohen (2010), and Vogel (2010). We cannot go into this here.

4 These proposals need not be *exclusive* of each other: we might have more than
just one route to self-knowledge. Boyle (2009) and Schwitzgebel (2011), arguing
from different perspectives, both recommend pluralism, while Byrne (2011)
recommends uniformity. It also goes without saying that proponents of distinctive
self-knowledge acknowledge that we can, and often do, acquire knowledge about
ourselves through *non-distinctive* means as well – for example, through self-
observation, self-interpretation, and the testimony of those around us.

5 The search for unconscious factors influencing behaviour has been a hot topic
in psychology. Some of this research – including landmark studies on 'priming'
effects, such as Bargh, Chen, and Burrows (1996) – is currently under a cloud,
as it has failed replication (Doyen et al. 2012; Pashler and Wagenmakers 2012).
Nevertheless, few would deny that our knowledge of the motives for our actions
has limits.

6 Even this can be contested, however. As Noë (2002, 2004) points out, we may
interpret naïve subjects as holding that they have visual experiences of a *richly
detailed world*, not that they have *richly detailed visual experiences*. This claim is not
undermined by the facts just cited.

7 The sceptics may admit that there is a sense in which we are at an epistemic
advantage when it comes to knowing our own minds, simply because in our own
case we typically have a richer and more comprehensive set of data to interpret. In
particular, in our own case we have access not just to our overt behaviour, but also
to 'inner promptings', such as mental images and bodily feelings (Lawlor 2009). But
the epistemic advantage of having a larger set of data to go on has to be weighed
against the disadvantage of being too invested in our own self-conceptions to
permit an unbiased evaluation of these data.

8 This is similar to an argument in Byrne's (2012) review of Carruthers' book.

9 Transparency approaches face a number of difficulties of their own, including how
they might generalize to attitudes other than belief: Ashwell (2013), Paul (2014),
and Baker (2015) address attempts at generalization by Moran (2001) and Byrne
(2011).

10 Such a capacity is unlikely to be infallible, of course, especially in cases where
our first-order point of view on the world is not fully settled, or contains internal

tensions; but nothing in the considerations Schwitzgebel puts forth shows that it is massively unreliable either.

11 Similar reasoning has also been used to argue that 'externalism' about content is incompatible with privileged self-knowledge (Boghossian 1989). This debate is beyond the scope of the present chapter.

References

Alston, W. P. (1971), 'Varieties of Privileged Access', *American Philosophical Quarterly*, 8: 223–41.

Armstrong, D. M. (1968), *A Materialist Theory of the Mind*, London: Routledge & Kegan Paul.

Ashwell, L. (2013), 'Deep, Dark … or Transparent? Knowing Our Desires', *Philosophical Studies*, 165: 245–56.

Baars, B. J. (1993), *A Cognitive Theory of Consciousness*, Cambridge: Cambridge University Press.

Baker, D. (2015), 'Why Transparency Undermines Economy', *Synthese*, 192: 3037–50.

Bargh, J. A., Chen, M., and Burrows, L. (1996), 'Automaticity of Social Behavior: Direct Effects of Trait Construct and Stereotype Activation on Action', *Journal of Personality and Social Psychology*, 71: 230–44.

Berker, S. (2008), 'Luminosity Regained', *Philosophers' Imprint*, 8: 1–22.

Block, N. (2003), 'Mental Paint', in M. Hahn and B. Ramberg (eds), *Reflections and Replies: Essays on the Philosophy of Tyler Burge*, Cambridge: The MIT Press.

Boghossian, P. A. (1989), 'Content and Self-Knowledge', *Philosophical Topics*, 17: 5–26.

BonJour, L. (2003), 'A Version of Internalist Foundationalism', in E. Sosa and L. BonJour, *Epistemic Justification: Internalism vs. Externalism, Foundations vs. Virtues*, Oxford: Blackwell.

Boyle, M. (2009), 'Two Kinds of Self-Knowledge', *Philosophy and Phenomenological Research*, 78: 133–64.

Brueckner, A. and Fiocco, M. O. (2002), 'Williamson's Anti-luminosity Argument', *Philosophical Studies*, 110: 285–93.

Burge, T. (1996), 'Our Entitlement to Self-Knowledge', *Proceedings of the Aristotelian Society*, 96: 91–116.

Burge, T. (1998), 'Reason and the First Person', in C. McDonald, B. C. Smith, and C. Wright (eds), *Knowing Our Own Minds*, Oxford: Clarendon Press.

Byrne, A. (2005), 'Introspection', *Philosophical Topics*, 33: 79–104.

Byrne, A. (2011), 'Transparency, Belief, Intention', *Aristotelian Society Supplementary Volume*, 85: 201–21.

Byrne, A. (2012), 'Review of Peter Carruthers, *The Opacity of Mind: An Integrative Theory of Self-Knowledge*', *Notre Dame Philosophical Reviews*.

Carruthers, P. (2009), 'How We Know Our Own Minds: The Relationship between Mindreading and Metacognition', *Behavioral and Brain Sciences*, 32: 121–38.

Carruthers, P. (2011), *The Opacity of Mind: An Integrative Theory of Self-Knowledge*, Oxford: Oxford University Press.

Cassam, Q. (2011), 'How We Know What We Think', *Revue de Métaphysique et de Morale*, 68: 553–69.

Cassam, Q. (2014), *Self-Knowledge for Humans*, Oxford: Oxford University Press.

Chalmers, D. J. (2003), 'The Content and Epistemology of Phenomenal Belief', in Q. Smith and A. Jokic (eds), *Consciousness: New Philosophical Perspectives*, Oxford: Clarendon Press.

Cohen, S. (2010), 'Luminosity, Reliability, and the Sorites', *Philosophy and Phenomenological Research*, 81: 718–30.

Dennett, D. C. (1992), *Consciousness Explained*, New York: Back Bay Books.

Dennett, D. C. (2002), 'How Could I Be Wrong? How Wrong Could I Be?' *Journal of Consciousness Studies*, 9: 13–16.

Doyen, S., Klein, O., Pichon, C.-L., and Cleeremans, A. (2012), 'Behavioral Priming: It's All in the Mind, But Whose Mind?', *PLOS ONE* 7.

Evans, G. (1982). *The Varieties of Reference*, Oxford: Clarendon Press.

Fernández, J. (2013), *Transparent Minds: A Study of Self-Knowledge*, Oxford: Oxford University Press.

Fodor, J. A. (2001), *The Mind Doesn't Work That Way: The Scope and Limits of Computational Psychology*, Cambridge: The MIT Press.

Gallois, A. (1996), *The World Without, The Mind Within*, Cambridge: Cambridge University Press.

Gertler, B. (2001), 'Introspecting Phenomenal States', *Philosophy and Phenomenological Research*, 63: 305–28.

Gertler, B. (2011a), *Self-Knowledge*, Abingdon: Routledge.

Gertler, B. (2011b). 'Reviewed Acquaintance', in D. Smithies and D. Stoljar (eds), *Introspection and Consciousness*, New York: Oxford University Press.

Harman, G. (1990), 'The Intrinsic Quality of Experience', *Philosophical Perspectives*, 4: 31–52.

Kind, A. (2003), 'What's So Transparent about Transparency?' *Philosophical Studies*, 115: 225–44.

Lawlor, K. (2009), 'Knowing What One Wants', *Philosophy and Phenomenological Research*, 79: 47–75.

Locke, J. (1975 [1690]), *An Essay Concerning Human Understanding*, ed. P. H. Nidditch, Oxford: Clarendon Press.

Lycan, W. G. (1996), *Consciousness and Experience*, Cambridge: The MIT Press.

Mack, A. and Rock, I. (1998), *Inattentional Blindness*, Cambridge: The MIT Press.

Moore, G. E. (1903), 'The Refutation of Idealism', *Mind*, 12: 433–53.

Moran, R. (2001), *Authority and Estrangement: An Essay on Self-Knowledge*, Princeton: Princeton University Press.

Moran, R. (2003), 'Responses to O'Brien and Shoemaker', *European Journal of Philosophy*, 11: 402–19.

Neta, R. and Rohrbaugh, G. (2004), 'Luminosity and the Safety of Knowledge', *Pacific Philosophical Quarterly*, 85: 396–406.

Nichols, S. and Stich, S. P. (2003), *Mindreading: An Integrated Account of Pretence, Self-Awareness, and Understanding Other Minds*, Oxford: Oxford University Press.

Nisbett, R. E. and Wilson, T. D. (1977), 'Telling More Than We Can Know: Verbal Reports on Mental Processes', *Psychological Review*, 84: 231–59.

Noë, A. (2002), 'Is the Visual World a Grand Illusion?' *Journal of Consciousness Studies*, 9: 1–12.

Noë, A. (2004), *Action in Perception*, Cambridge: The MIT Press.

Paul, S. K. (2014). 'The Transparency of Intention', *Philosophical Studies*, 172: 1529–48.

Pashler, H. and Wagenmakers, E.-J. (2012), 'Editors' Introduction to the Special Section on Replicability in Psychological Science: A Crisis of Confidence?', *Perspectives on Psychological Science*, 7: 528–30.

Peacocke, C. (1996), 'Entitlement, Self-Knowledge and Conceptual Redeployment', *Proceedings of the Aristotelian Society*, 96: 117–58.

Peacocke, C. (1998), 'Conscious Attitudes, Attention and Self-Knowledge', in C. McDonald, B. C. Smith, and C. Wright (eds), *Knowing Our Own Minds*, Oxford: Clarendon Press.

Pitt, D. (2004), 'The Phenomenology of Cognition, or, What Is It Like to Think That P?', *Philosophy and Phenomenological Research*, 69: 1–36.

Rorty, R. (1979), *Philosophy and the Mirror of Nature*, Princeton: Princeton University Press.

Russell, B. (1912), *The Problems of Philosophy*, London: Williams and Norgate.

Ryle, G. (2002 [1949]), *The Concept of Mind*, Chicago: University of Chicago Press.

Schwitzgebel, E. (2008), 'The Unreliability of Naive Introspection', *The Philosophical Review*, 117: 245–73.

Schwitzgebel, E. (2010), 'Acting Contrary to Our Professed Beliefs or the Gulf Between Occurrent Judgment and Dispositional Belief', *Pacific Philosophical Quarterly*, 91: 531–53.

Schwitzgebel, E. (2011), *Perplexities of Consciousness*, Cambridge: The MIT Press.

Shoemaker, S. (1963). *Self-Knowledge and Self-Identity*, Ithaca, NY: Cornell University Press.

Shoemaker, S. (1990), 'First-Person Access', *Philosophical Perspectives*, 4: 187–214.

Shoemaker, S. (1996), *The First-Person Perspective and Other Essays*, Cambridge: Cambridge University Press.

Simons, D. J. and Chabris, C. F. (1999), 'Gorillas in Our Midst: Sustained Inattentional Blindness for Dynamic Events', *Perception*, 28: 1059–74.

Stich, S. P. (1978), 'Beliefs and Subdoxastic States', *Philosophy of Science*, 45: 499–518.

Tye, M. (1995), *Ten Problems of Consciousness*, Cambridge: The MIT Press.

Valaris, M. (2013), 'Self-Knowledge and the Phenomenological Transparency of Belief',
    Philosophers' Imprint, 14: 1–17.
Vogel, J. (2010), 'Luminosity and Indiscriminability', *Philosophical Perspectives*,
    24: 547–72.
Weatherson, B. (2004), 'Luminous Margins', *Australasian Journal of Philosophy*,
    82: 373–83.
Williamson, T. (2000), *Knowledge and Its Limits*, Oxford: Clarendon Press.
Wittgenstein, L. (1958), *Philosophical Investigations*, trans. G. E. M. Anscombe,
    Englewood Cliffs, NJ: Prentice Hall.
Wong, W.-H. (2008), 'What Williamson's Anti-luminosity Argument Really Is', *Pacific
    Philosophical Quarterly*, 89: 536–43.

9

Knowledge as Contextual

Michael Blome-Tillmann

1. The beginning: epistemic contextualism

The most familiar approach in epistemology that postulates a form of contextuality is *epistemic contextualism*, the view that, in a first approximation, the truth-values of knowledge attributions may vary with the conversational context of ascription in a distinctly epistemic way. To illustrate epistemic contextualism further, let us begin with an example.

Imagine schoolteacher Jones in the zoo explaining to his class that the animals in the pen are zebras. Tom is unconvinced and challenges Jones: 'Are you sure that those aren't antelopes?' After Jones has explained the difference between antelopes and zebras, Tom assures his classmates:

1. He knows that the animals in the pen are zebras.

Has Tom spoken truly? Surely, Jones' epistemic position seems good enough for satisfying the predicate 'knows that the animals in the pen are zebras' (henceforth, 'knows *Z*'): Jones has visual experiences of a black and white striped horse-like animal, he can discriminate reliably between zebras and antelopes, he has read the sign on the pen that reads 'Zebra Pen', and so on. Thus, Tom's utterance of (1) seems to be a paradigm case of a true 'knowledge' attribution.

Next, imagine a couple, Bill and Kate, walking along. Bill, a would-be postmodernist artist, gives details of his latest ideas: he envisions himself painting mules with white stripes to look like zebras, putting them in the zebra pen of a zoo and thereby fooling visitors. The couple randomly considers Jones, and Kate claims the following, at the very same time as Tom is asserting (1):

2. He doesn't know that the animals in the pen are zebras.

In Kate's mind, for Jones to 'know Z', he must have better evidence or reasons in support of Z than are momentarily available to him. In particular, Kate has it that Jones' evidence must eliminate the possibility that the animals in the pen are painted mules. As long as his evidence is neutral with respect to whether or not the animals are cleverly painted mules, Kate claims, Jones doesn't qualify as 'knowing Z'.

What is going on in our little example? According to our intuitions, an utterance of (1) is true in the context of the school class, while an utterance of (2) is true in the context of the artistic couple. Moreover, the sentence (2) is the negation of (1): it doesn't differ from (1) except for containing the verbal negation 'doesn't'. And since the personal pronoun 'he' refers in both contexts to Jones, it seems that the schoolteacher satisfies the predicate 'knows Z' in the context of the school class but not so in the context of the artists.

How are we to account for these phenomena? First, note again that Tom and Kate are talking about one and the same person – Jones – at exactly the same time. Thus, we cannot resolve the situation by claiming, for instance, that Jones 'knows Z' in one context but not the other because he believes Z in one context but not in the other. Similarly, we cannot plausibly respond that Jones has certain visual experiences in one context that he lacks in the other, or that he has the ability to discriminate reliably between certain scenarios in one context but not the other, or, finally, that he has read the sign on the zebra pen in one context but not in the other. All factors pertaining to the subject are identical with respect to both contexts, as the speakers in both contexts – Tom and Kate – are talking about one and the same subject at one and the same time.

Thus, what the above example suggests is that the mentioned epistemic factors – Jones' visual experiences, his discriminatory abilities, and so on – are sufficient for him to satisfy 'knows Z' in one context, but not so in the other. And it is this view that epistemic contextualism (EC) takes at face value: how strong one's epistemic position towards p must be for one to satisfy 'know(s) p' may vary with the context of utterance. In the artists' conversational context, Jones needs to be in a stronger epistemic position – he needs more evidence in support of Z – than in the school class's conversational context in order for him to satisfy 'knows Z'. Now, some contextualists describe the situation by claiming that contexts of utterance are governed by so-called epistemic standards. Given this terminology, the epistemic standards in our example are lower in the context of the school class than in the context of the artists' conversation. In the former context, the standards are low enough for Jones to satisfy 'knows Z', while in the latter they are too high: in the artists' context, Jones doesn't satisfy 'knows Z' but instead satisfies 'doesn't know Z'.

The notion of an epistemic standard can be explicated in a variety of ways. On one of the more intuitive ways, which is inspired by relevant alternatives approaches to contextualism, epistemic standards are said to be higher in the school class's context because, as David Lewis (1996) puts it, satisfying 'knows *Z*' in that context doesn't require the elimination of the possibility that the animals are painted mules, while this is required in the context of the postmodernist artists. More alternatives must be eliminated or ruled out in the context with the higher standards than in the context with the lower standards.

Given the hypothesized context-sensitivity of the predicate 'know(s) *p*', it is in general possible that a subject satisfies the predicate in one conversational context but doesn't do so in another, or, in other words, that somebody in a given context speaks truly when uttering a sentence of the form '*x* knows *p*' while somebody in a different context speaks falsely when uttering the very same sentence – even though both speakers are speaking about the same subject *x* at the same time of utterance *t*. Epistemic contextualism is, as a consequence, a linguistic or a semantic view – namely, the view that the truth-values of 'knowledge'-ascriptions – sentences of the form '*x* knows *p*' – may vary with the context of utterance. According to EC, 'knowledge'-ascriptions are, as Stanley (2005: 17) puts it, context-sensitive in a distinctively epistemological way: the truth-values of a sentence *S* containing the predicate 'know(s) *p*' can change with context, independently of whether *S* is ambiguous or context-sensitive in any other way.

In a first approximation, we can thus define 'epistemic contextualism' as follows:

> (EC′) The truth-values of 'knowledge'-ascriptions may vary with the context of utterance, where this variance is traceable to the occurrence of 'know(s) *p*' and concerns a distinctively epistemic factor.

Given semantic compositionality – the view that the extensions of complex expressions are a function of the extensions of their ultimate constituents and the way in which they are combined – (EC′) entails (EC):

> (EC) The contribution that the predicate 'know(s) *p*' makes to the truth-value of a sentence it is embedded in may vary with the context of utterance in a distinctly epistemic way.

According to EC, the predicate 'know(s) *p*' *adds* context-sensitivity to a sentence it occurs in, and this context-sensitivity is distinctly epistemic – that is, it goes over and above the context-sensitivity that the verb contributes to the sentence in virtue of its tense.

There are several different ways to semantically model the context-sensitivity of 'know(s) p', but this topic is beyond the scope of this chapter. It is, however, worth noting that EC is not a lexical ambiguity theory – that is, it doesn't claim that 'know(s) p' is assigned multiple conventional meanings in English, as are the lexically ambiguous expressions 'bank' or 'orange'. On the contrary, contextualists have commonly compared 'know(s) p' to indexical expressions, such as 'I', 'that', and 'today', or to gradable adjectives such as 'flat' and 'empty': these expressions are widely taken to have only one conventional meaning – what Kaplan (1989) calls their 'character' – but different contents or semantic values in suitably different contexts of utterance.

To illustrate this further, many contextualists have employed an analogy to gradable adjectives that will prove fruitful for our purposes, even though the analogy has turned out to be a little rough-and-ready.[1] Just as what counts as satisfying 'flat', 'empty', or 'tall' may vary with context, contextualists have argued, what counts as satisfying 'know(s) p' may vary with context, too. Given this analogy, EC can be construed as claiming that the utterances of (1) and (2) in our above example stand in a relation similar to the relation between a basketball coach's utterance of 'MB-T isn't tall' and a jockey coach's utterance of 'MB-T is tall': while the surface syntax of these sentences suggests a contradiction, the propositions expressed are compatible, as the semantic value of 'tall' changes with the context of utterance. On the face of it, ordinary usage of 'tall' and 'knows p' seem to be similar: both expressions seem to be context-sensitive.[2]

The issue of how to precisely implement EC and the context-sensitivity of 'know(s) p' at the semantic level shall not be discussed in this chapter.[3] For now, let us consider evidence in support of EC that has been put forward by its defenders in the literature. The main evidence for EC derives from our intuitions about the truth-values of 'knowledge'-ascriptions in examples such as the above zebra case. However, there are further, more familiar examples that have been presented in the literature. Consider, for instance, Stewart Cohen's (1999: 58) *Airport Case*:

Airport
Mary and John are at the L.A. airport contemplating taking a certain flight to New York. They want to know whether the flight has a layover in Chicago. They overhear someone ask a passenger, Smith, if he knows whether the flight stops in Chicago. Smith looks at the flight itinerary he got from the travel agent and responds, 'Yes I know – it does stop in Chicago.' It turns out that Mary and John have a very important business contact they have to make at the Chicago airport. Mary says, 'How reliable is that itinerary? It could contain a misprint.

They could have changed the schedule at the last minute.' Mary and John agree that Smith doesn't really know that the plane will stop in Chicago. They decide to check with the airline agent.

As Cohen's example suggests, the sentence 'Smith knows that the flight stops over in Chicago' appears true as uttered in Smith's context but false as uttered in Mary's and John's context. Moreover, it seems as though the practical interests and goals of the conversational participants or how high the stakes are with regard to the proposition that the flight will stop over in Chicago influence the respective contexts' epistemic standards, and thus whether Smith satisfies 'knows'. In Smith's own context, he satisfies 'knows that the flight will stop over in Chicago', but in Mary and John's context, where the stakes are significantly higher, he doesn't.

Here is another example reinforcing this point – namely, Keith DeRose's (1992) famous *Bank Cases*, as presented by Stanley (2005: 3–4):

Low Stakes
Hannah and her wife Sarah are driving home on a Friday afternoon. They plan to stop at the bank on the way home to deposit their paychecks. It is not important that they do so, as they have no impending bills. But as they drive past the bank, they notice that the lines inside are very long, as they often are on Friday afternoons. Realizing that it isn't very important that their paychecks are deposited right away, Hannah says, 'I know the bank will be open tomorrow, since I was there just two weeks ago on Saturday morning. So we can deposit our paychecks tomorrow morning.'

High Stakes
Hannah and her wife Sarah are driving home on a Friday afternoon. They plan to stop at the bank on the way home to deposit their paychecks. Since they have an impending bill coming due, and very little in their account, it is very important that they deposit their paychecks by Saturday. Hannah notes that she was at the bank two weeks before on a Saturday morning, and it was open. But, as Sarah points out, banks do change their hours. Hannah says, 'I guess you're right. I don't know that the bank will be open tomorrow.'

The above examples and others like them have attracted a large amount of critical attention in the recent literature. Let us briefly consider four points of contention.

First, the above argument in support of EC takes the form of an inference to the best explanation. In evaluating the support EC receives from the examples, we must, therefore, compare EC's account of the data with competing explanations offered by rival theories. Such comparisons of explanatory virtue in philosophy, however, are often difficult and complicated, as it is not always clear how to compare competing advantages of different theories. To reach a final verdict, we would thus need to take into account alternative explanations of the data, which is, unfortunately, well beyond the scope of this chapter.

A second point of contention concerns the above data's evidential status. Some experimental philosophers have, in recent studies, aimed to undermine the above case for contextualism by arguing that professional philosophers' intuitions about the above cases do not coincide with the intuitions of the general public. These issues present interesting and legitimate challenges to EC, but they, too, go beyond the scope of this chapter.[4]

A third point that has attracted discussion concerns the exact contextual factors influencing the semantic content of 'know(s) *p*'. Cohen's *Airport Case* and DeRose's *Bank Case* seem to suggest that the practical stakes at the context of ascription influence what we earlier called the context's 'epistemic standards'. But it is not obvious that similar mechanisms are in place in the zebra example outlined above. Some theorists have, therefore, proposed that what raises the epistemic standards at a context are the alternatives or possibilities that are taken seriously or have been attended to in the context, or the possibilities whose denials are not presupposed in the context, while others have argued that it is the practical interests of the contributors to the conversation and what is at stake for them. The debate between stakes versus salience is ongoing.

A fourth issue to be mentioned here concerns the difference between first-person and third-person 'knowledge'-attributions. The 'knowledge'-attribution in DeRose's bank cases are made from the first-person perspective – they are so-called self-ascriptions – while the 'knowledge'-ascriptions in the zebra case are third-person ascriptions. Tom ascribes 'knowledge' to Jones, while Kate denies Jones 'knowledge'. The difference between first-person ascriptions and third-person ascriptions is important, as some of the rival views to EC – such as the pragmatic encroachment accounts discussed below – have the explanatory resources to explain the former, but are not so clear on the latter. In determining which view has the better explanation of the data, we thus need to make sure that we consider both first-person and third-person 'knowledge'-attributions.

A fifth and final issue to be mentioned here concerns a topic that is commonly taken to provide an important philosophical motivation for EC: namely, sceptical puzzles. According to most contextualists, their views offer a powerful solution to sceptical puzzles. Consider the following argument:

1. If I know that it's raining in Cambridge right now, then I know that I'm not a brain in a vat.
2. I don't know that I'm not a brain in a vat.
3. Therefore, I don't know that it's raining in Cambridge right now.

The conclusion of the argument is surprising and unintuitive. After all, looking out of the window seeing the rain coming down, few things seem more obvious than my knowing that it's raining in Cambridge right now. But the argument is valid and the premises appear plausible. How are we to resolve the tension created by the argument? The contextualist has an interesting suggestion. According to contextualism, premise (2) of the argument expresses a truth in high-standards contexts, such as the context of a philosophy classroom, but a falsehood in more ordinary, everyday contexts. Thus, the argument is sound in the philosophy classroom, but not so in everyday contexts. And when we consider the argument in a philosophical context, we tend to lose track of the fact that our everyday 'knowledge'-attributions remain true – they are, after all, made in different, lower-standards contexts.

The details of the contextualist solution to sceptical puzzles are intricate and somewhat controversial, as it relies on the contextualist's *error-theory* – the idea that competent speakers are sometimes unaware of the context-sensitivity of 'knows p'.[5] However, it should be noted at this point that if contextualism offers us a solution to sceptical puzzles then the view is of primary philosophical importance – despite the fact that one might, mistakenly, think that a theory about the semantics of the expression 'knows p' in English (i.e. a theory about the meaning of 'knowledge' rather than about knowledge itself) cannot really be of *epistemological* interest.[6]

2. Subject-Sensitive Invariantism

While epistemic contextualism was the first major theory to underline the importance of context in epistemology, a subtly different but related view emerged in the early-to-mid-2000s. According to what I shall call 'Subject-Sensitive Invariantism' (SSI), context determines partly whether or not we know, but it is the context of the subject rather than the context of the person ascribing 'knowledge' that influences whether or not the subject knows. Thus, it is not the ascriber's practical interests, goals, and presuppositions that determine whether one knows a given proposition on a given occasion of usage; it is the practical interests, goals, and presuppositions *of the subject* that do so. SSI is, as a consequence, an invariantist account of 'knowledge' – that is, it rejects the view that the predicate 'knows *p*' has an unstable Kaplan character.[7] According to SSI, 'knows *p*' expresses one and the same relation in every context, but the nature of this relation is such that whether it applies depends on the subject's context – to be precise, on the subject's goals, intentions, and practical interests. However, while SSI is not a contextualist theory, it nevertheless stipulates an epistemologically interesting kind of contextuality – namely, sensitivity to the subject's context. The view accordingly takes middle ground between contextualism and more traditional insensitive invariantist views in that it accepts contextuality but not context-sensitivity in the linguistic sense.

In the literature, a variety of different labels have been used for different versions of SSI. The label 'Subject-Sensitive Invariantism' itself is due to DeRose (2004), while Jason Stanley (2005) labels his version of SSI 'Interest Relative Invariantism'. Yet other theorists, most notably Jeremy Fantl and Matthew McGrath (2002, 2007), refer to SSI as 'impurism' or as 'pragmatic encroachment theories', since pragmatic factors of the subject's situation encroach on (and thereby impurify) the truth-related epistemic conditions that are traditionally taken to be placed on knowledge. In the remainder of this chapter, I shall make use of DeRose's coinage and employ the term 'SSI'.

SSI has been motivated in different ways in the literature. The main motivation for the view, however, stems from considerations concerning the normative roles of knowledge. Fantl and McGrath (2002, 2007), for instance, argue for SSI by defending what they call the knowledge-action principle:

(KA) *x* knows *p* only if *x* is rational to act as if *p*.

Further versions of the link between knowledge and action defended by Fantl and McGrath have been proposed by other philosophers. Hawthorne (2004: 30) and Hawthorne and Stanley (2008), for instance, have defended the view that knowledge is the norm of practical reasoning. Here is the *Knowledge Rule of Practical Reasoning*:

(PR) It is permissible for *x* to use *p* as a premise in her practical reasoning iff *x* knows *p*.

With (KA) and (PR) at hand, the defenders of SSI can explain our intuitions in certain cases of knowledge ascriptions. Consider, for instance, the following example in which you and your partner are about to back out of your driveway to go on a two-week vacation[8]:

Partner: Did you remember to turn the stove off after breakfast?

You: Yes.

Partner: You know you forgot to turn it off the other day. If we leave it on over our vacation, our house will burn down.

You: You're right. I don't know. I'd better go back and check.

Given that your house is at stake, it is not, in the example, rational for you to act as if the stove is off, and the explanation that Fantl and McGrath give for this datum is that you do not know that the stove is off. Similarly, one can argue along Hawthorne and Stanley's line that it is not permissible for you to act as if the stove is off because you do not know that the stove is off. Your epistemic position in the example is too weak to treat that proposition as a premise in your practical reasoning, and this is why it seems plausible to claim that you also fail to know that proposition.

What is crucial at this point, however, is that what is permissible for someone to use as a premise in practical reasoning varies with the subject's practical situation: if the stakes were lower because you are not about to go on a two-week holiday but you are only about to bring out the rubbish, it would be permissible for you to use the proposition that you turned off the stove as a premise in your practical reasoning. But if, as is uncontroversial, what is rational to use as a premise in practical reasoning varies with the subject's context or practical situation, then, given (PR), whether one knows must vary with the subject's context or practical situation, too. (PR) and (KA) establish a link between knowledge, on the one hand, and permissible or rational action, on the other, that ensures that the two sway together: if one varies with the subject's context, so does the other.

Many of the cases that have been used to motivate epistemic contextualism can also be explained by impurism. In the *High Stakes* version of DeRose's bank case, for instance, it is not rational for Hannah to act as if the bank will be open on Saturday, since she is not permitted to use that premise in her practical reasoning: the stakes are just too high and the consequences of getting it wrong are too severe. Similar considerations apply to Cohen's *Airport Case*.

Let us move on to some of the most widely discussed criticisms of SSI. One important objection to the view concerns the normative role of knowledge postulated by the above principles and thus the view's primary motivation. Many opponents of SSI reject the principles (KA) and (PR), which are, in fact, discussed rather controversially in the literature. Another response addressing the same issue has been levelled by some contextualists, who have argued that no competitive advantage arises from (KA) and (PR) for the impurists: contextualism, the argument goes, can accommodate the knowledge-action principles rather well by appealing to its error-theory.[9]

A second important line of criticism stems from the data presented above. While SSI has a plausible and appealing account of the data in the stove example and the bank cases, the view struggles with examples involving third-person 'knowledge' attributions in which the ascriber's context is governed by high epistemic standards and the subject's context by low epistemic standards. To see what is at issue here, remember the previous section's case of school teacher Jones and the postmodernist artists, which is precisely such a high-ascriber/low-subject case. In the example, Jones is in a context with low epistemic standards, while the artists are in a context with high epistemic standards. What is crucial, however, is that when the artists assert 'He doesn't know *Z*', they seem to speak truly – a datum that is in direct conflict with the predictions of impurism. According to impurism, the subject's – that is, Jones' – low epistemic standards determine whether or not he 'knows *Z*', and we have seen that Jones in fact satisfies those lower epistemic standards. Thus, given impurism, the artists speak falsely when denying Jones 'knowledge'.

In response to this challenge, some defenders of impurism have emphasized that the motivation of their view is not 'data-driven' but instead relies on the above principles linking knowledge and action.[10] It should be noted, however, that the data discussed in the previous section are in rather obvious conflict with the predictions made by impurism, and that the conflict appears to come at some cost to the view. Hawthorne (2004) and Stanley (2005) seem to agree with this conclusion and, in response, aim to offer an error-theory that explains why our intuitions in the relevant cases are mistaken. Whether the impurists' error-theories are successful or superior to those proposed by the contextualists must be left for another occasion.[11]

3. Relativism about 'knowledge' attributions: assessment-sensitivity

A third important development in the debate on 'knowledge'-attributions to be mentioned here is *epistemic relativism*, stemming from the work of John MacFarlane (2005a, 2011, 2014). Epistemic relativists, as the term is used in this debate, agree with the abovementioned general idea that knowledge is contextual and that our varying intuitions about the truth-values of 'knowledge'-attributions must be explained by reference to context. The crucial difference to the above views, however, is that, according to the relativist, it is neither the ascriber's nor the subject's context that accounts for the perceived variability in truth-conditions. Rather, the truth-values of 'knowledge'-attributions are determined relative to what MacFarlane calls a 'context of assessment'. In other words, epistemic relativism postulates so-called 'assessment-sensitivity'.

To illustrate the view further, consider Jones' utterance of 'I know Z' (in the zebra example). According to relativism, Jones' utterance has a truth-value only relative to a context of assessment, which may be distinct from both Jones' own context and the context of 'knowledge' ascription. In fact, different people may assess one and the same utterance – say, Jones' utterance – from different contexts and assign differing truth-values. For instance, relative to Jones himself as an assessor, his utterance of 'I know Z' is true, because Jones is in a low-standards context, but, relative to the artists as assessors, it is false, because the artists are in a high-standards context. Whoever the assessor may be, it is the epistemic standards in her, the assessor's, context that determine the utterance's truth-value. Without a context of assessment, Jones' utterance cannot be assigned a truth-value at all.

As MacFarlane's (2011) groundbreaking work on relativism has made clear, there are two principally distinct ways to semantically implement assessment-sensitivity that should be distinguished here – namely, *content relativism* and *truth relativism*. According to content relativism, the content expressed by an utterance – (usually) what is said by the utterance – varies with the context of assessment. There is, according to this view, no assessment-independent fact as to what was said or semantically expressed by an utterance. Content relativism thus rejects invariantism, the idea that – no matter what context we consider – exactly one proposition is expressed by a 'knowledge'-attribution. According to truth relativism, however, the content of a 'knowledge'-attribution is invariant and a sentence of the form 'x knows p' expresses one and the same proposition relative to any context of assessment. What is crucial, however, is that the propositions expressed by 'knowledge'-attributions are of a rather special kind in that they do not have truth-values in the way that ordinary propositions do – that is, relative to ordered pairs of worlds and times – but rather relative to ordered triples of worlds, times, and contexts of assessment. Either way, on both views Jones' utterance has a truth-value only relative to a context of assessment.

The motivation for assessment-sensitivity runs along very similar lines as does the motivation for epistemic contextualism: the view allows us to account for all of the data from the above cases, including the ones that turned out to be problematic for SSI. Since the context of assessment is, in the examples discussed, identical to the context of ascription, epistemic relativism will fare just as well as contextualist accounts do. However, MacFarlane points out that, with respect to the data, relativism has one crucial advantage over contextualism: relativism has, according to MacFarlane (2005a), a better account of so-called *retraction data*. Consider the following:

> If yesterday Sally asserted [in a low-standards context] 'I know that the bus will be on time', and today she admits [in a high-standards context] that she didn't know yesterday that the bus would be on time, I will expect her to retract her earlier assertion. I will find it exceedingly bizarre if she replies by saying that her assertion was true, even if she adds 'by the standards that were in place yesterday'. (203)

The problem for contextualism here, as MacFarlane points out, is that it is rather plausible that Sally should retract her earlier utterance, which is difficult to explain on a contextualist account. Contextualism entails, after all, that what Sally said yesterday is true. But if Sally spoke truly yesterday, then why should she retract yesterday's assertion? Unlike the contextualist, the truth relativist has no problem explaining this retraction phenomenon. According to truth relativism, Sally speaks truly today if she asserts, 'I was wrong yesterday. I didn't know that the bus would be on time.' This is because the proposition Sally asserted yesterday – namely, the proposition that she knew that the bus would be on time – is false relative to her current, high-standards, context of assessment. Thus, retraction data present an important point of divergence between contextualism and relativism: while contextualism predicts that one is making a mistake in retracting one's earlier utterance, relativism doesn't.

Contextualists have objected to the relativists' argument by pointing out that their views do, after all, have an explanation of retraction data and that, in the absence of a competitive advantage over their view, EC should be favoured in virtue of proposing the more conservative semantic theory.[12] Another, more important and direct, objection to relativism questions whether we are warranted in introducing assessment-sensitivity into the semantics of 'knows p' – and into our linguistic toolbox more generally. It is often assumed that the most plausible candidate expressions for a relativist semantics are predicates of personal taste, such as 'tasty' or 'fun'. Consider the following example:

John: 'That chilli is tasty.'
Hannah: 'That chilli is not tasty.'

When considering John's and Hannah's utterances, there is an intuition of so-called faultless disagreement. While John and Hannah seem to disagree about the chilli, there is also an intuition that neither of them is at fault: it is plausible that neither John nor Hannah is wrong about the chilli, despite the fact that they disagree and assert two seemingly incompatible propositions. The relativist explanation of this phenomenon seems appealing: the disagreement between John and Hannah is accounted for by the fact that Hannah does in fact assert the negation of what John asserts. The faultlessness, however, is accounted for by the fact that both Hannah's and John's utterances express truths – namely, relative to their respective contexts of assessment.

While a relativist semantics seems appealing in the case of predicates of personal taste, it doesn't seem so clearly appealing in the case of 'knowledge'-attributions. Consider the following two utterances from our zebra case:

Tom: 'Jones knows that the animals are zebras.'
Kate: 'Jones doesn't know that the animals are zebras.'

While the relativist about 'knows p' can account for the intuition that Tom and Kate both speak truly, and thus that neither of them is at fault, it isn't so obvious that we have an intuition of disagreement in this case. For, when considering the zebra case in Section 1, it seemed as if Tom and Kate were talking about different things – Tom about the ability to eliminate the possibility that the animals are antelopes, and Kate about the ability to eliminate the possibility that the animals are cleverly painted mules. The contents conveyed by their respective utterances seems to differ over and above the fact that one of them contains a negation, which is an intuition that isn't present in the chili example. If there is in fact such a disanalogy in our intuitions between the two cases, then that presents a cost to the relativist.

A third and rather interesting objection to relativism is due to Martin Montminy (2009). Consider again Kate's utterance of 'Jones doesn't know Z' that was made in a high-standards context. Montminy argues that, in her high-standards context, Kate would feel no commitment to withdraw (or retract) her 'knowledge'-denial if she should, in the future, find herself in a low-standards situation. For as long as Kate is in a high-standards situation, she will think it inappropriate to withdraw her utterance of 'Jones doesn't know Z' in some future low-standards context (354). In other words, if Kate were to consider moving into a low-standards context in the future, she wouldn't conclude that her current 'knowledge'-denial would have to be withdrawn. Instead, she would, the argument goes, conclude that her denial would still stand and remain true, despite the fact that the standards would differ in the imagined future context of assessment. Montminy concludes from these observations that, according to relativism, competent speakers are systematically mistaken about their commitments to retract utterances. Consequently, the relativist needs an error-theory, too, and has, therefore, no competitive advantage over a contextualist or subject-sensitive invariantist semantics for 'knows *p*'.

The details of the debate on relativism are intricate and highly abstract. While the debate is still ongoing, it seems fair to say that the opponents of relativism usually argue that the motivation for the view and its admittedly elegant explanations of the data is not sufficient to warrant what is perceived as a rather drastic divergence from orthodox semantics.

4. Strict invariantism

The final family of views to be discussed here is the formerly standard epistemological position according to which knowledge is not contextual: *strict invariantism*. According to strict invariantism, the truth-values of 'knowledge'-attributions do not vary with any context whatsoever – that is, neither with the ascriber's, nor the subject's, nor the assessor's. The question immediately arises as to how the strict invariantist will account for our intuitions concerning the variability in truth-values of 'knowledge'-attributions. How can the strict invariantist explain the data from the zebra case, the bank case, and related examples? There are two main invariantist approaches to the mentioned data; those that aim to explain the phenomena by means of psychological considerations and those that resort to pragmatics. Let us consider psychological accounts first.

The earliest version of psychological invariantism is that championed by Hawthorne (2004) and Williamson (2005), who attempt to explain our intuitions in the relevant examples by means of a bias known as the *availability heuristic*. According to the availability heuristic, we overestimate the probability of events that can be easily imagined and recalled.[13] Hawthorne and Williamson employ this bias as follows: in the zebra example, we overestimate the probability that the animals in the pen are painted mules and this overestimation causes us to mistakenly judge that alternative to be epistemically relevant. The mistaken belief that the alternative is epistemically relevant, however, causes us to mistakenly believe that Jones doesn't know Z. Thus, our intuition that Kate speaks truly when asserting 'Smith doesn't know *Z*' is accounted for by the availability heuristic. While initially promising, Hawthorne's and Williamson's proposal has been criticized in detail by Jennifer Nagel (2010), who also points out that 'it is unclear how so fragile a bias could continue to produce the intuitions driving scepticism and contextualism' (Nagel and Smith forthcoming).

Another psychological explanation of the data is Mikkel Gerken's (2013; forthcoming) *epistemic focal bias* account. An important part of his account is the idea that psychologically (or contextually) salient alternatives are normally cognitively processed as epistemically relevant alternatives. In other words, an alternative that is psychologically 'in focus' is automatically treated as epistemically relevant. On this view, the artists in the zebra example, for instance, treat the alternative that the animals are cleverly painted mules as epistemically relevant only because it is cognitively 'in focus' – they have attended to the possibility. The very fact that it is in focus or attended to, however, doesn't make the alternative epistemically relevant. In fact, according to Gerken, the artists make a mistake in treating it as relevant, and the resulting 'knowledge'-denial results again in the assertion of a falsehood.

Further sophisticated psychological explanations have been proposed and criticized in the work of Nagel (2007, 2010; Nagel and Smith 2017). Instead of going into more detail at this point, however, note that one worry about psychological explanations more generally is that they run the risk of being unable to account for the stability and recalcitrance of the data at issue. To be precise, if the acceptance of an alternative as epistemically relevant is the result of the mistaken application of a cognitive heuristic or bias of the fragile type mentioned above, why is it so difficult to correct ordinary speakers and to convince them of the irrelevance of those alternatives?[14] Moreover, with respect to Gerken's account, it seems that in some situations alternatives are 'in focus' or salient but are nevertheless clearly considered epistemically irrelevant.[15] What explains this datum, if not the idea that speakers are sensitive to the fact that some alternatives are epistemically relevant in some contexts but not so in others?[16]

The second version of strict invariantism to be mentioned here is *pragmatic invariantism*. According to pragmatic invariantism, the contextual variations in our willingness to ascribe 'knowledge' are to be accounted for by means of pragmatic theories. Patrick Rysiew (2001, 2007), for instance, has forcefully argued that the truth-conditions of 'knowledge'-attributions are invariant with the context of ascription while the conditions under which 'knowledge'-sentences are felicitously assertable may vary with the ascriber's context. According to Rysiew, some assertions of 'knowledge'-sentences give rise to Gricean implicatures that account for our intuitions in the cases used to support contextualism. Thus, what varies with the conversational context is, according to the pragmatic invariantist, not the proposition semantically expressed by a particular 'knowledge'-sentence, but rather the proposition pragmatically imparted or implicated by an utterance of that 'knowledge'-sentence: context affects assertibility-conditions, not truth-conditions.[17]

There are two principally different ways to model the pragmatic view. According to *moderate pragmatic invariantism* (MPI) we are speaking truly when ascribing 'knowledge' in everyday low-standards situations, while a false implicature is triggered in high-standards situation. For instance, according to Rysiew's version of MPI, the artist's utterance of 'Jones knows that the animals are zebras' in the zebra case asserts the true proposition expressed by (1) but implicates the falsehood expressed by (2):

1. Jones' evidence eliminates all *epistemically relevant* alternatives to the animal being a zebra.
2. Jones' evidence eliminates all *conversationally salient* alternatives to the animal being a zebra.

Thus, the impropriety of a 'knowledge'-attribution in high-standards contexts is accounted for by a false implicature.[18]

On a second version of PI – *sceptical pragmatic invariantism* (SPI) – our positive 'knowledge'-attributions in everyday contexts are false, but their felicity is accounted for by means of true implicatures. Wayne Davis (2007: 395), for instance, argues that ordinary 'knowledge'-attributions are instances of *loose use*: they are strictly speaking false – in virtue of semantically expressing a false proposition – but convey or pragmatically impart a truth, such as the proposition that one is 'close enough to knowing p for contextually indicated purposes'. The details of these pragmatic views and the pragmatic mechanisms that they employ are intricate and complicated.

The views themselves, like each of the views discussed in this chapter, are controversial. Thus, I conclude by noting that the state of the literature is currently such that we are far from speaking a final world on the semantics of 'knowledge'-attributions.

Notes

1 Cf. Schaffer and Szabó (2014).
2 For a detailed discussion of the analogy, see Blome-Tillmann (2008, 2014).
3 But see Blome-Tillmann (2009b, 2014).

4 But see Boyd and Nagel (2014) for interesting discussion.

5 See Blome-Tillmann (2014) for extensive discussion.

6 See Sosa (2000) for this objection and Blome-Tillmann (2007, 2014) for a response.

7 An unstable Kaplan (1989) character is, in brief, a conventional meaning that determines different contents in different contexts.

8 The example is a slight variant of a case used by McBrayer (2014).

9 See Greenough and Kindermann (forthcoming) for the contextualist's error-theory.

10 Stanley (2005), who seems to mainly motivate his Interest Relative Invariantism by means of examples, seems to be an exception to this claim.

11 For further objections to SSI, see MacFarlane (2005b) and Blome-Tillmann (2009a).

12 See, for instance, Blome-Tillmann (2013b).

13 See Tversky and Kahneman (1973).

14 See Nagel and Smith (2017) for this point.

15 Consider the following case for illustration:

    Cyborg Bank Case:

    A: 'I know the bank will be open tomorrow.'

    B: 'The thing could be a cyborg and just walk away overnight.'

    A: 'What are you talking about!?'

16 For further promising versions of the psychological view, see Nagel (2010). Gerken (forthcoming) addresses the above worries in some detail. Unfortunately, there is not enough room here for a discussion of these views.

17 DeRose (1999) refers to pragmatic invariantist strategies as 'Warranted Assertibility Manoeuvres' or 'WAMs'. For an introductory discussion of conversational implicatures, see Blome-Tillmann (2008, 2013a).

18 Note that the datum from the zebra case, however, isn't yet explained: the datum of the zebra case was that a 'knowledge'-denial appears true and felicitous, not that a (positive) 'knowledge'-attribution appeared false and infelicitous. See Blome-Tillmann (2008, 2013b) for discussion.

References

Blome-Tillmann, M. (2007), 'Contextualism and the Epistemological Enterprise', *Proceedings of the Aristotelian Society*, 107: 387–94.

Blome-Tillmann, M. (2008), 'The Indexicality of 'Knowledge', *Philosophical Studies*, 138: 29–53.

Blome-Tillmann, M. (2009a), 'Contextualism, Subject-Sensitive Invariantism, and the Interaction of "Knowledge"-Ascriptions with Modal and Temporal Operators', *Philosophy and Phenomenological Research*, 79: 315–31.

Blome-Tillmann, M. (2009b), 'Knowledge and Presuppositions', *Mind*, 118: 241–94.

Blome-Tillmann, M. (2013a), 'Conversational Implicatures (and How to Spot Them)', *Philosophy Compass*, 8: 170–85.

Blome-Tillmann, M. (2013b), 'Knowledge and Implicatures', *Synthese*, 190: 4293–319.

Blome-Tillmann, M. (2014), *Knowledge and Presuppositions*, Oxford: Oxford University Press.

Boyd, K. and Nagel, J. (2014), 'The Reliability of Epistemic Intuitions', in E. Machery and E. O'Neill (eds), *Current Controversies in Experimental Philosophy*, New York: Routledge.

Cohen, S. (1999), 'Contextualism, Skepticism, and the Structure of Reasons', *Philosophical Perspectives*, 13: 57–89.

Davis, W. A. (2007), 'Knowledge Claims and Context: Loose Use', *Philosophical Studies*, 132: 395–438.

DeRose, K. (1992), 'Contextualism and Knowledge Attributions', *Philosophy and Phenomenological Research*, 52: 913–29.

DeRose, K. (1999), Contextualism: An Explanation and Defense', in J. Greco and E. Sosa (eds), *The Blackwell Guide to Epistemology*, Oxford: Blackwell.

DeRose, K. (2004), 'The Problem with Subject-Sensitive Invariantism', *Philosophy and Phenomenological Research*, 68: 346–50.

Fantl, J. and McGrath, M. (2002), 'Evidence, Pragmatics and Justification', *The Philosophical Review*, 111: 67–94.

Fantl, J. and McGrath, M. (2007), 'On Pragmatic Encroachment in Epistemology', *Philosophy and Phenomenological Research*, 75: 558–89.

Gerken, M. (2013), 'Epistemic Focal Bias', *Australasian Journal of Philosophy*, 91: 41–61.

Gerken, M. (forthcoming), *On Folk Epistemology: How We Think and Talk about Knowledge*, Oxford: Oxford University Press.

Greenough, P. and Kindermann, D. (forthcoming), 'The Semantic Error Problem for Epistemic Contextualism', in J. J. Ichikawa (ed.), *The Routledge Handbook of Epistemic Contextualism*, London: Routledge.

Hawthorne, J. (2004), *Knowledge and Lotteries*, Oxford: Clarendon Press.

Hawthorne, J. and Stanley, J. (2008), 'Knowledge and Action', *The Journal of Philosophy*, 105: 571–90.

Kaplan, D. (1989), 'Demonstratives', in J. Almog, J. Perry, and H. Wettstein (eds), *Themes from Kaplan*, New York: Oxford University Press.

Lewis, D. (1996), 'Elusive Knowledge', *Australasian Journal of Philosophy*, 74: 549–67. [Reprinted in: DeRose, K. and Warfield, T. A. (eds) (1999), *Skepticism: A Contemporary Reader*, New York: Oxford University Press. Page references are to the reprint edition.]

MacFarlane, J. (2005a), 'The Assessment Sensitivity of Knowledge Attributions', in T. Gendler and J. Hawthorne (eds), *Oxford Studies in Epistemology, Vol. 1*, Oxford: Oxford University Press.

MacFarlane, J. (2005b), 'Knowledge Laundering: Testimony and Sensitive Invariantism', *Analysis*, 65: 132–8.

MacFarlane, J. (2011), Relativism and Knowledge Attributions', in S. Bernecker and D. Pritchard (eds), *The Routledge Companion to Epistemology*, New York: Routledge.

MacFarlane, J. (2014), *Assessment Sensitivity: Relative Truth and Its Applications*, Oxford: Oxford University Press.

McBrayer, J. P. (2014), 'Review of Aaron Rizzieri, *Pragmatic Encroachment, Religious Belief and Practice*', *Notre Dame Philosophical Reviews*.

Montminy, M. (2009), 'Contextualism, Relativism and Ordinary Speakers' Judgments', *Philosophical Studies*, 143: 341–56.

Nagel, J. (2007), 'Epistemic Intuitions', *Philosophy Compass*, 2(6): 792–819.

Nagel, J. (2010), 'Knowledge Ascriptions and the Psychological Consequences of Thinking about Error', *The Philosophical Quarterly*, 60: 286–306.

Nagel, J. and Smith, J. J. (2017), 'The Psychological Context of Contextualism', (with Julia Jael Smith), in Jonathan Ichikawa (ed.), *Routledge Handbook to Contextualism*, New York: Routledge, 94–104.

Rysiew, P. (2001), 'The Context-Sensitivity of Knowledge Attributions', *Nôus*, 35: 477–514.

Rysiew, P. (2007), 'Speaking of Knowing', *Noûs*, 41: 627–62.

Schaffer, J. and Szabó, Z. G. (2014), 'Epistemic Comparativism: A Contextualist Semantics for Knowledge Ascriptions', *Philosophical Studies*, 168: 491–543.

Sosa, E. (2000), 'Skepticism and Contextualism', *Philosophical Issues*, 10: 1–18.

Stanley, J. (2005), *Knowledge and Practical Interests*, Oxford: Clarendon Press.

Tversky, A. and Kahneman, D. (1973), 'Availability: A Heuristic for Judging Frequency and Probability', *Cognitive Psychology*, 5: 207–32.

Williamson, T. (2005). 'Knowledge, Context and the Agent's Point of View', in G. Preyer and G. Peter (eds), *Contextualism in Philosophy: Knowledge, Meaning, and Truth*, Oxford: Clarendon Press.

10

Knowledge and Probability

Weng Hong Tang

1. Introduction

Knowledge is traditionally thought to entail justified true belief, and the kind of belief in question is typically taken to be binary in nature – either we believe a proposition, or we disbelieve it, or we suspend judgement as to its truth. But there is also room for a more nuanced notion of belief. Among propositions that we believe, we might be more confident of some than of others. For example, we might believe the proposition that 2 + 2 = 4 and the proposition that the world will not end in 2030, and yet be more confident of the former than of the latter. In such a case, we have a greater *degree of belief* in the first proposition than in the second. There are also propositions that we neither believe nor disbelieve outright, but in which we might still invest varying degrees of belief. For instance, we might have a degree of belief of 0.7 in the proposition that it'll rain, and we might have a degree of belief of 0.5 in the proposition that a fair coin will land heads if tossed.[1]

Degrees of belief are also known as *subjective probabilities*. Or, to be more careful, *ideally rational* degrees of belief are often taken to be subjective probabilities – that is, they are often taken to obey the probability axioms.[2] For example, a standard axiom of probability says that the probability of any tautology is 1, whereas another axiom says that the probability of a disjunction equals the sum of the probability of each disjunct, given that the disjuncts are inconsistent with each other. If our degrees of belief obey the probability axioms, then our degree of belief in any tautology will be 1, and our degree of belief in '*p* or *q*' will be equal to our degree of belief in *p* plus our degree of belief in *q*, given that *p* and *q* are jointly inconsistent.

Some philosophers think that the notion of subjective probability or degree of belief renders the notion of knowledge toothless. Jeffrey (1968: 166), for instance, holds that we should 'deny that the notion of knowledge has the importance generally attributed to it' and that we should 'try to make the concept of [degree of] belief do the work that philosophers have generally assigned the grander concept'. Similarly, but in a slightly more conciliatory vein, Lewis (1996: 563) suggests that the ascription of knowledge is 'one of the messy short-cuts – like satisficing, like having indeterminate degrees of belief – that we resort to because we are not smart enough to live up to really high, perfectly Bayesian, standards of rationality'; although ascriptions of knowledge 'may yet be indispensable in practice', 'they are a handy but humble approximation.'[3]

One might not want to go as far as Jeffrey and Lewis do. First, Jeffrey (1968: 166) thinks that 'knowledge is sure, and there is little that we can be sure of outside logic and mathematics and truths related immediately to experience'. Given such a view, it is unsurprising that Jeffrey holds that knowledge should be downplayed in favour of degrees of belief. After all, while there might be few propositions that we are sure of, there are many propositions – concerning various matters other than those having to do with logic, mathematics, or our experiences – to which we assign varying degrees of belief. But arguably, *pace* Jeffrey, knowledge does not require certainty. For example, you might know that you had a sandwich for lunch without being absolutely sure that you did, and you might know that the library is open even if you won't bet the farm on it.[4] Second, in response to Lewis, one might deny that the ascription of knowledge is a mere short-cut. For instance, just as one might think that there is more epistemic value in knowing that *p* than in merely having a justified true belief that *p*, one might think that there is more epistemic value in knowing that *p* than in merely having a rational degree of belief in *p*.[5]

Nonetheless, even while granting that the notion of knowledge plays important roles in epistemology, one might maintain that it plays no significant role in practical deliberation. After all, a prominent account of rational action is offered by Bayesian decision theory. According to the theory, what is rational for us to do is determined by what maximizes expected utility, which is in turn determined by the relevant degrees of belief and utilities.[6] If so, there seems to be no need to invoke the notion of knowledge at all – where rational action is concerned, it seems that degrees of belief, in combination with utilities, do all of the heavy lifting.

But while the preceding line of thought is a natural one, it has been challenged. For instance, Hawthorne (2004: 30) claims that 'one ought only to use that which one knows as a premise in one's deliberations', whereas Stanley (2005: 9) holds that 'one should only act on what one knows'.[7] If Hawthorne and Stanley are right, then knowledge has its pride of place in practical deliberation, after all.[8]

In this chapter, I will consider some objections to the kind of view espoused by Hawthorne and Stanley. I will also discuss an intriguing defence of the view that has recently been advanced by Moss (2013). Moss' defence appeals to the notion of *probabilistic knowledge* – knowledge that is constituted by one's degrees of belief. Although the defence, if successful, will give knowledge its pride of place in practical deliberation, it brings with it its own challenges to the very notion of knowledge.

2. Knowledge and action

Stanley (2005: 10) writes:

> A standard use of knowledge attributions is to justify action … When my wife asks me why I turned left rather than going straight, I reply that I knew that it was the shortest direction to the restaurant. When it turns out that it was not a way to go to the restaurant at all, my wife will point out that I only *believed* that it was the shortest way to the restaurant. To say that an action is only based on a belief is to criticize that action for not living up to an expected norm. (Emphasis in the original)

But, granting that it is standard to use knowledge attributions to justify action, one might still question the claim that, if an action is based on a belief that does not amount to knowledge, that action is to be criticized. For, the thought goes, we often act on our degrees of belief, and it is often proper to do so – no norm is violated in doing so – even though such degrees of belief do not constitute knowledge. To use Schiffer's (2007: 189–90) example, suppose Jane has a 0.4 degree of belief in the proposition that it will rain. Then, given certain desires and given that her degree of belief is justified, her carrying an umbrella need not violate any norm. This is so, even though her degree of belief, not being truth apt, does not constitute knowledge.

In response, Hawthorne and Stanley (2008: 581–2) hold that one 'possible maneuver' is to maintain that, in such cases, one is acting on one's knowledge of the relevant chances.[9] For example, on this view, if Jane's carrying an umbrella violates no norm, it is because she is acting on her knowledge that there is a 0.4 chance that it will rain. It should be noted that Hawthorne and Stanley are not using the word 'chance' to refer to some kind of objective probability; rather, they are using the word 'to express *epistemic probabilities*, where one's epistemic probability for a proposition is determined by *the total body of one's knowledge*' (emphases in the original). Against the worry that animals or children might rationally act on their degrees of belief even though they might not be able to grasp the concept of (epistemic) chance (Schiffer 2007: 190), Hawthorne and Stanley (2008: 585) reply that we 'should not overintellectualize the concept of chance' – they maintain that 'there are very basic concepts of chance that we employ' even if we might not be able to understand its nature or understand philosophical analyses of chance.

Let's grant that we should not over-intellectualize the concept of epistemic chance. Still, there are other worries. Cresto (2010: 329) thinks that Hawthorne and Stanley owe us an account of what epistemic chances are – that they should tell us, for example, how the value of the epistemic chance of p given K is obtained, for any p and any K. Even if a subject may know what the relevant chances are, without knowing much about confirmation theory or inductive logic, a theorist *qua* theorist cannot just appeal to the notion of epistemic chance without spelling it out in more detail. Cresto also thinks that the appeal to our knowledge of epistemic chances 'adds an unnecessary complication, and ultimately distorts the nature of the underlying phenomenon' (327). If we ask someone why she is carrying an umbrella, a natural reply is that she desires not to get wet, and she knows (or believes) that it is going to rain. A less natural reply would be that she has the higher-order knowledge that she desires not to get wet, and she has the higher-order knowledge that her total body of evidence or knowledge supports the proposition that it will rain.[10] Baumann (2012: 20) seems to be expressing a similar worry when he holds that it is 'unclear why the agent has to know their probabilities and why it is not sufficient just to rely on them'.[11]

Hawthorne and Stanley (2008: 585) have a ready reply to the worries. They think that, when we base an action on our knowledge of chances, such knowledge is in turn based on knowledge of some other facts about the world. To use their example, our knowledge that there is a 0.6 chance that the restaurant is on the left might be based on our knowledge that three out of five people whom we have asked for directions indicated that the restaurant is on the left. Further, even someone who does not have the concept of chance will be able to act on knowledge of such facts about the world. Ultimately, Hawthorne and Stanley think that the appeal to knowledge of epistemic chances is not essential. But if that is right, then it is not essential, after all, that they give us a detailed account of epistemic chance. They will also avoid the worry that an act of carrying an umbrella or an act of going to the left is based on higher-order knowledge about our own mental states rather than first-order knowledge about the world.

Baumann (2012: 20) thinks that Hawthorne and Stanley's attempt to avoid appealing to knowledge of probabilities fails: why is our knowledge that three out of five people indicated to us that the restaurant is on the left relevant to whether we should go right or left, he asks, 'if not because it implies something about or simply reduces to a belief about the relevant probabilities?'

Perhaps someone sympathetic to Hawthorne and Stanley's position might respond as follows. A creature without the concept of chance may act on its degrees of belief. But the performance of such an act is proper only if its degrees of belief are justified by the relevant pieces of knowledge. For example, if it is proper to act on a 0.6 degree of belief in the restaurant being on the left, such a degree of belief, according to the current response, must be justified by some relevant piece of knowledge, such as the knowledge that three out of five people have indicated that the restaurant is on the left. Perhaps, in this sense, we can be said to be acting on the relevant piece of knowledge even though, in the first instance, we are acting on a 0.6 degree of belief in the restaurant being on the left.

I shall not dwell on whether the response works. For, even if we answer Baumann's worry, another one lurks. There seem to be cases in which it is in perfect order for us to act on our degrees of belief even though there is no relevant knowledge to be had. Consider cases in which one obtains a certain degree of belief in a proposition through the 'deliverances of experience' (van Fraassen 1980: 167–9). For instance, Jeffrey (1968: 172–3) holds that 'in examining a piece of cloth by candlelight, one might come to attribute [subjective] probabilities 0.6 and 0.4 to the propositions G that the cloth is green and B that it is blue', where such an assignment of degrees of belief is a 'direct result of the observation [by candlelight]'. Presumably, there are cases in which such degrees of belief are rational and we can act appropriately on them. If one holds that, in these cases, we must have knowledge of the relevant epistemic chances, then one faces Cresto's and Baumann's worries about the appeal to such knowledge. But it is not clear if there is any other relevant knowledge to be had. Perhaps one might hold that we must have knowledge that an experience of such-and-such qualities has a certain tendency to indicate the presence of an object with a certain colour. But this brings us back to the worry that, on Hawthorne and Stanley's account, whether it is proper for someone like Jane to perform a particular action depends not on her first-order knowledge about the world, but rather on her knowledge about her own mental states.

Consider also another kind of case that involves memory beliefs. Several epistemologists hold that one's belief may be justified even if one has forgotten one's original justification for it and has not gained any new relevant evidence. For example, Goldman (1999: 280) holds that many 'justified beliefs are ones for which an agent once had adequate evidence that she subsequently forgot'. And Bernecker (2008: 113–14) writes:

> Suppose at t_1, you come to justifiably believe (and know) that p on the basis of a trustworthy friend's having told you so. At t_2, as is normal, you have forgotten a great deal of what you once knew. Among those things that you have forgotten is that it was your trustworthy friend who told you that p. For all you know you could have acquired the belief that p by reading an article in the *National Inquirer* or from some other unreliable source. You no longer remember the original justification for believing p and you have not gained new evidence concerning the proposition in question. But since you remember p most of us would feel comfortable saying that you are still justified in believing p.

Although Goldman and Bernecker seem to have in mind a binary notion of belief, one might think that a similar point holds with respect to degrees of belief. Suppose that we justifiably come to have a degree of belief of 0.7 in *p* on the basis of a somewhat reliable friend telling us that *p*. Sometime later, we retain this degree of belief in *p*. Now, we might no longer remember our original evidence for having such a degree of belief, and we might not have gained any new evidence concerning *p*. But insofar as our memory allows us to remain justified in having a binary belief that *p* even if we have forgotten our original evidence for it, it should also allow us to remain justified in having a certain degree of belief in *p* even if we have forgotten our original evidence for it.

How does the discussion concerning memory beliefs bear on the discussion of knowledge and rational action? Well, suppose that one may have a justified degree of belief in a proposition even if one has forgotten one's original evidence (and has not gained any new relevant evidence) for it. If such a degree of belief is justified, then an action that is based on it – as well as on the relevant desires – may be justified as well. But there is no relevant knowledge about external facts to be had. After all, the case is precisely one in which one has forgotten the relevant evidence. Now, given the discussion above, a binary belief may be justified and may amount to knowledge even if one has forgotten one's original evidence for it. But presumably, since it is a categorical error to hold that a degree of belief of 0.7 in *p* is true or false, and since knowledge entails true belief, such a degree of belief cannot amount to knowledge.[12] Perhaps one might appeal to knowledge of the reliability of one's memory or knowledge of the vividness of one's memory impressions concerning *p*. But this move is unlikely to appeal to Hawthorne and Stanley, given that, ultimately, they want to tie rational action to first-order knowledge about the world.

3. Probabilistic knowledge to the rescue?

Moss (2013) has recently put forward an account of *probabilistic knowledge* that promises to deal with the worries raised against Hawthorne and Stanley. According to her, even though a degree of belief in p, unlike a binary belief that p, may not be something that is true or false, it can nonetheless constitute knowledge (1).[13] For instance, if Moss is right, a degree of belief of 0.6 in a piece of cloth being green can constitute knowledge concerning the cloth's being green, and a degree of belief of 0.7 in p can constitute knowledge even if one has forgotten one's original evidence for p. In such a case, one might maintain a strong connection between rational action and knowledge. For example, in the case of Jane, one might claim that her act of carrying an umbrella is proper only if her degree of belief of 0.4 in the proposition that it will rain constitutes knowledge. If Moss is right, there is no need to appeal to knowledge of epistemic chances or knowledge of other relevant facts.

Moss argues for the view that degrees of belief can constitute knowledge by contending that it 'yields simple solutions to some difficult problems'. She focuses on two main problems. The first problem concerns how to understand the language of subjective uncertainty. The second problem concerns cases that involve probabilistic analogues of Gettiered beliefs. I will go through each problem and then discuss Moss' solution.

3.1 The first problem

As Moss notes, we often utter sentences such as the following:

1. It's probably not raining.
2. Joe's more likely to be in the library than to be in his office.

Drawing on the work of Yalcin (2007), Moss (2013: 5) maintains that such sentences are not truth apt. For her purposes, she proposes to understand the sentences via 'a very simple expressivist semantics' according to which, in uttering the first sentence, one expresses the advice to give a high degree of belief to the proposition that it is not raining, and, in uttering the second sentence, one expresses the advice to give a higher degree of belief to Joe's being in the library than to Joe's being in his office.[14]

Why think that (1) and (2) are not truth apt? Consider the following sentences:

3. Suppose that it's raining, and it's probably not raining.
4. If it's raining and it's probably not raining, then . . .

Both (3) and (4) are infelicitous. But they should not be so if (1) were truth apt. If (1) were truth apt, then, when I utter (1), I would be asserting, for instance, the proposition that the epistemic probability that it is raining, given my total body of evidence, is low. But there is no infelicity in uttering the following:

5. Suppose that it is raining and the epistemic probability that it is raining, given my total body of evidence, is low.
6. If it's raining and the epistemic probability that it is raining, given my total body of evidence, is low, then . . .

This suggests that, in uttering a sentence such as (1), we are not trying to report a probabilistic fact about the world.

Given that the above is right, how should we understand a sentence such as the following?

7. Sue believes that it's probably not raining.

On expressivist theories, (7) does not ascribe a relation between Sue and a proposition concerning probability. In particular, (7) does not say that Sue has a binary belief concerning the probability of rain. Instead, it is really a claim about Sue's degrees of belief. It says that Sue's degrees of belief conform to a certain constraint – that she assigns a high degree of belief to the proposition that it is not raining.

But now there is a problem concerning a sentence such as the following:

8. Sue knows that it's probably not raining.

Traditionally, knowledge that p is understood to entail that p is true. Traditionally, when we ascribe knowledge to a subject, we ascribe a relation between that subject and a true proposition. However, given that 'It's probably not raining' is not truth apt, (8) does not ascribe an attitude towards truths.

3.2 The second problem

The second problem is that there are probabilistic analogues of Gettiered beliefs, and there is a question of how we should account for them. Consider the following example from Moss (2013: 9–10):

> Several assistants at a reputable entomology supply company select specimens from cultures in response to mail order requests for cereal flies. There are two cultures, one consisting mainly of *G. hackmani* specimens and one consisting

mainly of *G. balachowskyi* specimens. A diligent lab assistant sends out specimens from the former culture along with a letter to the recipient saying that their specimens are more likely *G. hackmani* than *G. balachowskyi*. Meanwhile, several disgruntled lab assistants have started sending out the very same sort of letter along with specimens from the latter culture. On receiving your letter, which happens to be from the diligent lab assistant, you assign more credence [assign greater degree of belief] to the proposition that your specimens are *G. hackmani* than to the proposition that they are *G. balachowskyi*.

Moss observes that in such a case, our believing that our specimens are more likely *G. hackmani* than *G. balachowskyi* – our assigning a higher degree of belief to the proposition that our specimens are *G. hackmani* than to the proposition that they are *G. balachowskyi* – seems justified on the basis of the letter we receive. Yet, Moss claims, there is nonetheless something 'epistemically incorrect' about our doxastic state (10). Although our specimens are indeed more likely to be *G. hackmani* than to be *G. balachowskyi*, this seems to be due to luck – in the way that, in Carl Ginet's fake barn case (Goldman 1976), it is due to luck that we are looking at a real barn. Further, we are not inclined to say that we *know* that our specimens are more likely to be *G. hackmani* than *G. balachowskyi*. Suppose that, just as there are Gettiered beliefs, there are Gettiered degrees of belief. It would be nice if we have a theory that picks out certain common properties that non-Gettiered beliefs and non-Gettiered degrees of belief share, and that tells us why such properties are absent in the example above (Moss 2013: 11).

3.3 Moss' solution and a worry concerning factivity

Moss (2013: 12–13) thinks that both problems can be solved by positing probabilistic knowledge – by holding that one's degree of belief can constitute knowledge.[15] Probabilistic knowledge helps solve the first problem. If degrees of belief can constitute knowledge, then Sue's believing that it's probably not raining can constitute knowledge, and she can know that it's probably not raining even though 'It's probably not raining' is not truth apt. Probabilistic knowledge also helps to solve the second problem. We assign a higher degree of belief to the proposition that our specimens are *G. hackmani* than to the proposition that they are *G. balachowskyi* just in case we believe it is more likely that our specimens are *G. hackmani* than that they are *G. balachowskyi*. Such a belief is epistemically incorrect, in just the way that a standard Gettiered belief is epistemically incorrect – they both fail to constitute knowledge.

One might wonder: how, exactly, is the positing of probabilistic knowledge supposed to help solve the first problem? After all, one might think, the worry is precisely that knowledge is factive but so-called probabilistic knowledge is not factive. This, as Moss is well aware, is the biggest worry for her. To mitigate it, she distinguishes two senses in which an attitude might be factive, and argues that, although knowledge is not factive in the first sense, it is factive in the second sense. In the first sense, for knowledge to be factive is for 'S knows that p' to be true only if p is true (14). If Moss is right, knowledge is not factive in this sense – on her view, it might be true that Sue knows that it's probably not raining even though the sentence 'It's probably not raining' is not truth apt.[16] But knowledge may still be factive in the sense that the inference from 'S knows that p' to p is valid, where validity is not defined in terms of truth preservation (14).[17] According to Moss, '[A]ny expressivist must develop notions of consequence, validity, and inconsistency within the context of an expressivist semantic theory' (15–16); instead of defining validity in terms of truth, an expressivist might hold that an inference from 'S knows that p' to p is valid in the following sense: 'if you follow the advice that "S knows that p" expresses, you thereby follow the advice that p expresses.'[18]

Moss considers the objection that the first sense of factive is the important one, 'since *factive* verbs should relate their subjects to *facts*' (17; emphases in the original). In response, she holds that she is not interested in settling a verbal dispute as to what 'factive' means; she thinks that the second sense of 'factive' does the work that we want a notion of factivity to do.[19] Nonetheless, one might worry that something important has been left out. It is often said that belief aims at truth.[20] One might think that there is something epistemically good or correct about a true belief, regardless of whether or not the belief is justified. Now, if knowledge entails true belief, then knowledge that p brings with it whatever a true belief that p brings (and more). There is something good about knowing that p, in part because there is something good about having a true belief. Can we account for this, given Moss' favoured sense of 'factive'?

It is not immediately clear how we might do so. Suppose we follow the advice that 'Sue knows that it's probably not raining' expresses, and thereby follow the advice that 'It's probably not raining' expresses. On Moss' view, 'It's probably not raining' expresses the advice to give a high degree of belief to the proposition that it is not raining. But what is epistemically good about following such advice – what is good about the mere adoption of such a high degree of belief? Moss does not say.

In light of the above, one might suggest that we need an analogue of truth for degrees of belief – that we need to say what makes for good advice. Hájek (manuscript) has argued that truth is to belief as objective chance is to degree of belief. Just as there is something epistemically good about a true belief – regardless of whether it is justified or whether it constitutes knowledge – there is something epistemically good about a degree of belief that matches the relevant objective chance – regardless of whether it is justified or whether it constitutes knowledge. Given this, one might suggest that a degree of belief of x in p constitutes knowledge only if the objective chance that p is true is x. For example, on the current suggestion, the advice to give low credence to the proposition that it is raining counts as good advice only if the objective chance that it is raining is low.

Here is a worry with the suggestion. Given that the objective chance of a past event is either 1 or 0, depending on whether the event occurred, we cannot have probabilistic knowledge of past events if the relevant degrees of belief are neither 1 nor 0.[21] But presumably proponents of probabilistic knowledge would want to maintain that we can have such knowledge – presumably, on their view, Sue's degree of belief of 0.9 in the proposition that it did not rain yesterday can constitute knowledge even if the objective chance of the proposition being true is not 0.9.

To get around the above worry, one might suggest that instead of appealing to objective chance, we appeal to epistemic probability. Moss (2013: 23) does consider the suggestion that 'your credence in a proposition constitutes knowledge just in case it equals your epistemic probability for that proposition'. But she points out that the suggestion does not work. Recall the lab specimens example. Suppose that the diligent lab assistant states in the letter that the specimens are very likely to be *G. hackmani*, and the disgruntled lab assistants do the same in their letters. Suppose that, as a result of reading the letter sent by the diligent lab assistant, we come to have a very high degree of belief in our specimens being *G. hackmani*. It seems that the epistemic probability of the specimens being *G. hackmani*, given the relevant evidence, is similarly high. But intuitively, Moss claims, our degree of belief does not constitute knowledge.

Now, one might wish to retreat to the weaker claim that one's degree of belief in a proposition constitutes knowledge only if it equals the epistemic probability of that proposition given one's evidence or background knowledge. However, a larger problem remains: namely, the epistemic probability of a proposition given one's evidence or background knowledge does not seem to serve as a good analogue of truth. As Moss points out, we might understand epistemic probability in terms of the degree of belief that it is rational for us to have in a proposition or in terms of the justification or evidence that we have for believing a proposition (23). So, the weaker claim is akin to saying that one's degree of belief constitutes knowledge only if it is rational or justified by one's evidence.

Perhaps the appeal to some kind of epistemic probability will still work if we follow Yalcin (2011) in distinguishing between *rational* speech acts and *advisable* speech acts. A speech act is 'rational in the sense that someone equipped with the evidence of the speaker would be responding appropriately to the evidence by accepting the content of the speech act', whereas it is 'advisable in the sense that a person equipped with full information about the relevant situation would be responding appropriately to that information by accepting the content of the speech act' (311). Now, consider the slightly modified lab specimens example. Suppose that we are one of those who get a letter from a disgruntled lab assistant, and we claim, 'It's very likely that our specimens are *G. hackmani*.' Is our claim rational? Is it advisable?

There is a way to understand rationality and advisability in terms of different kinds of epistemic probability. Since the epistemic probability of the specimens being *G. hackmani* given *our evidence* is high, we would be responding appropriately to our evidence by accepting that it's very likely that our specimens are *G. hackmani*. So, our claim is rational. But it is not advisable. Since the epistemic probability of the specimens being *G. hackmani* given *full information about the relevant situation* is low, someone equipped with such full information will *not* be responding appropriately to that information by accepting that it's very likely that our specimens are *G. hackmani*. It easy to see that there can also be advisability without rationality. Suppose that we get a letter from the diligent lab assistant, but, without reading it, we assign a high degree of belief to our specimens being *G. hackmani* because of wishful thinking (we really needed to get our hands on *G. hackmani*). Then it is not rational for us to claim, 'It's very likely that our specimens are *G. hackmani*.' But the claim is nonetheless advisable (in the sense spelt out by Yalcin). For the epistemic probability of the specimens being *G. hackmani*, given full information about the relevant situation, is high.

Given the distinction between rational and advisable speech acts, one might suggest that advisability serves as the analogue of truth for degrees of belief: whereas a binary belief aims at truth, a degree of belief aims at advisability. To illustrate, a belief that it's raining attains its aim of truth if it is true that it's raining. Analogously, a belief that it's probably raining attains its aim of advisability if the epistemic probability that it's raining, given full information about the relevant situation, is high.

The suggestion is promising. As mentioned, knowledge is epistemically good in part because it entails true belief, and there is something epistemically good about having a true belief, regardless of whether such a belief is justified or whether it amounts to knowledge. If the suggestion works, it will enable us to hold that, similarly, probabilistic knowledge is epistemically good in part because it entails believing a claim that is advisable, regardless of whether or not the belief is justified or amounts to knowledge.

However, more has to be done to spell out what it is to have full information about a relevant situation. Presumably, in many situations, due to the limited information available to us, we can at most believe that a proposition is very likely to be the case – we shouldn't be absolutely certain of the proposition. But someone with *full* information about the relevant situation might well have information that the proposition is in fact true. So, the epistemic probability of the proposition being true given such full information is 1. But then, if a degree of belief constitutes knowledge only if it equals the relevant epistemic probability, it would seem that most intermediate degrees of belief will not constitute knowledge.

3.4 Two other worries

Setting the issue of factivity aside, one might also worry about how to understand a sentence such as the following:

9. Sue knows that either it's very likely to rain or it's very unlikely to rain (but does not know which).

Suppose that Sue hears a weather forecaster whom she knows to be very reliable make an announcement about rain. Due to loud background noise, Sue isn't sure whether the forecaster said 'It's very likely to rain' or 'It's very *un*likely to rain,' although she knows that it was one of the two. Given this, it seems that we should accept (9). But if Sue's knowledge is probabilistic knowledge, what are the relevant degrees of belief?[22]

It won't do to hold that either Sue has a very high degree of belief or she has a very low degree of belief in the proposition that it will rain. In the first case, if her degree of belief were to constitute knowledge, it would constitute knowledge that it's very likely to rain. In the second case, if her degree of belief were to constitute knowledge, it would constitute knowledge that it is very unlikely to rain. But Sue neither knows that it's very likely to rain nor knows that it's very unlikely to rain.

One might think that, since Sue does not know whether it's more likely to rain or more likely not to rain, she might end up assigning a 0.5 degree of belief to the proposition that it will rain. As we'll see soon, I think that such a scenario is possible. Nonetheless, if such a degree of belief were to constitute knowledge, it would constitute knowledge that it's 50 per cent likely to rain, and not knowledge that either it's very likely to rain or it's very unlikely to rain.

Rothschild (2012: 109–12) considers a similar problem and suggests that the solution lies in *imprecise* degrees of belief. In particular, suppose that we model a person's degrees of belief by a set of probability functions rather than a single probability function. Then we can hold that Sue's doxastic state is modelled by a set of probability functions which are such that some of them assign a very high value to the proposition that it will rain and the rest assign a very low value to the same proposition. Such a doxastic state, one might hold, constitutes knowledge that it's very likely to rain or it's very unlikely to rain.

Those who think that degrees of belief should be precise will not be satisfied with this suggestion.[23] For they will hold that Sue is irrational if she has imprecise degrees of belief, but knowing that it's very likely to rain or it's very unlikely to rain (without knowing which) does not make her irrational. Of course, if one denies that degrees of belief can even be imprecise to begin with, one will also be dissatisfied with the suggestion.

Perhaps one might counter by holding that it is clear that Sue can know that either it's very likely or it's very unlikely to rain. One might then hold that, since the best way to account for this is by holding that such knowledge is constituted by rational imprecise degrees of belief, there is good reason to hold that the latter exist. (Thus, we have a new argument for imprecise degrees of belief.)

But here's a worry. It seems possible for Sue to know what she knows and yet lack the relevant imprecise degrees of belief. Consider the following exchange:

Joe: How confident are you that it'll rain?
Sue: I'm 50 per cent confident.
Joe: Is there any reason why?
Sue: Well, **I know that either it's very likely to rain or it's very unlikely to rain**. But I don't know which, and I've no more reason to think that it'll rain than I've reason to think that it won't.

Sue's claims **in bold** seem consistent. One might object that, given her evidence, she is irrational in being 50 per cent confident that it will rain; instead, her degree of belief in rain should be imprecise. However, even if this is right, the point remains that it is possible for Sue to know that either it's very likely to rain or it's very unlikely to rain (without knowing which), and then to assign a precise degree of belief to the proposition that it will rain – regardless of whether or not she is rational to do so. But then Sue's knowledge is not constituted by imprecise degrees of belief.

Yet another worry has to do with one's confidence in one's claims. (But this might be more of a request for clarification rather than a worry per se.) Consider the following exchange:

Sue: It's going to rain.
Joe: How confident are you?
Sue: Very confident.

The exchange above is intelligible. In replying to Joe, Sue is saying that she's very confident that it's going to rain. Now, consider a slightly different exchange:

Sue: It's probably raining.
Joe: How confident are you?
Sue: Very confident. (Or: somewhat confident)

This exchange seems intelligible too, and no less intelligible than the previous one. In replying to Joe, Sue is saying that she's very confident that it's probably raining. But how are we to understand the latter? Supposing that 'Sue believes that it's probably raining' tells us that Sue has a high degree of belief in the proposition that it's raining, what does 'Sue is confident that it's probably raining' or 'Sue is somewhat confident that it's probably raining' tell us about Sue's degrees of belief? Presumably, since each sentence is significantly different from the other two, they shouldn't all be telling us exactly the same thing – that Sue has a high degree of belief in rain. The worry, then, is that to distinguish between the sentences, we have to understand the latter two as reporting Sue's degree of belief in the proposition that it's probably raining. But such a view is presumably antithetical to the expressivist's position. If the latter two sentences are to be understood in such a way, it is at least puzzling why the first sentence should not be understood as reporting Sue's belief in the same probabilistic proposition.

4. Conclusion

One might think that, far from being rendered toothless, the notion of knowledge continues to bare its fangs. In particular, one might think that knowledge plays an important role in deliberation. I have focused on the view that one should act only on what one knows, and discussed some objections to it, as well as Hawthorne and Stanley's responses to those objections. I have also considered a defence of the view offered by Moss. Her defence avoids several of the worries faced by Hawthorne and Stanley. On her view, there is no conflict between acting on one's degrees of belief and acting on what one knows. For, according to her, one's degrees of belief may constitute knowledge. But, interestingly, her view introduces some challenges to the very notion of knowledge itself. Although she thinks that the main challenge – which has to do with the factivity of knowledge – can be answered, I have argued that her response might be a bit too quick.

Notes

1 Colloquially: We might be 70 per cent confident that it'll rain and 50 per cent confident that a fair coin will land heads if tossed.

2 For some arguments that ideally rational degrees of belief obey the probability axioms, see Vineberg (2016).

3 Here's one really high, perfectly Bayesian, standard of rationality. Assign a degree of belief of 1 to any tautology, no matter how complex. It seems that ordinary human agents will fall short of such a standard.

4 For an argument that knowledge requires certainty, see Unger (1971). For an argument that it doesn't, see Stanley (2008).

5 For instance, Conee (1988: 57) holds that the 'ultimate goal of pure inquiry' is knowledge, and not mere justified belief or mere justified true belief. Kaplan (1985: 350), however, argues that 'what you know doesn't matter' – that what matters, epistemically speaking, is justified true belief.

6 To elaborate, an act that we perform might have several possible outcomes. The utility that we assign to an outcome indicates how much we desire or prefer that outcome (relative to the other outcomes). The expected utility of an act A is calculated by taking the weighted average of the utilities of each of A's possible outcomes, where the weight associated with an outcome is given by our degree of belief in A leading to that outcome. The act that maximizes expected utility is, according to decision theory, the rational act to perform.

7 Similar views have also been put forward by Williamson (2000) and Fantl and McGrath (2009).

8 See Weatherson (2012) for another reason as to why knowledge plays an important role in decision-making. In this chapter, I focus on the kind of reason put forward by Hawthorne and Stanley.

9 Also, see Stanley (2005: 10).

10 For my purposes I follow Cresto (2010) in using terms such as 'higher-order knowledge' or 'second-order belief' to refer to knowledge or beliefs about one's attitudes, where such attitudes need not be beliefs.

11   Also, see Schiffer (2007: 190).

12   We'll see below that Moss (2013) would challenge such a claim.

13   Moss is not claiming that knowledge is a gradable notion. But for such a view, see
     Hetherington (2011) – in particular, chapters 2 and 5.

14   On a standard truth-conditional semantics, the meaning of a sentence is cashed
     out in terms of the conditions under which the sentence is true. But Yalcin (2007)
     has argued that a sentence like (1) is neither true nor false: when one utters it, one
     is not reporting a fact about the world but is instead expressing a certain attitude
     towards rain (just as someone who says 'Ouch!' is not saying anything true or false
     about the world but is merely expressing pain). An expressivist semantics attempts
     to account for the meaning of such sentences in non-truth-conditional terms.

15   Weisberg (2013: 11) also argues that degrees of belief can constitute knowledge, but
     on slightly different grounds – he thinks that a 0.4 degree of belief can constitute
     'a belief that there's a decent chance that P, or even a belief that P is 0.4 probable',
     where the notion of probability he has in mind is that of epistemic probability. As
     we have seen earlier, however, some might worry that children and animals can
     have a degree of belief in a proposition without being able to grasp the concept of
     epistemic probability.

16   But, to be more careful, Moss (2013: 14) does note that expressivists might endorse
     theories of truth on which probabilistic knowledge counts as factive even in the
     first sense. For reasons of space, I cannot discuss such theories here.

17   Moss (2013: 18–20) also considers versions of the safety condition and the
     sensitivity condition for probabilistic knowledge.

18   What about the worry that, traditionally, knowledge that p entails having a justified
     binary belief that p, but that, on Moss' view, it doesn't? She does not consider this
     worry explicitly. But it's plausible that she would say that what is important about
     the concept of knowledge is that 'S knows that p' entails 'S justifiably believes that p',
     and on her view such an entailment is preserved.

     For instance, on her view, 'Sue knows that it's probably not raining' does not
     entail that Sue has a justified binary belief that the probability that it's not raining is
     high. But it is plausible that Moss would hold that it entails 'Sue justifiably believes
     that it's probably not raining', which, on her view, is true just in case Sue justifiably
     assigns a high degree of belief to the proposition that it's not raining.

19   See Moss (2013: 15–17) for some examples illustrating how the second sense of
     'factive' does such work.

20   For discussion of this claim, see, for example, Wedgwood (2002) and Engel (2004).

21   Lewis (1980) and Schaffer (2007) think that past events are not chancy. But, for a
     dissenting view, see Loewer (2001) and Hoefer (2007).

22   This is a version of the Frege-Geach problem for expressivism with respect to
     probability talk. Traditionally, the problem is discussed with respect to certain
     metaethical theories according to which the utterance of a sentence such as

'Stealing is wrong' does not report a fact about the world but merely expresses a certain attitude (such as that of disapproval) towards stealing (Geach 1965). For instance, on such a kind of view, uttering the sentence is akin to uttering 'Stealing – boo!' But now there arises a question as to how we may account for the relation between the sentence 'Stealing is wrong' and a more complex sentence in which the former is embedded, such as 'If stealing is wrong, encouraging someone to steal is wrong, too' and 'He knows that stealing is wrong but is tempted to steal anyway.' To see why there is at least a prima facie problem, consider, for instance, the conditional sentence. Typically, the antecedent of a conditional is taken to be a proposition, which is either true or false. But, on the kind of view under consideration, 'Stealing is wrong' is neither true nor false. Perhaps the meaning of 'Stealing in wrong' in an unembedded context is different from its meaning in an embedded context. But one might worry that such a suggestion is implausible.

23 See Elga (2010) and White (2009) for arguments that rational degrees of belief should be precise.

References

Baumann, P. (2012), 'Knowledge, Practical Reasoning and Action', *Logos & Episteme*, 3: 7–26.

Bernecker, S. (2008), *The Metaphysics of Memory*, Dordrecht: Springer.

Conee, E. (1988), 'Why Solve the Gettier Problem?', in D. F. Austin (ed.), *Philosophical Analysis: A Defense by Example*, Dordrecht: Kluwer.

Cresto, E. (2010), 'On Reasons and Epistemic Rationality', *The Journal of Philosophy*, 107: 326–30.

Elga, A. (2010), 'Subjective Probabilities Should Be Sharp', *Philosophers' Imprint*, 10: 1–11.

Engel, P. (2004), 'Truth and the Aim of Belief', in D. Gillies (ed.), *Laws and Models in Science*, London: King's College Publications.

Fantl, J. and McGrath, M. (2009), *Knowledge in an Uncertain World*, Oxford: Oxford University Press.

Geach, P. T. (1965), 'Assertion', *The Philosophical Review*, 74: 449–65.

Goldman, A. I. (1976), 'Discrimination and Perceptual Knowledge', *The Journal of Philosophy*, 73: 771–91.

Goldman, A. I. (1999), 'Internalism Exposed', *The Journal of Philosophy*, 96: 271–93.

Hájek, A. (manuscript), 'A Puzzle about Degrees of Belief'.

Hawthorne, J. (2004), *Knowledge and Lotteries*, Oxford: Clarendon Press.

Hawthorne, J. and Stanley, J. (2008), 'Knowledge and Action', *The Journal of Philosophy*, 105: 571–90.

Hetherington, S. (2011), *How to Know: A Practicalist Conception of Knowledge*, Malden, MA: Wiley-Blackwell.

Hoefer, C. (2007), 'The Third Way on Objective Probability: A Sceptic's Guide to Objective Chance', *Mind*, 116: 549–96.

Jeffrey, R. C. (1968), 'Probable Knowledge', in I. Lakatos (ed.), *The Problem of Inductive Logic*, Amsterdam: North-Holland Publishing.

Kaplan, M. (1985), 'It's Not What You Know That Counts', *The Journal of Philosophy*, 82: 350–63.

Lewis, D. (1980), 'A Subjectivist's Guide to Objective Chance', in R. Carnap and R. C. Jeffrey (eds), *Studies in Inductive Logic and Probability, Volume II*, Los Angeles: University of California Press.

Lewis, D. (1996), 'Elusive Knowledge', *Australasian Journal of Philosophy*, 74: 549–67.

Loewer, B. (2001), 'Determinism and Chance', *Studies in History and Philosophy of Science Part B*, 32: 609–20.

Moss, S. (2013), 'Epistemology Formalized', *The Philosophical Review*, 122: 1–43.

Rothschild, D. (2012), 'Expressing Credences', *Proceedings of the Aristotelian Society*, 112: 99–114.

Schaffer, J. (2007), 'Deterministic Chance?' *The British Journal for the Philosophy of Science*, 58: 113–40.

Schiffer, S. (2007), 'Interest-Relative Invariantism', *Philosophy and Phenomenological Research*, 75: 188–95.

Stanley, J. (2005), *Knowledge and Practical Interests*, Oxford: Clarendon Press.

Stanley, J. (2008), 'Knowledge and Certainty', *Philosophical Issues*, 18: 35–57.

Unger, P. (1971), 'A Defense of Skepticism', *The Philosophical Review*, 80: 198–219.

van Fraassen, B. C. (1980), 'Rational Belief and Probability Kinematics', *Philosophy of Science*, 47: 165–87.

Vineberg, S. (2016), 'Dutch Book Arguments', in E. N. Zalta (ed.), *The Stanford Encyclopedia of Philosophy* (Spring 2016 Edition): http://plato.stanford.edu/archives/spr2016/entries/dutch-book/.

Weatherson, B. (2012), 'Knowledge, Bets, and Interests', in J. Brown and M. Gerken (eds), *Knowledge Ascriptions*, Oxford: Oxford University Press.

Wedgwood, R. (2002), 'The Aim of Belief', *Philosophical Perspectives*, 16: 267–97.

Weisberg, J. (2013), 'Knowledge in Action', *Philosophers' Imprint*, 13: 1–23.

White, R. (2009), 'Evidential Symmetry and Mushy Credence', in T. S. Gendler and J. Hawthorne (eds), *Oxford Studies in Epistemology, Vol. 3*, Oxford: Oxford University Press.

Williamson, T. (2000), *Knowledge and Its Limits*, Oxford: Clarendon Press.

Yalcin, S. (2007), 'Epistemic Modals', *Mind*, 116: 983–1026.

Yalcin, S. (2011), 'Nonfactualism about Epistemic Modality', in A. Egan and B. Weatherson (eds), *Epistemic Modality*, Oxford: Oxford University Press.

11

The Analysis of Knowledge

Duncan Pritchard

1. The analytical project in epistemology

For much of the past fifty years, the project of offering an analysis of propositional knowledge was thought to be central to the epistemological enterprise. Call this the *analytical project*, for short. The reason why this project came to the fore of epistemological discussion around fifty years ago is of course due to the famous article by Edmund Gettier (1963) which demonstrated that the traditional tripartite account of knowledge in terms of justified true belief was unsustainable. In countering the tripartite account, Gettier also cemented the idea that there was indeed a traditional account of knowledge in the literature along just the lines that he sets out in his critique of it. This might well be contentious, so let us first pause to explore a little what is supposedly involved in the 'traditional' tripartite account.

In what follows, I will take it as entirely uncontentious that knowledge entails truth, in the sense that it is *factive* – if one knows that p, then p is true. It is also reasonably uncontentious that knowledge entails belief – or at least some sort of belief-like propositional attitude – in the sense that if one knows that p, then one believes that p.[1] We should thus focus our attention on the third condition in the tripartite analysis, the justification condition. Gettier himself says very little about this condition. He attributes it to Roderick Chisholm (1957: 16) and to A. J. Ayer (1956), although in both cases he grants that they do not quite use the terminology of 'justification' themselves, writing instead (respectively) in terms of the knowing subject having 'adequate evidence' for their belief in the target proposition or 'having the right to be sure' that the target proposition is true.[2] What seems to be the common thread here as far as Gettier is concerned is that knowledge requires true belief that is supported by good reasons that the subject can offer in favour of the truth of her belief.

Crucially, however, it is also vital to the counterexamples that Gettier offers to the tripartite account, as he himself notes, that justification cannot itself be factive (i.e. one can have a justified belief that p and yet p be false). This is important because so-called Gettier-style cases essentially involve a subject justifiably believing a proposition in a manner that would have ordinarily resulted in a false belief, but where the subject ends up with a true belief regardless, albeit one that is completely disconnected from the justification.

To take one of Gettier's own examples, suppose that one has a good justification for believing that p is true, when in fact it is false. Now imagine that one infers from p the (inclusive) disjunction, either p or q, where q is a proposition which one has no reason for thinking is true. Normally, inferring a disjunction in this way would lead to a false belief (viz. where one's original belief is in fact false, and where one is adding a disjunct that one has no reason to think is true). Nonetheless, one's belief ought to be justified, at least if the original belief that p is justified, because if one has good reasons for thinking that p is true, then one also has good reasons for thinking that p or q is true. All we now need to do is stipulate that the inferred disjunction is true, on account of q being true (unbeknown to our subject). Hey presto, we now have a justified true belief, where the truth of the belief is completely disconnected from the original justification (which, recall, was a justification for thinking that p, and hence that p or q, is true).

We will examine the structure of Gettier-style cases a little more thoroughly in a moment. First, I want to reflect on whether Gettier is right to suppose that it was widely accepted, prior to his article, that knowledge has been analysed along these particular tripartite lines. In fact, there is reason to be sceptical of this claim, as it seems far from straightforward that pre-Gettier epistemologists would have been happy to accept a conception of justification that was compatible with the target belief being false. Ayer, for example, sets out his position in opposition to what he refers to as the 'quest for certainty', which would suggest that he took the standard view to be much more demanding than his own. Moreover, there is a clear philosophical tradition, at least in the United Kingdom, of treating knowledge as involving an *infallible* grasp of the truth.[3] This is a tradition that goes back at least to the writings of John Cook Wilson (which have been tremendously influential on twentieth-century British philosophy) and those directly influenced by him, such as H. A. Prichard.[4] Accordingly, it might plausibly be argued that the tripartite account of knowledge that Gettier attacked with his counterexamples was in fact not the standard view at all. Moreover, notice that the idea that knowledge involves an infallible grasp of the truth appears to go hand-in-hand with a conception of justification which is similarly infallible, and which would thus be completely unaffected by Gettier-style counterexamples. On this view, after all, the agents in Gettier-style cases are not justified in what they believe, precisely because their justification is compatible with the falsity of what they believe.[5]

Even so, one can see why those who initially responded to Gettier's article in the mid-1960s were willing to grant that justification must be understood along fallibilist lines. Wouldn't such an infallibilist conception of justification lead directly to radical scepticism, and hence be unsustainable?[6] In that case, the stark choice facing those responding to Gettier's counterexamples seems to either be to endorse an infallibilist conception of justification, and so deal with the very real threat of radical scepticism, or else to embrace a fallibilist conception of justification and to inherit the problem of offering an adequate analysis of knowledge that Gettier-style cases expose.

In any case, what is clear from the post-Gettier literature is that commentators very quickly took on board the idea that justification must be understood along fallibilist lines, and hence that the 'traditional' tripartite conception of knowledge was as Gettier described. For example, if one were to open an epistemology textbook written from a post-Getter perspective, then one would expect to see the tripartite account of knowledge being described just as Gettier described it. Moreover, we see this point in action in terms of the initial wave of responses to Gettier counterexamples, which involve, not a renewed defence of an infallibilist conception of justification, but rather the offering of ways of effectively bolstering the tripartite account that has a fallibilist conception of justification at its core.[7] With this point in mind, let us look a little closer at the problem that Gettier identifies.

2. The Gettier problem

As we saw in the previous section, Gettier's own cases essentially involve an inference, and so one natural response to these cases is to suppose that this is where one should focus in trying to fix the tripartite account.[8] In particular, in the case that we looked at earlier, the subject forms her justified true belief in the disjunction by inferring it from a false premise (i.e. her justified belief that p). Thus, one might suppose that all we need to do to get around the problem is to insist that knowledge is justified true belief – where justification is still understood along the non-factive lines that Gettier attributed to the tripartite account – that is not inferred from any false premises. This general style of approach to the Gettier problem is known as the *no false lemmas* approach.[9] Although initially appealing, it quickly runs into difficulties, and hence acts as a good 'case-study' when it comes to appreciating why solving the Gettier problem is trickier than it looks.

The first thing to note is that while Gettier's own two counterexamples to the tripartite account of knowledge essentially involve an inference from a false premise, this seems incidental to the general structure of a Gettier-style example. Consider, for example, the 'sheep' case that Chisholm (1977: 105) offers. Imagine a farmer – whom we'll call 'Roddy' – who is looking into a field and sees what looks to be a sheep. On this basis, Roddy comes to justifiably believe that there is a sheep in the field. As it happens, though, what he is looking at is not a sheep at all but merely a big hairy dog that looks like a sheep. Ordinarily, then, if one were to form this belief on this basis one would end up with a false belief. Nonetheless, Roddy has excellent (although fallible) grounds in favour of his belief – the big hairy dog does, after all, look just like a sheep, and Roddy has no reason to doubt what he sees – which is why his belief is justified. Moreover, as it happens, Roddy's belief is true since there is a sheep in the field hidden from view behind the big hairy dog. Roddy thus has a justified true belief that does not count as knowledge (since one can't come to know that there is a sheep in the field simply by looking at a big hairy dog).

Note that there is no essential inference involved in this case – Roddy just looks into the field and directly forms the belief that there is a sheep in the field. Moreover, notice that this case has just the kind of structure of a standard Gettier-style case, in that we effectively have good epistemic luck cancelling out bad epistemic luck, such that the target belief is both true and justified, but where the latter is completely disconnected from the former. That is, the bad epistemic luck that Roddy happens to be looking at a sheep-shaped object rather than an actual sheep is cancelled out by the good epistemic luck that there happens to be a genuine sheep in the field. This is why his justification for his belief is disconnected from the truth of the belief.[10]

The existence of such cases entails that the no false lemmas approach will need to be much more subtle in order to be effective.[11] In particular, it must allow for false assumptions that are in some sense operative in the background, even if the subject doesn't actively employ them in an inference. In the case just described, for example, Roddy is falsely supposing that what he is looking at is a genuine sheep, even if this is not a premise in his reasoning towards his belief that there is a sheep in the field.

But the fundamental challenge facing any development of the no false lemmas view is to offer a principled way of understanding what constitutes a false lemma in this regard which is neither too broad as to exclude genuine cases of knowledge, nor too thin as to be unable to deal with Gettier-style cases. In order to see the force of the latter horn, notice that one can construct Gettier-style cases where the subject is not misled at all, at least in a direct fashion. Consider, for example, the famous *barn façade case*.[12] Here we are to imagine a subject – let's call him Barney – who looks at a genuine barn in good cognitive conditions, and thereby forms the justified true belief that what he is looking at is a barn. The twist in the tale is that, although this barn is genuine, it is in fact the only genuine barn in the vicinity, all of the others apparent barns in fact being mere barn façades. Had Barney happened to look at any of the other apparent barns, then he would have formed a false belief.

This case has just the same feature of good epistemic luck cancelling out bad epistemic luck that we find in other Gettier-style cases. Barney has the bad epistemic luck to be forming a belief that there is a barn before him by looking at the front of the object in an environment where this is not a reliable guide as to whether there is a genuine barn there. But this bad epistemic luck is cancelled out by the good epistemic luck that he happens to be looking at the one genuine barn in the vicinity. Accordingly, his justification for what he believes is disconnected from the truth of his belief.

But what is the false assumption in play in the barn façade case supposed to be, on the no false lemmas view? Is Barney really assuming that he is not in barn façade country? Moreover, if we do attribute this stance to the proponent of the no false lemmas thesis, then the other horn of our dilemma becomes apparent. For if the notion of a false lemma is this broad, then isn't it often the case that when we genuinely come to know propositions there will be *some* false assumptions in play, however tacit? The worry is thus that a lot of our bona fide knowledge is now under threat.[13]

The point of the foregoing is not to suggest that the no false lemmas approach is completely unsustainable, but merely to highlight the difficulties involved in dealing with the Gettier problem.[14] Indeed, I think we are now in a better position to say a bit more about what the Gettier problem amounts to. In particular, while in the first instance it was treated as the challenge of explaining how we go about fixing the traditional tripartite account of knowledge, once we recognize that there is no easy fix in this regard a deeper construal of the Gettier problem emerges. This concerns our very notion of knowledge. Gettier cases highlight the point that when one knows one's cognitive success – that is, one's true belief – ought not to be just down to luck in any significant way. Instead, it should be arising out of our cognitive agency.

This is exactly what goes wrong in Gettier-style cases, and thus why the tripartite account of knowledge is unsustainable as it stands. That is, we might have initially thought that having a justification, even a fallible one, would ensure that our beliefs are due to our cognitive agency in such a way that they are not simply down to luck. And yet the good-luck-bad-luck structure of the Gettier-style cases exposes how one can have a justified true belief and yet the truth of one's belief is entirely down to luck and nothing to do with one's manifestation of cognitive agency. Roddy is manifesting his cognitive agency by using his reliable perceptual faculties to pick out (what he takes to be) the sheep before him. And he ends up with a true belief, but the truth of his belief is just down to the good epistemic luck that there happens to be a sheep in the field hidden from view behind the sheep-shaped object at which he is looking. Similarly, Barney is manifesting his cognitive agency by using his reliable perceptual faculties to pick out the barn before him. And he ends up with a true belief, but the truth of his belief is just down to the good epistemic luck that he happens to be looking at the one genuine barn in the vicinity. And so on.

If this is the right way of characterizing the Gettier problem, then it suggests that our natural way of thinking about knowledge is in terms of a cognitive success that is not down to luck, but is rather in some substantive way due to our manifestation of cognitive ability. This raises some interesting questions about why we think about knowledge in this fashion. Moreover, given that the moral of the Gettier problem is that (fallible) justification cannot fit the bill in this regard, then the hunt is on to find a way of thinking about knowledge that is adequate.[15]

3. Scepticism about the analytical project

Interestingly, however, while there has been a thriving philosophical industry devoted to resolving the Gettier problem, there is also a growing mood of scepticism about the very possibility – and even desirability – of offering such a solution. There are various sources of this scepticism. One source of scepticism is not specific to the analytical project in epistemology, but rather concerns all analytical projects in philosophy. Perhaps they are all wrong-headed, in that no philosophically interesting notion can be made subject to such an account? One might, for example, advance broadly Wittgensteinian reasons in support of this claim.[16]

Whatever the rationale for this sceptical line, I think we can fairly set it to one side for our purposes, given that it is not specific to the analytical project in epistemology. Moreover, it is also notable that this way of critiquing the analytical project tends to take it as given that what it would take to resolve this project is a non-circular set of necessary and sufficient conditions. But it is far from clear that our ambitions should be nearly so ambitious. An analysis of knowledge might well be informative even though it interdefined several notions, and hence was not ultimately non-circular. Nonetheless, such an account might cast a lot of light on the nature of these notions and how they relate to one another. Conversely, it is also worth noting that non-circular analyses of knowledge can sometimes be *un*informative, as when they are ad hoc, so it is not as if eliminating circularity is a guarantee of a good analysis anyway.[17]

A more interesting sceptical line regarding the analytical project for our purposes – and which is specific to knowledge – arises out of the post-Gettier literature itself. It involves a kind of pessimistic induction, whereby the continued failure of epistemologists engaged in this literature to offer a counterexample-proof analysis of knowledge is meant to provide inductive support for the idea that there is something inherently wrong-headed about this approach.[18] In effect, the idea is that offering an analysis of knowledge is akin to being involved in a degenerating research programme.[19] Interestingly, this complaint often goes hand-in-hand with a distinct sceptical line to the effect that the kinds of analyses of knowledge that have been offered in post-Getter epistemology tend to be so convoluted and plain ugly that one struggles to see how they could ever be plausible, much less account for why knowledge is such a fundamentally important notion.

Although these two complaints tend to be run together, I think we would be wise to keep them apart. The latter complaint is the weaker one. Why can't an analysis of knowledge be entirely adequate but also ugly? Indeed, why can't it be simultaneously true that knowledge is the kind of thing that we value a great deal, and that also has a complex, and thus ugly, analysis?[20] What makes this complaint even less compelling is that, although some solutions that have been offered to the Gettier problem have been complex, there are in fact some elegant solutions available too, as we will see in a moment.

This last point is also relevant to the pessimistic induction complaint. This is because whether such an inductive inference is sensible very much depends on whether we think that progress has been made in the post-Gettier literature. That a research programme has failed does not itself entail that it is a degenerating research programme, after all, since this could be a failure that has been inching towards success. Again, that there are some elegant solutions to the problem available in the literature is thus a good ground to be suspicious of this sceptical line regarding the analytical project.

A final source of scepticism about the analytical project in epistemology arises out of the *knowledge-first* research programme as defended by Timothy Williamson (2000). Unlike the other critiques of the analytical project, this is focused on offering a positive defence of an alternative approach. Williamson argues that once we recognize the conceptual primacy of knowledge with regard to related concepts like belief and evidence, such that we attempt to define the latter in terms of the former rather than vice versa, then we will be able to make significant headway on the key epistemological problems. This doesn't just include resolving the Gettier problem – which effectively disappears on this view, at least insofar as we treat that problem as essentially trading on the idea that we should analyse knowledge in terms of true belief plus some further epistemic conditions – but also extends to other difficulties such as the problem of radical scepticism.

It would take me too far afield to critically engage with knowledge-first epistemology here, particularly since it is a proposal that has so many important moving parts.[21] Instead, I am going to take a slightly different tack, and briefly outline two recent responses to the analytical project that I think are plausible. As we will see, in doing so I am not necessarily objecting to knowledge-first epistemology, since both of these proposals could be recast along knowledge-first lines (even while – arguably at any rate – remaining potential resolutions of the analytical problem).[22]

4. Resolving the analytical project: robust and anti-luck virtue epistemology

We noted above that the moral of the Gettier problem is that one can appropriately manifest one's cognitive agency (such that one's belief is justified), and in the process be cognitively successful (viz. form a true belief), even though there is a complete disconnection between one's cognitive success and one's manifestation of cognitive agency. In particular, even despite one's appropriate manifestation of cognitive agency, one's cognitive success can nonetheless be due to luck. If that's right, then this suggests that the way to respond to the Gettier problem is to insist that the cognitive success be appropriately related to the manifestation of cognitive agency.

How might one do this? One popular proposal – advanced, in various guises, by such figures as Ernest Sosa (1991, 2007, 2009, 2016), Linda Zagzebski (1996, 1999), and John Greco (2009) – is to contend that knowledge should be understood as cognitive success that is *because of* the subject's manifestation of relevant cognitive agency. Take, for example, the Roddy case described above. Although Roddy is cognitively successful and appropriately manifests cognitive agency (such that his belief is justified), his cognitive success is not in any sense because of his manifestation of cognitive agency. Rather, it seems to be because of the happenstance that there is a sheep hidden from view in the field, which is nothing to do with his cognitive agency.

This proposal is known in the literature as *robust virtue epistemology*. It is a form of virtue epistemology in that it defines knowledge in terms of the manifestation of cognitive agency (or intellectual virtue, broadly conceived). It is a robust form of the view, in that it only appeals to cognitive agency in its account of knowledge, rather than incorporating a non-virtue-theoretic condition as well (we will be looking at a non-robust, or *modest*, form of virtue epistemology in a moment).[23] There are lots of technicalities regarding how best to understand this proposal – for example, how best to unpack the 'because of' relation which figures in this account – but we will need to restrict ourselves to making a few general points about the view.

First, it is important to note some of the attractive features of the proposal. In particular, it is able to offer a striking diagnostic story as to why knowledge might be structured in this fashion. The idea is that knowledge is simply a subclass of the broader category of *achievements*, where an achievement is a success that is because of the subject's manifestation of relevant skilful agency. This explains why one can construct analogous Gettier-style cases outside epistemology. Take someone firing an arrow at a target. Merely hitting the target would not suffice for an achievement, since perhaps there is no skill involved. But achievements are also undermined when there is both success and the relevant manifestation of skilful agency but where the latter is not because of the former. This is where the Gettier-style luck comes into play. An archer who skilfully fires an arrow at a target, and hits the target, but only hits the target because (say) a dog jumped up mid-flight, snatched the bolt and placed it in the target, would not be credited with an achievement.

A further advantage of this proposal is that it seems able to account for the special value that we place on knowledge. Achievements, after all, are of special value to us – a good life is surely one that is rich in achievements, for example – and hence it is unsurprising that knowledge, qua cognitive achievement, should also be prized.[24]

Robust virtue epistemology thus offers a compelling response to the analytical project, and thus the Gettier problem. Note, though, that the analysis of knowledge that it offers may well turn out to be non-reductive. Perhaps, for example, there is no way of defining cognitive agency that doesn't appeal to knowledge. In that case, the proposal would be ultimately circular. Nonetheless, it could still be informative, for the reasons given above, and hence an adequate response to the analytical project. (Relatedly, notice that robust virtue epistemology and knowledge-first epistemology need not be in conflict, in that a proponent of the latter could consistently endorse a version of the former.)

Despite the attractions of robust virtue epistemology, it does face some problems. One issue is that, although it fares well with regard to standard Gettier-style cases like the Roddy scenario, it struggles with some non-standard cases, particularly the Barney example. Wouldn't we naturally describe this case as being one where the subject's true belief is indeed because of his manifestation of relevant cognitive agency (he is looking at a real barn after all)? More generally, some have objected that knowledge and achievements come apart in terms of their relationship to luck. While an achievement can be *fragile* – in the sense that, although it is a success that is because of one's skilful agency, it nonetheless could have easily been a failure – the same doesn't seem true of knowledge. The archer who skilfully hits the target, but who could have easily missed (had the mischievous dog just described not been held back, for example), nonetheless exhibits an achievement. But would we ever treat a cognitive success that could have very easily been a cognitive failure – as in the Barney case – as an instance of knowledge?[25]

This problem concerns whether robust virtue epistemology is too weak as an account of knowledge, in that it treats some agents as having knowledge which intuitively they do not possess. But the account has also been charged with being too strong, in that it seems to deprive some agents of knowledge that they genuinely possess. Often, for example, testimonial knowledge is gained, to a large extent, by trusting the word of another. But would we want to say that in such cases one's cognitive success is because of one's manifestation of cognitive agency? The point is that although one does manifest some degree of relevant cognitive agency in such cases – testimonial knowledge isn't acquired by simply trusting anyone, after all – nonetheless in such scenarios it seems as if one's cognitive success is because of one's *informant's* manifestation of cognitive agency, if anyone's.

As is usual in philosophy, none of these objections, at least taken alone, is fatal, as there are plausible counter moves that the proponent of robust virtue epistemology can make. For example, some commentators have observed that the intuition that knowledge is lacking in the Barney case is far less strong than in more standard Gettier-style cases, like the Roddy scenario. Accordingly, one could reasonably argue that, rather than being an objection to the proposal, one should instead embrace the consequence that Barney has knowledge in this case, on account of the fact that he has exhibited a genuine cognitive achievement.[26]

If one is unconvinced by robust virtue epistemology, however, there is another proposal available in the general vicinity. This is a modest form of virtue epistemology, in that it doesn't exclusively define knowledge in terms of a virtue-theoretic condition. According to this proposal, we should take seriously the idea that there are two distinct constraints operative on knowledge. One is that one's cognitive success should be appropriately related to one's cognitive agency. The other is that one's cognitive success shouldn't be due to luck; alternatively, that it shouldn't be a risky success (viz. a success that could have very easily been a failure). Gettier-style cases demonstrate that one can satisfy the first constraint without thereby satisfying the second constraint. Indeed, Barney-style cases seem to demonstrate that one can exhibit a genuine cognitive achievement even while lacking knowledge on account of the epistemic luck involved. Conversely, it is uncontentious that one's cognitive success can be neither due to luck nor anything to do with one's manifestation of cognitive agency – perhaps there are environmental factors that simply guarantee that one's belief will be true, regardless of its epistemic pedigree.

If we take these observations seriously, then they suggest a more complex analysis of knowledge than that offered by robust virtue epistemology. According to this proposal – what is known as *anti-luck* (or *anti-risk*) *virtue epistemology* – knowledge is to be understood as non-lucky/non-risky cognitive success that is significantly attributable to one's manifestation of relevant cognitive agency. Notice that this account is both in one aspect more demanding, and in another aspect less demanding, than robust virtue epistemology. It is more demanding in that it is not just one's cognitive success that needs to be significantly attributable to one's manifestation of relevant cognitive agency, but rather one's non-lucky/non-risky cognitive success. It is less demanding, in that the relation in play here is not the because-of relation employed by robust virtue epistemology. Instead, all that is demanded is that one's manifestation of relevant cognitive agency should play some significant explanatory role in one's non-lucky cognitive success.[27]

Anti-luck virtue epistemology is designed to avoid the kinds of problems that face robust virtue epistemology. Barney-style cases are dealt with on account of how they involve lucky success. But one can also account for why cases of testimonial knowledge that involve a high degree of trust are genuine, since although the subject's cognitive agency does not play an overarching explanatory role in her cognitive success, it does play a significant explanatory role.

Anti-luck virtue epistemology is thus able to offer an alternative way of responding to the analytical project, and hence the Gettier problem (although, like robust virtue epistemology, this doesn't mean that it is thereby offering a reductive account of knowledge). Admittedly, however, anti-luck virtue epistemology lacks the elegant simplicity of robust virtue epistemology, and that might be thought to be a substantive strike against it.

5. Concluding remarks

That there exist plausible responses to the analytical project that arose in response to the Gettier problem obviously doesn't entail that this project has been resolved, much less that it is a coherent philosophical project to undertake. But it does suggest that we shouldn't be too quick to dismiss this project, or else to take it for granted that it represents a degenerating research programme. It also highlights that the challenge that Gettier posed for epistemology in 1963 is still alive today.[28]

Notes

1   This condition has been disputed – for example, by Radford (1966) – but is nonetheless widely accepted.

2   In addition, Gettier suggests that Plato's discussion of knowledge in the *Theaetetus* in terms of true opinion, or judgement, with an account as potentially also being an endorsement of the traditional tripartite account of knowledge.

3   And of course there is also an earlier, and far more influential, Cartesian tradition of seeking certain foundations for one's knowledge.

4   See Cook Wilson (1926) and Prichard (1950). I am grateful to Charles Travis for first alerting me to the work of Cook Wilson and its influence on UK philosophy, particularly via Prichard, but also in the writings of such figures as J. L. Austin, John McDowell, and Timothy Williamson. See especially Travis (2005).

5   For a detailed defence of the idea that an infallibilist conception of justification was part of the standard pre-Gettier account of knowledge, see Dutant (2015). For a helpful discussion of the role of the notion of fallible justification in the Gettier problem, see Zagzebski (1994).

6 This is the line that Ayer (1956: 21) took, for example.

7 See Zagzebski (1994). A good example of this general tendency is the *no false lemmas* approach that we will examine below. Note, however, that in the recent literature there has been a resurgence of interest in a factive conception of justification, largely inspired by McDowell's (e.g. 1995) defence of (a position which is these days called) epistemological disjunctivism. See, for example, Pritchard (2012b).

8 For a detailed account of the first wave of responses to the Gettier counterexamples in the literature, see Shope (1983).

9 For an early version of this approach, see Clark (1963).

10 I think the first person to characterize Gettier-style cases in terms of this recipe of good epistemic luck cancelling out bad epistemic luck was Zagzebski (1994). See also Zagzebski (1999). For more on the notion of epistemic luck and its role in Gettier-style cases, see Pritchard (2005, 2015).

11 Note, too, that there are lots of cases of this general type in the literature, and hence it would not be a promising strategy to try to side-step this difficulty by claiming that in this particular example the subject is making a hidden inference from a false premise (e.g. such as from *that's a sheep*, to *there is a sheep in the field*).

12 This was first offered by Goldman (1976), although he credits the example to Carl Ginet.

13 Note that one response to the barn façade case is to deny that it is a Gettier-style case at all, and thus to insist that the agent acquires knowledge. Although this approach was not initially seen as very plausible, it has gained some traction in the recent literature. For a high-profile proponent of this line, see Sosa (2007: 31–2). For a recent critical discussion of this line of argument, see Pritchard (2016). A more radical line – one that applies not just to the barn façade case but also to other Gettier-style cases – is to insist that knowledge is compatible with the agent forming her true belief entirely by luck. For a defence of this view, see Hetherington (2013). For a response, see Pritchard (2013).

14 For a particularly interesting recent development of the no false lemmas line, see Lycan (2006).

15 For further discussion about the right way to conceive of the 'Gettier problem', see Pritchard (2015, 2017).

16 See, especially, Wittgenstein's (1953) famous remarks on family resemblance concepts.

17 See Zagzebski (1999) for an insightful discussion of how we should think about the project of analysing knowledge. More generally, see Strawson's (1992) influential account of elucidation in philosophical analysis.

18 There are many exponents of this complaint, but the most prominent is Williamson (2000: ch. 1).

19 See Lakatos (1978).

20 See DePaul (2009) for a very interesting discussion of just this point.

21 For a very helpful recent book-length critique of knowledge-first epistemology, see McGlynn (2014).

22 A further source of scepticism about the analytical project can be found in the particular wing of virtue epistemology that explicitly rejects the idea that defining knowledge should be central to the epistemological enterprise. See, for example, Code (1987), Kvanvig (1992), Montmarquet (1993), Hookway (2003), and Roberts and Wood (2007). Sometimes this proposal is allied to one of the complaints regarding the analytical project just noted, but often the claim is simply that focusing on the analytical project in some fundamental way distorts what the epistemological enterprise ought to be about (i.e. epistemically virtuous agents). For further discussion of the methodology of epistemology, and the role of the analytical project within it, see Pritchard (2012c).

23 I introduced the distinction between robust (or 'strong') and modest (or 'weak') forms of virtue epistemology in earlier work. See especially Pritchard (2009) and Pritchard, Millar, and Haddock (2010: chaps 1–4).

24 For further general discussion of the value of knowledge, see Pritchard (2007). For further discussion of the specific topic of the value of achievements, see Pritchard (2010).

25 For a recent development of this general line of objection in terms of an epistemic twin earth argument, see Kallestrup and Pritchard (2014).

26 See also note 13.

27 For the main defences of this proposal, see Pritchard (2009, 2012a, 2016, 2017) and Pritchard, Millar, and Haddock (2010: chaps 1–4).

28 I am grateful to Stephen Hetherington for helpful comments on an earlier version of this chapter.

References

Ayer, A. J. (1956), *The Problem of Knowledge*, Harmondsworth: Penguin.

Chisholm, R. M. (1957), *Perceiving: A Philosophical Study*, Ithaca, NY: Cornell University Press.

Chisholm, R. M. (1977), *Theory of Knowledge*, 2nd edn, Englewood Cliffs, NJ: Prentice-Hall.

Clark, M. (1963), 'Knowledge and Grounds: A Comment on Mr. Gettier's Paper', *Analysis*, 24: 46–8.

Code, L. (1987), *Epistemic Responsibility*, Hanover, NH: University Press of New England.

Cook Wilson, J. (1926), *Statement and Inference*, Oxford: Clarendon Press.

DePaul, M. R. (2009), 'Ugly Analyses and Value', in A. Haddock, A. Millar, and D. Pritchard (eds), *Epistemic Value*, Oxford: Oxford University Press.

Dutant, J. (2015), 'The Legend of the Justified True Belief Analysis', *Philosophical Perspectives*, 29: 95–145.

Gettier, E. (1963), 'Is Justified True Belief Knowledge?' *Analysis*, 23: 121–3.

Goldman, A. (1976), 'Discrimination and Perceptual Knowledge', *Journal of Philosophy*, 73: 771–91.

Greco, J. (2009), *Achieving Knowledge: A Virtue-Theoretic Account of Epistemic Normativity*, Cambridge: Cambridge University Press.

Hetherington, S. (2013), 'Knowledge Can Be Lucky', in M. Steup, J. Turri, and E. Sosa (eds), *Contemporary Debates in Epistemology*, 2nd edn, Malden, MA: Wiley Blackwell.

Hookway, C. (2003), 'How to Be a Virtue Epistemologist', in M. DePaul, and L. Zagzebski (eds), *Intellectual Virtue: Perspectives from Ethics and Epistemology*, Oxford: Oxford University Press.

Kallestrup, J. and Pritchard, D. (2014), 'Virtue Epistemology and Epistemic Twin Earth', *European Journal of Philosophy*, 22: 335–57.

Kvanvig, J. L. (1992), *The Intellectual Virtues and the Life of the Mind: On the Place of the Virtues in Epistemology*, Savage, MD: Rowman & Littlefield.

Lakatos, I. (1978), *The Methodology of Scientific Research Programmes: Philosophical Papers Volume 1*, ed. J. Worral and G. Currie, Cambridge: Cambridge University Press.

Lycan, W. G. (2006), 'On the Gettier Problem Problem', in S. Hetherington (ed.), *Epistemology Futures*, Oxford: Clarendon Press.

McDowell, J. (1995), 'Knowledge and the Internal', *Philosophy and Phenomenological Research*, 55, 877–93.

McGlynn, A. (2014), *Knowledge First?* London: Palgrave Macmillan.

Montmarquet, J. A. (1993), *Epistemic Virtue and Doxastic Responsibility*, Lanham, MD: Rowman & Littlefield.

Prichard, H. A. (1950), *Knowledge and Perception*, Oxford: Clarendon Press.

Pritchard, D. (2005), *Epistemic Luck*, Oxford: Oxford University Press.

Pritchard, D. (2007), 'Recent Work on Epistemic Value', *American Philosophical Quarterly*, 44: 85–110.

Pritchard, D. (2009), 'Knowledge, Understanding and Epistemic Value', in A. O'Hear (ed.), *Epistemology: Royal Institute of Philosophy Supplement: 64*, Cambridge: Cambridge University Press.

Pritchard, D. (2010), 'Achievements, Luck and Value', *Think*, 9: 1–12.

Pritchard, D. (2012a), 'Anti-luck Virtue Epistemology', *The Journal of Philosophy*, 109: 247–79.

Pritchard, D. (2012b), *Epistemological Disjunctivism*, Oxford: Oxford University Press.

Pritchard, D. (2012c), 'On Meta-Epistemology', *The Harvard Review of Philosophy*, 18: 91–108.

Pritchard, D. (2013), 'Knowledge Cannot Be Lucky', in M. Steup, J. Turri, and E. Sosa (eds), *Contemporary Debates in Epistemology*, 2nd edn, Malden, MA: Wiley Blackwell.

Pritchard, D. (2015), 'Anti-luck Epistemology and the Gettier Problem', *Philosophical Studies*, 172: 93–111.

Pritchard, D. (2016), 'Epistemic Risk', *The Journal of Philosophy*, 113: 550–71.

Pritchard, D. (2017), 'Knowledge, Luck and Virtue: Resolving the Gettier Problem', in C. Almeida, P. Klein, and R. Borges (eds), *Explaining Knowledge: New Essays on The Gettier Problem*, Oxford: Oxford University Press, 57–73.

Pritchard, D., Millar, A., and Haddock, A. (2010), *The Nature and Value of Knowledge: Three Investigations*, Oxford: Oxford University Press.

Radford, C. (1966), 'Knowledge: By Examples', *Analysis*, 27: 1–11.

Roberts, R. C. and Wood, W. J. (2007), *Intellectual Virtues: An Essay in Regulative Epistemology*, Oxford: Clarendon Press.

Shope, R. K. (1983), *The Analysis of Knowing: A Decade of Research*, Princeton: Princeton University Press.

Sosa, E. (1991), *Knowledge in Perspective: Selected Essays in Epistemology*, Cambridge: Cambridge University Press.

Sosa, E. (2007), *A Virtue Epistemology: Apt Belief and Reflective Knowledge*, Volume I, Oxford: Clarendon Press.

Sosa, E. (2009), *Reflective Knowledge: Apt Belief and Reflective Knowledge*, Volume II, Oxford: Clarendon Press.

Sosa, E. (2016), *Judgment and Agency*, Oxford: Oxford University Press.

Strawson, P. F. (1992), *Analysis and Metaphysics: An Introduction to Philosophy*, Oxford: Oxford University Press.

Travis, C. (2005), 'A Sense of Occasion', *The Philosophical Quarterly*, 55: 286–314.

Williamson, T. (2000), *Knowledge and Its Limits*, Oxford: Clarendon Press.

Wittgenstein, L. (1953), *Philosophical Investigations*, ed. G. E. M. Anscombe and R. Rhees, trans. G. E. M. Anscombe, Oxford: Blackwell.

Zagzebski, L. (1994), 'The Inescapability of Gettier Problems', *The Philosophical Quarterly*, 44: 65–73.

Zagzebski, L. T. (1996), *Virtues of the Mind: An Inquiry into the Nature of Virtue and the Ethical Foundations of Knowledge*, Cambridge: Cambridge University Press.

Zagzebski, L. T. (1999), 'What Is Knowledge?', in J. Greco and E. Sosa (eds), *Blackwell Guide to Epistemology*, Oxford: Blackwell.

12

Conceiving of Knowledge in Modal Terms?

Stephen Hetherington

1. Two generic modal dimensions to knowing?

When contemporary epistemologists contemplate the nature of knowledge, standardly they claim to discern its having at least two interlinked modal dimensions. One of those dimensions is of strength; the other is of structure. What links each to the other is a shared concern to characterize aspects of knowledge as a distinctive form of connection to truth. Two general questions then arise. How *strong* a connection to truth is knowledge? And in what specific *ways* is knowledge a connection to truth?

When philosophers talk of modality *simpliciter*, they are generally aiming to reflect upon forms of possibility and necessity. Usually, the initial such form that is discussed is *metaphysical* modality. For instance, consider a particular frog, existing within this world. Are there other ways that it *might* have been? If so, is that also part of what makes it a frog at all – here, now, in this world? Equally, are there features that the frog not only has but *had* to have? If so, is that also part of what makes it a frog at all – here, now, in this world? We may gaze at the frog, sitting silently, gulping phlegmatically. No matter how closely we observe it, though, perhaps we will never be observing all of it, in the sense that we will never be observing its modal dimensions as such – its being such that there is also some feature that it *could* have, and its having some feature *necessarily*. Does it nonetheless have those modal dimensions? Of course, philosophers are supposedly not confined to observation when posing and answering those questions; and so, in particular, we might accord ourselves the conceptual freedom to wonder non-observationally about the modal dimensions of various beings and phenomena. The frog is one such being; knowing is one such phenomenon. What are *knowledge's* modal dimensions, then?

2. Being less generic about those possible modal dimensions of knowledge

Let us render Section 1's generic remarks somewhat less so, by mentioning some of the more prominent pertinent ideas that epistemologists have proposed.

The strength dimension. Here we meet the fallibility/infallibility distinction – and we see its being combined with the concept of knowledge. We ask whether, in knowing a truth or state of affairs p, your link to p must somehow be infallible. Or, more moderately, is fallibility allowed within knowing? Clearly, the answer to that question will depend on how we should understand what fallible knowledge *would* be. A standard first conception of it could well be this:[1]

> One's knowledge that p is *fallible* when the knowledge's presence coexists with the possibility that one's evidence (or whatever other epistemic justification one might have) for believing that p was not strong enough to eliminate entirely the prospect of the belief's being false. And one's knowledge that p is *in*fallible if and only if it is not fallible: the evidence (or whatever other epistemic justification one has for the belief that p) is too strong to admit even the possibility of the belief's being false.

The fallibility as such would thus be the belief's possibly being mistaken – its possibly being false, that is, for all that the evidence (or whatever other epistemic justification that the person has for the belief) proves to the contrary. Correlatively, the knowledge's being fallible would be its presence coexisting somehow with the belief's possibly being mistaken.

The structure dimension. Can there be any fallible knowledge – or, for that matter, infallible knowledge – if it is to be understood in that way? If we are to understand why knowledge that p needs to be infallible, or instead why it is able to be fallible, we might need to understand something about its structurally modal features. A picture of those features will – at least if it is relevantly explanatory – either include or preclude mention of fallibility, as it describes how various other phenomena combine in constituting an instance of knowledge. Several such pictures have been sketched, with each being built around some supposedly explanatory central notion. In that respect, epistemologists have been especially interested in the notions of epistemic safety, veritic luck, and epistemic sensitivity.

3. Possible worlds

But before we can understand those notions, we need to understand something about modality itself. So, let us take a moment, in this section, to do that.

When contemporary philosophers seek to understand modality, most commonly they talk of *possible worlds*. Philosophical use of the idea of a possible world – of there somehow and in some sense being worlds, other than this one, that are equally possible – dates back to Gottfried Leibniz in the seventeenth century. How could there be a God, given the apparent evil that so readily permeates this world? Leibniz's famous – still famous – answer to this theologically and humanly pressing question involved the view that this is *the best of all possible worlds*.[2] That was – still is – an evocative metaphysical picture.

It has also been a philosophically adaptable picture. Beginning in the mid-twentieth century, the concept of a possible world has been applied – increasingly so – to a wide range of philosophical tasks. The result has been *many* evocative pictures, supposedly of the modal dimensions of many phenomena. Rudolf Carnap (1947) talked influentially of state descriptions. In the 1950s, several logicians, including Jaakko Hintikka, turned their attention to modal models. Then came the 1960s and beyond: again Hintikka was prominent, especially with his *Knowledge and Belief* (1962), along with – most notably – Saul Kripke (1963, 1972) and David Lewis (1968, 1973, 1986). Philosophy quickly became replete with analyses and applications – including epistemological ones – of the idea of a possible world.[3]

In Leibniz's hands, that idea was purely metaphysical. In contemporary hands, it became part of a semantic package. At the centre of that package was this sort of idea:

> A statement of the form 'Possibly, p' is true in a world if and only if there is at least one possible world, accessible from that first world, where it is true that p. A statement of the form 'Necessarily, p' is true in a world if and only if in no world accessible from that first one is it false that p.

The accessibility relation between worlds was intended to reflect different strengths of possibility and thereby of necessity. When, but only when, it is an equivalence relation being applied at once to *all* possibilities (so that every world is accessible from every world) does necessity become truth in all possible worlds, for instance.

The accessibility relation could also be used to reflect different kinds of possibility and thereby of necessity. One such kind is *epistemic*. And (it was proposed, such as by Hintikka) knowing could be semantically modelled *as* a kind of necessity: 'one knows that p at time t' is true if and only if it is true that p in every world that is epistemically accessible for one at t. We might then say that such a world is one that includes (i) all of one's evidence at t for p and (ii) nothing incompatible with what (else) one knows at t. There is room for debate as to the nature of epistemic possibility. There is also room for debate (see Hetherington 2016b) as to whether knowing should be analysed semantically in quite such modally strong terms – needing p to be true in all (rather than just in many) of the epistemically accessible worlds. But few epistemologists would doubt that – if modal terms are to be used at all in thinking about knowing – we will need to look to *some* further possible worlds, beyond this one, in analysing 'one knows at t that p'.

4. Gettier cases

The 1960s experienced a special spur to the growth in modal accounts of knowledge. That spur was Edmund Gettier's (1963) challenge to how epistemologists had been conceiving of what it is to have some knowledge. It was a striking challenge to the accuracy of a specific approach to defining what it is to have knowledge.

Now, a definition of knowledge would purport (at least by implication) to pronounce accurately upon *each* actual or possible instance of knowledge or of non-knowledge: 'yes, it's knowledge', implied of each and only each instance of knowledge; similarly for 'no, it's not knowledge' for each and only each instance of non-knowledge. And the particular kind of definition that was Gettier's prey also seemed to be especially *efficient* in its use of other conceptual resources: it called upon just three other concepts, seemingly simple ones. Gettier began his landmark paper by highlighting this way of seeking to define knowledge. It soon became known as the *justified-true-belief* definition of knowledge (for any person S, time t, and proposition p):

> At t, S knows that p =df At t, it is true that p, S believes that p, and S has good justification for believing that p (for instance, S has good evidence for its being true that p).

If Gettier was right, this definition had long been presumed or defended by philosophy. Even so, he found a surprisingly simple way to question the *sufficiency* of the definition's picture of what it is to know. Gettier described two apparent counterexamples to the definition – to its sufficiency as an account of knowing's nature. These were thought experiments. They portrayed imaginary situations where a person has a justified true belief that nonetheless – surmised Gettier (and epistemologists in general have since agreed with him about this) – fails to be knowledge. Such situations – be they real or be they hypothetical;

be they Gettier's two, or be they similar ones thought of subsequently by other epistemologists – soon became known as *Gettier cases*. The main belief at the core of a Gettier case was called, correlatively, a *Gettiered* belief.

Gettier's own first case (often termed *the job-coins case*) was as follows. He imagines someone, Smith, being told by the company president that Jones will be getting a particular job within the company. Smith combines that evidence with his knowing – we are not told why he has this knowledge – that there are ten coins in Jones's pocket. Smith infers that Jones, with ten coins in his pocket, will be getting that job – and then infers, too, that *the person who will be getting the job has ten coins in his pocket*. Lo and behold: that final belief is true. It is made true, however, by Smith himself: *he* will be getting the job and *he* has ten coins in his pocket – neither of which is something that he knows about himself. Should we allow that his final belief – that the person who will get the job has ten coins in Jones's pocket – is knowledge? Not at all (says Gettier). However, notice that it is true and justified: it is made true by two facts about Smith; and it is justified by the testimony from the president, by Smith's having counted the coins in Jones' pocket, and by his inferring his final belief from all of this via some simple (and good) reasoning. Hence, the belief is true and justified without being knowledge; in which event, the justified-true-belief definition of knowledge cannot be revealing *enough* of what it takes, in general, for a belief to be knowledge.

Gettier and his cases were inspirational for epistemologists: 'the Gettier problem' was born – the epistemological challenge, still unresolved, of uncovering a *better* definition of knowledge than the justified-true-belief definition now seemed to have been. Some epistemologists have questioned aspects of Gettier's challenge.[4] Still, most have accepted that it succeeded. Let us consider the main post-Gettier suggestions, therefore, that took an explicitly modal turn while trying to conceive of knowledge in ways that reflected an acceptance that Gettier had genuinely uncovered something about knowledge and the inadequacy of understanding it in terms of the justified-true-belief definition.

5. Post-Gettier modal accounts of fallible knowledge

Fallibility is an explicitly modal phenomenon, since the suffix 'ible' connotes some sort of possibility. Now compare the idea of a fallible inquirer with that of a fallible knower. The former could be exemplified by someone who is somewhat liable to make mistakes – in particular, to form some false beliefs (which are thereby not knowledge). A fallible *knower* could be understood similarly: one can know sometimes even if not always, in spite of earnest effort. What is more subtle, however, is the idea of fallible *knowledge* – some knowledge being achieved yet somehow remaining fallible in itself. Epistemologists are still striving to understand this idea.[5]

Section 2 introduced us to a traditional conception of fallibility. It was also one of the two key epistemic principles with which Gettier (1963) developed his counterexamples to the justified-true-belief definition of knowledge. Here is how he formulated that fallibilism: 'in that sense of "justified" in which S's being justified in believing P is a necessary condition of S's knowing that P, it is possible for a person to be justified in believing a proposition that is in fact false' (121). And from that we can derive a simple account of fallible knowledge – as being a fallibly justified true belief (since this was the account that was about to be questioned by the rest of Gettier's paper):

> S knows that p =df S has a true belief that p that is justified well-even-if-fallibly (in the sense that S's justification somehow leaves open the possibility of not-p).

But Gettier proceeded to challenge that definition; and epistemology has not been the same since he did so. One aspect of post-Gettier conceptions of knowledge has been an increased awareness of alternative possible conceptions of the fallibility as such within any instance of fallible knowledge. Another kind of response has, it seems, sought a modally stronger connection to truth, within any instance of knowledge, than Gettier was considering. I will describe, briefly, an example of each of these approaches.

Failability. Why is fallibility even a prima facie threat to knowing (as many epistemologists would allow it to be)? The underlying reason is that possibly being mistaken is possibly not knowing; for possibly being mistaken is possibly failing to satisfy knowledge's truth condition. More precisely, possibly being mistaken is possibly not knowing even when all else that is part of knowing *is* present. And this, I have argued (1999; 2001: ch. 2), is the more fundamental sort of failing that is present when fallibility is. In any event, we need to move beyond the traditional conception of fallibility. For if a given p is necessarily true then it cannot be false, no matter what justification is also present for one's belief that p. Nevertheless, it seems that we would want to say that there is at least a fallibility-*like* weakness that could be embedded within one's justification for some necessarily true belief that p – and hence that the necessarily true belief that p of one's would be knowledge in at least a fallible-*like* way. How should we recognize this enriched sense of the relevant modal details within an adequate definition? My proposal was this:[6]

> S knows failably that p =df S knows that p, but there is at least one aspect of S's knowing that p which could have been absent even with the others being present (in which event, S would *not* have known that p).

Failability is thus the genus of which fallibility is a species: knowledge's being fallible is just one way for it to be failable. And so knowledge could be fallible-like by being failable. How is that so? On the traditional conception of fallibility (the one on which Gettier called), the truth that p could be absent even when the belief that p and the justification for that belief remain: in at least one accessible possible world, one still has the belief and the justification, but the belief is not true. *That* is how knowledge would be failable by being fallible. Yet knowledge can be failable also by being modally fragile in how it has one or both of its components *other* than truth.[7] For example, perhaps one has justification that supports one's true belief that p, yet there are accessible possible worlds where one retains the true belief even in the absence of that justification. This would induce a modal fragility – a fallibility-*like* quality – in one's knowing that p: one does know, although one might not have done so; and even when not doing so, one would still have been constitutively close to doing so (because one's justified belief need only have also been true, say, if it was to be knowledge).

Conclusive reasons. Gettier's challenge can be regarded as undermining our ability to define fallible knowledge, not simply knowledge per se. Correlatively, one response to Gettier cases has been to deny that knowledge *ever* is understandable in a fallibilist way. Linda Zagzebski (1994), for one, argued that, so long as one's concept of knowledge is fallibilist, one will never find a definition of knowledge that survives Gettier's sort of challenge: any fallibilist conception is susceptible to actual or new Gettier cases. Should we therefore seek to understand knowledge in *in*fallibilist terms – as being akin more to necessity than to (mere) possibility?

An influential exemplar of that approach was Fred Dretske (1971). He focused on a line of modal thought about knowledge that has often been remarked on by philosophers. Consider this form of claim: 'If you know that p, then you cannot be wrong about p.' There are two ways *not* to be epistemologically impressed by such a claim. First, it could be reflecting a triviality – that knowledge entails truth: necessarily, if you know that p then it is true that p. Second, that sort of claim could be overly restrictive by saying that if you know that p then it is necessarily true that p. But Dretske found another interpretation of such claims.

He characterized knowledge that p in terms of having conclusive reasons for believing that p (so that, in *this* sense, if you know that p then you cannot be wrong about p) – with R being a conclusive reason for p if and only if R would not be the case unless p were the case.

How is that a modal condition? Well, recall Section 3's presentation of the most central modal concepts in terms of possible worlds. Other concepts, too, were soon seen to admit of being understood in those terms. A few years prior to Dretske's proposal, Robert Stalnaker (1968) had shown philosophers how they could analyse *conditionals* semantically in terms of possible worlds: 'If p then q' is true at a world if and only if, in the possible world most like that first world where it is true that p, it is true that q. Around that time, too, Lewis (1973) modified Stalnaker's approach. On this theory of counterfactual conditionals, 'If p were true, q would be true' is true at a world if and only if, in the possible worlds most like that first world where it is true that p, it is true that q. (Lewis thus talks of 'worlds' where Stalnaker had written of a single world, in each case where it is true that p.) The Stalnaker-Lewis kind of theory, as it is often called, is now philosophers' default way of conceiving of the semantics of conditionals. But the immediate point is that Dretske's account of knowledge was at least partly modal (and so we are about to examine recent modal accounts of knowledge that have continued some of Dretske's thinking).[8]

6. Post-Gettier modal accounts of knowledge's structure

Tracking. In 1981, Robert Nozick's account of knowledge appeared – an account that, like Dretske's, conceived of knowledge partly by way of subjunctive conditionals. Nozick (1981: 172–85) called his a *tracking* account of knowledge. It added these two distinctive conditionals to the usual (1) truth condition and (2) belief condition for knowledge that p:

3. If p were not true, then S would not believe that p.
4. If p were true (not only in this world, but in other close possible worlds), then S would (continue to) believe that p.

Nozick's motivation for these conditions included resolving Gettier's challenge but also engaging satisfyingly with *sceptical* challenges. This dual motivation would, if successful, give us an even richer conception of knowledge. Nozick was aiming to show, for example, that although a sceptic could be correct to deny you the knowledge that you are not a brain in a vat on Alpha Centauri (a brain being stimulated to think that you are living a normal life on Earth), this would not entail your not knowing your everyday surroundings (206–10). Dretske (1970) had also argued for this conceptual combination, as Nozick (1981: 689n53) acknowledged. It is a tempting vista. Nozick's account has sparked much debate.[9]

Safety. Focusing less on scepticism than on Gettier, Ernest Sosa (e.g. 1999) proposed a slightly different modal link as being needed within knowing. Consider Gettier's job/coins case. Smith's final belief is Gettiered (on that proposal of Sosa's) because it has been formed *unsafely*. Consider the other possible worlds that are the most like this world from among those worlds where Smith relies in the same way on the same evidence as he does in this world. In too many of them, it seems, he will be led by that belief-forming method (the same one as he has used here) to form a *false* belief, instead of – as it happens – the true belief that he has formed in this world via that same belief-forming method. Smith's belief-forming method is thus unsafe. This is why even the true belief that he has generated by using it is not knowledge.

Veritic luck. Sosa's adverting modally to the role of belief-forming methods within knowledge was part of what has become a recent tradition. Nozick was likewise careful to include within his conditions (3) and (4) – when these were fully formulated – a reference to the belief-forming *method* that was used by the person: the method via which she had formed her belief that p within this world was also how, in applying conditions (3) and (4), she was to be considered as forming – or not forming – her belief within those other possible worlds. That emphasis upon belief-forming methods is also at the heart of recent accounts of knowledge in terms of *veritic luck* – this being a kind of *epistemic* luck. This sort of account is associated especially with Duncan Pritchard (e.g. 2005).[10] He, too, is much motivated by reflection upon Gettier cases. Within each such case (we are told), the reason why the case's Gettiered belief is not knowledge is its being true only veritically luckily. This is explained modally:

> In *not enough* of the accessible possible worlds where a belief is generated via the same belief-forming method as has been used in the specific Gettier case within this world, say, is a true belief formed. (By hypothesis, a true belief has been formed via that method within this world, since the belief is part of a Gettier case; not in enough other relevant possible worlds, though.)

In Gettier's job/coins case, for example, given the evidence on which Smith has relied in forming his belief, and given the circumstances in which he has used that evidence, he has been lucky to reach his true final belief (that the person who will get the job has ten coins in his pocket). Smith's evidence was about

Jones, not himself. And there are accessible possible worlds where Smith has that same final belief on the basis of that same evidence – but where the belief is false because neither he nor Jones will get the job, say. This is a simple modal variation on what actually occurs within Gettier's case; and so there are accessible possible worlds where variations such as this occur. The belief has also thereby been formed unsafely: even when – as in Gettier's case – a true belief is the result of Smith's sort of reasoning in his circumstances, this outcome is infrequent enough within accessible possible worlds that we may classify the Gettier case's belief as being true only luckily. And knowledge – we are told – is never a belief that is true like *that*.

7. The redundancy problem for modal accounts of knowing

The previous sections have conveyed some of the variety existing among overtly modal accounts of knowledge. Are there general morals that we are now in a position to derive about such accounts, even thereby about knowledge itself? I will close this chapter by developing one such moral. The result will be a programmatic challenge to one of epistemology's treasured presumptions about the nature of knowledge.

This much is immediately clear from the earlier sections: when epistemologists highlight knowledge's supposed modal aspects, they are emphasizing and seeking to understand knowledge's link to truth. Each of the accounts we have met strives to explicate knowledge's nature in some way that links the belief in question (the belief that p, that supposedly is the knowledge that p) not only to the truth that p but also to truths (including the same truth that p) in other possible worlds. For instance, we saw (in Section 5) how the traditional characterization of *in*fallible knowledge that p requires the true belief that p to be replicated in all other possible worlds where the person has the same evidence. Correlatively, *fallible* knowledge would be held to require such replication in not-all-but-still-enough such possible worlds, if the true belief is to be (fallible) knowledge that p in this world. A similar thesis was on display with the concept of veritic luck, for example (in Section 6): if a belief is to be knowledge, it is not enough for the belief to be true in this world; the belief needs to have been formed in a way that mostly, when also being used in other possible worlds, generates a true belief. In such ways, therefore, we see that epistemological attempts to conceive of knowledge in modal terms seek to explicate how a belief is knowledge only if it is more than actually true – that is, only if it is true yet not only so within *this* world.

Now, that thesis – saying that knowledge involves more than being correct merely within this world – may be treated as either equivalent to, or entailed by, the venerable epistemological truism that, in some way, knowledge is a true *and (epistemically) justified* belief.[11] I say 'in some way' because epistemologists have remarked at length on what a belief needs to be – other than true – if it is to be knowledge. They have suggested various theories of epistemic justification, such as theories built around the concept of *evidence* for the truth of the belief or the concept of a faculty's or a person's truth-linked *reliability* in forming the belief.[12] All such suggestions share this view:

> Knowledge is more than true belief, by also including something that at least entails an appropriate configuration of true beliefs in other accessible possible worlds. For instance, *using good evidence* to reach one's true belief is a means whereby one's actually reaching a true belief is a member of this set: {in this world, you form the true belief that p by using that evidence; in world 1, that also happens; as it does in world 2; likewise in world 3; not quite so in world 4, say, where the outcome is a false belief that p; etc., with that sort of distribution of many-more-true-than-false beliefs that p recurring throughout the worlds where that evidence is being used}.

Yet *must* knowledge be conceived of in that way? In effect, epistemologists are thereby offering us instances of the following picture when they conceive of knowledge modally (so as to portray it as being more than mere true belief): 'In knowing that p, both an *actual* true belief that p and various *possible* true beliefs, including true beliefs that p, are needed. The latter need not all be possessed by the one person in the one world. They are possessed modally, spread across individuals – including the same individual – in various possible worlds – including this one.' Knowledge in one world is thus at least a true belief in that world. But – we are being told – it also involves the existence of true beliefs in other possible worlds.

Why should we be tempted by such a picture? The standard epistemological answer, I believe, would be that – by being thus modally 'fattened', most likely by the use of some sort of justification for the belief that p – the knowledge that p is a relevantly *stronger link* to the truth that p than is constituted by a mere true belief that p. I suggest, however, that even this apparently natural answer should be treated with caution. There is a reason why we are *not* obliged to accord the modal fattening of the person's link to the truth that p an epistemic weight that has to be conceived of as being part of her knowing that p. That reason is, in effect, a generalization of epistemology's *swamping* problem for those who would include process reliability as a component within knowing. The swamping problem is as follows:[13]

> It is an epistemological datum that there is epistemic value in knowledge – including some epistemic value beyond whatever value there is in simply the true belief within the knowledge. Presumably, the justification – including any of its modal consequences – within knowledge helps to give the knowledge that increased value. Yet when the justification is reliabilist, the value in the justification's presence is its having rendered *more likely* the true belief's presence. But once the true belief *is* present, how is the resulting combination thereby any better because of the reliability's continuing presence? It is not. Accordingly, we do not advance our understanding of knowledge's value – or therefore our understanding of knowledge itself – by conceiving of its justification component in a reliabilist way.

Now let us generalize that argument, so that we are discussing not only reliabilists but also that larger body of epistemologists who advocate modal accounts of knowledge. I call this the *redundancy* problem:[14]

> Consider the epistemic value of being linked to truth by one's belief. And compare the state that is *a belief that p's being true and justified* (be it fallibly or be it infallibly justified) with the state that is *a belief that p's being true*. Standard epistemology tells us that the former state should – courtesy of the justification within it – be more strongly linked than the latter state to p's *being true*. Necessarily, though, neither of those states is more strongly linked than the other to that state of affairs: trivially, there is no possible world where a true belief is not true – just as there is no possible world where a justified true belief is not true. Hence, insofar as the value of the justification's presence within the knowledge that p is to *be* the knowledge's being the sort of link to the truth that p that it should be (given its being knowledge, after all), the justification adds *no* value by its presence within the knowledge. (Its presence is redundant, in that sense.)

What does that argument suggest about the possible nature of knowledge? It points us towards a way of conceiving anew of the relationship between knowledge and its modal associations.

1. We might begin by allowing any instance of knowledge to be, strictly speaking, *simply a true belief*. For this is all that is needed, insofar as being in the state of knowing that p is to be a link to the truth that p. The

redundancy problem shows that, once one has a true belief that p, one has a modal link to the truth that p that is not strengthened by adding justification to the true belief.

2. Is justification thereby irrelevant to the knowing that p? Not necessarily. Once we no longer require justification's presence within knowledge, we have the conceptual licence to accord justification a slightly different role within this general epistemic neighbourhood. Evidence for p's being true, like reliability in the belief-forming method that one uses in gaining the belief that p, could still be deemed to be epistemically valuable for a *potential* knower that p. For instance, evidence could be useful in a self-regulative way – when one is *considering* and *choosing between* possibilities, as part of *forming* a belief that p. And reliability could be cited as an explication of why we look to this person rather than that one, when wondering whether to form one's own belief that p on the basis of testimony, say. We might continue to regard justification as essential for such roles, insofar as – for whatever reason – we wish to reach knowledge that is justified. There are many social settings where, and reasons why, we often seek not only to be correct but to have good evidence for our being correct. We might also believe that, as a matter of contingent fact about people and our wider world, the use of justification is how we are *more likely* to reach the true beliefs that – by (1) – are our cases of knowledge.

More generally, then, I am proposing this conceptual reorganization of the relevant epistemic phenomena:

> Evidence or other justification could *help us* to know – and might even be the best way for us to gain knowledge, given facts about how our world functions – without the evidence or other justification thereby being *part* of the resulting knowledge (the knowledge that is present once a true belief has been formed). In short, justification could be *causally* constitutive of knowledge without being *metaphysically* constitutive of it. In this way, knowledge's modal aspect would be part of that *causal background*, without being literally a *component within* the knowledge (once the knowledge has come into existence).

This programmatic picture is a knowledge-*minimalism*. It conceives of any instance of knowledge as being, strictly speaking, a mere true belief; whatever else there is in the knowledge's neighbourhood, such as its modal accompaniments, would not be a *component* of the knowledge as such. So, even if in practice we believe that knowledge is present only when there are accompanying modal features, this does not entail that those features are *part* of the knowledge itself. Hence (continues this thinking), these further features *could* in principle be absent even when some knowledge is present. (Of course, it might be objected that, even if the modal accompaniments are not literally part of the knowledge, they remain necessary to the knowing's existence. But that is a misleading objection. The justified-true-belief definition that we met in Section 4, for example, *was* seeking to describe whatever it is that constitutes any given instance of knowing. A person's having a brain might well be a causally, even a conceptually, necessary accompaniment of her having some knowledge. But the brain's presence is never part of the knowing as such. So, the presence of a brain is not mentioned by any potentially useful epistemological articulation of *what it is* for some specific belief to be knowledge. The point of the definition of knowledge was to say *what knowing is*, not merely to describe whatever is necessary and sufficient *in the world* for some knowing to exist.)

Knowledge-minimalism has proponents: Crispin Sartwell (1991, 1992), and perhaps Alvin Goldman (1999: 23–6), Richard Foley (1996, 2012), and myself (Hetherington 2001: ch. 4; 2011: ch. 4). Sartwell (1991: 161) explicitly endorsed (2) above, describing justification as a *criterion* of knowledge, a way of checking on whether knowledge – true belief – is present.[15] But most epistemologists would be wary of knowledge-minimalism, thinking of it as allowing a confidently but dogmatically held true belief – any correct conviction that is based on nothing more than confidence, for example – to be knowledge. Few epistemologists would tolerate that implication.

Still, their reluctance is not a decisive reason for rejecting knowledge-minimalism. The redundancy problem provides a theoretical reason – rather than a mere 'competing intuition' – for conceiving of knowledge in that way. And, as I have acknowledged, even a knowledge-minimalist can concur with other epistemologists as to the epistemic benefits in using justification – whereby justification is held to assist us in gaining knowledge – without accepting the usually accompanying *metaphysical* picture – whereby justification is held to be *part* of the knowledge, once some knowledge has been attained. My conjecture, more generally, is that this should be our model for how to conceive of knowledge's *modal* aspect – namely, as a story about *how to gain* knowledge, not about *what it is* to know. How well justification ever helps us to be linked to truth – by helping us to gain knowledge at all – will, I am also conjecturing, depend on *contingent* aspects of how this world functions.[16]

Notes

1 See Dougherty (2011) and Hetherington (2005, 2016b) for critical surveys of the nature of fallibility and of fallible knowledge.

2 On the associated intellectual ferment of Leibniz's time, see Nadler (2008). On Leibniz on 'the best of all possible worlds', see Lin (2011: 202–7).

3 For general overviews of that segment of recent philosophical history, see Loux (1979) and Divers (2002). On modality and epistemology, see Hendricks (2006).

4 See, for example, Kirkham (1984), Kaplan (1985), Hetherington (1998; 2001: ch. 3; 2011: ch. 3; 2016a), and Williamson (2000: ch. 1). See also Weinberg, Nichols, and Stich (2001) for the main paper that initiated what has since become known as experimental philosophy: a recurring challenge in that literature has been to test the claim by Weinberg, Nichols, and Stich that perhaps the 'intuitive' response by Western epistemologists to Gettier cases – namely, that no Gettiered belief is knowledge – is not shared across all ethnic cultures and all socioeconomic groups, and hence that we are not epistemically *obliged* to regard Gettiered beliefs as failing to be knowledge.

5 For discussion of it, see Hetherington (2016b).

6 Trent Dougherty (2011: 140) calls it, approvingly, the 'it could have failed to be knowledge' conception. For critical discussion of it, see Reed (2002).

7 Pre-Gettier, epistemologists in general would have said that there are two other such components – justification and belief. If – post-Gettier – further components are thought to be needed, these will simply fall within my general account of failability: instead of 'one or both', I would write 'one or another'.

8 For recent developments of Dretske's approach, see Cross (2015) and Lando (2016).

9 See, for example, Luper-Foy (1987). On condition (3) – the *sensitivity* condition, as it has become known – see Becker and Black (2012). For a non-modal version of the condition, see Roush (2005), who parses it in probabilistic terms.

10 These various accounts – such as Dretske's, Nozick's, Sosa's, and Pritchard's – are instances of what Levi (1980: 1–2) called *pedigree* epistemology, which remains the dominant approach taken by contemporary philosophers to conceiving of knowledge. For an alternative approach, see Section 7.

11 Why 'venerable'? Epistemologists generally trace it to Plato's *Meno* (97a–99d). For discussion of that reasoning in the *Meno*, see Hetherington (forthcoming a).

12 For recent influential versions of these ideas, see, respectively, Conee and Feldman (2004) on evidentialism, and Goldman (1979, 1986) on reliabilism.

13 For early discussion of this problem, see Swinburne (1998: 57–66) and Kvanvig (2003: 46–52). For one response to it, see Pritchard (2010).

14 Elsewhere (forthcoming b), I present it in more detail.

15 I say 'perhaps' for those other epistemologists, because they do not clearly say that *all* knowledge is only true belief. I have now joined Sartwell in endorsing this stronger thesis about all knowledge (forthcoming a,b).

16 For more on this sort of contingency in how knowledge and justification are to be conceptually joined with each other, see Hetherington (2011: ch. 4).

References

Becker, K. and Black, T. (eds) (2012), *The Sensitivity Principle in Epistemology*, Cambridge: Cambridge University Press.

Carnap, R. (1947), *Meaning and Necessity: A Study in Semantics and Modal Logic*, Chicago: The University of Chicago Press.

Conee, E. and Feldman, R. (2004), *Evidentialism: Essays in Epistemology*. Oxford: Clarendon Press.

Cross, C. B. (2015), 'A Logical Transmission Principle for Conclusive Reasons', *Australasian Journal of Philosophy*, 93: 353–70.

Divers, J. (2002), *Possible Worlds*, London: Routledge.

Dougherty, T. (2011), 'Fallibilism', in S. Bernecker and D. Pritchard (eds), *The Routledge Companion to Epistemology*, New York: Routledge.

Dretske, F. I. (1970), 'Epistemic Operators', *The Journal of Philosophy*, 67: 1007–23.

Dretske, F. I. (1971), 'Conclusive Reasons', *Australasian Journal of Philosophy*, 49: 1–22.

Foley, R. (1996), 'Knowledge Is Accurate and Comprehensive Enough True Belief', in J. L. Kvanvig (ed.), *Warrant in Contemporary Epistemology: Essays in Honor of Plantinga's Theory of Knowledge*, Lanham, MD: Rowman & Littlefield.

Foley, R. (2012), *When Is True Belief Knowledge?* Princeton: Princeton University Press.

Gettier, E. L. (1963), 'Is Justified True Belief Knowledge?', *Analysis*, 23: 121–3.

Goldman, A. I. (1979), 'What Is Justified Belief?' in G. S. Pappas (ed.), *Justification and Knowledge: New Studies in Epistemology*, Dordrecht: D. Reidel.

Goldman, A. I. (1986), *Epistemology and Cognition*, Cambridge, MA: Harvard University Press.

Goldman, A. I. (1999), *Knowledge in a Social World*, Oxford: Clarendon Press.

Hendricks, V. F. (2006), *Mainstream and Formal Epistemology*, Cambridge: Cambridge University Press.

Hetherington, S. (1998), 'Actually Knowing', *The Philosophical Quarterly*, 48: 453–69.

Hetherington, S. (1999), 'Knowing Failably', *The Journal of Philosophy*, 96: 565–87.

Hetherington, S. (2001), *Good Knowledge, Bad Knowledge: On Two Dogmas of Epistemology*, Oxford: Clarendon Press.

Hetherington, S. (2005), 'Fallibilism', *The Internet Encyclopedia of Philosophy*: http://www.iep.utm.edu/f/fallibil.htm.

Hetherington, S. (2011), *How to Know: A Practicalist Conception of Knowledge*, Malden, MA: Wiley-Blackwell.

Hetherington, S. (2016a), *Knowledge and the Gettier Problem*, Cambridge: Cambridge University Press.

Hetherington, S. (2016b), 'Understanding Fallible Warrant and Fallible Knowledge: Three Proposals', *Pacific Philosophical Quarterly*, 97: 270–82.

Hetherington, S. (forthcoming a), 'Knowing as Simply Being Correct'. *Proceedings of International Conference on Facts and Evidence in Law and Philosophy*, Shanghai 2016.

Hetherington, S. (forthcoming b), 'The Redundancy Problem: From Knowledge-Infallibilism to Knowledge-Minimalism', *Synthese*.

Hintikka, J. (1962), *Knowledge and Belief: An Introduction to the Logic of the Two Notions*, Ithaca, NY: Cornell University Press.

Kaplan, M. (1985), 'It's Not What You Know That Counts', *The Journal of Philosophy*, 82: 350–63.

Kirkham, R. L. (1984), 'Does the Gettier Problem Rest on a Mistake?' *Mind*, 93: 501–13.

Kripke, S. A. (1963), 'Semantical Considerations on Modal Logic', *Acta Philosophica Fennica*, 16: 83–94.

Kripke, S. A. (1980 [1972]), *Naming and Necessity*, Oxford: Blackwell.

Kvanvig, J. L. (2003), *The Value of Knowledge and the Pursuit of Understanding*, Cambridge: Cambridge University Press.

Lando, T. (2016), 'Conclusive Reasons and Epistemic Luck', *Australasian Journal of Philosophy*, 94: 378–95.

Levi, I. (1980), *The Enterprise of Knowledge: An Essay on Knowledge, Credal Probability, and Chance*, Cambridge: The MIT Press.

Lewis, D. (1968), 'Counterpart Theory and Quantified Modal Logic', *The Journal of Philosophy*, 65: 113–26.

Lewis, D. (1973), *Counterfactuals*, Oxford: Blackwell.

Lewis, D. (1986), *On the Plurality of Worlds*, Oxford: Blackwell.

Lin, M. (2011), 'Leibniz's Philosophical Theology', in B. C. Look (ed.), *The Bloomsbury Companion to Leibniz*, London: Bloomsbury.

Loux, M. J. (ed.) (1979), *The Possible and the Actual: Readings in the Metaphysics of Modality*, Ithaca, NY: Cornell University Press.

Luper-Foy, S. (ed.) (1987), *The Possibility of Knowledge: Nozick and His Critics*, Totowa, NJ: Rowman & Littlefield.

Nadler, S. (2008), *The Best of All Possible Worlds: A Story of Philosophy, God, and Evil*, New York: Farrar, Straus and Giroux.

Nozick, R. (1981), *Philosophical Explanations*, Cambridge, MA: Harvard University Press.

Pritchard, D. (2005), *Epistemic Luck*, Oxford: Clarendon Press.

Pritchard, D. (2010), 'Knowledge and Understanding', in D. Pritchard, A. Millar, and A. Haddock (eds), *The Nature and Value of Knowledge: Three Investigations*, Oxford: Oxford University Press.

Reed, B. (2002), 'How to Think about Fallibilism', *Philosophical Studies*, 107: 143–57.

Roush, S. (2005), *Tracking Truth: Knowledge, Evidence, and Science*, Oxford: Clarendon Press.

Sartwell, C. (1991), 'Knowledge Is Merely True Belief', *American Philosophical Quarterly*, 28: 157–65.

Sartwell, C. (1992), 'Why Knowledge Is Merely True Belief', *The Journal of Philosophy*, 89: 167–80.

Sosa, E. (1999), 'How Must Knowledge Be Modally Related to What Is Known?', *Philosophical Topics*, 26: 373–84.

Stalnaker, R. C. (1968), 'A Theory of Conditionals', in N. Rescher (ed.), *Studies in Logical Theory*, Oxford: Basil Blackwell.

Swinburne, R. (1998), *Providence and the Problem of Evil*, Oxford: Clarendon Press.

Weinberg, J. M., Nichols, S., and Stich, S. (2001), 'Normativity and Epistemic Intuitions', *Philosophical Topics*, 29: 429–60.

Williamson, T. (2000), *Knowledge and Its Limits*, Oxford: Clarendon Press.

Zagzebski, L. (1994), 'The Inescapability of Gettier Problems', *The Philosophical Quarterly*, 44: 65–73.

13

Knowledge and Normativity

Clayton Littlejohn

1. Introduction

In a standard epistemology course, students are told that Gettier's (1963) cases demonstrate that knowledge cannot be identified with or defined as justified true belief.[1] Two thinkers might share the same beliefs, these beliefs might be equally justified, but even if both beliefs are true it's possible that only one belief constitutes knowledge. Students are then introduced to a massive literature in which philosophers struggled to find the extra conditions needed that would close the gap between knowing and merely having a justified, true belief.

According to the standard story, propositional knowledge requires justified belief and further conditions that justified beliefs might lack. If we think of the justified belief as the normatively appropriate belief, the standard story accepts the first thesis but rejects the second:

Necessity: Necessarily, if S knows that *p*, S's belief in *p* is justified.
Sufficiency: Necessarily, if S's belief in *p* is justified, S knows *p*.

According to the Necessity Thesis, propositional knowledge has a normative dimension or aspect because it requires justified belief.[2] If the proponents of the standard story are right in rejecting the Sufficiency Thesis, there is more to propositional knowledge than normatively appropriate belief. The conditions that would make it appropriate for Agnes to believe that it is raining in London or that it will rain again in London tomorrow can obtain even if Agnes' beliefs are only accidentally correct (if correct), and even if Agnes' beliefs are mistaken. If, as most epistemologists think, Agnes' beliefs might be incorrect or only accurate as a matter of luck and still be justified or appropriately held, the extra conditions that distinguish justified belief from knowledge turn out to be normatively insignificant.

If we accept this much of the standard story, it might seem that the part of the epistemology that has to do with appropriate belief and addresses questions about what we should believe will have little if anything to do with the part of epistemology that has to do with questions about the nature and extent of knowledge.[3] This chapter addresses questions that have recently come to the fore in contemporary discussions about the relationship between these two parts of epistemology. If these two parts of epistemology truly are distinct, we shouldn't have to draw on the theory of knowledge in offering a theory of justified or normatively appropriate belief. The recent discussions of knowledge-first epistemology show that it will be incredibly difficult to maintain this separation. I shall point to some difficulties that arise for the standard story, starting with the Necessity Thesis and turning to an extended discussion of the Sufficiency Thesis.

2. Justification and knowledge

Justification is not always understood as normatively appropriate belief, but this deontological theory serves as a good starting point for this discussion:

> DJ: S's belief in p is justified iff S believes p and it is not the case that S should not believe p.[4]

Epistemic norms identify the conditions under which some thinker should or should not believe p. So, DJ could be restated in terms of the beliefs that thinkers hold while conforming to epistemic norms or hold without violating any epistemic norms.

Drawing on Gettier's discussion, a proponent of the standard view might argue against the Sufficiency Thesis as follows:

The Subtraction Argument
1. If S is in a position to know p, it is permissible for S to believe p.
2. Holding fixed the supporting reasons that S has for this belief while subtracting away any combination of truth, belief, and being unGettiered makes no difference to whether it is permissible for S to believe p.
C. Thus, the Sufficiency Thesis is false since it implies that S has justification to believe p only if S is in a position to know p.[5]

This argument, if sound, shows that the conditions necessary for propositional knowledge are a mixture of normatively significant and insignificant conditions. (While having good reason might be normatively significant in that it is necessary and sufficient for having the right to believe, the truth of your belief might be neither necessary nor sufficient for the realization of any normative property.) The former conditions tell us what we should believe, and the latter serve only to tell us why some but not all of the things we should believe are things we can know. The argument's first premise, if suitably restricted, should appeal to proponents of DJ. The second premise might be supported by an appeal to intuitions about error cases. Consider this passage from Cohen's (1984: 281) discussion of reliabilism:

> Imagine that unbeknown to us, our cognitive processes (e.g. perception, memory, inference) are not reliable owing to the machinations of the malevolent demon. It follows on a Reliabilist view that the beliefs generated by those processes are never justified. Is this a tenable result? I maintain that it is not . . . [P]art of what the hypothesis entails is that our experience is just as it would be if our cognitive processes were reliable. Thus, on the demon hypothesis, we would have every reason for holding our beliefs that we have in the actual world. It strikes me as clearly false to deny that under these circumstances our beliefs could be justified.[6]

What does this argument show us about the relationship between justification and knowledge? If sound, would it establish a thesis as strong as this one?

> *Irrelevance*: The concept of knowledge plays no essential role in the theory of justified or normatively appropriate belief.

The subtraction argument would not establish that strong thesis on its own. The argument rests on the controversial assumption that when we hold fixed the supporting reasons in the pair of cases we will find that the subjects' beliefs will not differ in justificatory status between the two cases. Let's suppose for the time being that this is correct. It might still be that we will not be able to identify the relevant pair of cases without identifying subjects that stand in some interesting relation to a knower.

Suppose that propositional justification supervenes upon a subject's total reasons at a time, so that it is impossible to have differences in what two subjects have justification to believe without any difference in their reasons. There are two theoretical roles for knowledge to play in this account that would make the concept of knowledge indispensable in fleshing out the details of the account. First, we haven't yet said anything about what supporting reasons are. We might need to invoke the concept of knowledge to give an account of reasons. Second, we haven't yet said anything about what makes some sets of supporting reasons sufficient. We might need to invoke the concept of knowledge in giving an account of sufficient support.

We will look at recent discussions of the nature of reasons and of the aim of belief to assess the status of the Irrelevance Thesis. We shall see that there are interesting ways to challenge the Irrelevance Thesis without questioning the standard story and without challenging the Subtraction Argument. It shouldn't surprise readers to learn that the Subtraction Argument is itself controversial. We shall also consider challenges to this argument and look at some recent defences of the Sufficiency Thesis. We'll return to these issues in the next sections of the chapter.

Do the considerations that underwrite the Subtraction Argument tell us anything about the Necessity Thesis? It does seem that the first premise is stated in such a way that it presupposes the Necessity Thesis, but it's fair to ask for some reason to think that a subject's being in a position to know ensures that she's permitted to believe. It might seem that DJ lends some support to the Necessity Thesis. Suppose that Agnes believes that it is raining in London. Amy wonders whether Agnes should believe this. If I assure Amy that Agnes knows that it is raining in London, could Amy accept this and then insist that Agnes shouldn't believe that it is raining in London? If not, do we now have some reason to accept the Necessity Thesis?

Perhaps not. Agnes is a dog. Amy is a mature adult human. If Amy knew that Agnes was a dog, it would be strange for her to think that Agnes shouldn't believe what she believes. Do dogs have the rational capacities that they would need if they are to be answerable for their actions or attitudes? If not, it seems that Agnes wouldn't have responsibilities that she should meet and it might be a mistake to say that she should not do or believe certain things. If this is right, it would be a mistake for Amy to say that Agnes should not believe that it is raining in London, but it would equally be a mistake for Amy to say that Agnes' beliefs are justified or unjustified, just as it would be a mistake for Amy to say that Agnes' anger wasn't justified or that she has a duty not to sleep on the sofa. Some animals might be exempt from normative appraisal in such a way that they don't have duties or responsibilities and cannot have justified or unjustified attitudes. Such creatures, however, might know that things are so. Even if Agnes doesn't know that it is raining in London, she might know that it is raining when she is in London, suffering through it on a long walk.[7] (If you think that it helps, try to imagine that Agnes is a fish, a gerbil, a cat, an infant, a toddler, an undergraduate, etc., and see if there is some set of mental capacities typical of these kinds of creatures where it seems plausible to say that Agnes knows that it is raining and implausible to say that she has justified beliefs about the weather.)

If some creatures can have propositional knowledge without justified belief, we have our first challenge to the standard story. The story would be mistaken if it tried to characterize propositional knowledge as a special case of normatively appropriate belief. The objection to the standard view might require only a small revision to DJ:

> DJ*: S's belief in p is justified iff S believes p, S can be held accountable for her attitudes, and it is not the case that S should not believe p.

Because this emendation is minor, it might seem that this challenge to the standard story won't be terribly significant. This point might prove to be significant later.

If there is a kernel of truth in the Necessity Thesis, it might be this. When we're thinking about mature adult humans (and other creatures, if there are any, that can be held accountable for their actions and attitudes), the thinker's beliefs couldn't fail to be justified if they constitute knowledge. The conditions that ensure that this thinker knows p would ensure that she violated no epistemic norms by virtue of believing p. The case of animals that are exempt from rational criticism is interesting because it suggests that knowledge might be non-normative in its nature but have a normative upshot, in that its presence ensures that the right thinkers could be in a good position to believe what they ought to believe. We will discuss the Necessity Thesis further in Section 5.

3. Reasons, justification, and knowledge

The Subtraction Argument might appeal to those who accept this supervenience thesis:

> *Evidentialism*: Propositional justification supervenes upon a subject's evidence (that is, if two thinkers have the very same evidence, they will have justification to believe the very same propositions).

This thesis, if true, would only support the Irrelevance Thesis if we didn't need the concept of knowledge to fill out the details of the view. In this section, we'll look at the relationship between knowledge and reasons. In the next, we'll look at the relationship between knowledge and rational support.

If you look at Gettier's original examples, they involve cases in which a subject's evidence supports a false belief and, according to Gettier, provide the kind of support that would justify the false belief. Gettier doesn't tell us what the subject's evidence is or what has to happen for the subject to possess this evidence, but questions about the ontology of epistemic reasons and the conditions that have to be met to possess them have recently come to the fore. Thanks largely to Williamson's (2000) work, there has been a great deal of discussion recently about his identification of evidence and knowledge:

E=K: S's evidence includes *p* iff S knows *p*.[8]

If we combine E=K with Evidentialism, we get a quick refutation of the Irrelevance Thesis. The concept of knowledge would play an important role in the theory of justification because a subject's evidence is just her knowledge. Propositional justification would supervene upon propositional knowledge if it supervened upon evidence.

E=K is deeply controversial. According to E=K, a subject's evidence or a subject's reasons should be identified with the objects of her knowledge, and knowledge is taken to be necessary and sufficient for the possession of a reason or piece of evidence. Critics have levelled a number of objections against this view, including the following:

1. The subject's evidence or reasons should be identified with the subject's states of mind. It should be possible for a subject's belief to be based on her evidence and the basing relation holds between mental states and events.[9]

2. The subject's evidence or reasons should be identified with the objects of our attitudes, not the attitudes themselves, but the contents of these attitudes will constitute evidence even if these attitudes are inaccurate. Thus, we do not need knowledge to possess evidence because belief or justified belief is sufficient for the possession of evidence.[10]

3. The subject's evidence or reasons can be provided by experience or perception, and the subject is not required to believe or know that the target proposition is true.[11]

4. Gettier cases show that a belief might just fail to constitute knowledge and still provide us with reasons or evidence.[12]

The success of these objections is still very much up for discussion. The critics of E=K need to address two powerful lines of argument. First, against (1), Dancy (2000) notes that it should be possible in principle to not just do or believe what there is good reason to do but instead to do or believe things for good reasons. If, as he suggests, good reasons are the things that figure in reasoning and seem to count in favour of doing what we do, they would be the objects of our attitudes; they would not be the attitudes themselves. Thus, it seems that reasons should be propositionally specified using that-clauses and not propositional attitudes or mental events. Second, Unger (1975) observed long ago that when we attribute reasons to a subject in specifying her reasons for thinking, feeling, or doing things, these ascriptions appear to entail correlative knowledge ascriptions. If Unger was right about the linguistic considerations, proponents of E=K might not have to worry too much about (2)–(4).[13]

Those sympathetic to E=K will often say that reasons of all kinds are either facts or true propositions. To possess or have some reason is to stand in relation to a reason (i.e. a fact or true proposition) such that you can be guided by it in thinking, feeling, and doing what you do.

> Some critics might raise one final objection to E=K:
>
> (5) E=K implies that we have too much evidence or too many reasons, in that the reach or scope of our knowledge is potentially quite great even though the reasons or evidence we possess consist(s) of things to which we have a special kind of access.[14]

This objection might or might not be connected to the familiar point that the normatively significant conditions have to be able to guide or direct us in a way that external things might not.

One way to respond to such worries is to think about what knowledge is supposed to be. According to Hyman (1999), propositional knowledge is an ability, the ability to be rationally guided by reasons that are facts. Sometimes it seems that the main idea behind (5) is that the objects of knowledge cannot guide you in what you think, feel, or do because what *really* guides us are things that are more subjective than the external facts that we normally take ourselves to know. Your reasons couldn't include external facts that, say, subjects in similar mental states mistakenly believed to obtain, but would have to be something that you and these subjects shared (e.g. your beliefs about how things were or your experiences that made things seem a certain way). On a view like Hyman's, there is a tension in saying that (a) you know many things about your external situation but (b) it could not be that such things constituted your reasons for thinking, feeling, or doing what you do, because knowledge *just is* the ability to be guided by certain facts in coming to think, feel, or do what you do. If the critic understood that knowledge is an ability, they should either insist that we really don't know anything about the situations we're in because we cannot be rationally guided by facts about our situations, or admit that the things that are known can guide us by entering into the rational processes that lead us to believe, feel, and act.

To some, the *real* objection that underwrites (5) has to do with the problematic nature of the access we have to external things. According to E=K, you could have better evidence for your beliefs than, say, someone in similar subjective states who happens to be mistaken in their beliefs about their surroundings. Critics of E=K might say that it's wrong to suggest that such internally similar subjects *should* respond differently to the apparent facts. If our subjectively similar subjects are *perfectly* similar subjectively, shouldn't they be equally confident in their attitudes? If so, aren't there two obvious lessons to take from this? First, we should conclude that the external facts we know do not put us under rational pressure to modify our beliefs, change how we feel, or decide to do certain things. Second, we should conclude that the subjective things are what create the *real* rational pressure to revise our beliefs, change how we feel, and do what we do.

It seems that this kind of objection works only if we assume that there is some important difference between the kind of access we have to external things and the kind of access we have to the more subjective things we might share in common with mental duplicates of ourselves embedded in different surroundings. A defender of E=K might argue that there really aren't any interesting principled differences between, say, the kind of access I have to the things that are plainly in view and the kinds of things that I can learn about through introspection. In both cases, it seems that we're typically well placed to say how things are. In neither case does it seem that we're infallible when it comes to judging how things are. Without any compelling reason to think that the kind of access we have to external things and internal things differs in kind, it's hard to see that there's much to this line of attack on E=K.[15]

4. Rational support and knowledge

In the previous section, we saw how someone who accepts E=K might challenge the Irrelevance Thesis. In this section, we'll look at a second challenge to the Irrelevance Thesis, one that has to do with the nature of rational support. We expect philosophers who accept Evidentialism (understood as it is here) to say that a belief is justified or rationally held if based on sufficient evidence. How should we understand this notion of sufficiency? Can we understand what makes the support sufficient, without invoking the concept of knowledge?

One approach that we might consider is the Lockean approach.[16] A Lockean could argue that the degree of belief that a thinker ought to have in a proposition should match the evidential probability of that proposition, and that it is rational for a thinker to believe (outright) p iff she rationally has a sufficiently high degree of confidence in the truth of p. In stating this account, it seems we wouldn't need to invoke the concept of knowledge. This kind of approach might be appealing to philosophers who think that our epistemic aim is to believe what's true and avoid believing what's false. It captures an important aspect of rationality: 'A rational agent should be doing well by her own lights, in a particular way: roughly speaking, she should follow the epistemic rule that she rationally takes to be most truth-conducive. It would be irrational, the thought goes, to regard some epistemic rule as more truth-conducive than one's own, but not adopt it' (Horowitz 2014: 43). Lottery propositions (viz. the proposition that the ticket you hold for the lottery just held did not win) are an interesting test case for approaches to rational support that focus on truth-conducivity, or the rational means for pursuing truth and avoiding error. While it seems that we should be highly confident that a ticket for an upcoming lottery is not the one that will be chosen, opinion seems to divide on two questions about full belief. First, can we know that our ticket will not win if we're just going on the odds? Second, can we justifiably believe (outright) that our ticket will not win if we're just going on the odds?

Suppose that we know a priori that we aren't in a position to know whether our ticket will lose. Since we do know that adopting a rule against believing in such cases would not be as truth-conducive as adopting a rule that permits or requires belief in such cases, it might seem from a certain perspective that we would be justified in believing outright that a ticket would lose. From a different perspective, however, it might seem irrational to believe what you know you cannot know. To be sure, if we assigned values to getting things right and getting things wrong and aimed to form beliefs in such a way as to maximize expected value (restricted to these values!), it would seem that rationality should permit belief in these cases. Indeed, it should permit believing conjunctions of the form: this ticket will lose and I don't know if it will. Since this strikes many as an irrational thing to think, it might give us some reason to worry about the idea that rationality and rational support should be characterized in terms of some connection to the truth and without any concern for whether our beliefs would stand in some interesting relationship to knowledge.[17]

Some philosophers have proposed that there is a rational requirement that forbids believing *p* while believing that you aren't in a position to know whether *p*. If such a requirement exists, cases like the lottery suggest that we do need to invoke the concept of knowledge to understand what makes rational support sufficient for full belief. Two beliefs might be equally likely on the evidence, but it might be rational to fully believe in only one case if, say, one belief is a good candidate for knowledge and the other is hopeless. This has led Bird (2007: 84) to propose an interesting account of rational belief or judgement, according to which (roughly) a judgement is rationally held if either it constitutes knowledge or is similar in certain important respects to a judgement that would constitute knowledge.

One nice feature of Bird's account is that it explains an intuitive difference between the lottery and preface cases. In both cases, we have propositions that are highly probable on the subject's evidence. In one version of the preface case, an author believes on good evidence each claim in her work of non-fiction and is told by a highly reliable source that her work contains one error. It seems that she could rationally believe this piece of testimony and still rationally believe each claim in the book. While it seems that the Lockean tells us a nice story about how this is possible, it also seems to imply that it should be rational to believe lottery propositions. This second claim, however, strikes some as counterintuitive and leads some authors to insist that the cases should be treated differently. Bird's account vindicates this intuition if, as many philosophers think, the entries in the book (including the preface statement) are things that the subject could know but lottery propositions are not.[18]

Instead of thinking of belief as aimed at just the truth, some philosophers would argue that belief aims at knowledge. Stated in a different way, they might say that beliefs are supposed to be knowledge or that a belief can only do what it is supposed to do when it constitutes knowledge.[19] If we revise our view of belief and its aim accordingly, it is easy to see why a view of rationality akin to Bird's might seem attractive. If it is attractive, though, note that we have used the concept of knowledge to understand when rational support is sufficient, and abandoned the project of understanding the sufficiency of support in terms of nothing but some connection to the truth.

Lynch (2004: 17) suggests that we value true belief, in part, because we value being in touch with reality:

[I]f we didn't have a basic preference for the truth, it would be hard to explain why we find the prospect of being undetectably wrong so disturbing. Think about a modification of the experience-machine scenario we began with. Some super neuroscientists give you the choice between continuing to live normally, or having your brain hooked up to a supercomputer that will make it seem as if you are continuing to live normally ... When in the vat, you will continue to have all the same experiences you would have in the real world. Because of this, you would believe that you are reading a book, that you are hungry, and so on. In short, your beliefs and experiences will be the same, but most of your beliefs will be false.

Part of what's disturbing about this, he says, is that we don't just want certain experiences or appearances, we 'want certain realities behind those experiences' (139). If we see Gettier-type cases as situations in which our true beliefs fail to put us in touch with these realities, this might explain why beliefs are supposed to be knowledge and aim at something more than mere accuracy. If they aim at more than mere accuracy, we should expect that we wouldn't be able to cash out the notion of sufficient support for being in a state that aims at knowledge in terms of nothing but some relation to truth. Beliefs are supposed to provide us with reasons that can guide our thinking, feeling, and doing; and, arguably, our beliefs do this iff they constitute knowledge.[20]

5. Knowledge norms

We have considered two ways of challenging the Irrelevance Thesis without challenging any of the operative assumptions in the Subtraction Argument. Even if it's possible to justifiably believe what you don't know, it might be that the concept of knowledge plays an important role in our understanding of epistemic normativity because that concept plays an important role in understanding the nature of reasons and the kind of rational support necessary for rational or justified belief. In this section, we shall look at some of the ways that philosophers have challenged the operative assumptions in the Subtraction Argument.

McDowell (1998: 395) tells us that knowledge is a standing in the space of reasons, and I think that we can read him as saying two things in saying this. First, he thinks that it's important that knowledge is supported by reasons, that we acquire knowledge by responding appropriately to the reasons in our possession. Second, he thinks that knowledge is a standing of normative significance in that he believes that if you believe *p* without knowing *p*, then you believe something you shouldn't and your belief cannot be justified. On the first point, McDowell tells us that 'one's epistemic standing ... cannot intelligibly be constituted, even in part, by matters blankly external to how it is with one subjectively. For how could such matters be other than beyond one's ken? And how could matters beyond one's ken make any difference to one's epistemic standing?' (390). As he sees it, the conditions that ensure that we know must all be present to the mind, and the factors that play this role in ensuring that our beliefs constitute knowledge are reasons for our belief. These reasons have to ensure that we're in a position to know, for otherwise there would be a gap between believing for these reasons and knowing, a gap that makes the difference between knowledge and ignorance turn on something that is 'beyond our ken'. Such matters might make you lucky, healthy, or wealthy, but they shouldn't be the crucial factors that explain how you're 'in the know'. As for the second point, he seems to think that if we adopt the standard account of knowledge, one that rejects the Sufficiency Thesis, we will fail to accommodate the crucial internalist insight contained in the passage just quoted:

> In the hybrid conception [of knowledge that allows that two subjects might both believe for adequate reasons but differ in what they know], a satisfactory standing in the space of reasons is only part of what knowledge is; truth is an extra requirement. So two subjects can be alike in respect of their satisfactoriness of their standing in the space of reasons although only one of them is a knower, because only in her case is what she takes to be actually so. But if its being so is external to her operations in the space of reasons, how can it not be outside the reach of her rational powers? And if it is outside the reach of her rational powers, how can its being so be the crucial element in the intelligible conception of her knowing that it is so? (403)

McDowell embraces the Sufficiency Thesis and takes it that if a subject's reasons provide sufficient support for her beliefs, then they ensure that the subject's beliefs constitute knowledge.

Critics will of course argue that this conception of knowledge is problematic because the subject's reasons could always fall short and fail to ensure that the subject's beliefs are accurate. McDowell thinks that such objections miss their mark insofar as they reflect the mistaken assumption that the reasons that we would possess in the good and bad cases would be identical. They might be similar in certain respects, and we might not be able to tell by reflecting on our reasons that we're in the bad case when we're in that case, but it is nevertheless a mistake to think that the rational support we have for our beliefs doesn't differ in the good and bad cases.

It might seem that we get some support for this idea by thinking about the arguments we considered earlier in support of E=K. Such arguments, if sound, would show that if a subject knows *p* and a second subject mistakenly believes *p*, the first subject's evidence would provide better support for his belief, however similar these subjects might otherwise be.[21] In fact, E=K might cause trouble for McDowell. If we read him as saying that all propositional knowledge involves believing something for reasons that provide the kind of rational support that ensure that your beliefs would constitute knowledge, it is hard to see how to square this with E=K. This is because it is hard to see how cases of non-inferential knowledge would be possible.[22] E=K tells us that knowledge is a necessary condition for the possession of reasons or evidence. If, as seems plausible, you cannot believe *p* for some specific reasons if the possession of these reasons requires believing *p*, it's hard to see how to square E=K with McDowell's conception of knowledge. It isn't surprising, then, that he offers an account of the possession of reasons according to which perception can provide us with reasons that constitute the rational basis of our perceptual beliefs.

Why, then, would Williamson embrace the Sufficiency Thesis? He does so because, like McDowell, he thinks that knowledge is a standing in the space of reasons in the sense that he thinks that this norm governs belief:

You should believe *p* only if you know *p* (Only Knowledge).[23]

If you think that belief is governed by this norm, there is a simple and straightforward argument for the Sufficiency Thesis:

The Deontological Argument
1. S's belief in *p* is justified only if S believes *p* and it is not the case that S should not believe *p*. [DJ]
2. If S believes *p* but does not know *p*, she should not believe *p*. [Only Knowledge]
C. S's belief is justified only if S knows *p*.[24]

If a thinker violates norms that govern belief, the thinker might be excused, but the deontological theory understands 'justified' as 'permitted'.

If we assume that DJ is correct, critics will naturally focus on Only Knowledge. Why, they might ask, should we think that belief is governed by such a norm? We have already seen some of the evidence. It might be that Only Knowledge does a better job explaining our intuitions than alternative norms that have no natural or ready explanation as to why we shouldn't believe Moorean absurdities or lottery propositions, or why it might be acceptable to come to believe *p* but not believe *q* when the evidence that supports *q* makes *q* more probable than *p*.[25]

Philosophers sympathetic to the idea that the concept of knowledge figures in norms that govern assertion, and the use of premises in practical or theoretical reasoning, have observed that we often challenge the use of premises or the assertion of a claim by asking an individual whether she knows that something is true. This suggests that there is some mutual recognition that it is normatively significant whether the thinker knows that the premises in her reasoning are true or whether she knows that what she says is true.[26]

Many epistemologists would still insist that the Sufficiency Thesis is mistaken. Some would argue that justification doesn't require conforming to all of the norms that govern belief, only those that have internal or subjective application conditions.[27] Some would argue that the very same kinds of cases that originally led philosophers to reject the Sufficiency Thesis (e.g. cases of error, cases of accidentally true belief) should lead philosophers to reject the idea that the concept of knowledge figures in the formulation of genuine epistemic norms.[28]

The difficulty we face in resolving the dispute at this point in the dialectic is similar to the difficulty we face in trying to resolve the internalism-externalism dispute. It seems that one camp will insist that everything of normative significance is in place if we're internally similar to knowers. Another camp will insist that belief is only normatively appropriate if the internal and external conditions necessary for knowledge are satisfied. One way to try to break the deadlock is to think about what happens *after* the violation of some putative norm. If we assert something we do not know, and assertion is governed by a norm similar to Only Knowledge, then do speakers have special responsibilities for misleading their audience, or should we say that something bad has happened, and that the speaker, strictly speaking, did not do anything wrong? Perhaps further research into these kinds of questions will help us to decide whether the arguments for internalism about justification should lead us to reject the Sufficiency Thesis or they might help us to see that the Sufficiency Thesis is actually in better shape than its critics would have us believe.[29]

Notes

1   Those who accept the standard view often describe Gettier's criticism of the JTB view as a criticism of a traditional conception or understanding of knowledge. Dutant (2015) discusses the propriety of describing Gettier's attack an attack on a traditional view of knowledge. It provides significant evidence that the view was

not traditionally held and discusses some of the Gettier-type cases that appeared prior to 1963, including some from non-Western philosophical traditions.

2 See Kim's (1988) classic discussion of naturalized epistemology.

3 See Foley (2012) for an attempt to develop these two parts of epistemology separately.

4 Some authors have argued that justification should be understood as responsible belief. See Naylor (1988). I do *not* intend DJ to be read that way. I will not assume that a thinker that can be held responsible for her attitudes should be held responsible whenever she violates a norm. We should allow for excuses, and should not assume in advance that any thinker that is responsible in the regulation of her beliefs will invariably conform to the norms that govern belief.

5 Inspired by Fantl and McGrath's (2009: 72) subtraction argument against the knowledge norm for practical reasoning.

6 Cohen's target is the kind of reliabilist view defended in Goldman (1979), so this intuition pump is stronger than needed for the job.

7 Maria Alvarez persuaded me to abandon the Necessity Thesis in discussing non-human animal knowledge. For further critical discussion of the Necessity Thesis, see Audi (1997), Kornblith (2008), Marcus (2012), Littlejohn (2015), Schellenberg (forthcoming), and Sylvan (manuscript).

8 See also Unger (1975), Hyman (1999), and Hornsby (2008) for discussion.

9 This statist conception of reasons is inspired by Davidson's (1963) seminal discussion of causes and reasons for action. See Turri (2009), Gibbons (2013), and McCain (2014) for versions of this objection, and Dancy (1999), Alvarez (2010), and Littlejohn (2012) for responses.

10 See Schroeder (2011), Hofmann (2014), and Mitova (2015) for discussion of the idea that we can possess evidence by virtue of what we believe even if our beliefs do not constitute knowledge. See Fantl and McGrath (2009) for a critical discussion of the truth-requirement on evidence.

11 See McDowell (1994) and Brueckner (2005). For critical discussion of the operative assumptions about the nature of perceptual experience, see Brewer (2011) and Travis (2013).

12 See Hughes (2014) and Locke (2015) for discussion. See Hyman (1999) for a defence.

13 For a state of the art discussion of the linguistic evidence, see Hawthorne and Magidor (forthcoming).

14 We find versions of this objection in Fumerton (1995) and Silins (2005). This doesn't seem to be essential to Cohen's (1984) new evil demon objection, but he does characterize a subject's reasons as things common to the good and the bad cases.

15 For helpful discussions of these issues, see Williamson's (2000) anti-luminosity argument and Gertler (2010), Littlejohn (2012), and Srinivasan (2015).

16   See Foley (2009). For a subtle version of the Lockean view that might avoid the standard objections levelled against it, see Locke (2014).

17   For further discussion of these kinds of cases, see Nelkin (2000), Williamson (2000), Adler (2002), Sutton (2007), McGlynn (2011, 2014), and Littlejohn (2015). I argue that the lottery causes difficulty for the Lockean because it shows that full beliefs and partial beliefs are under different rational pressures (Littlejohn 2015). In these discussions, authors typically assume that the lottery propositions are, in Sutton's terminology, 'known unknowns'. For dissent on this point, see Sosa (2015). Sosa suggests that we can know that some specific tickets will lose when the probabilities are high enough.

18   For two very different perspectives on Makinson's (1965) preface paradox, see Ryan (1991) and Christensen (2004).

19   For arguments that belief 'aims' at the truth, see Williams (1973) and Wedgwood (2002). For arguments that the aim of belief is knowledge, see Hyman (1999), Williamson (2000), Bird (2007), Sutton (2007), Smithies (2012), and Littlejohn (2013).

20   This line of argument – found in Hyman (1999), Williamson (2000), and Littlejohn (2015) – provides a response to Sartwell's (1991) challenge to orthodox accounts of knowledge that distinguish knowledge from mere true belief. It also avoids Lackey's (2009) objections to credit-based accounts of the value of knowledge. For alternative accounts of the value of knowledge, see Zagzebski (1996) and Kvanvig (2003).

21   Indeed, on Williamson's (2000) view, this is trivial because p is always evidence for itself. Thus, if E=K is true and p is known, it follows that the evidential probability of p on your total evidence is 1. See Brown (2013) for criticism of this claim.

22   Many writers now (including McDowell) think that perceptual knowledge is typically non-inferential and that our perceptual beliefs are about external things, not about the experiences that give rise to them. For arguments that we should not assume that, whenever a subject acquires knowledge, she does so by believing something for a reason, see Anscombe (1962) and McGinn (2012).

23   While the idea that the fundamental norm of belief is Only Knowledge is increasingly popular, this view faces two prima facie difficulties. According to the Necessity Thesis, a belief is knowledge only if it is justified. According to DJ, if it is justified then it violates no norm. If justified belief requires more than knowledge, it seems that a justified belief might both satisfy and violate the fundamental epistemic norm. This is bad enough, but there is a second worry that has to do with grounding. If the Necessity Thesis is correct, Only Knowledge only applies once something or other determines whether a belief is justified. If Only Knowledge is the fundamental norm, *it* should determine whether a belief is justified. If we reject the Necessity Thesis and see knowledge as a relation between a thinker and

a fact that involves no normative dimension or part, these problems go away. We can think of the relationship between knowledge and permission, justification, or rightness as akin to the relationship that the utilitarian thinks holds between the optimific and the right. If Agnes performs an action that is optimific, it has the properties that would make it right if she were a responsible agent. The optimific act (if performed by a responsible agent) might also imply rightness, but the property of being optimific is independent of the property of being right and can play a kind of grounding role.

24 For an interesting discussion of whether knowledge should be sufficient for justified belief, see Lasonen-Aarnio (2010). For a discussion of whether knowledge ensures that the thinker conforms to epistemic norms, see Brown (2011). For defences of the view that all justified beliefs have to be knowledge, see Unger (1975), McDowell (1998), Sutton (2007), Littlejohn (2013), and Williamson (2017). Unger's is a puzzling case because he argues that we could not rationally believe *p* unless we knew it and then argues that virtually nothing is known.

25 See Williamson (2000).

26 See Hawthorne and Stanley (2008) for a defence of a knowledge norm for practical reasoning. For defences of the knowledge norm for assertion, see Slote (1979), Unger (1975), Williamson (2000), and Turri (2011). See Montminy (2013) for arguments that a common norm will govern assertion and the use of premises in practical reasoning.

27 Bird (2007), Smithies (2012), and Huemer (forthcoming) defend views akin to this one.

28 See Lackey (2007), Fantl and McGrath (2009), Gerken (2011), and McKinnon (2013).

29 This line of research has been explored in Robinson and Darley (1998), Littlejohn (2012), and Turri (2015).

References

Adler, J. E. (2002), *Belief's Own Ethics*, Cambridge: The MIT Press.

Alvarez, M. (2010), *Kinds of Reasons: An Essay in the Philosophy of Action*, Oxford: Oxford University Press.

Anscombe, G. E. M. (1962), 'On Sensations of Position', *Analysis*, 22: 55–8.

Audi, R. (1997), 'The Place of Testimony in the Fabric of Knowledge', *American Philosophical Quarterly*, 34: 405–22.

Bird, A. (2007), 'Justified Judging', *Philosophy and Phenomenological Research*, 74: 81–110.

Brewer, B. (2011), *Perception and Its Objects*, Oxford: Oxford University Press.

Brown, J. (2011), 'Fallibilism and the Knowledge Norm for Assertion and Practical Reasoning', in Jessica Brown and Herman Cappelen (eds), *Assertion: New Philosophical Essays*, Oxford: Oxford University Press.

Brown, J. (2013), 'Infallibilism, Evidence, and Pragmatics', *Analysis*, 73: 626–35.

Brueckner, A. (2005), 'Knowledge, Evidence, and Skepticism According to Williamson', *Philosophy and Phenomenological Research*, 70: 436–43.

Christensen, D. (2004), *Putting Logic in Its Place: Formal Constraints on Rational Belief*, Oxford: Clarendon Press.

Cohen, S. (1984), 'Justification and Truth', *Philosophical Studies*, 46: 279–95.

Dancy, J. (2000), *Practical Reality*, Oxford: Oxford University Press.

Davidson, D. (1963), 'Actions, Reasons, and Causes', *The Journal of Philosophy*, 60: 685–700.

Dutant, J. (2015), 'The Legend of the Justified, True Belief Analysis', *Philosophical Perspectives*, 29: 95–145.

Fantl, J. and McGrath, M. (2009), *Knowledge in an Uncertain World*, New York: Oxford University Press.

Foley, R. (2009), 'Beliefs, Degrees of Belief, and the Lockean Thesis', in F. Huber and C. Schmidt-Petri (eds), *Degrees of Belief*, Dordrecht: Springer.

Foley, R. (2012), *When Is True Belief Knowledge?* Princeton: Princeton University Press.

Fumerton, R. (1995), *Metaepistemology and Skepticism*, Lanham, MD: Rowman and Littlefield.

Gerken, M. (2011), 'Warrant and Action', *Synthese*, 178: 529–47.

Gertler, B. (2010), *Self-Knowledge*, New York: Routledge.

Gettier, E. L. (1963), 'Is Justified True Belief Knowledge?' *Analysis*, 23: 121–3.

Gibbons, J. (2013), *The Norm of Belief*, Oxford: Oxford University Press.

Goldman, A. I. (1979), 'What Is Justified Belief?', in G. S. Pappas (ed.), *Justification and Knowledge: New Studies in Epistemology* , Dordrecht: D. Reidel.

Hawthorne, J. and Magidor, O. (forthcoming), 'Reflections on Reasons', in D. Star (ed.), *Oxford Handbook of Reasons and Normativity*, Oxford: Oxford University Press.

Hawthorne, J. and Stanley, J. (2008), 'Knowledge and Action', *The Journal of Philosophy*, 105: 571–90.

Hofmann, F. (2014), 'Gettier for Justification', *Episteme*, 11: 305–18.

Hornsby, J. (2008), 'A Disjunctive Conception of Acting for Reasons', in A. Haddock and F. Macpherson (eds), *Disjunctivism: Perception, Action, Knowledge*, Oxford: Oxford University Press.

Horowitz, S. (2014), 'Immoderately Rational', *Philosophical Studies*, 167: 41–56.

Huemer, M. (forthcoming), 'Defending a Brain in a Vat', in F. Dorsch and J. Dutant (eds), *The New Evil Demon*, Oxford: Oxford University Press.

Hughes, N. (2014), 'Is Knowledge the Ability to φ for the Reason that P?', *Episteme*, 11: 457–62.

Hyman, J. (1999), 'How Knowledge Works', *The Philosophical Quarterly*, 50: 433–51.

Kim, J. (1988), 'What Is "Naturalized Epistemology"?' *Philosophical Perspectives*, 2: 381–405.

Kornblith, H. (2008), 'Knowledge Needs No Justification', in Quentin Smith (ed.), *Epistemology: New Essays*, Oxford: Oxford University Press.

Kvanvig, J. L. (2003), *The Value of Knowledge and the Pursuit of Understanding*, Cambridge: Cambridge University Press.

Lackey, J. (2007), 'Norms of Assertion', *Noûs*, 41: 594–626.

Lackey, J. (2009), 'Knowledge and Credit', *Philosophical Studies*, 142: 27–42.

Lasonen-Aarnio, M. (2010), 'Unreasonable Knowledge', *Philosophical Perspectives*, 24: 1–21.

Littlejohn, C. (2012), *Justification and the Truth-Connection*, Cambridge: Cambridge University Press.

Littlejohn, C. (2013), 'The Russellian Retreat', *Proceedings of the Aristotelian Society*, 113: 293–320.

Littlejohn, C. (2015), 'Who Cares What You Accurately Believe?' *Philosophical Perspectives*, 29: 217–48.

Locke, D. (2014), 'The Decision-Theoretic Lockean Thesis', *Inquiry*, 57: 28–54.

Locke, D. (2015), 'Knowledge, Explanation, and Motivating Reasons', *American Philosophical Quarterly*, 52: 215–32.

Lynch, M. (2004), *True to Life: Why Truth Matters*, Cambridge: MIT Press.

Makinson, D. C. (1965), 'The Paradox of the Preface', *Analysis*, 25: 205–7.

Marcus, E. (2012), *Rational Causation*, Cambridge, MA: Harvard University Press.

McCain, K. (2014), *Evidentialism and Epistemic Justification*, New York: Routledge.

McDowell, J. (1994), *Mind and World*, Cambridge, MA: Harvard University Press.

McDowell, J. (1998), 'Knowledge and the Internal', in his *Meaning, Knowledge, and Reality*, Cambridge, MA: Harvard University Press.

McGinn, M. (2012), 'Non-inferential Knowledge', *Proceedings of the Aristotelian Society*, 112: 1–28.

McGlynn, A. (2011), 'Believing Things Unknown', *Noûs*, 47: 385–407.

McGlynn, A. (2014), *Knowledge First?* Basingstoke: Palgrave Macmillan.

McKinnon, R. (2013), 'The Supportive Reasons Norm of Assertion', *American Philosophical Quarterly*, 50: 121–35.

Mitova, V. (2015), 'Truthy Psychologism about Evidence', *Philosophical Studies*, 172: 1105–26.

Montminy, M. (2013), 'Why Assertion and Practical Reasoning Must be Governed by the Same Epistemic Norm', *Pacific Philosophical Quarterly*, 94: 57–68.

Naylor, M. B. (1988), 'Epistemic Justification', *American Philosophical Quarterly*, 25: 49–58.

Nelkin, D. K. (2000), 'The Lottery Paradox, Knowledge, and Rationality', *Philosophical Review*, 109: 373–409.

Robinson, P. H. and Darley, J. M. (1998), 'Testing Competing Theories of Justification', *North Carolina Law Review*, 76: 1095–143.

Ryan, S. (1991), 'The Preface Paradox', *Philosophical Studies*, 64: 293–307.

Sartwell, C. (1991), 'Knowledge Is Merely True Belief', *American Philosophical Quarterly*, 28: 157–65.

Schellenberg, S. (forthcoming), 'Perceptual Capacities, Knowledge, and Gettier Cases', in R. Borges, C. de Almeida, and P. Klein (eds), *Explaining Knowledge: New Essays on the Gettier Problem*, Oxford: Oxford University Press.

Schroeder, M. (2011), 'What Does It Take to "Have" a Reason?', in A. Reisner and A. Steglich-Petersen (eds), *Reasons for Belief*, Cambridge: Cambridge University Press.

Silins, N. (2005), 'Deception and Evidence', *Philosophical Perspectives*, 19: 375–404.

Slote, M. (1979), 'Assertion and Belief', in Jonathan Dancy (ed.), *Papers on Language and Logic: Proceedings of the Conference on the Philosophy of Language and Logic Held at the University of Keele in April, 1979*, Keele: Keele University Library.

Smithies, D. (2012), 'The Normative Role of Knowledge', *Noûs*, 46: 265–88.

Sosa, E. (2015), *Judgment and Agency*, Oxford: Oxford University Press.

Srinivasan, A. (2015), 'Normativity without Cartesian Privilege', *Philosophical Issues*, 25: 273–99.

Sutton, J. (2007), *Without Justification*, Cambridge: The MIT Press.

Sylvan, K. (manuscript), *Knowledge as a Non-Normative Relation*.

Travis, C. (2013), *Perception: Essays after Frege*, Oxford: Oxford University Press.

Turri, J. (2009), 'The Ontology of Epistemic Reasons', *Noûs*, 43: 490–512.

Turri, J. (2011), 'The Express Knowledge Account of Assertion', *Australasian Journal of Philosophy*, 89: 37–45.

Turri, J. (2015), 'Knowledge and the Norm of Assertion: A Simple Test', *Synthese*, 192: 385–92.

Unger, P. (1975), *Ignorance: A Case for Scepticism*, Oxford: Clarendon Press.

Wedgwood, R. (2002), 'The Aim of Belief', *Philosophical Perspectives*, 16: 267–97.

Williams, B. (1973), 'Deciding to Believe', in his *Problems of the Self*, Cambridge: Cambridge University Press.

Williamson, T. (2000), *Knowledge and Its Limits*, Oxford: Clarendon Press.

Williamson, T. (2017), 'Ambiguous Rationality', *Episteme*, 14: 263–74.

Zagzebski, L. T. (1996), *Virtues of the Mind: An Inquiry into the Nature of Virtue and the Ethical Foundations of Knowledge*, Cambridge: Cambridge University Press.

14

Intellectual Virtue and Knowledge

Heather Battaly

1. Introduction

The notion of intellectual virtue made its contemporary debut in Ernest Sosa's 'The Raft and the Pyramid' (1980). At that time, analytic epistemology was teeming with proposed solutions to the Gettier Problem (Gettier 1963), newly minted objections to internalism and externalism, and seemingly intractable disagreements between foundationalists and coherentists. Sosa drew what was then the iconoclastic conclusion that the notion of intellectual virtue might help us resolve the foundationalism-coherentism debate.[1] Following suit, Linda Zagzebski (1996) argued that the notion of intellectual virtue could help us circumvent the debate between internalism and externalism,[2] and both Sosa (1991, 2007, 2015a) and Zagzebski (1996, 2009) have championed virtue-based solutions to the Gettier problem.[3] In short, they offered analytic epistemologists a potential way out of the problems that were plaguing their belief-based theories. Roughly, *belief-based epistemologies* take knowledge and justification, which are evaluations of beliefs, to be more theoretically fundamental than intellectual virtues, which are evaluations of agents.

To explicate, the belief-based epistemologies of the mid-twentieth and late twentieth century rarely mentioned intellectual virtues, but, if they had, they would have defined intellectual virtues in terms of knowledge and justification, rather than the other way around. In contrast, Sosa's and Zagzebski's proposed alternative, *virtue epistemology*, invites us to take intellectual virtues and vices to be the fundamental concepts and properties of our epistemic theories. In this manner, the theoretical structure of virtue epistemology is analogous to that of virtue ethics. Virtue epistemology invites us to start with evaluations of agents, as intellectually virtuous or vicious, and to define knowledge, and other belief-evaluations, in terms of intellectual virtues. It 'revers[es] the direction of analysis'

(Greco 2000: 248), and, in so doing, hopes to bypass or resolve the above debates over knowledge and justification.

Whether virtue epistemology succeeds in bypassing or resolving any of the above debates is an open question. It may fail in this endeavour. In that vein, this chapter raises objections to Sosa's and Zagzebski's solutions to the Gettier problem. But the chapter also demonstrates that virtue epistemology is already making *other* important contributions to the analysis of knowledge, particularly to its expansion. First, by inviting us to start elsewhere – with intellectual virtue – and to define knowledge in terms of intellectual virtue rather than the reverse, virtue epistemology has succeeded in shining a spotlight on active knowledge. Neglected by mid- and late-twentieth-century belief-based epistemologies (which instead emphasized the passive knowledge that we share with non-human animals and children), active knowledge is thought to express our agency. Roughly, it is thought to manifest our ability to actively reflect on our epistemic lives, and to use these reflections to guide the epistemic actions we perform in inquiries. Second, a subset of virtue epistemologists have invited us to re-evaluate the importance of locating necessary and sufficient conditions for knowledge. They have suggested that, despite the emphasis on such conditions in mid- and late-twentieth century belief-based epistemology, these are not the only analytical game in town and may not even be the most important. These epistemologists think that, even if intellectual virtues prove unnecessary for knowledge, there will still be probabilistic connections between the virtues and knowledge that can be applied in educational settings. Thus, it will be important to home in on these probabilistic connections, even if they aren't captured by necessary and sufficient conditions. Arguably, these ways of expanding the analysis of knowledge, so as to include active knowledge and looser methods of analysis, are worthy of exploration. Accordingly, even if our initial impetus for pursuing virtue epistemology ends up as a bust – even if virtue epistemology fails to bypass or solve the problems that have plagued belief-based epistemology – virtue-theoretic analyses of knowledge would still be worthy of pursuit.

2. Two sorts of knowledge and two sorts of intellectual virtue

Sosa and Zagzebski, the two leading figures in virtue epistemology, both argue for necessary and sufficient connections between knowledge and intellectual virtue. Both also distinguish between two sorts of knowledge – roughly, active knowledge and passive knowledge. They also share the intention to analyse *both* of these sorts of knowledge in terms of intellectual virtue. But, since Sosa and Zagzebski conceive of the intellectual virtues differently, Sosa's theory ends up being better-suited to analyse passive knowledge, while Zagzebski's ends up being better-suited to analyse active knowledge.

Let's begin to unpack this. For starters, Sosa and Zagzebski agree that there are *two sorts of knowledge*. One of these is *passive*, involuntary, and automatic – it is the sort of knowledge that we share with children and non-human animals. Sosa (1991: 240) dubs this 'animal' knowledge; for Zagzebski (1996: 273–83), it is 'low-grade'. To avoid playing favourites, I call it 'passive'. Its paradigms include perceptual knowledge and memory knowledge – for example, knowing that the wall is white, or that you had cereal for breakfast. To illustrate, suppose you are in a well-lit room whose walls are painted white. Arguably, you can come to know that they are white without doing anything at all. You don't need to conduct an inquiry, or to reflect on your perceptual capacities. Given that your eyes are open, and your eyes and brain are functioning properly, you automatically come to know that the walls are white. This knowledge is passive and involuntary – it is 'something that happens to you' (Dougherty 2011: 80). In contrast, *active* knowledge is volitional – it requires agency and action. Roughly, it requires an agent to actively reflect on her epistemic situation – her beliefs, cognitive environment, and cognitive abilities and limitations – and to 'reflectively guide her epistemic behavior' (Zagzebski 2014: 141). Sosa (2015a: 25, 74, 86–7) calls this sort of knowledge 'reflective', 'judgmental', and 'knowing full well'; Zagzebski calls it 'reflective' (2014: 141–2) and 'high-grade' (1996: 273–83). Its paradigms include discoveries in (for instance) science, medicine, and philosophy, and the 'investigative applied' knowledge that professionals acquire in the workplace (Battaly 2008: 652). To illustrate, suppose you are a police detective investigating a murder, to which there are no witnesses. In order to know who committed the murder, you must perform epistemic actions. You must reflect on your epistemic situation, and conduct an inquiry: you must form a hypothesis, search for confirming and disconfirming evidence, consider alternative suspects, and so on. The key idea is this: one can't acquire active knowledge simply by opening one's eyes in an appropriate environment; its acquisition requires active reflection and inquiry.

Historically, Sosa and Zagzebski are hardly the only epistemologists to draw attention to this distinction. Some epistemologists – arguably, Plato and Aquinas – even deny the very existence of passive knowledge. Against this background, Sosa and Zagzebski point out that analytic epistemology's recent focus on passive knowledge breaks with the tradition. In Sosa's (2017: 2609) words, 'I do think that the epistemology of judgment has suffered neglect in recent times, by comparison with its place in the broad sweep of the historical tradition, from the Greeks, especially the Pyrrhonists, through Descartes.'[4] Sosa and Zagzebski want to rectify this recent neglect of active knowledge, making space for it in contemporary analytic epistemology.

Though Sosa and Zagzebski share the same general outlook, they endorse *two different analyses of intellectual virtue*: Virtue-Reliabilism and Virtue-Responsibilism. Zagzebski's Responsibilism argues that intellectual virtues require dispositions of intellectual motivation and action, over which the agent has some control, and for which the agent is (at least partly) responsible. Zagzebski contends that intellectual virtues are analogous in structure to Aristotelian moral virtues. Accordingly, she conceives of them as character traits; as dispositions of intellectual motivation, action, emotion, and perception. The paradigms of Responsibilist virtue include open-mindedness, intellectual courage, and intellectual humility. There are four points to emphasize. (1) Zagzebski (1996: 102–5) argues that we are *praiseworthy* for possessing intellectual virtues, and that we can only be praised for things within our control. Accordingly, she thinks that intellectual virtues must be *acquired* qualities; they cannot be hard-wired faculties like vision. (2) She argues that intellectual virtues are *personal*: they express one's epistemic character – what one values, and cares about, as a thinker. For this reason, too, she rules out hard-wired faculties, which are sub-personal (104). Relatedly, (3) she contends that intellectual virtues require *acquired dispositions of motivation*: specifically, the motivation for truth, which is itself valuable. She thinks we often lack sufficient motivation for truth, and must learn to care more. On her view, we have some control over whether we end up caring about truth, since we acquire our epistemic motivations via practice and the imitation of exemplars. She argues that all intellectual virtues share an underlying motivation to care appropriately about truth. This, in turn, generates the motivations that are distinctive of each individual virtue – for example, the motivation to consider alternative ideas appropriately (distinctive of open-mindedness). But, for Zagzebski, good intellectual motivations are insufficient for virtue. One must also be *disposed to act* in accordance with those motivations. Thus, 'if [an agent] is truly open-minded, she must actually be receptive to new ideas'; caring about being receptive isn't enough (177). Finally, (4) intellectual virtues must also be reliable.[5] Zagzebski thinks that success matters for virtue (99–100, 137). In her words, 'not only is an open-minded person motivated to consider the ideas of others without prejudice ... and is reliably successful in doing so, but her reliable success in being open-minded is truth-conducive' – she reliably gets true beliefs as a result of considering the ideas she should (185). Putting all of this together, she thinks the intellectual virtue of open-mindedness is a disposition to (a) care appropriately about truth, (b) care about considering alternative ideas appropriately, (c) consider appropriate alternatives, and (d) reliably produce true beliefs.

Sosa's Virtue-Reliabilism argues that intellectual virtues are reliable dispositions – they are dispositions to produce more true beliefs than false ones.[6] Unlike Zagzebski, Sosa does not restrict intellectual virtues to character traits. He argues that intellectual virtues are *any* stable qualities that enable us to perform our intellectual functions well, or (*sans* teleology) to produce good intellectual effects, like true beliefs. These qualities can be hard-wired faculties, acquired skills, or acquired character traits. The paradigms of Reliabilist virtue include reliable faculties of (e.g.) vision and memory, and reliable skills of (e.g.) reading MRI films. In his early work, Sosa (1991, 2007) focused on virtues that were faculties or skills. In more recent work, he has begun to focus on 'agential' virtues like proper care and attentiveness, and character virtues like open-mindedness (2015a: 48; 2017). There are four corresponding points to emphasize. (1) Sosa (2007) argues that intellectual virtues need not be praiseworthy and need not be acquired; they can be *hard-wired faculties*. Thus, some of our intellectual virtues 'come courtesy of Mother Nature and her evolutionary ways, but many others must be learned' (85). Despite Sosa's (2017) recent shift towards agential virtues, he still counts reliable faculties among the intellectual virtues. (2) Sosa thinks that intellectual virtues *need not be personal*, and need not express one's epistemic character. Virtues *can* express one's epistemic character, but when they do so they are unlikely to be constitutive of knowledge (2015a: 41–3). Relatedly, (3) he argues that intellectual virtues *do not require acquired dispositions of motivation or action.* Children and animals can possess the hard-wired virtue of vision even though they have not (yet) acquired the motivation to care appropriately about truth. Nor do hard-wired virtues, like reliable vision, involve dispositions of voluntary action (acquired or otherwise). Finally, (4) Sosa argues that intellectual virtues require *reliability.* To be an intellectual virtue, a quality must be disposed to produce a preponderance of true beliefs. But it need only be disposed to do so in the sorts of conditions we typically encounter. To illustrate, Sosa argues that the reliability of vision is not impugned by its failure to produce true beliefs in the dark. But it is impugned by its failure to produce true beliefs about medium-sized objects seen in broad daylight.[7] Roughly, he argues that, for vision to be reliable and thus a virtue, it must be disposed to produce more true beliefs than false ones about the basic shapes and colours of medium-sized objects, when they are seen nearby, without occlusion, and in good light (Sosa 1991: 139).[8]

3. Defining knowledge in terms of intellectual virtue: Sosa's view and objections

Sosa defines knowledge in terms of Reliabilist virtue. For starters, he argues that knowledge is a kind of success – the cognitive success of arriving at a true belief. Of course, it is possible to arrive at a true belief due to luck, in which case one wouldn't have knowledge. In an effort to exclude luck, Sosa argues that knowledge requires true belief to be a credit to *the agent*, and not due to luck or some other extraneous factor. This is where virtue plays a key role. Sosa thinks that, to have knowledge, an agent must arrive at a true belief because of her own intellectual virtues, and not because of luck (or other extraneous factors). Specifically, he defines knowledge as apt belief, whereby an agent knows that p if and only if her belief that p is (1) accurate – true; (2) adroit – is produced by one of her intellectual virtues; and (3) apt – she obtains the truth *because* her belief is produced by one of her intellectual virtues (2007: 23). Sosa explains that, like shots in archery, beliefs can be both accurate and adroit without being apt. To illustrate, an archer's shot might hit the target and be produced by her skill in archery, but simultaneously fail to hit the target *because* it was produced by her skill – for example, when it hits the target due to doubly shifting winds (22).[9] Analogously, an agent's belief might be both true and produced by one of her intellectual virtues, and yet she might arrive at that true belief because of luck, not virtue (as one does in Gettier cases). Sosa contends that only when beliefs are apt is the correctness of the belief creditable to the agent, and only then does the agent have knowledge. Accordingly, Sosa's analysis of knowledge is a version of the credit theory.[10]

Much of Sosa's work has emphasized hard-wired virtues, like reliable vision. But if virtues are hard-wired, then Sosa's definition is better-suited to analyse passive knowledge than active knowledge. Indeed, Sosa offers it in precisely this vein: namely, as an analysis of 'animal' knowledge (2007: 24). Recall that active knowledge requires active reflection and action-guidance. In contrast, apt beliefs that are produced by hard-wired virtues require neither. In fact, they don't require voluntary actions of any kind; nor do they require agency in any strong sense (animals and children can have apt beliefs).[11] To put the last point differently, Sosa's 'agents' can be mere 'subjects'. On his view, subject S will know that a fast-moving large object (e.g. a truck) is approaching if she arrives at a true belief to that effect due to her reliable vision. She need not know that her vision is reliable, nor need she *do* anything. Given that she is in broad daylight, her virtue of vision will automatically and involuntarily produce beliefs about her surroundings. And, given that those beliefs are true and that luck is inoperative, she will passively come to have apt beliefs. Aptness will 'happen to her'. Granted, arriving at a true belief must be a credit to her. But this is not the sort of credit that requires control – it is not Responsibilist praise. Rather, in assigning credit to her, Sosa is answering the question, 'What caused her to arrive at a true belief?' His answer is that her virtues are the most salient cause. He is attributing the cause of true belief to her, rather than to extraneous factors like luck. Sosa sees all of these points as strengths of his view. He explicitly wants to make space for a kind of knowledge that is passive and externalist, and distinct from reflective knowledge, the latter of which he defines as 'apt belief aptly [believed]' (2007: 34).

But doesn't Sosa's analysis of *reflective* knowledge do a better job of capturing the key features of active knowledge? After all, one might object, Sosa never intended his analysis of animal knowledge to capture those features; moreover, his reflective knowledge is nothing if not reflective! In reply, the problem is that Sosa's reflective knowledge (as it is analysed in his 1991, 2007, and much of his 2009) doesn't seem to require voluntary action. To explicate, Sosa thinks of reflective knowledge as a way for adults to know that they know. For instance, an adult can have reflective knowledge that the wall is white – she can know that she knows that the wall is white. She will have such knowledge if and only if (RK1) she has animal knowledge that 'the wall is white' (see above), (RK2) she believes that 'she knows that the wall is white', (RK3) her belief that 'she knows that the wall is white' is itself accurate – true, (RK4) her belief that 'she knows that the wall is white' is itself adroit – produced by one of her intellectual virtues, and (RK5) her belief that 'she knows that the wall is white' is itself apt – true because virtuous. In less technical terms, to have reflective knowledge that the wall is white, she must know that the wall is white, know that vision is the source of her belief that the wall is white, and know that her vision is reliable.[12] Sosa's reflective knowledge clearly requires higher-level beliefs, but it doesn't clearly require voluntary action. Arguably, one could acquire these 'reflective' beliefs without actively doing anything, since the virtues that produce these beliefs might themselves be passive. Very roughly, if one's vision *is* reliable, one might come to know that it is reliable through its continued passive use, given that this use (in combination with the use of other passive reliable faculties) gradually produces coherent higher-level beliefs about one's place in the world and about how one gains knowledge from it.[13] In short, such higher-level beliefs could 'happen to us' without our having sought them out. The main point is that Sosa's reflective knowledge doesn't seem to require active reflection, or epistemic action, or agency in any strong sense. There is nothing to prevent reflective knowledge from devolving into passively knowing that one passively knows.[14] In sum, the difference between animal and reflective knowledge (in Sosa 1991, 2007, and much of 2009) is arguably a difference in degree, not in kind; whereas the difference between passive and active knowledge is a difference in kind, not degree. It is worth noting that Sosa's analysis of reflective knowledge may make progress in resolving the internalist-externalist debate. Even so, it fails to capture the key features of active knowledge.[15] As we will see below, Sosa's (2015a) recent work on judgemental knowledge does a much better job of accounting for active knowledge.

Let's return to Sosa's analysis of passive knowledge as apt belief. Is this definition successful? There are two main objections to Sosa's view (and to credit theories in general). First, Duncan Pritchard (2009) objects that apt belief is insufficient for passive knowledge, since it fails to exclude environmental luck. In short, Pritchard contends that Sosa's view is still subject to Gettier counterexamples. To illustrate, imagine that Barney is driving through a rural region. He sees what appears to be the side of a barn, and forms the belief 'There is a barn'. Suppose that Barney's belief is true: he has seen a real barn. His belief is also adroit – it is produced by his virtue of vision. Moreover, it is apt – he actually arrives at a true belief because of his virtue of vision. But now add that, unbeknown to Barney, the region he is in contains very few real barns and a plethora of barn façades.[16] His apt belief that 'There is a barn' now seems to fall short of knowledge, since his belief could easily have been false. He could easily have looked at a barn façade instead of one of the few real barns in the region. In technical terms, even though Barney's belief is apt, it isn't 'safe', and thus doesn't seem to count as knowledge (Battaly 2008).

Sosa's reply is that Barney lacks reflective knowledge, but still has animal knowledge. He thinks reflective knowledge requires safety, but animal knowledge doesn't (2007: 31, 2015a: 79). To explicate, he argues that, despite the fact that an archer's shot is unsafe (the wind might too easily have diverted the arrow), if the wind *didn't* gust, and the archer *actually* hit the target because of her skill, then the shot's success is a credit to her. Analogously, despite the fact that Barney's belief that 'there is a barn' is unsafe – it might too easily have been false because he might too easily have looked at a barn façade – if he *didn't* look at a barn façade and *actually* arrived at a true belief because of his virtue of vision, then the belief's correctness is a credit to him. Unsurprisingly, Pritchard disagrees, arguing that animal knowledge requires safety in addition to virtue.[17] In short, it is an open question as to whether passive knowledge requires safety.

The second main objection to Sosa's view comes from Jennifer Lackey. She argues that apt belief is not necessary for passive knowledge, since testimonial knowledge need not be apt. Recall that, for Sosa, aptness requires the agent to arrive at a true belief because of her own intellectual virtues, and not because of luck or other extraneous factors. Believing correctly must be a credit to the agent in question, and to virtues in her. This means that it must not be creditable to something outside the agent, or to virtues in someone else. Enter Morris. Lackey asks us to imagine that Morris has just arrived at the train station in Chicago. Being unfamiliar with the city, he asks the nearest adult passer-by for directions to the Sears Tower, which the passer-by provides. Indeed, knowing the city quite well herself, the passer-by provides Morris with superb directions, which he unhesitatingly believes (Lackey 2007: 352). Lackey argues that Morris knows the location of the Sears Tower, even though his true beliefs about its location are not a credit to him. In her words, 'what explains why Morris got things right has nearly nothing of epistemic interest to do with him and nearly everything … to do with the passer-by … it is the passer-by's experience with and knowledge of the city … that explains why Morris ended up with a true belief rather than a false belief' (352). In short, Morris' true belief is a credit to the passer-by and *her* virtues; it is not a credit to Morris. And yet we would be hard-pressed to deny that Morris has knowledge. Moreover, this seems to hold for testimonial knowledge more generally – typically, it is the *speaker* who deserves credit for the testimonial knowledge acquired by the hearer. Briefly, credit theorists might reply that *hearers* have a testimonial virtue of sorts, a virtue that tracks the credibility of speakers or a 'virtuous testimonial sensibility' (Fricker 2007: 77). The epistemology of testimony is itself a burgeoning field. Whether hearers have a testimonial virtue, and what such a virtue would look like, are open questions.

In his recent work, Sosa (2015a) intentionally shines a spotlight on active knowledge in an effort to rectify its neglect.[18] He argues that unlike passive 'functional' knowledge (25), judgemental knowledge requires 'free, volitional endorsement by the subject who judges', or at least dispositions to make such volitional endorsements (3). In other words, it requires judgement, which is itself an act of endorsement that is under the agent's direct voluntary control (93). Accordingly, to have judgemental knowledge that, for example, the butler committed the crime, a police detective must make the corresponding judgement. Moreover, the truth of the detective's judgement must be due to her intellectual virtues; and due to them 'in a way that constitutes knowledge' (Sosa 2015b: 67). Crucially, Sosa here argues that these virtues must be agential. He conceives of agential virtues as 'active [and] volitional' (2015a: 35). He contends that they are 'obviously' distinct from non-agential faculties like reliable vision, and also distinct from the 'personal-worth-involving motivationally appropriate' character virtues of Responsibilism (48). Agential virtues do not require an acquired motivation for truth (49–50), but do seem to be acquired traits for whose exercise the agent is responsible (48). Moreover, they seem to require acquired dispositions of action. Sosa tells us that agential virtues, like proper care and attentiveness, are *not* 'virtues of inquiry' (e.g. open-mindedness and intellectual perseverance), which merely put one in a position to know. Rather, agential virtues are 'virtues of judgment proper', whose exercise constitutes knowledge (45).[19]

Clearly, Sosa has made considerable progress in accounting for active knowledge. Is his analysis of active knowledge in terms of agential virtue successful? It would help to have more details about agential virtues themselves, and exactly how they differ from Responsibilist virtues, and also from acquired skills. If agential virtues like proper care and attentiveness are stable traits whose dispositions of action are acquired over time, then they will be much more difficult to possess than hard-wired faculties. And if their *possession* is required for active knowledge – as Sosa seems to think – then his view might make active knowledge too difficult to get. As we will see below, Zagzebski's analysis of active knowledge is still arguably subject to the Gettier problem, and to an objection involving testimony. Sosa's analysis of judgemental knowledge will be subject to these worries as well.

4. Defining knowledge in terms of intellectual virtue: Zagzebski's view and objections

Zagzebski (1996) defines knowledge in terms of Responsibilist virtue. Specifically, she argues that knowledge is true belief that arises from an act of intellectual virtue (271). She uses 'act of intellectual virtue' as a technical term. Performing such an act requires more than simply doing what an intellectually virtuous person would do. But it requires less-than-full possession of intellectual virtue. In her words, 'an act of intellectual virtue A is an act that arises from the

motivational component of A, is something a person with virtue A would ...
do in the circumstances, is successful in achieving the end of the A motivation,
and is such that the agent acquires a true belief ... through these features of the
act' (270).

To illustrate, consider an act of open-mindedness. To perform an act of
open-mindedness, the agent must (1) possess the motivational component of
the virtue of open-mindedness. We have seen that the motivational component
of each Responsibilist virtue is twofold. It includes the acquired motivation to
care appropriately about truth, which spawns a motivation distinctive of the
virtue in question – in this case, the motivation to consider alternative ideas
appropriately. The agent must also, on this occasion, succeed in attaining the
ends of this dual motivation. That is, she must (2) succeed in considering
appropriate alternatives – she must do what an open-minded person would do.
(She must perform a voluntary epistemic action.) And she must (3) succeed in
attaining a true belief. Finally, she must (4) attain a true belief because of her
motivation and action, and not because of luck. On Zagzebski's view, one can
perform acts of intellectual virtue from time to time, without fully possessing
the intellectual virtue in question. Recall that, for Zagzebski, intellectual virtues
are stable dispositions. To fully possess the virtue of open-mindedness, an agent
must *consistently* (a) care about truth, (b) care about considering alternatives,
(c) consider appropriate alternatives, and (d) produce true beliefs. Performing
an act of open-mindedness requires the agent to consistently care about truth
and about considering alternatives, but it does not require her to consistently
consider appropriate alternatives or to be reliable (as a result of so doing).
To explicate, the agent need not have acquired a stable *disposition* to do what
an open-minded person would do; given that she possesses the motivational
component of the virtue, she need only succeed in doing what an open-minded
person would do and in getting the truth on *this occasion*.

Though Zagzebski offers her definition as an analysis of both passive (low-
grade) and active (high-grade) knowledge (1996: 277–81; 2014: 144), it is better-
suited as an analysis of the latter. Indeed, Zagzebski is largely responsible for
putting active knowledge back on the epistemological map. (Sosa is a late arrival.)
Her analysis of knowledge is nothing if not active: for her, knowledge clearly
requires agency and voluntary epistemic action. But these same features make
her definition unsuitable for analysing passive knowledge. Adults, children,
and animals can know that a fast-moving large object is approaching, without
possessing any acquired motivation for truth or performing any voluntary
epistemic actions. As John Greco (2002: 296) puts the point, '[Y]ou know that

there is a truck moving toward you independent of any control.' Nor does such knowledge require motivations to be 'open-minded, careful, or the like. On the contrary, it would seem that you know there is a truck coming towards you even if you are motivated not to be open-minded' (ibid.). Similarly, Jason Baehr (2014: 137) argues that one can spontaneously know that the lights in the room have just gone out without 'any sort of attention or curiosity whatsoever', without 'any virtuous motives', and without performing any voluntary actions. In short, Zagzebski's definition of knowledge arguably fails to capture passive knowledge.

Is Zagzebski's definition successful as an analysis of active knowledge? There are two key objections to her view. First, Baehr (2006) argues that her analysis is still subject to the Gettier problem. Zagzebski intends the fourth condition of an act of intellectual virtue – whereby 'the agent acquires a true belief ... through the [virtuous] features of the act' – to immunize knowledge from Gettier counterexamples. Baehr argues that it fails to do so. To adapt an example from Baehr, suppose that Jane is a police detective investigating the murder of an accountant who worked for a multinational corporation. There were no witnesses. Jane cares appropriately about truth, cares about considering alternative suspects, and cares about being thorough in searching for and evaluating evidence. In other words, she satisfies the motivational condition of an act of intellectual virtue. For simplicity's sake, imagine that there are only two viable suspects: the CEO of the corporation, and the accountant's husband. The evidence reveals that the accountant 'cooked' the corporation's books, that the government was conducting an investigation of the corporation, and that the CEO's fingerprints were on the murder weapon. It also reveals that the accountant was loathed by her husband. Suppose that most of the evidence points towards the CEO, and that Jane is thus inclined to believe that the CEO is the murderer. But, because she cares about truth and about considering alternatives, she consults her team of detectives and considers their views. In so doing, she meets the second condition of an act of intellectual virtue – she does what an intellectually virtuous person would do. Further, suppose that, unbeknown to Jane and her team, the corporation has brainwashed her team into believing that the husband did it. Accordingly, when she consults them, they confidently claim that the husband is the murderer, and that she has misinterpreted the evidence. In weighing the options, Jane 'out of an earnest openness to [her] colleagues' views and a keen awareness of [her] own fallibility' comes to believe that the husband is the murderer (Baehr 2006: 488). Her belief turns out to be correct, thus meeting the third condition of an act of intellectual virtue. Moreover, she acquires a true belief about the murderer's identity because of her virtuous motivations and actions – if she hadn't consulted her team, then she would have ended up with a false belief. So, Jane arguably satisfies all four conditions of an act of intellectual virtue. And yet she doesn't seem to know that the husband did it. The corporation just happened to brainwash her team into believing something that was true (Battaly 2015: 124–5).

Zagzebski's reply is that the example above does not actually satisfy the fourth condition of an act of intellectual virtue. Jane does not arrive at a true belief because of the virtuous features of her act; rather, she arrives at a true belief primarily because of luck. Luck is the most salient cause of her arriving at the truth. It is an open question as to whether this reply succeeds. Its success depends on locating an independent analysis of causal saliency that can explain why luck is *more salient* than Jane's virtuous motivations and actions. Credit theories are also beholden to analyses of causal saliency. Accordingly, it may be telling that Sosa (2015a: 40–3) has recently moved away from the view that virtue must be *the most salient cause* of true belief, and towards the view that virtue must *constitute* knowledge.

The second set of objections contends that acts of intellectual virtue are not necessary for active knowledge. Recall that acts of intellectual virtue require the agent to possess the motivational component of the virtue. But it is difficult to acquire a stable motivation to care appropriately about truth – it takes time and practice. Many of us fall short of possessing this stable motivation, and yet we still have active knowledge (Battaly 2015: 128). In a similar vein, Sosa (2015a: 49) argues thus:

> Hedge fund managers, waste disposal engineers, dentists, and their receptionists, can all attain much knowledge in the course of a … workday despite the fact that they seek the truths relevant to their work only for their instrumental value. That is why they want them, not because they love truth … It is not love of truth that drives their professional activities, by contrast with desire for professional standing, wanting to help someone, or trying to make a living.

That is, one can acquire active knowledge even when one doesn't care about truth, or at least doesn't care about truth for its own sake.[20] Relatedly, one can acquire active knowledge even when one's motivations are intellectually vicious. For instance, a scientist who is motivated by vanity, the desire to win the Nobel prize, and 'competitive opportunism' can still acquire active knowledge (Roberts and Wood 2007: 144). The motivation to beat his competitors, or win awards, may be what causes the scientist to conduct a thorough investigation and to make new discoveries. As Sosa (2015a: 50) puts the point, people who are motivated to believe whatever will help them 'gain fame, wealth, and power' can still attain active knowledge. They can attain active knowledge even though truth does not enter into their motivations, or only enters into them insofar as it instrumentally serves their 'twisted ends' (ibid.). Burnt-out students and professionals might even come to despise pursuing truths in subjects they once loved. And yet they may continue to jump through the requisite hoops so as to successfully obtain such truths. (They may be motivated to keep their jobs, or to pass their classes.) We would be hard-pressed to deny that any of the agents above attain active knowledge. Consequently, it appears that active knowledge does not require intellectually virtuous motivations.

Acts of intellectual virtue also require the agent to act – to do what an intellectually virtuous person would do. Here, too, testimonial knowledge provides a putative counterexample. Suppose the Higgs-Boson does exist, and that scientists at the LHC know this. Their knowledge is active – it is the culmination of decades of inquiry. While listening to the news, you hear that the Higgs-Boson exists. It seems that you now know that the Higgs-Boson exists, even though you didn't conduct an inquiry. Nor, arguably, did you perform a voluntary action of any kind – let alone an action that a virtuous person would perform. You just had the news on (Battaly 2015: 129). So, if active knowledge is transmissible via testimony, then it doesn't require action on the part of the hearer.[21] The hearer can acquire active knowledge without performing a voluntary action herself.

In reply, Zagzebski (2014: 143; 2009: 127) has recently argued for a more forgiving analysis of knowledge, whereby an agent has knowledge whenever she arrives at a true belief 'because she acts in an epistemically conscientious way'. How does an epistemically conscientious person act? Zagzebski (2014: 144) tells us that the conscientious person is not 'continuously reflective' – he does not actively reflect on *every* belief. Instead, he has basic self-trust, and only actively reflects when it is appropriate. Else, he would be neurotic, not conscientious. Nor is he *always* consciously motivated to get the truth. Instead, he is only consciously motivated to get the truth 'when the appropriate occasion arises' (ibid.). In short, his active reflection and conscious motivation for truth kick-in when and only when he has reason to be suspicious of himself, others, or his environment. In the definition above, an agent is said to have knowledge whenever she arrives at the truth in the same way a conscientious person would. Accordingly, an agent can have knowledge even when she is *not* consciously motivated to get truth, and even when she does *not* actively reflect, provided that the occasion does not call for conscious motivation or active reflection, and provided that she *would* be so motivated and *would* actively reflect should such an occasion arise.

In one sense, these new conditions on knowledge are somewhat easier to satisfy – they allow an agent to have knowledge on some occasions when she hasn't acted and wasn't consciously motivated to get truth. But, in another sense, they are not easier to satisfy, and thus do not make much progress in assuaging the objections above. The main problem is that it will still be quite difficult to meet the counterfactual condition – arguably, to do so, one must learn when it is, and when it is not, appropriate to actively reflect and consciously pursue truth. In this sense, the new conditions may be even stronger than the old ones – it now seems that one must possess something tantamount to the dispositions of the conscientious person, at least insofar as those are required to satisfy the counterfactual. In any case, most of us will still fall short of satisfying the counterfactual. Granted, for the few agents who do satisfy the counterfactual, Zagzebski's new definition makes progress in answering the objection from testimony. It also helps to mitigate concerns about agents whose conscious motivations, though not for truth, are benign. But it does not mitigate concerns about the majority of agents who fail to satisfy the counterfactual, including agents whose conscious motivations are vicious. It is noteworthy that agents whose motivations are vicious – opportunistic scientists and burnt-out professionals – still seem to acquire active knowledge.[22]

With these objections in mind, several Responsibilists have emphasized probabilistic connections between the intellectual virtues and active knowledge.[23] They think the virtues are unlikely to be strictly necessary or sufficient for active knowledge. But they also think that necessary and sufficient conditions have been overemphasized. After all, if we are interested in attaining active knowledge, and in teaching our students to do so, then it will be important for us to explore probabilistic connections between the virtues and knowledge. First, regarding sufficient conditions, they argue that Gettier cases rarely arise in the real world. Accordingly, it is reasonable to think that (e.g.) detectives, scientists, and students *often* acquire active knowledge when they manage to care enough about truth and succeed in performing the acts that an intellectually virtuous person would perform. For instance, we can easily imagine a detective who cares about correctly identifying who-done-it (perhaps with benign ulterior motives), who tenaciously tracks down leads and follows the evidence, and who arrives at a true belief as a result (Battaly 2015: 126–7). Since her case does not involve any bizarre twists of luck, we shouldn't hesitate to claim that she knows.

Second, they contend that intellectually virtuous motivations and actions are not strictly necessary for acquiring active knowledge – we can sometimes get active knowledge without them. But they think there are also cases in which we *won't* get active knowledge without such motivations and actions. We *sometimes* need virtuous motivations and actions to acquire active knowledge. To illustrate, Robert Roberts and Jay Wood (2007) argue that Jane Goodall could not have made her discoveries about chimps without intellectually virtuous motivations and actions. On their description, Goodall's love of science and love of chimps motivated her to laboriously and meticulously chronicle the details of their lives, which in turn enabled her to make several breakthroughs (145–8). Using a different kind of example, knowing one's own sexual orientation sometimes requires intellectually virtuous motivations and actions, especially in societies that pressure people to believe that they are heterosexual. To combat this pressure, and to avoid arriving at false beliefs, LGBT people may need to perform intellectually virtuous actions – for example, actively reflecting and considering the possibility that they are not heterosexual. Such actions are likely to require a sufficiently strong motivation for truth, without which agents would likely succumb to the motivation to believe whatever is easiest (Battaly 2015: 130).

In sum, this chapter has argued that Sosa's definition of knowledge, in terms of Reliabilist virtue, is better-suited to analyse passive knowledge, while Zagzebski's definition, in terms of Responsibilist virtue, is better-suited to analyse active knowledge. More broadly, I hope to have shown that virtue-theoretic analyses of knowledge are worthy of pursuit. Virtue epistemology has put active knowledge back on the map, and has encouraged us to explore probabilistic connections between active knowledge and intellectual virtue. In short, it is already making a valuable contribution to the analysis of knowledge.

Notes

1 On the foundationalism-coherentism debate, see Alston (1976) and BonJour (1978).
2 On the internalism-externalism debate, see Goldman (1979), BonJour (1980), and Alston (1993). Goldman argues for externalism; BonJour for internalism; and Alston for the claim that the debate is at an impasse. Goldman (1992) and BonJour (2002) have since moderated their views.
3 Gettier (1963) famously argues that true justified belief is insufficient for knowledge.
4 On the neglect of active knowledge, see Zagzebski (1996: 45–50; 2014: 142).

5   Baehr (2011: 123–6) is a Responsibilist who argues that reliability is not necessary
    for intellectual virtue.

6   See also Greco (2000, 2010).

7   Also see Greco's (2010: 77) analysis of an ability.

8   See Sosa's (2015a: 95) SSS (seat, shape, and situation) conditions.

9   Unluckily, one gust of wind happens to direct the arrow off course; luckily, another
    gust of wind happens to direct it back on course.

10 These are also called 'achievement' theories: see Greco (2010).

11 Sosa (2015a: 94) remarks that such hard-wired virtues are 'devoid of agency'.

12 See Sosa (2009: 151).

13 Sosa (2009: 149–52) suggests as much. See also Battaly (2010, 2012).

14 Sosa (2015a: 84) replies to this objection. There, his analysis of 'reflective'
    knowledge is active.

15 This means that internalist knowledge does not entail active knowledge. One can
    meet the conditions for internalism without meeting the conditions for active
    knowledge. It may be difficult to see this, both because active knowledge entails
    internalism and because Descartes' hugely influential epistemology combines
    the two.

16 Barney has no reason to think that he is in 'fake barn country' or that
    such a 'country' exists (nor can he distinguish fake barns from real ones from
    the road).

17 Sosa (2004) used to think that safety was required for animal knowledge.

18 His epistemology still includes passive knowledge: see Sosa (2017).

19 Breaking with his earlier work, Sosa (2015a: 40–3) distinguishes between a virtue's
    being the most salient cause of arriving at a true belief and a virtue's *constituting*
    knowledge. He argues that virtues of inquiry, like open-mindedness and intellectual
    perseverance, may be necessary for, and may even be the most salient cause of,
    one's arrival at a true belief. But their exercise won't constitute knowledge. They
    regulate the process of inquiry without issuing in judgement. They merely put
    one in a position to exercise one's virtues of judgement, like proper care and
    attentiveness. It is the exercise of these latter virtues that constitutes knowledge. For
    objections, see Baehr (2015).

20 Zagzebski's view is committed to caring about truth for its own sake. Else, her
    view will not be able to ground the value of intellectual virtue on the value of its
    motivational component. See Baehr (2015: 78).

21 This raises the question of whether active knowledge becomes passive knowledge
    in its transmission via testimony.

22 Nor will children or animals satisfy the counterfactual condition.

23 See Code (1987: 63), Roberts and Wood (2007), and Baehr (2014: 138;
    2015: 126–30).

References

Alston, W. P. (1976), 'Two Types of Foundationalism', *The Journal of Philosophy*,
   73: 165–85.
Alston, W. P. (1993), 'Epistemic Desiderata', *Philosophy and Phenomenological Research*,
   53: 527–51.
Baehr, J. (2006), 'Character in Epistemology', *Philosophical Studies*, 128: 479–514.
Baehr, J. (2011), *The Inquiring Mind: On Intellectual Virtues and Virtue Epistemology*,
   Oxford: Oxford University Press.
Baehr, J. (2014), 'Are Intellectually Virtuous Motives Essential to Knowledge?', in M.
   Steup, J. Turri, and E. Sosa (eds), *Contemporary Debates in Epistemology*, 2nd edn,
   Malden, MA: Wiley Blackwell.
Baehr, J. (2015), 'Character Virtues, Epistemic Agency, and Reflective Knowledge', in
   M. Alfano (ed.), *Current Controversies in Virtue Theory*, New York: Routledge.
Battaly, H. (2008), 'Virtue Epistemology', *Philosophy Compass*, 3: 639–63.
Battaly, H. (2010), 'Review of Reflective Knowledge', *Analysis*, 70: 388–91.
Battaly, H. (2012), 'Sosa's Reflective Knowledge: How Damaging Is Epistemic
   Circularity?' *Synthese*, 188: 289–308.
Battaly, H. (2015), *Virtue*, Cambridge: Polity Press.
BonJour, L. (1978), 'Can Empirical Knowledge Have a Foundation?' *American
   Philosophical Quarterly*, 15: 1–13.
BonJour, L. (1980), 'Externalist Theories of Empirical Knowledge', *Midwest Studies in
   Philosophy*, 5: 53–73.
BonJour, L. (2002), 'Internalism and Externalism', in P. K. Moser (ed.), *Oxford
   Handbook of Epistemology*, New York: Oxford University Press.
Code, L. (1987), *Epistemic Responsibility*, Hanover, NH: Brown University Press.
Dougherty, T. (2011), 'Knowledge Happens: Why Zagzebski Has Not Solved the Meno
   Problem', *The Southern Journal of Philosophy*, 49: 73–88.
Fricker, M. (2007), *Epistemic Injustice: Power and the Ethics of Knowing*, Oxford: Oxford
   University Press.
Gettier, E. (1963), 'Is Justified True Belief Knowledge?', *Analysis*, 23: 121–3.
Goldman, A. I. (1979), 'What Is Justified Belief?' in G. S. Pappas (ed.), *Justification and
   Knowledge: New Studies in Epistemology*, Dordrecht: D. Reidel, 1–23.
Goldman, A. I. (1992), 'Strong and Weak Justification', in his *Liaisons: Philosophy Meets
   the Cognitive and Social Sciences*, Cambridge: The MIT Press.
Greco, J. (2000), *Putting Skeptics in Their Place: The Nature of Skeptical Arguments and
   their Role in Philosophical Inquiry*, Cambridge: Cambridge University Press.
Greco, J. (2002), 'Virtues in Epistemology', in P. K. Moser (ed.), *The Oxford Handbook of
   Epistemology*, New York: Oxford University Press.
Greco, J. (2010), *Achieving Knowledge: A Virtue-Theoretic Account of Epistemic
   Normativity*, Cambridge: Cambridge University Press.

Lackey, J. (2007), 'Why We Don't Deserve Credit for Everything We Know', *Synthese*, 158: 345–61.

Pritchard, D. (2009), 'Apt Performance and Epistemic Value', *Philosophical Studies*, 143: 407–16.

Roberts, R. C. and Wood, W. J. (2007), *Intellectual Virtues: An Essay in Regulative Epistemology*, Oxford: Oxford University Press.

Sosa, E. (1980), 'The Raft and the Pyramid: Coherence versus Foundations in the Theory of Knowledge', *Midwest Studies in Philosophy*, 5: 3–26.

Sosa, E. (1991), *Knowledge in Perspective: Selected Essays in Epistemology*, Cambridge: Cambridge University Press.

Sosa, E. (2004), 'Replies', in J. Greco (ed.), *Ernest Sosa and His Critics*, Oxford: Blackwell.

Sosa, E. (2007), *A Virtue Epistemology: Apt Belief and Reflective Knowledge*, Volume I, Oxford: Oxford University Press.

Sosa, E. (2009), *Reflective Knowledge: Apt Belief and Reflective Knowledge*, Volume II, Oxford: Oxford University Press.

Sosa, E. (2015a), *Judgment and Agency*, Oxford: Oxford University Press.

Sosa, E. (2015b), 'Virtue Epistemology: Character vs. Competence', in M. Alfano (ed.), *Current Controversies in Virtue Theory*, New York: Routledge.

Sosa, E. (2017), 'Replies to Comments on *Judgment and Agency*', *Philosophical Studies*, 174(10): 2599–611.

Zagzebski, L. T. (1996), *Virtues of the Mind: An Inquiry into the Nature of Virtue and the Ethical Foundations of Knowledge*, Cambridge: Cambridge University Press.

Zagzebski, L. T. (2009), *On Epistemology*, Belmont, CA: Wadsworth.

Zagzebski, L. T. (2014), 'Knowledge and the Motive for Truth', in M. Steup, J. Turri, and E. Sosa (eds), *Contemporary Debates in Epistemology*, 2nd edn, Malden, MA: Wiley Blackwell.

Index

Pichon, C. 170 n.5
Pisoni, D. B. 145
Pitt, D. 157
Plato 28, 53, 60, 226 n.2, 245 n.11, 271
Poincaré, H. 96
Popper, K. 3, 92, 94
possible worlds *see* metaphysics
pragmatic encroachment *see* subject-
 sensitive invariantism
pragmatism 6, 9
 and knowledge-attribution 9, 19–20, 22
 and neopragmatism 9, 18, 20
 and pragmatic encroachment 9, 20–3
 see also Dewey, J.; James, W;
 Peirce, C. S.
preface, paradox of 44 n.5, 258
Prichard, H. A. 216
Pritchard, D. 123, 139, 144, 239, 245 n.10,
 245 n.13, 276, 277
probability 3, 16, 245 n.9, 283
 epistemic 197–8
 and probabilistic knowledge 201–5
 and problem of prior probabilities 104
 subjective 195–6
 see also Bayes' rule; confirmation;
 degrees of belief
proprioception 147–8, 149
protocol sentences 92–3
psychology 70–2, 73, 74, 77, 79, 84–5,
 118
 see also Peirce, C. S.; science;
 self–knowledge
Pyrrhonian scepticism 33, 44 n.7, 272
 see also Sextus Empiricus

Quine, W. V. O. 3, 70–1, 72, 73, 74, 75–6,
 77–8, 79, 80, 96–100, 105, 106

Radford, C. 226 n.1
realism 11, 23 n.10
 vs anti-realism 28, 89–90
reductionism 60–2, 115–19, 139
 see also intellectualism vs anti-
 intellectualism, and knowledge-how
Reed, B. 6 n.6, 245 n.6
Reid, T. 70, 115–16, 125, 127 n.1
Reichenbach, H. 70–1, 100–4
reliabilism 73, 80–1, 84–5, 115, 116, 241,
 242, 245 n.12, 251, 272, 273, 274, 284

see also naturalism; reliability;
 testimony, and reliability
reliability 19, 37, 54–5, 92, 116, 118, 121,
 125, 127 n.2, 129 n.9, 130 n.14, 133
 n.22, 200, 243, 273
 see also reliabilism
Rescher, N. 22–3
responsibility, epistemic 54, 55, 119,
 252, 262
 see also virtues, intellectual
Roberts, R. 228 n.22, 284, 285 n.23
Robinson, P. 265 n.29
Rock, I. 157
Rohrbaugh, G. 170 n.3
Rorty, R. 18, 19, 169 n.2
Ross, A. 114
Rothschild, D. 208
Roush, S. 245 n.9
Rowling, J. K. 51, 54, 65 n.5, 66 n.13
Russell, B. 5, 27–8, 67 n.18, 82, 112, 157
 and anticipation of Gettier cases
 30–2, 38
 and anti-scepticism 31–8
 and fallibility vs infallibility 33–4
 and foundationalism vs
 coherentism 33–7
 and problem of induction 28–9
Ryan, S. 264 n.18
Ryle, G. 52, 59, 60, 63, 65 n.4, 66 n.13,
 67 n.14, 67 n.16, 67 n.19, 67 n.20,
 139, 155
Rysiew, P. 70, 76, 130 n.10, 189, 190

Saarinen, J. 145, 147
Sainsbury, M. 29
Salmon, W. 105
Sarrou, M. 147
Sartwell, C. 244, 264 n.20
scepticism 5, 6 n.6, 52, 58–63, 66 n.13,
 81–2, 83, 90–1, 180–1, 189, 190, 217,
 220–2, 238–9
 and self-knowledge 155–9, 162, 165,
 166, 168, 169
 see also Moore, G. E., and scepticism;
 Russell, and anti-scepticism
Schaffer, J. 190 n.1, 211 n.21
Schellenberg, S. 263 n.7
Schiffer, S. 197–8, 211 n.11
Schlick, M. 91, 93–4, 97